Insurgency and Counterinsurgency in South Asia

Praise for

Insurgency and Counterinsurgency in South Asia

"These excellent case studies shift the counterinsurgency focus to the origins and gestation of insurgencies and show how they grew into major regional conflicts. With helpful maps and chronologies, data-rich chapters by South Asia specialists reveal how four insurgencies became intractable. Having traced their emergence through the lens of the 'conflict curve,' the book's findings challenge the peacebuilding, development, democracy-building, and human rights communities to concentrate more of their energies on the precrisis stage of 'unstable peace' in the many existing quasi-democratic weak states, when their tools can be more effective in avoiding the carnage and threats from potential insurgencies."
—**Michael S. Lund,** senior associate, Management Systems International, Inc.

"Understanding insurgency in South Asia is essential to making sense of the region's politics. This volume provides a valuable comparative study of conflicts in Kashmir, northwestern Pakistan, Sri Lanka, and Nepal. The chapters identify key factors that drove the onset of wars, discuss the nature of the violence within them, and explore actual and prospective mechanisms for creating durable peace. This is important reading that will benefit both specialists in South Asia and scholars interested in broader questions of violence and peacebuilding."
—**Paul Staniland**, assistant professor, department of political science, The University of Chicago

"This timely and accessible volume astutely employs the lens of peacebuilding to analyze the issue of insurgency in South Asia, a phenomenon which has, until now, received proportionately little attention. The contributors provide first-rate analysis and practical conclusions that will be of use to both scholars and policymakers. The case study approach is particularly welcome, as it will benefit both regional specialists as well as peacebuilders seeking wider lessons about the elements of successful interventions across the conflict cycle."
—**Abiodun Williams**, president, The Hague Institute for Global Justice

Insurgency and Counterinsurgency in South Asia

Through a Peacebuilding Lens

Edited by

Moeed Yusuf

UNITED STATES INSTITUTE OF PEACE

WASHINGTON, D.C.

FOUNDATION BOOKS

FOUNDATION BOOKS

Foundation Books is an imprint of Cambridge University Press, India.

Cambridge House, 4381/4 Ansari Road, Daryaganj, New Delhi 110 002

www.cambridgeindia.org

First South Asia edition 2015

Printed in India at Thomson Press India Ltd., New Delhi 110001

ISBN 978-93-84463-03-8 Paperback

Contents

Part IV. Sri Lanka

Acknowledgments

This book project has had a long journey. It would simply not have been possible without the perseverance, dedication, and patience of the authors who have contributed to the volume. I am truly indebted to them—far more than an average editor would be.

The volume has its origins in our collective desire to allow indigenous South Asian voices to debate organized conflict in their region. What has emerged is a "Southasian" understanding of four major contemporary insurgencies and counterinsurgency approaches but with applicability to a much broader set of cases globally.

This project has traveled with me as I have moved along in my professional life from Pakistan to Boston and finally to the U.S. Institute of Peace in Washington, D.C. It underwent numerous iterations, finally culminating in what we hope will be a useful collection of empirical analyses with practical utility for peacebuilders operating in conflict environments. Given the volume's focus on peacebuilding, it is only fitting that it was ultimately housed at the U.S. Institute of Peace. USIP's Pakistan program inherited the project and devoted time and resources to it. But more importantly, the project gained tremendously from input from peacebuilding experts who happened to be colleagues at the Institute. I especially wish to thank Andrew Wilder and Abi Williams, who saw merit in this project and remained supportive in their respective capacities at the Institute.

I have been very fortunate to avail excellent research and administrative assistance throughout the life of this project. Special gratitude is due to my very able and diligent associates, Stephanie Flamenbaum and Ayesha Chugh, who provided excellent research support. Sairah Yusuf worked with me in the very early stages of the project and helped coneptualize it. Emily Horin was a great help in all housekeeping matters. I also owe gratitude to Valerie Norville, Michelle Slavin, Marie Marr, Kay Hechler, and their team in the USIP Publications department for all their support and to Michael Carr for excellent editorial support.

Introduction

Insurgency and Counterinsurgency in South Asia

Moeed Yusuf

South Asia is home to one-fifth of the world's population. It comprises eight nation-states, from the swiftly rising powerhouse India to the struggling nuclear power Pakistan to the little-known kingdom of Bhutan. Despite the region's frequently highlighted potential, South Asian states have failed to forge a truly synergic existence. In fact, the region today is the least economically integrated in the world. South Asia's great diversity notwithstanding, its people possess noticeable historical and cultural similarities, making this lack of integration all the more lamentable. The most apparent commonalities have been undesirable ones, chief among them the reality of sustained violence across the region in the postcolonial era. Over the past six decades, South Asia has experienced the breakup of a state, repeated interstate tensions and wars, and myriad intrastate conflicts with various reasons, agendas, and goals. All these have threatened the territorial integrity of states.

Before the September 11, 2001, attacks on the United States, much of the popular conflict coverage in South Asia focused on the India-Pakistan conflict—four wars between 1947 and 1999, one of which led to the breakup of Pakistan—and international attention has focused primarily on the U.S.-led campaign in Afghanistan ever since. Belying the picture of interstate conflict suggested by this focus is the reality that warfare *within* South Asian states has been far more prevalent, with far more conflict-related casualties, than war *between* states. According to the Uppsala Armed Conflict

Database, South Asia experienced 298 conflicts between 1946 and 2002, a staggering 277 of which have been intrastate in nature (Gleditsch et al. 2002). The casualty figures attributed to interstate conflict pale in comparison to those for intrastate conflict.[1] The total number of deaths in South Asia's three major interstate wars since 1947 is listed at 20,000 (Dahal et al. 2003). To compare, intrastate conflict-related casualties in Pakistan alone over the past decade have been close to 50,000 (SATP 2013).

Of specific interest to this volume are the large number of sustained insurgent movements that form a subset of the region's intrastate conflict. Apart from the small island state of Maldives (population 143,000), every state in South Asia has faced one or more sustained insurgencies since decolonization. Indeed, just a decade ago, in 2003, all the South Asian countries except Maldives and Bangladesh were confronting at least one active insurgent movement.

The persistence of conflict in South Asia is worrisome, especially since the region's vital importance for regional and global peace is widely recognized. Former U.S. president Bill Clinton called South Asia the "world's most dangerous place" (Marcus 2000). After all, the region contains Afghanistan, where the 9/11 attacks were planned, and Pakistan, which is regularly referenced as the global hub of Islamist terrorists. But the ultimate concern for future stability is not just one-off spectacular acts of terrorism. More troublesome is the prospect of large-scale insurgent movements taking advantage of the conflictual nature of South Asian interstate ties and state vulnerabilities to initiate what could end up being a catastrophic breakdown of state authority in much of the region. At the very least, this would mean that South Asia could lose the opportunity to harness its positive potential to let its people progress in a peaceful environment. At worst, it could threaten the territorial integrity of two nuclear-weapon states and their neighbors—the dream scenario for a wide array of terrorist actors.

Peacebuilding and the Study of South Asian Insurgencies and Counterinsurgencies

The dilemma points to the need for South Asian decision makers and relevant actors elsewhere in the world to systematically examine, learn from, and apply lessons from past insurgencies and counterinsurgency campaigns in order to prevent or mitigate future occurrences in the most sustainable

1. There is a significant discrepancy in figures for battle-related deaths and their breakdowns across types of conflicts in the various databases available. But all confirm the astronomically higher number of intrastate conflicts and deaths in South Asia. See, for example, various iterations of the Uppsala Armed Conflict Database, the Stockholm Peace Research Institute's yearbooks, and the World Bank's data on battle-related deaths.

ways. Towards this endeavor, this volume is conceptually grounded in the discipline of peacebuilding and the concept's focus on nonviolent means of resolving potential, ongoing, or past conflict.

After the Cold War, peacebuilding emerged as a major field of study, and practice focused on post-conflict resolution and intrastate fragility. Although "post-conflict peacebuilding" was first coined in the 1970s, UN secretary-general Boutros Boutros-Ghali defined it in his seminal 1992 report *An Agenda for Peace* as "action to identify and support structures which will tend to strengthen and solidify peace in order to avoid a relapse into conflict" (UNGA 1992). The term has since broadened in scope to include a broad array of interventions aimed at promoting social justice as the means of transforming societies toward permanent peaceful coexistence. The U.S. Institute of Peace defines "peacebuilding" in its glossary of peace terms: "Peacebuilding involves a transformation toward more manageable, peaceful relationships and governance structures—the long-term process of addressing root causes and effects, reconciling differences, normalizing relations, and building institutions that can manage conflict without resorting to violence" (Snodderly 2011, 40–41).[2] Peacebuilders recognize that violence is part and parcel of war and that sometimes *not* employing violent coercion may lead to greater conflict. The use of force is therefore considered legitimate and necessary in specific circumstances. And yet the peacebuilding approach differentiates itself from such disciplines as war-and-conflict studies through its relatively greater emphasis on nonviolent and peaceful interventions to prevent or end conflict and to allow for sustained post-conflict peace. It is this aspect of peacebuilding that is of special interest to this volume.

The original focus of the peacebuilding framework on post-conflict interventions has largely remained. Even conflict prevention has been traditionally understood as a means of preventing recurrence of conflicts where violent crises and wars have erupted in the past (Cutter 2005, 779–80). But a strong plea for broadening the horizon has come from those studying prevention and realizing the qualitatively different requirements of mechanisms aimed at preventing "initial onset of large-scale violent conflict" (Woocher 2009, 3). Moreover, "conflict management" and "peacemaking"—terms used to describe activities that could limit, contain, or resolve

2. Peacebuilding includes a broad canvas of interventions. The U.S. Institute of Peace's glossary lists these: providing humanitarian relief, protecting human rights, ensuring security, establishing nonviolent modes of resolving conflicts, fostering reconciliation, providing trauma healing services, repatriating refugees and resettling internally displaced persons, supporting broad-based education, and aiding in economic reconstruction (Snodderly 2011, 40–41). Promoting viability of political processes in conflict-prone environments is also seen as part of peacebuilding (Cousens and Kumar 2001).

ongoing conflicts and generate agreement among warring parties through nonviolent tools—are also central to peacebuilders as they seek to maintain or restore peace (Snodderly 2011, 15, 41).

Peacebuilding's applicability to a wide array of conflict situations, and its ability to subsume approaches to prevent and mitigate conflict or rebuild sustained peace after conflict has occurred, can best be understood in terms of "conflict curves" or "progression of conflict." Michael Lund defines five stages, moving along the conflict curve from total calm to all-out war:

1. *durable peace,* which signifies a just order
2. *stable peace,* where peace ensues but the potential for rising tensions exists
3. *unstable peace,* where tensions have risen and some confrontation may also take place
4. *crisis,* where violence breaks out
5. *war,* marked by large-scale violent conflict (Lund 1996, 38–39)

These are textbook representations of how conflicts evolve; the stages are seldom as neatly demarcated in the real world. Thus, empirical cases involve considerable overlap among various approaches. Still, in each stage, a particular type of peacebuilding approach is most relevant and plays a dominant role. While durable peace requires no action, as tensions rise *peacetime diplomacy* ensues during stable peace, *conflict prevention* is central during times of unstable peace, and *crisis management and peacemaking* are needed during crisis and war. As the violence begins to decrease, the situation requires *conflict mitigation, conflict termination,* and then *post-conflict peacebuilding*—and *conflict resolution* to arrive eventually at stable or, better yet, durable peace once again (Lund 1996, 38–44; 2009, 290).[3]

This volume contains four case studies of the most salient armed insurgencies in South Asia over the past three decades and the counterinsurgency response to each. The authors have studied one insurgency each from India, Pakistan, Nepal, and Sri Lanka. They assess the ongoing insurgency in the Indian state of Jammu and Kashmir (J&K), whose beginnings were marked by mass protests and violence in 1989 in Kashmir Valley. In Pakistan, the authors focus on the post-9/11 rise of the Pakistani Taliban (Tehrik-e-Taliban Pakistan, or TTP) and its insurgent activities in Pakistan's northwest. The other two cases consider recently concluded insurgent movements: the Nepalese Maoist insurgency, which lasted from 1996 to 2006 and ended with a victory for the insurgents, and the Sri Lankan insurgency led by the Liberation Tigers of Tamil Eelam (LTTE), which

3. For definitions of these "peace terms," see Snodderly (2011).

began in 1983 and persisted for a quarter century until the Sri Lankan government eventually decimated the violent opposition.

Why This Book?

Asymmetric conflicts such as these four cases, where the power differentials between warring factions are all too obvious, continue to interest scholars and practitioners alike, not least because the outcomes have not always favored the powerful. Typologies of asymmetric conflict have proved to be a contested battleground in literature. Often, "asymmetric conflict," "insurgency," "guerrilla warfare," "terrorism," "ethnic warfare," "communal conflict," and like terms are used loosely, even interchangeably (Gates and Roy 2011, ixxi). This volume focuses specifically on full-fledged insurgency and counterinsurgency, defined respectively as a major armed uprising directed against the state to achieve political objectives, ranging from regime change to secession from a state, and counteractions by an established and recognized legal entity (usually the state) to tackle that threat (Snodderly 2011). Insurgents may use guerrilla or terrorism tactics, among others, and states may use conventional forces, paramilitary units, or law enforcement agencies or undertake nonmilitary interventions to defeat the insurgent movement.

Literature already abounds on the topic of insurgency and counterinsurgency. Many researchers have studied the root causes of insurgencies or specific manifestations of insurgent tactics, as well as typical state responses. Anger and frustration, ideology, political grievances, relative or absolute deprivation, identity issues, religion, greed, geographic factors, external environment, and resource mobilization have all been highlighted as root causes for insurgencies (Ballentine 2003; Borooah 2008; Collier 2006; Collier and Hoeffler 2002; Abeyratne 2004; Muller and Seligson 1987; Regan and Norton 2005; Gurr 1970). For counterinsurgencies, the focus is on military tactics, law enforcement measures, intelligence, monetary and other incentives, improved socioeconomic and governance conditions, policies aimed at appeasing populations in troubled areas, public information campaigns, long-term commitments to reforms, humanitarian relief, and, most frequently, some combination of these as potent means of quashing insurgent challenges (Donnelly and Serchuk 2003; Mackinlay and Al-Baddawy 2008; Sepp 2005; Findley and Young 2007; Van Creveld 1991).

The choice, timing, modes of application, and results of these strategies may depend heavily on the specific historical and cultural context, the nature of the insurgent movement, the type of state, and the state's counterinsurgent capabilities. Even as we have seen a strong push to generalize lessons, and sensationalized phrases such as "winning hearts and minds" show up frequently, the relativist nature of lessons learned from studies of insurgencies and counterinsurgencies really lends itself to a case study approach to comprehend the specific dynamics most applicable to the region under observation.[4]

Each case study in this volume is a self-contained piece, examining either the buildup from the stable peace stage to the crisis stage on the conflict curve or the move up the curve from crisis to war and, where applicable, conflict termination and post-conflict peacebuilding. Each chapter examines the considerations, strategies, decisions, and expectations of the relevant actors at various stages of the conflict, uncovering in the process the dynamics and behavior patterns of the conflicting parties that were instrumental in moving the situation up or down the conflict curve.

The questions guiding the case studies, along with the stipulation to take a holistic perspective of the factors explaining conflict trajectories, give the authors enough freedom to hone in on the aspects most crucial to their respective cases. And yet these guiding principles are focused enough to produce policy-relevant conclusions on the kinds of behavior and interventions that help rather than hinder the quest to arrive at a permanent state of stable, if not durable, peace. A collective reading of the case studies not only provides insights into why insurgencies occurred and in what ways they were managed in South Asia but also helps policymakers better understand what kinds of initiatives from within the peacebuilding toolkit are likely to be most effective in avoiding or minimizing violence.

This volume has been compiled for three primary reasons. First, while some important works have come out that are relevant to insurgent movements and counterinsurgent efforts in South Asia, much of the international attention on violence in South Asia over the past decade has tended to focus on terrorism. Ultimately, though, South Asia's stability lies not only in addressing terrorism but also in preventing coordinated and sustained insurgencies that threaten to undermine the affected state. Concurrent with this attention to terrorist threats is a geographic fixation in recent years because of the international engagement in Afghanistan and Pakistan. But Afghanistan's insurgency is linked to the presence of foreign forces—a temporary phenomenon not applicable to the rest of the region.

Second, given the diverse trajectories and outcomes of major South Asian insurgencies in the post-Cold War, post-9/11 environment, now is the opportune moment to examine them. Within the past twenty-five years, the four significant insurgencies considered in this volume started and followed diverse trajectories. Two concluded, while two are ongoing with varying intensities.

---

4. Virtually all literature on successful counterinsurgencies includes talk about winning over the people. For examples, see Galula (1964), Nagl (2005), Kilcullen (2006), and Sepp (2005).

Third, previous examination has often placed these insurgencies and counterinsurgencies in discrete "silos," limiting the opportunity to explore links between the causes and characteristics of particular insurgencies and between the states' countertactics. Moreover, much of the literature in the South Asian context takes a "war studies" approach (Midlarsky 1989). This narrow analytical scope often focuses disproportionately on the types and tools of violence used by insurgents and on defense policy, strategic planning, and tactical and operational aspects of the counterinsurgency campaigns. Much less attention is paid to deep-rooted structural problems enabling resentments and tensions to coalesce into a violent insurgency or to options for prevention or for a proactive, nonviolent state response.

This volume departs from others in a number of ways. It focuses not on the tactical or operational aspects of insurgencies and counterinsurgencies but on those policy-relevant conclusions and lessons gleaned from the case studies that are pertinent to the discipline of peacebuilding. Contributors study the cases holistically so that the collective findings remain relevant across the entire conflict curve.

Unlike authors of a number of other works interested in peacebuilding, the contributors to this volume have not deliberately set out to underscore the importance of the peacebuilding concept or its virtues. Such a singular focus runs the risk of artificially amplifying this or that aspect of peacebuilding, even if, in reality, it may not have been central to the dynamics of the conflict case—thus blurring or distorting the picture. Instead, the authors were asked to write case studies based on two central questions: What incentives led resentful groups to resort to armed insurgency against the state? And once insurgency was under way, how did the insurgents and the state go about managing it?

Lessons relevant to peacebuilding are crystallized in the concluding chapter. The conclusions drawn will be useful not only to traditional peacebuilders—international organizations, regional blocs acting as mediators, individual states external to the conflict, international and local nongovernment bodies, and individual mediators, among others—seeking to help clashing parties avoid conflict or seek its reasonably peaceful and swift mitigation. But they will also prove useful to policymakers of the state and the insurgents—who, after all, have the greatest influence on the conflict situation.

This volume's effort to study insurgencies and counterinsurgencies in parallel through a peacebuilding lens is largely absent from comparable works. Most of the case studies are stand-alone efforts at understanding a particular insurgency or counterinsurgency (Lawoti and Pahari 2010; Florig 2008; Bandarage 2009; Cassidy 2012; Chima 2010; Gellner 2002; Hutt 2004). Some studies look at conflict in general, combining interstate and intrastate violence in a single volume (Johnson 2005). Others have examined armed militias and their impact on societies, using innovative analytical techniques, such as studying militants' careers (Gayer and Jaffrelot 2009). Some are more interested in exploring the role of specific potential causes of conflicts. In the South Asian context, this often focuses on religion and ethnicity (Roberts 2005; Gombrich 2006; Gould 2012; Kundu 1994; Hinnells and King 2007; Roy 2007; Rowell 2006). Even narrower studies have focused on aspects such as urban violence or post-9/11 terrorism (Sahadevan 2002; Varshney 2002; Jones and Fair 2010). Some literature on violence and human security takes a broader perspective on conflict and examines, foremost, its effects on individuals and societies (Behera 2008; Dahal et al. 2003). Finally, even studies that specifically study peace processes and efforts at peacebuilding often consider the period only from the onset of large-scale violence to its termination. Even here, the emphasis is often on the final negotiations that end the conflict and on post-conflict peacebuilding efforts (Darby and MacGinty 2000). By applying the underutilized conceptual lens to bring together lessons for peacebuilders across the life cycle of a conflict, this volume adds to the present understanding of opportunities and means of preventing, managing, and resolving conflicts without necessarily having to bank on a war studies approach.

Cases and Structure of the Book

Even though this volume can study only a very small subset of the many insurgencies that have confronted South Asian states over the years, the cases selected have arguably been the most serious insurgent challenges that these countries have faced. Each of the four insurgencies was initiated by local groups against the state. This criterion precluded inclusion of the insurgency in Afghanistan, since it emerged in response to a direct intervention by an external actor seeking to depose the ruling regime.

The time frame of the chosen insurgencies spans the greater part of the past three decades, even though the roots of these conflicts reach back to events decades earlier. Two of the case study insurgencies began during the Cold War, one between its end and 9/11 and one after 9/11. Observations are therefore possible on appreciable differences in the approaches by insurgents and the states in different historical circumstances. But all four cases are contemporary and, thus, relevant to today's policy backdrop.

Further, the cases provide significant diversity in their trajectories—two are active insurgencies, and the other two concluded very differently from each other—allowing us to look at the conflict curve's full spectrum and identify potential variables that explain the different outcomes from a peacebuilding lens. But all the included cases represent protracted conflicts where ample opportunities for nonviolent interventions to achieve crisis objectives were theoretically available to both parties to the conflicts. Among the four cases, differences across numerous key variables make the analysis even more interesting and significant. We have insurgencies under functioning democracy, troubled democracy, military rule, and monarchy. The included states also have a mix of secular and religious orientations in their formal stance on the division between church and state. India and Pakistan have exceptionally strong militaries that were employed for the counterinsurgency efforts, whereas Sri Lanka and Nepal were hardly known for their military might. Further, the studied cases mark Nepal's first major experience with counterinsurgency, whereas Sri Lanka, Pakistan, and especially India faced earlier insurgent challenges. Finally, the cases represent conflicts that are predominantly internal and yet feature external involvement as a secondary, added complication, as well as conflicts officially recognized as bilateral disputes.

The volume contains nine empirical chapters, each written by a practitioner or academic who is a native of South Asia, lending the volume deep contextual and cultural understanding. The book is arranged sequentially by country, moving from the ongoing insurgencies in India and Pakistan to the concluded insurgencies in Nepal and Sri Lanka, with paired chapters on each insurgency and counterinsurgency. The chapters on the insurgencies look at the genesis of the insurgency, the interaction between the state and the insurgents before the onset of violence, the potential opportunities to prevent escalation of tensions and reasons for not using them, and the trigger events that ultimately led to large-scale violence. The chapters dealing with counterinsurgencies look holistically at the military, political, and economic dimensions of the states' responses. Where applicable, they also examine the post-conflict phases.

Examining the roots of the insurgency in J&K, Happymon Jacob characterizes it as a "federal relationship that went drastically wrong." Jacob identifies internal drivers—New Delhi's mismanagement of the state of J&K and, specifically, its denial of the Kashmiris' constitutional and democratic rights—as the primary cause of the insurgency. Pakistan's role is seen as crucial in sustaining the insurgency but is considered only an exacerbating factor. Rekha Chowdhary analyzes the Indian state's counterinsurgency response and notes a progressive improvement from a purely militaristic approach to one with a more pronounced political-economic component. Chowdhary credits the application of lessons learned by the state in the initial phases of the counterinsurgency campaign for the improvement of conditions in J&K. As the Indian state moved along the six phases of response identified by Chowdhary, it gradually made room for political efforts, reintegrated and strategically used militants who had opted out of the insurgency, allowed a fair democratic process to take place, began a sincere political dialogue with the Kashmiri leadership, and engaged in dialogue with Pakistan to find a mutually acceptable resolution to the problem, enabling the conflict to de-escalate from the war phase.

Khalid Mahmood's chapter is the only one that breaks the pattern of paired chapters on insurgency and counterinsurgency for each case study. It was included in recognition of the importance of the interstate dimension to the insurgency in J&K. By focusing on the dialogue process between Pakistan and India over Kashmir, the chapter expounds on a key effort at peacebuilding that came close to resolving one of the world's most intractable disputes. Mahmood's Pakistani perspective complements Jacob's and Chowdhary's discussion of India's outlook toward dialogue with Pakistan on Kashmir. As an insider to the India-Pakistan back-channel negotiations on Kashmir during 2004–07, Mahmood explains how a series of bilateral and regional developments led the two sides to acknowledge that a military solution to Kashmir was impossible. From a peacebuilding perspective, the reader can decipher how Pakistan, a state that had traditionally held on to a maximalist position on Kashmir, found circumstances and leadership committed to identifying a mutually acceptable compromise solution.

The two chapters on Pakistan examine the challenge that the Pakistani Taliban has posed for the state in the semiautonomous Federally Administered Tribal Areas (FATA) and the Khyber Pakhtunkhwa (KPK) province. Muhammad Amir Rana's chapter reminds us that the present insurgency in FATA and KPK cannot be understood without considering its historical underpinnings in the Soviet-Afghan war of the 1980s. The chapter details how the Pakistani state's simultaneous patronage and complacency enabled the emergence of an industry of jihad, with FATA acting as the de facto hub. Rana charts the ways that FATA's anomalous governance structures facilitated militants' ingress and let the Pakistani Taliban promote a "pro-jihad" narrative since 9/11. He also examines the role of the geostrategic milieu—in which the Pakistani state acted as both manipulator and victim—in enabling the Pakistani Taliban not only to generate momentum for its movement but also to spread quickly beyond the boundaries of FATA.

Examining the state's response, Shaukat Qadir, a retired Pakistani army officer, conveys a sense that the policies of the Pakistani state under President Musharraf exacerbated the insurgent challenge and escalated the conflict by employing a heavy-handed approach to deal with the challenge in FATA. Qadir's focus on the Pakistani military's operations and strategies reflects the narrow approach taken by Pakistan in its campaign in FATA and KPK. Even though the military tactics proved successful in reversing the insurgency's advance, Qadir succinctly articulates a fear that the insurgent challenge may be far from over, noting that the Pakistani military's victories alone cannot win a war that continues to lack civilian-military coordination and a complementary political-socioeconomic strategy.

The next pair of chapters considers the recently settled insurgency in Nepal. At the heart of S. D. Muni's analysis of the rise of Nepal's Maoist insurgents lies the country's deeply flawed political and governance system. The stifling nature of the Nepalese monarchy and its persistent repression of party-based democracy alienated the people from the state and reinforced the dream of a "New Nepal" espoused by the Maoists. The relative deprivation and marginalization—and, interestingly, the geographic location of the most disgruntled parts of Nepalese society—helped coalesce the resentment against the state into a full-fledged uprising. The move toward an insurgency was greatly facilitated by the Maoists' ability to monopolize this popular antistate resentment in the midwestern part of the country.

Bishnu Raj Upreti's chapter dissects the difficulties of peacemaking and conflict resolution efforts in Nepal's protracted conflict. Unlike in the Indian and Pakistani cases, the Nepalese state initially refrained from using the army in its counterinsurgency campaign when it sought to present the uprising merely as a law-and-order problem. Ultimately, however, the many contradictions of the Nepalese political system, and the monarchy's propensity to overplay its hand, contributed to the Maoists' success in abolishing the monarchy and taking power in a democratic process. This chapter also examines post-conflict developments and sounds a cautionary note: Nepal's continued political tensions indicate that transforming a conflict landscape into a state of stable, let alone durable, peace after a conflict has ended requires approaches and initiatives very different from those instrumental in the conflict's termination.

The final case study examines the Sri Lankan state's struggle against the LTTE. Rooted in the country's ethnic makeup—namely the tensions between the Sinhalese majority and the Tamil minority—the rift deepened thanks to the actions of myopic, self-serving politicians who made decisions only to satisfy communal and electoral interests. This is a common theme underpinning the analyses of all the insurgencies in this volume: Numerous opportunities arose when the conflicting parties could have obviated the spiral of ethnic tensions, yet they chose not to do so for electoral reasons. As Chalinda Weerasinghe shows us, a majoritarian system created perverse incentives that forced the moderates among the minority Tamils into silence and all but guaranteed a move up the conflict curve.

Kumar Rupesinghe examines the only counterinsurgency campaign among the included cases that ended in what is widely acknowledged as a military victory by the state over the insurgents. As in Qadir's chapter, the disproportionate focus on the military aspect of the Sri Lankan government's strategy represents the virtual absence of a holistic political-economic approach to complement the use of force. Unlike the other authors, however, Rupesinghe takes a statist view and attributes the Sri Lankan government's military victory to its unwavering political commitment to this goal; its refusal to negotiate once the final phase of the counterinsurgency was under way; and its defiance of liberal commentators, human rights activists, and others advocating nonviolent approaches right through to the very end. Indeed, Rupesinghe blames the absence of that same political will for the government's failure to end the insurgency much earlier. Rupesinghe's praise for the Sri Lankan government's performance is atypical and rather controversial and must be disturbing for peacebuilders. But in arguing that active insurgent violence was ended by a strategy that flies in the face of all that peacebuilders hold dear, the chapter presents an interesting intellectual challenge. Despite its controversial take on the counterinsurgency campaign in Sri Lanka, the chapter's inclusion in this volume is merited since it emphasizes the failure of nonviolent approaches as a precursor to the state's military-led approach and does not necessarily argue against their use per se. It is a critique of nonviolent approaches' failure to deliver, not a glorification of ruthless force. The chapter thus serves the useful purpose of challenging peacebuilders to convince those proposing a militaristic approach that there are ways around the failure of nonviolent interventions experienced by the Sri Lankan state. Moreover, the sustainability of Sri Lanka's military victory must be questioned since militaristic approaches often can only suppress the conflict drivers without resolving them.

Peacebuilding ultimately aims for sustainable conflict transformation. The concluding chapter draws lessons from the four case studies on the opportunities and constraints in applying peacebuilding approaches across the conflict curve, identifying in particular recommendations for the conflicting parties and traditional peacebuilders working to prevent or mitigate conflict through nonviolent means. It also points to aspects in the case studies that challenge the traditional thinking of the peacebuilding discipline.

The hope is that the analyses in this volume and the lessons drawn in the conclusion will give peacebuilders and the conflicting parties a holistic empirical understanding of the life cycle of insurgencies and the opportunities and pitfalls in preventing, managing, and resolving them sustainably.

References

Abeyratne, Sirimal. 2004. "Economic Roots of Political Conflict: The Case of Sri Lanka." *World Economy* 27 (8): 1295–1314.

Ballentine, Karen. 2003. "Reconstructing the Economic Dynamics of Armed Conflict." In *The Political Economy of Armed Conflict: Beyond Greed and Grievance,* ed. Karen Ballentine and Jake Sherman. Boulder, CO: Rienner.

Bandarage, Asoka. 2009. *The Separatist Conflict in Sri Lanka: Terrorism, Ethnicity, and Political Economy*. New York: Routledge.

Behera, Ajay Darshan. 2008. *Violence, Terrorism, and Human Security in South Asia*. Dhaka: Bangladesh Institute of International and Strategic Studies.

Borooah, Vani K. 2008. "Deprivation, Violence, and Conflict: An Analysis of Naxalite Activity in the Districts of India." *International Journal of Conflict and Violence* 2 (2): 317–33.

Cassidy, Robert. 2012. *War, Will, and Warlords: Counterinsurgency in Afghanistan and Pakistan, 2001–2011*. Carlisle, PA: U.S. Army War College.

Chima, Jugdep S. 2010. *The Sikh Separatist Insurgency in India: Political Leadership and Ethnonationalist Movements*. Los Angeles: SAGE.

Collier, Paul. 2007. "Economic Causes of Civil Conflict and Their Implications for Policy." In *Leashing the Dogs of War: Conflict Management in a Divided World,* ed. Chester A. Crocker, Fen Osler Hampson, and Pamela Aall. Washington, DC: U.S. Institute of Peace Press.

Collier, Paul, and Anke Hoeffler. 2004. "Greed and Grievance in Civil War." *Oxford Economic Papers* 56 (4): 563–95.

Cousens, Elizabeth, and Chetan Kumar, with Karin Wermester, eds. 2001. *Peacebuilding as Politics: Cultivating Peace in Fragile Societies*. Boulder, CO: Rienner.

Cutter, Ana. 2005. "Peace Building: A Literature Review." *Development in Practice* 15 (6): 778–84.

Dahal, Shiva Hari, Haris Gazdar, S. I. Keethaponcalan, and Padmaja Murthy. 2003. *Internal Conflict and Regional Security in South Asia: Approaches, Perspectives and Policies*. Geneva: UN Institute for Disarmament Research.

Darby, John, and Roger MacGinty. 2000. *The Management of Peace Processes*. New York: St. Martin's Press.

Donnelly, Thomas, and Vance Serchuk. 2003. "U.S. Counterinsurgency in Iraq: Lessons from the Philippine War." *AEI Online,* Nov. 1. www.aei.org/article/foreign-and-defense-policy/regional/middle-east-and-north-africa/us-counterinsurgency-in-iraq/.

Findley, Michael, and Joseph Young. 2007. "Fighting Fire with Fire? How (Not) to Neutralize an Insurgency." *Civil Wars* 9 (4): 378–401.

Florig, William R. 2008. *The Red Scourge Returns: The Strategic Challenge of Maoist Insurgency in India and South Asia*. Carlisle, PA: U.S. Army War College.

Galula, David. 1964. *Counterinsurgency Warfare: Theory and Practice*. New York: Praeger.

Gates, Scott, and Kaushik Roy, eds. 2011. *Unconventional Warfare in South Asia, 1947 to the Present*. London: Ashgate.

Gayer, Laurent, and Christophe Jaffrelot. 2009. *Armed Militias of South Asia: Fundamentalists, Maoists and Separatists*. New York: Columbia Univ. Press.

Gellner, David N. 2002. *Resistance and the State: Nepalese Experiences*. Ann Arbor, MI: Univ. of Michigan Press.

Gleditsch, Nils Petter, Peter Wallensteen, Mikael Eriksson, Margareta Sollenberg, and Håvard Strand. 2002. "Armed Conflict 1946–2001: A New Dataset." *Journal of Peace Research* 39 (5).

Gombrich, Richard. 2006. "Is the Sri Lankan War a Buddhist Fundamentalism?" In *Buddhism, Conflict and Violence in Modern Sri Lanka*, ed. Mahinda Deegalle, 22–37. London: Routledge.

Gould, William. 2012. *Religion and Conflict in Modern South Asia*. New York: Cambridge Univ. Press.

Gurr, Ted R. 1970. *Why Men Rebel*. Princeton, NJ: Princeton Univ. Press.

Hinnells, John R., and Richard King. 2007. *Religion and Violence in South Asia: Theory and Practice*. London: Routledge.

Hutt, Michael. 2004. *Himalayan People's War: Nepal's Maoist Rebellion*. Bloomington, IN: Indiana Univ. Press.

Johnson, Rob. 2005. *A Region in Turmoil: South Asian Conflicts since 1947*. London: Reaktion Books.

Jones, Seth G., and C. Christine Fair. 2010. *Counterinsurgency in Pakistan*. Santa Monica, CA: RAND.

Kilcullen, David. 2006. "Counter-insurgency Redux." *Survival* 48 (4): 111–30.

Kundu, Apurba. 1994. "The Indian Armed Forces' Sikh and Non-Sikh Officers' Opinion of Operation Blue Star." *Pacific Affairs* 67 (1): 46–69.

Lawoti, Mahendra, and Anup K. Pahari, eds. 2010. *The Maoist Insurgency in Nepal: Revolution in the Twenty-first Century*. London: Routledge.

Lund, Michael S. 1996. *Preventing Violent Conflicts: A Strategy for Preventive Diplomacy*. Washington, DC: U.S. Institute of Peace Press.

———. 2009. "Conflict Prevention: Theory in Pursuit of Policy and Practice." In *The SAGE Handbook of Conflict Resolution*, ed. Jacob Bercovitch, Victor Kremenyuk, and I. W. Zartman, 287–308. London: SAGE.

Mackinlay, John, and Alison Al-Baddawy. 2008. *Rethinking Counterinsurgency*. RAND Counterinsurgency Study. Vol. 5. Santa Monica, CA: RAND.

Marcus, Jonathan. 2000. "Analysis: The World's Most Dangerous Place?" *BBC News*, Mar. 23. http://news.bbc.co.uk/2/hi/south_asia/687021.stm.

Midlarsky, Manus, ed. 1989. *Handbook of War Studies*. Winchester, MA: Unwin Hyman.

Muller, Edward N., and Mitchell A. Seligson. 1987. "Inequality and Insurgency." *American Political Science Review* 81 (2): 425–52.

Nagl, John A. 2005. *Learning to Eat Soup with a Knife: Counterinsurgency Lessons from Malaya and Vietnam*. Chicago: Univ. of Chicago Press.

Regan, Patrick M., and Daniel Norton. 2005. "Greed, Grievance, and Mobilization in Civil Wars." *Journal of Conflict Resolution* 49 (3): 319–36.

Roberts, Michael. 2005. "Tamil Tiger 'Martyrs': Regenerating Divine Potency?" *Studies in Conflict and Terrorism* 28 (6): 493–514.

Rowell, James L. 2006. "Gandhi and bin Laden: Religious Conflict at the Polar Extremes." *Journal of Conflict Studies* 26 (1): 35–54.

Roy, Kaushik. 2007. "Just and Unjust War in Hindu Philosophy." *Journal of Military Ethics* 6 (3): 232–45.

Sahadevan, P. 2002. "Ethnic Conflicts and Militarism in South Asia." *International Studies* 39 (2): 103–38.

South Asia Terrorism Portal (SATP). 2013. "Fatalities in Terrorist Violence in Pakistan 2003–2013." June 23. www.satp.org/satporgtp/countries/pakistan/database/casualties.htm.

Sepp, Kalev I. 2005. "Best Practices in Counterinsurgency." *Military Review* 85 (3): 812.

Snodderly, Dan, ed. 2011. *Peace Terms: Glossary of Terms for Conflict Management and Peacebuilding*. Academy for International Conflict Management and Peacebuilding. Washington, DC: U.S. Institute of Peace.

UN General Assembly (UNGA). 1992. *An Agenda for Peace: Preventive Diplomacy, Peacemaking and Peace-keeping* (A/47/277). Summit meeting, Jan. 31. www.unrol.org/files/A_47_277.pdf.

Van Creveld, Martin. 1991. *The Transformation of War*. New York: Simon and Schuster.

Varshney, Ashutosh. 2002. *Ethnic Conflict and Civic Life: Hindus and Muslims in India*. New Haven, CT: Yale Univ. Press.

Woocher, Lawrence. 2009. "Preventing Violent Conflict: Assessing Progress, Meeting Challenges." U.S. Institute of Peace Special Report no. 231, www.usip.org/files/resources/preventing_violent_conflict.pdf.

I

India

Map 1. Jammu and Kashmir

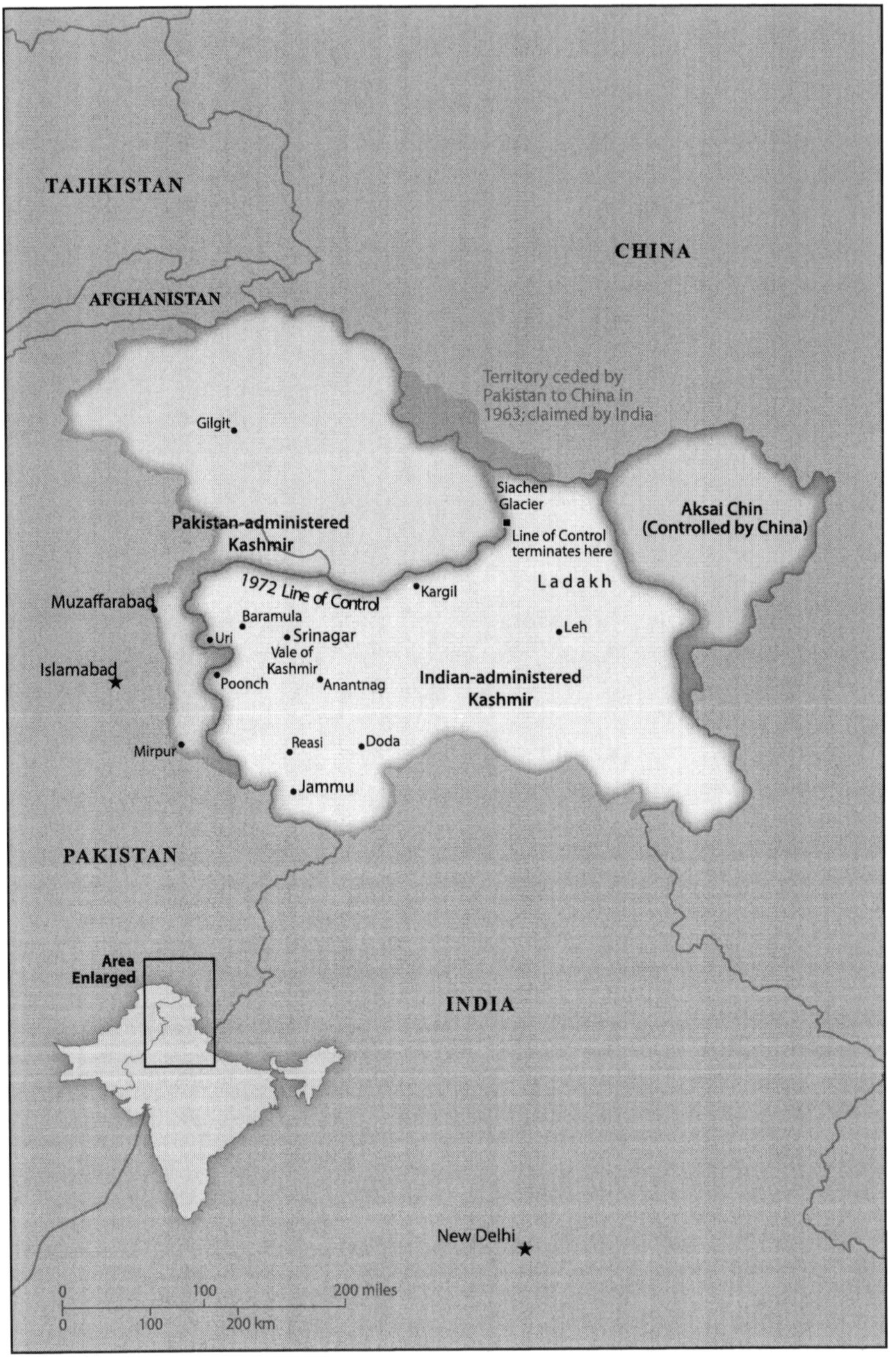

Kashmir: Timeline of Events

1947

August	Partition of British India creates independent India and Pakistan.
October	Maharaja Hari Singh, ruler of princely state of J&K, signs the Instrument of Accession, formally acceding to the Dominion of India. Pakistan disputes accession.

1947–48

First Kashmir war between India and Pakistan leads to division of the state into Azad Jammu and Kashmir, and J&K, to be administered by Pakistan and India respectively.

1948

August	UN mandates plebiscite in Kashmir and withdrawal of Pakistani troops from J&K. No plebiscite is held.

1952

July	Kashmiri National Conference leader Sheikh Abdullah signs Delhi Agreement, extending the rights of Indian Constitution, jurisdiction of Indian Supreme Court, to J&K.

1953

August	Sheikh Abdullah is dismissed as prime minister of J&K. Central government begins to erode various provisions of Article 370 of Indian Constitution, which limited central government's power to make laws for J&K.

1954

April	Presidential order removes customs barrier between J&K and the rest of India. Forty-three other orders are issued extending central legislation to the state.

1963

Bhutto-Swaran Singh negotiations: Pakistan's Zulfiqar Ali Bhutto puts forward concept of joint sovereignty for Kashmir, offering autonomy in domestic affairs and providing joint Indo-Pak control over foreign affairs and defense. India's Swaran Singh refuses in fifth round of negotiations.

1965

April–September	Second Kashmir war between India and Pakistan.

1975

February	Kashmir Accord returns Sheikh Abdullah as chief minister. But Kashmiris perceive this as a huge disappointment because now Abdullah must share power with Congress Party, a symbol of New Delhi's domination of J&K.

1982

September	Death of Sheikh Abdullah. Farooq Abdullah, his son, replaces him the following year.

1984

July	New Delhi dismisses Farooq Abdullah government for allegedly organizing a conclave of Indian opposition parties in Srinagar.

1986

March	New Delhi declares governor's rule in J&K.
November	Rajiv Gandhi-Farooq Abdullah Accord formalizes an alliance between Farooq Abdullah's National Congress (NC) and the Congress Party. Farooq is appointed chief minister of the NC-Congress coalition in J&K. Kashmiris see his appointment as another insult from a center that cares nothing for their rights.

1987

Muslim United Front enters the 1987 J&K Assembly Elections against the NC-Congress coalition but fails to gain its expected number of seats. Many Kashmiris, resentful of the political process, feel that NC-Congress has rigged the elections.

1989

Onset of Kashmir insurgency. Islamist "freedom fighters" step up activities in J&K.

1990

New Delhi handpicks Jagmohan Malhotra as governor of J&K. Under governor's rule, he uses an iron hand to quell the protests that have erupted against New Delhi's treatment of Kashmiris.

1993

Formation of the All Parties Hurriyat Conference, a group of twenty-six political and militant organizations, gives dissenters a political platform to express their grievances.

September New Delhi tries to stave off international pressure from human rights groups by introducing the Protection of Human Rights Act (1993). This act becomes the basis for establishing the National Human Rights Commission.

1996

March J&K Assembly elections are announced. Indian state perceives them as a success. NC government takes power.

1997

May Indian prime minister I. K. Gujral's United Front government tries to engage Pakistan through "composite dialogue" process. Prime Ministers Gujral and Sharif issue joint statement committing to address all bilateral issues, including J&K, and agree on format of the composite dialogue.

1998

Northern Command of the Indian army launches Operation Sadhbhavana, an attempt to target positive interventions in the Kashmiris' socioeconomic life.

May India, then Pakistan, tests nuclear weapons.

1999

February Indian prime minister Vajpayee and Pakistani prime minister Sharif sign Lahore Declaration. Both countries commit to resolve all bilateral issues, including Kashmir. A Memorandum of Understanding establishes eight confidence-building measures for both countries to undertake.

May–July Pakistani intrusion into Kargil region of J&K triggers Kargil conflict.

2000

July Hizbul-Mujahideen, the leading militant organization in Kashmir, announces unilateral three-month cease-fire. It is willing to negotiate if India will suspend its repressive security-centered approach and enter dialogue with Pakistani and Kashmiri separatists. New Delhi lets the opportunity pass.

2001–02

December Terrorist attack on the Indian Parliament is blamed on Pakistan-based militant organization Jaish-e-Mohammed. India's military mobilization in response brings the two countries to the brink of war again.

2003

April	Indian prime minister Vajpayee extends "a hand of friendship" to Pakistan in effort to revive dialogue on Kashmir.

2004

	Indian deputy prime minister L. K. Advani holds talks with moderate factions of the All Parties Hurriyat Conference in run-up to 2004 Indian general elections.
January	India and Pakistan release joint statement formally initiating peace process. The two nations begin back-channel discussions on Kashmir.
April–May	General elections take place in J&K. They are generally seen as fair, free of electoral manipulation from New Delhi.

2008

May 26	J&K government agrees to transfer 99 acres of Kashmir Valley forestland to the Shri Amarnathji Shrine Board to build facilities for Hindu pilgrims. The act sparks mass demonstrations in Kashmir Valley against the land transfer and protests from Jammu region supporting it.
November	Eleven coordinated shooting and bombing attacks in city of Mumbai are traced to Pakistan-based militant group Lashkar-e-Taiba. This stalls the official dialogue between India and Pakistan.

2010

Summer	Largest protest against Indian control of Kashmir since early 1990s occurs. It finally subsides in September, after Indian government defuses the crisis and compensates bereaved families.
December	India sends ten-member delegation of parliamentarians and civil society activists to interact with separatists and the Kashmiri people.

2012

September	India's foreign minister, S. M. Krishna, visits Pakistan.

2013

January	Indian and Pakistani soldiers are killed during crossfire along the Line of Control (LoC). Tensions rise momentarily.
February 9	Mohammad Afzal Guru, one of those convicted in the December 2001 attack on the Indian Parliament, is hanged in Delhi's Tihar Jail. Protests erupt in Kashmir because the hanging is perceived to be politically motivated.
August	Tensions rise again on the LoC as five Indian soldiers are killed.

1

Conflict in Kashmir

An Insurgency with Long Roots

Happymon Jacob

The conflict in and over Jammu and Kashmir is a legacy of the partition of British India into independent India and Pakistan in 1947. The first Indo-Pakistani war over Kashmir, in 1947–48, led to the division of the state into two entities—Azad Jammu and Kashmir (hereafter Pakistan-administered Kashmir [PAK]) and Jammu and Kashmir (J&K)—with the former staying within Pakistan and the latter becoming an Indian state. The LoC between India and Pakistan is the de facto border between these two parts.

Located in northwestern India, J&K borders Pakistan in the west, China in the north and east, and the Indian states of Punjab and Himachal Pradesh in the south. The state comprises three regions: the Vale of Kashmir (or Kashmir Valley), Jammu, and Ladakh. According to the 2001 census, Kashmir Valley has a population of 5,476,970; Jammu has 4,430,191; and Ladakh has 236,539 (MHA 2013). The eastern territory of Ladakh is ethnically Tibetan and mostly Buddhist, and Jammu, in the south, has a mixed population of Hindus, Muslims, and Sikhs. The Kashmir Valley, with its overwhelmingly Muslim majority population, has been at the center of the tensions in J&K through the years. It is also where the heart of the insurgency under discussion lies. In this chapter, much of the discussion about "Kashmiris" and "Kashmir" refers to the dynamics in the Valley and, to a lesser extent, troubled pockets of Jammu. The 1989 insurgency can be even more narrowly understood as referring to Kashmiri Muslims residing within the Valley (see map 1).

J&K has experienced a violent insurgency since 1989. The conflict has its roots in the various political and constitutional differences that have lingered since 1947 between the Indian central government in New Delhi and the people of Kashmir. That said, Kashmir is not just a case of an antistate insurgent movement. Its real importance on the international stage has come primarily from its being an internationally recognized dispute and, now, a nuclear flashpoint. It has earned South Asia the title as "the most dangerous place on earth" (Marcus 2000). In the name of Kashmir, India and Pakistan have fought wars, waged diplomatic battles at the United Nations, and claimed parts of J&K from each other's territory. The Indo-Pak crisis in 1990 and the Kargil conflict in 1999, both conducted under the shadow of nuclear weapons, were enacted in the Kashmir theater.[1] Pakistan's support to the insurgency in J&K since 1989 has, therefore, taken center stage in international discussions on Kashmir, to the neglect of the other major issue in Kashmir: India's failure to address the domestic grievances of Kashmiris nonviolently over the years.

In analyzing the reasons behind the onset of the Kashmir insurgency, this discussion will emphasize the domestic explanations, though without overlooking the Pakistan factor. The overarching argument is that New Delhi's denial of democracy to Kashmiris and its repeated attempts to destroy the sanctity of various democratic institutions in J&K are the proximate reasons for the Kashmir insurgency. The interstate dimension is important because Pakistan's claim over Kashmir created ambivalence among Kashmiri Muslims regarding their allegiance to the Indian state in the first place, and because direct Pakistani interference in the state, including support and training of armed groups, exacerbated the problems. Still, the bilateral context intensified but did not create the insurgency. A full understanding of why the insurgency erupted in Kashmir in 1989 requires both explanations.

According to Cousens and Kumar, helping institute "resilient and authoritative" political processes and providing for actors to consensually create and adapt their own political institutions to sustain viable political dynamics are central to peacebuilding (Cousens and Kumar 2001, 187–88). If so, the Indian state's efforts can be characterized as abysmal failures. For decades, the central government made many promises to accord Kashmiris their fundamental constitutional and political rights and redress the alienation they felt toward New Delhi, but these promises proved insincere and half-baked. Successive Indian governments since 1947 manipulated the political process in Kashmir to ensure that the ruling regimes in the state

1. For background and analysis on these crises, see Chari, Cheema, and Cohen (2007); Hagerty (1998).

remained favorable to New Delhi. This constant manipulation only deepened the feelings of alienation and disgruntlement among Kashmiris and was the single biggest factor in building up the momentum to the violent uprising of 1989.

Background to the Conflict

The story of this insurgency can never be fully told without explaining the India-Pakistan conflict over Kashmir and its origins and evolution. It is the interstate dimension of the Kashmir conflict that has received the most attention. It is what media and scholars alike have in mind when they speak of the "Kashmir dispute." According to the Indian Independence Act passed by the British Parliament in 1947, the princely states in British India, around 565 in number, could decide their own fate: whether to be part of India, part of Pakistan, or independent. But the last British viceroy of India, Lord Mountbatten, advised the princely states to join either India or Pakistan, thereby weakening the independence option. Most princely states negotiated with either India or Pakistan, depending on their geographical contiguity, and merged with one state or the other. The few significant exceptions were Hyderabad, Balochistan, Chitral, Junagadh, and J&K (Verghese 2010).

J&K was a Muslim-majority state ruled by a Hindu who wanted the state to remain independent from India and Pakistan. Both the Indian Congress Party, the predominant political force in India at independence and for many years thereafter, and Mountbatten advised him against independence. Nonetheless, Maharaja Hari Singh signed a "standstill" agreement with Pakistan, under which Pakistan guaranteed that the flow of essentials, such as trade, travel, and communication, through Pakistani territory would not be interrupted. Even as the ruler continued to hold on to his independence option, communal tensions rose within the state. Poonch district in the princely state was most affected, and some of the Muslim rebels who were not happy with the Hindu maharaja's rule and his reluctance to join Pakistan sought help from the Pashtun tribesmen across the border in Pakistan's Northwest Frontier Province (now called the Khyber Pakhtunkhwa). Pakistan made hay with this opportunity, sending in Pakistani army regulars in the guise of the tribesmen to take control of J&K (Dasgupta 2002).[2] By October 1947, thousands of Pakistani tribesmen and army regulars were fighting in Kashmir.

This forced Maharaja Hari Singh to ask the Indian government for help to stop the invaders from taking over the state. India demanded the princely state's accession as a precondition for help. The maharaja duly signed the

2. Pakistan contests this version. For a Pakistani perspective, see Hussain (1998).

treaty, joining the Indian Union on October 26, 1947, and Indian troops were airlifted to Srinagar. The local Kashmiris welcomed them. When a cease-fire was signed in January 1949, the cease-fire line approximated the ground positions of the Pakistani fighters/army and the Indian troops. As the dispute continued, the cease-fire line meant that PAK was left under Pakistani control and J&K under India's.[3]

On January 1, 1948, India made a formal complaint of aggression against Pakistan in the United Nations. The complaint was lodged under Article 35 of Chapter VI of the UN Charter, under which parties to the dispute would seek pacific settlement of disputes by "negotiation, enquiry, mediation, conciliation, arbitration, judicial settlement, resort to regional agencies or arrangements, or other peaceful means of their own choice" (UN Charter art. 35). UN deliberations and several resolutions followed. The spirit of the various resolutions concerning J&K, most importantly the key UN resolution of August 13, 1948, mandated a plebiscite and the withdrawal of invading troops of Pakistan from the princely state. However, neither the evacuation of invading troops nor the plebiscite ever took place. In the following years, both countries maintained the status quo in J&K without really resolving the problem. The Kashmir conflict has proved to be one of the most intractable disputes the world has seen over the past six decades.

Tracing the Roots of the Insurgency

After 1947, the global narrative on Kashmir remained fixated on the conflict's interstate dimension. The Indian Union's official line on the problems in J&K concurred by pointing to the bilateral context and Pakistan's meddling in the state as the underlying issues. But the Kashmir conflict, with its international and domestic dimensions, is multilayered and complex. At the core of the causes that led to the 1989 insurgency in J&K lie the many political anomalies created by the Indian state's mishandling of Kashmir over the years. Pakistan's role in keeping the Kashmir issue alive, and in the shape that the Kashmir insurgency ultimately took, has also been a major factor, though certainly less important than the domestic aspect.

A number of other factors have often been thrown up as causes of the Kashmir insurgency. Indeed, most Indian government-sponsored studies and scholarly analyses produced by research institutes in New Delhi, when analyzing the contours of the Kashmir problem, tend to present a vast canvas of issues. While this has certainly brought out the nuanced and complex nature of Kashmiri politics and has, to some extent, enhanced the understanding of the Kashmir issue, such analyses have also deflected attention

3. For some of the early history of the Kashmir dispute, see Schofield (2000); Korbel (1954).

from the core reasons for the insurgency, thereby impeding any meaningful identification of the remedies needed for sustainable conflict resolution.

Perhaps most frequently mentioned are misgovernance, lack of infrastructure development, the central government's unwillingness to devolve powers to local authorities, and administrative neglect.[4] But these are mere "add-on" factors, characteristically different from the two core issues mentioned earlier. The Kashmir conflict is not about good governance or infrastructure development. Governance and economic issues are not unique to J&K or, indeed, in any way special. These problems are found in all parts of the country and are dealt with by the various levels of government.

While most of the add-on aspects of the Kashmir conflict are contemporary in nature, the core conflict has clearly identifiable historical roots. These can be traced back to the circumstances surrounding the accession of J&K state to India, the failed promise of a plebiscite in the state, the watering down of Article 370 of the Indian Constitution, the imprisonment of Sheikh Abdullah (the charismatic Kashmiri leader and head of the most popular Kashmiri political party, the NC), the installing of puppet regimes in Srinagar by New Delhi, rigged elections, and rampant violations of the Kashmiris' human rights.

This section examines these many political and constitutional failures of the successive governments in New Delhi from 1947 to 1989 and analyzes the critical constitutional and political dynamics since J&K's accession to the Indian Union in 1947.

Constitutional Failure: Article 370 and Complicated Center-State Relations

The Indian state's biggest failure was in the realm of constitutional rights. Given the troubled circumstances surrounding J&K's accession to India, whereupon Pakistan immediately challenged the princely ruler's decision and claimed the state as its territory, it was critical for the Indian Union to define the contours of its relationship with Srinagar. Article 370 was introduced in the Indian Constitution, according J&K "special" status within the Indian Union. Putting this special treatment into effect essentially entailed stringent restrictions on the central government in New Delhi to legislate on matters concerning the state. Article 370 states:

> The power of Parliament to make laws for the said State shall be limited to:

---

4. Several official documents have taken this line in the past. Recently, the Indian government appointed interlocutors to explore ways to resolve the Kashmir issue. The committee's report goes to great lengths about the Kashmiris' economic and other related grievances. It also raises the issue of discrimination against Jammu and Ladakh by Kashmir Valley. The report is an apt example of how fundamental political issues are passed off as being merely economic or administrative problems. See Kumar, Padgaonkar, and Ansari (n.d.). Some other writings that point to nonpolitical aspects as causes of the problems in Kashmir are Pandit (2013); Morup (2010); Maini (2010).

> (i) Those matters in the Union List and the Concurrent List which, in consultation with the Government of the State are declared by the President to correspond to matters specified in the Instrument of Accession governing the accession of the State to the Dominion of India as the matters with respect to which the Dominion Legislature may make laws for that State; and
>
> (ii) Such other matters in the said Lists as, with the concurrence of the Government of the State, the President may by order specify. (SATP 2001a)

In other words, Article 370 clarifies that the Union government of India can make laws applicable to J&K State only in areas specifically mentioned in the Treaty of Accession of 1947. The treaty delineates only three areas where the government of India can legislate laws concerning J&K: defense, external affairs, and communications. The special relationship that J&K enjoyed with India also enabled it to have its own constitution, flag, prime minister (Wazir-e-Azam), and constitutional head of state (Sadr-e-Riyasat).

Writing on the origins of Article 370, well-known scholar Balraj Puri commented in his book, *Kashmir: Insurgency and After:*

> The special constitutional status of Jammu and Kashmir was, thus, not granted by the Government of India, but was sanctioned by the relevant provisions of the Government of India Act of 1935, the India Independence Act of 1947, the India (Provisional Constitution) Order of 1947 and the Instrument of Accession. . . . The Constituent Assembly of India or its successor Parliament had no constitutional right to abrogate or modify Article 370. The right belonged solely to the Constituent Assembly of the state. (Puri 2008, 25)

Article 370 has been the cause of significant controversy in India. A lack of consensus on the implications of according J&K special status has meant that Kashmiris were never truly accorded what the Article promised. Influential political circles and many others in India have continued to make the argument that the special status for J&K can affect the integration of the Indian Union—giving special status to one state may attract similar demands from other states as well, eventually weakening the center's control. Echoing this view, the right-wing nationalist Bharatiya Janata Party (BJP), which ruled India in the late 1990s and early 2000s, has always maintained that giving Kashmir special treatment will loosen India's control there, creating a domino effect in the other troubled parts of the country. The party has long argued that such actions would contravene the spirit of national integration (*Indian Express* 2012; Hassan 2010). This view, coming from many other quarters as well, has held sway even though several Indian states enjoy special provisions in varying degrees and are still as much a part of the Union as any other. Moreover, the Indian Supreme Court was also categorical in its judgment in *Khazan Chand v. State of Jammu and Kashmir* (1984), reiterating that J&K held "a special position in the constitutional set-up of our country" and that Article 370 formed the very basis for a constitutional relationship between the Indian Union and J&K (Indiacourts 2012).

Nonetheless, New Delhi has held a more skeptical view on Article 370. The Indian National Congress Party led India for all but three years between 1947 and 1980 and, thus, is singularly responsible for the Union's outlook toward J&K during this period. Its commitment toward Article 370 wavered constantly. Worried about loosened control over the state, New Delhi chipped away at the spirit of Article 370. Over time, most of the key features of this provision were distorted or removed until it was no longer recognizable. Interestingly, this was done in active collusion with J&K state governments that often acted at New Delhi's behest for political gain. The central government's constant encroachment has been a highly emotive issue for the various political formations and movements within Kashmir and, in turn, for the average Kashmiri.

Throughout much of 1947–80, J&K's point of view in negotiations with the center was represented chiefly by the NC, who, under Sheikh Abdullah, commanded widespread popularity throughout the state. The NC was a secular Kashmiri party whose politics were built around *Kashmiryat,* or Kashmiri identity.[5] New Delhi had appointed Abdullah the head of the emergency administration installed in J&K in 1947 and, later, the state's prime minister. In 1950, the president of India issued a constitutional order about J&K, specifying thirty-five Union entries (subjects on which legislation could be made) that fell broadly under the three subjects that the central government was empowered to legislate according to Article 370 and the 1947 Instrument of Accession (Jammu & Kashmir 1947). Despite this, the government of India, to quote Puri, "continued to persuade and pressurize the state government to accept more provisions of the Indian Constitution" (Puri 2008, 28). In July 1952, Indian prime minister Nehru and the sheikh entered into the Delhi Agreement on Centre-State Constitutional Relations. It was decided that under this agreement, the "Union flag will occupy the supremely distinctive place in the state" (which also had its own flag). "The fundamental rights of the Indian Constitution would apply to the state, and the jurisdiction of the Supreme Court would be extended in regard to the fundamental rights as well as in respect to disputes between states and between state and the centre" (Puri 2008, 28).

The Delhi Agreement's spirit was not honored for long. In August 1953, the towering political figure of Shiekh Abdullah was dismissed by the Sadr-i-Riyasat, Karan Singh (son of the former maharaja, Hari Singh), at the behest of the central government. Not only was Abdullah not given an

5. For a brief discussion of the NC's journey in J&K politics, see Chowdhary and Rao (2004), 1521–27.

opportunity to prove his support on the floor of the state assembly but he was arrested and later jailed for eleven years, accused of treason and conspiracy against the Indian Union in the famous *Kashmir Conspiracy Case* (Shah 1964).[6] Most Kashmiris saw the government's treatment of Abdullah as an insult; many even trace the beginning of serious Kashmiri resentment toward New Delhi to this time.

After Abdullah's dismissal, one of his former cabinet colleagues, Bakshi Ghulam Mohammed, was appointed prime minister. Mohammed, with little genuine support in J&K compared with Abdullah, was only too keen to obey New Delhi's diktats diluting important provisions of Article 370 by accepting the many presidential and constitutional orders that New Delhi issued thereafter. As Verghese points out, around forty-three constitutional orders with application to J&K and seeking extension of central legislation to the state have been issued since 1954 (Verghese 2010). Most significantly, the state government in J&K, at New Delhi's behest, made articles 356 and 357 applicable to the state, which meant that the central government could now dismiss the state government and assume power itself (Verghese 2010). Moreover, the state legislature was no longer empowered to elect its own governor. In due course, the title for the prime minister's post was also changed to "chief minister."

Sheikh Abdullah was released from prison in 1964. An attempt by New Delhi to negotiate with him on the future of the state was cut short when Indian prime minister Nehru died while negotiations were still ongoing. As Abdullah again became active in advocating rights for J&K, the central government attempted to crush him at every opportunity. All along, the Kashmiris continued to see New Delhi as a heavy-handed actor unwilling to honor the constitutional commitment made by the Indian Union through Article 370.

The next thaw in New Delhi-J&K relations came with the Kashmir Accord of 1974, signed between Abdullah's representative Mohammad Afzal Beg and Indian prime minister Indira Gandhi's representative G. Parthasarathy. Under the Accord, the sheikh was made chief minister of J&K. The Accord also provided for the restoration of Article 370, but the agreement was not specific enough to keep New Delhi honest. Consider, for example, the following paragraph from the accord:

> With a view to assuring freedom to the State of Jammu and Kashmir to have its own legislation on matters like welfare measures, cultural matters, social security, personal law and procedural laws, in a manner suited to the special conditions in

---

6. For more on this case, under which Sheikh Abdullah and many of his colleagues were jailed, see Sehgal (n.d.).

> the State, it is agreed that the State Government can review the laws made by Parliament or extended to the State after 1953 on any matter relatable to the Concurrent List and may decide which of them, in its opinion, needs amendment or repeal. Thereafter, appropriate steps may be taken under Article 254 of the Constitution of India. The grant of President's assent to such legislation would be sympathetically considered. (SATP 2001b)

Also, there was no agreement on the titles of the rulers of the state—the title of "prime minister" was not restored for J&K's chief political leader. The agreement read, "No agreement was possible on the question of nomenclature of the Governor and the Chief Minister and the matter is therefore remitted to the Principals" (SATP 2001b).

Even though the Kashmir Accord returned Sheikh Abdullah as chief minister, many Kashmiris considered the Accord itself a huge disappointment. Abdullah ended up sharing power with the Congress Party, which, to many, was a symbol of New Delhi's domination of J&K. Moreover, later NC governments did not try to restore Article 370 in its original essence. Verghese makes an important argument: "It is noteworthy that adjustments in Center-J&K relations have primarily been made through Presidential and Administrative orders rather than by means of constitutional amendments. The same route is therefore available for retractions, if any, that might be agreed upon in the future" (Verghese 2010, 20). That is to say, had the political will been there, the special provisions provided for J&K in Article 370 could have been restored with relative ease. But none was on display at any point between 1947 and 1989, when the insurgency broke out. Article 370 saw much debate and negotiation but little implementation in spirit.

Subversion of Kashmir's Political Processes

Intrinsically wedded to the constitutional gaps—in fact facilitated by them—was the mockery that New Delhi made of J&K's democratic process. From the outset, the Congress Party constantly subverted democratically elected governments in J&K and installed puppet regimes that lacked any local political support. Sten Widmalm points out, "From Jawaharlal Nehru's and Indira Gandhi's perspective, the sensitive border state simply was not ready for democracy. Building Indian nationalism and expanding democracy simultaneously, it seems, were sometimes considered incompatible goals, and it appears as if this reasoning was applied to Jammu and Kashmir in particular. An autonomous political opposition was regarded as a hindrance to national integration" (Widmalm 1997, 1007). But as Sumit Ganguly points out, this does not absolve Kashmir's own leadership of blame in stunting democratic evolution in the state and alienating the masses:

> In Kashmir, the process of institutional decay started even before Indira Gandhi. The singular political tragedy of Kashmir's politics was the failure of the local and the national political leaderships to permit the development of an honest political opposition. From the time of independence to his dismissal from office in 1953, Sheikh Abdullah dominated the politics of Kashmir. Subsequent NC regimes used the prerogatives of office to prevent the growth of any meaningful opposition. (Ganguly 1996, 100)

Successive regimes in New Delhi rigged elections in J&K time and again, jailed many Kashmiri leaders, installed puppet regimes in Srinagar, floated all sorts of political and nonpolitical outfits in the state to outwit the existing ones—only to float newer ones to replace these—violated human rights of Kashmiris, and killed hundreds of people in cold blood—all in the name of "national interest."[7] New Delhi—and the Congress Party in particular—believed that given the history of J&K and its proximity to Pakistan, the center had to micromanage the state's political activities and even manipulate them to keep Kashmir from slipping out of India's control.

Ever since 1953, New Delhi's heavy-handed measures toward J&K continued to build up underlying frustrations among Kashmiris. But it was the 1980s that turned out to be critical in sending this resentment over the brink and transforming it into a violent uprising. From the signing of the Kashmir Accord until Sheikh Abdullah's death in 1982, the status quo prevailed between the Center and J&K. State elections were held in 1977 without much notice. But the next elections, in 1983, proved definitive in determining Kashmir's future. Sheikh Abdullah's son, Farooq Abdullah, succeeded him as leader of the NC during the sheikh's lifetime. Under its new leader, the NC won the 1983 state elections against the Congress Party, taking forty-seven of the seventy-six state assembly seats (Puri 2008, 55–58). NC's outright victory did not sit well with Congress's continued obsession with micromanaging Kashmiri politics. As far as Congress was concerned, Farooq also committed another major transgression: He organized a conclave of Indian opposition parties in Srinagar. His romance with the opposition went squarely against the Congress's conception of national interest, which it quite clearly equated with its own dominance rather than with true democratic norms. The Congress rulers in New Delhi immediately sprang into action, maneuvering through the political landscape and quickly succeeding in enticing a twelve-member faction of the NC to defect and pledge allegiance to the Congress. Farooq's NC government was thereafter summarily dismissed in July 1984, and the Congress-led coalition comprising the ex-NC members was installed in its place (Koithara 2004, 61–62; Habibullah 2008, 52).

7. The best source for understanding the government of India's many misdeeds in Kashmir is Puri (2008).

Ironically, Kashmiri self-esteem was to be dealt an even greater blow—by none other than Farooq Abdullah himself. Son of the man who stood as the icon of J&K's rights for many Kashmiris, he was soon to join hands with the Congress to ensure his return to power. The Congress government in New Delhi managed to entice Farooq into a formal agreement, the Rajiv Gandhi-Farooq Abdullah Accord, in November 1986 (Puri 2008, 56–57). Ostensibly, the Accord was concluded to allow a focus of this partnership on economic development of the state and on tackling subversive forces (read *Pakistan*)—creating widespread resentment among Kashmiris. In reality, the Accord assured Farooq's return to power. In 1986, G. M. Shah, installed as chief minister after NC's dismissal in 1984, was shown the door, and after a brief period of "governor's rule," Farooq Abdullah was made chief minister of an NC-Congress coalition government in anticipation of the March 1987 state elections. The Kashmiris were not only disappointed in Abdullah but also more convinced than ever that New Delhi would ultimately continue manipulating the political process to the detriment of the Kashmiris' fundamental political rights.

The coup de grâce was to come with the widespread rigging engineered by the NC-Congress combine in the 1987 elections. It is now widely held that the 1984 dismissal of Farooq Abdullah's NC government, Farooq's subsequent U-turn regarding his relations with the Congress, and the rigging of the 1987 elections were the immediate triggers turning the Kashmiris' sense of alienation into violence in 1989.

The 1987 state assembly elections had a new political entrant that challenged the NC-Congress coalition. The Muslim United Front (MUF) was a broad coalition of Muslim groups seeking to energize voting along communal lines and, thus, had its greatest appeal in the Kashmir Valley. Despite little prior political support, the MUF, led by the religious political party Jama'at e-Islami and joined by other groups identifying with the Islamic cause, managed to mobilize youth from both urban and rural parts of the Valley in the wake of the disillusionment caused by the Rajiv-Farooq Accord (SAFHR 2012).[8] MUF "represented the first real challenge to the NC" since the Kashmir Accord (SAFHR 2012, 11). For the first time, Kashmiri politics was not about Kashmiryat only; it was now meshed with an unmistakable Islamic identity (Chowdhary 1998).

Despite its popularity, the MUF managed to bag only four seats in the Valley. The Congress-NC coalition, on the other hand, ended up with sixty-six of the seventy-six seats it contested statewide. The Rajiv-Farooq

8. The MUF included groups that identified themselves through their Muslim identity, such as the Jama'at-e-Islami, Ummat-e-Islami, and Anjuman-e-Ittehad-ul-Musalmeen. The People's Conference of Abdul Ghani Lone and the People's National Conference, led by G. M. Shah, supported the MUF but soon fell out (SAFHR 2012, 11).

combine had rigged the elections, manipulated the electoral process, and even beat up MUF's polling agents. An *India Today* article in 1987 revealed that before the elections, "600 opposition workers were arrested in areas where the MUF, independents, and People's Conference (PC) candidates were showing strength" (Badhwar 1987).[9] Many of the MUF cadres were disgusted by this and went on to form the core of the militant movement in Kashmir. For instance, Syed Salahuddin, the present head of the Islamist group United Jihad Council, based in PAK, had also contested the 1987 elections from the MUF platform. He agitated against the rampant rigging of the elections and was subsequently jailed. Later, he and many other disgruntled individuals decided that mainstream politics was unlikely to deliver legitimate rights for the Kashmiris and ended up joining the armed insurgency (Ganguly 1997, 92).

Farooq Abdullah's justification for being part of the center's designs is found in one of his earlier statements: "Anyone who wants to form a government in Kashmir cannot do so without sharing power with New Delhi. For the people did not matter much" (Puri 2000). Puri calls it the "Farooq doctrine." He writes:

> Farooq reframed his doctrine on Kashmir's relation with the centre by declaring his loyalty to any party that came to power in New Delhi; thus reaffirming his basic thesis that people of his state did not matter in forming a government. . . . If the Farooq doctrine is applied to any other state, it is doubtful if it would remain loyal to India. For it denies to the people the fundamental right of citizenship to change, choose and oppose the government of India and the party in power. By denying this fundamental right to the people of his state, he merely reminds them that they are less than full citizens of the country. Moreover, the people in no other state or in the country will give to any regional leader a monopoly of loyalty to India. For that is the surest way to divert popular discontent against monopolistic power in Kashmir to a secessionist channel and to a communal channel in Jammu. Before attempting any lasting solution of the Kashmir problem, the people of the state should first be allowed to exercise those minimum rights which people elsewhere in India take for granted. (Puri 2000, 2218–19)

What is tragic is that the security forces, policemen, election officials, and others who rigged the elections at various points in Kashmir seemed to have bought into the Indian Union's characterization of the Kashmir conflict. It was essentially portrayed as a Pakistan problem rather than as a consequence of New Delhi's mismanagement. The implementers of New Delhi's vision seemingly believed that they were serving the national interest. For the most part, public opinion in India was, amazingly, willing to buy these claims of national interest conveniently framed by the Congress

9. People's Conference is a Kashmiri political party established by Abdul Ghani Lone in the late 1970s. For Lone's political trajectory before and after the 1987 elections, see *Frontline* (2002).

leadership and New Delhi's ruling class. Indeed, much of what went on in the 1980s was the result of this narrow, biased, partisan, and imprudent understanding of national interest.

From Dormancy to Violence

Despite the long and uninterrupted history of center-state tensions over J&K, the insurgency in Kashmir remained dormant from 1953 to 1989. Perhaps the most obvious difference was that before the 1980s, even as New Delhi chipped away at various important aspects of Article 370, it always held out the pretense and offers of negotiations to J&K state governments. The 1980s saw far more direct manipulation of the political sphere and the NC's reconciliation with the Congress on terms humiliating to the Kashmiri people. The Rajiv-Farooq Accord, for one, meant that Kashmiris had lost their principal interlocutor with New Delhi. Erosion of NC's moral legitimacy in the mid-1980s opened up space for new, younger political actors who were not willing to kowtow to New Delhi's diktats. Communal lines hardened as parties such as the MUF pandered to the Valley's Muslims against the symbol of domination and subjugation: New Delhi. Reeta Chowdhari Tremblay points out:

> The NC party, whose various factions had ruled the state during the previous five decades, lost its hegemony over politics. Kashmir's traditional leaders, who had derived their legitimacy from the nationalist movement against the Dogra ruler in the forties, were replaced by the likes of the younger generation's Shabir Shah, Yasin Malik and Mirwaiz Umar Farooq whose appeal derived from the movement's successes in challenging the Indian state and from its pursuance of the goal of self-determination for the people of Kashmir. (Tremblay 1996, 471)

Moreover, as Ganguly notes, "Kashmiris, routinely denied their voting rights in deeply flawed elections, witnessed the increasingly free exercise of franchise in other parts of India. Realization of this distinction grew with the expansion of education and mass media in Kashmir and contributed to a growing sense of resentment against the malfeasances of the Indian state" (Ganguly 1996). The educated, unemployed, and disillusioned Kashmiri youth, who, as Victoria Schofield puts it, were neither part of the bureaucracy nor the elite, started talking the language of uprising and secession against the Indian state. Schofield also argues that the 1987 return to Pakistan of Amanullah Khan—the cofounder (along with Maqbool Bhatt) of the pro-independence militant organization Jammu and Kashmir Liberation Front (JKLF), established in Britain in 1964—also gave impetus to the Kashmiri nationalists based in PAK. Upon his return, Khan began to direct operations from across the border (Schofield 2010, 138–39). This was the beginning of a steady flow of Kashmiris into PAK for training and arms to fight the Indian state.

From 1988 on, a series of isolated incidents further aroused popular resentment and armed militancy in the state. With the state government having lost its legitimacy and authority in the wake of the 1987 elections, militants who were now steadily returning from PAK to J&K made occasional attacks against government installations in Srinagar. Anti-India demonstrations were on the rise as well. As Puri recalls, the Republic Day of 1989 was an important date, for that day was observed as a *bandh* (shutdown) throughout the Kashmir Valley. He weaves together the various instances: "A number of protest demonstrations followed: on the death anniversary of the JKLF founder, Maqbool Bhatt, on February 11, 1989; against Salman Rushdie's book, *The Satanic Verses;* against the death of the father of the People's League President, Shabir Shah, in police custody at Anantnag on April 5, 1989. All these protest demonstrations were marked by incidents of cross-firing between the police and the militants" (Puri 2008, 61). In the months to come, there were targeted political killings by militants, killings of Kashmiri Pandits (and the group's eventual exile), and numerous human rights violations by the security forces. With increasing frequency, the Kashmir Valley's streets were filled with defiant protesters; the situation was quickly turning into a mass mobilization.

It was within this context that even greater numbers of disillusioned Kashmiri youth went over to PAK, where they were trained by the Pakistani intelligence services and sent back along with veterans from the recently ended, Pakistan-backed Afghan war against the Soviet Union to carry out an armed insurgency in the state. Once the insurgency started, the militants were further emboldened by the Farooq Abdullah-led state government's and New Delhi's capitulation when, in December 1989, Union Home Minister Mufti Mohammad Sayeed's daughter Rubaiya Sayeed was kidnapped by members of the JKLF (Evans 1999, 24). It was almost certain that the militants would not harm the minister's daughter; that would have drained any sympathy for them among common Kashmiris. More importantly, a lot of people considered it un-Islamic and against the spirit of the indigenous Kashmiri culture to kidnap a young unmarried girl. However, the government met all of the abductors' demands, including the release of five militants, which not only emboldened the JKLF but also silenced those willing to speak out against the violence the organization was beginning to perpetrate.

The imposition of governor's rule and appointment of Jagmohan Malhotra as the state governor in January 1990 proved to be the final straw. Under his repressive handling, the situation further deteriorated. Jagmohan, handpicked by New Delhi, sought to restore order by authorizing the forces to use an iron hand in quelling the protests that by then had engulfed the whole Valley. The strategy led to large numbers of killings, long curfews, disappearances, and a string of human rights violations. Eventually, the insurgency entered a new phase in 1990, when it "was no longer a fight between the militants and the security forces. It gradually assumed the form of total insurgency of the entire population. The new phase was also marked by demoralization within the political system, followed by the collapse of the administration" (Puri 2008, 66).

The Interstate Dimension: Pakistan's Role in J&K

These, then, were the primary factors underlying the Kashmir insurgency. But the story is incomplete without the other core element underpinning the Indian state's woes in Kashmir. The Pakistani state never reconciled with the territorial distribution of Kashmir and has constantly sought a redrawing of the boundaries. Its outlook toward J&K implies that is has operated as a "revisionist" power seeking a change in the territorial status quo. Since J&K could have been a normal state of the Indian Union if not for the dispute with Pakistan in 1947, Pakistan remains central to creating ambivalence in Kashmiri minds about their identity as Indians. Pakistan has gone further, however, by proactively pushing its case through diplomatic and coercive means.

As discussed earlier, the initial occupation of what is today PAK by Pakistani tribesmen and troops is what divided Kashmir in the first place. Thereafter, Pakistan, while persistently pressing for a plebiscite, also made a number of arbitrary decisions over the years that not only increased the acrimony with India but also kept the pot boiling in J&K. In March 1963, Pakistan unilaterally signed an agreement with China and handed over to Beijing around 1,235,000 acres of territory in the Shaksgam area of the former princely state of Kashmir—land that had been under Islamabad's administration since 1947. Among other strategic repercussions for India, the agreement signaled to many Kashmiris that the territorial redistribution of J&K was a realistic possibility. Pakistan then sought to instigate an uprising in Kashmir and wrest control of J&K by sending armed infiltrators into J&K in 1965. According to Ganguly, the Pakistani leadership had assumed that both India's weakness, manifested in its defeat in the 1962 Sino-Indian war, and the troubled relations between the Center and J&K, represented by their failure to make political progress at the time—this was a year after Abdullah-Nehru talks were cut short by Nehru's death—would translate into Kashmiri support for the infiltrators. He argues that the politically quiescent nature of this particular Kashmiri generation failed Pakistan even though Islamabad's planners had correctly grasped the widespread resentment against New Delhi among Kashmiris in the Valley (Ganguly 1996). Nothing truly significant happened afterward until the India-Pakistan war, sparked by the crisis in East Pakistan in 1971, during which both sides crossed the cease-fire line. Pakistan lost the war, and East Pakistan became the independent country of Bangladesh.[10] Postsurrender deliberations led the two sides to sign the Simla Accord, which stated "that the two countries are resolved to settle their differences by peaceful means through bilateral negotiations. . . . Pending the final settlement of any of the problems between the two countries, neither side shall unilaterally alter the situation and both shall prevent the organization, assistance or encouragement of any acts detrimental to the maintenance of peaceful and harmonious relations" (MEA 2013). In essence, the fate of the Kashmir issue was deferred, but with the mutual promise to resolve it bilaterally.

Pakistan was largely absent from the scene until domestic events in J&K in the 1980s handed it an attractive opportunity to press its case once again. Pakistan not only backed the militants who were beginning to come together amid the political turmoil in J&K in the mid-1980s but also provided sanctuary and training to Kashmiri militants who then returned to J&K to assume key positions in the movement that ultimately grew into a full-fledged insurgency. Taking advantage of the popular uprising in Kashmir, Pakistan's intelligence agency, the Directorate for Inter-Services Intelligence (ISI), contributed by training hundreds of militants. In the beginning, these fighters were ethnic Kashmiris (Davis 1991; Ganguly 1997). Over time, foreign militants replaced the local Kashmiri youth. Perhaps Pakistan's biggest contribution was to gradually alter the tenor of the Kashmiri militancy from a nationalist movement to an Islamist one. Most of the foreign mercenaries shipped in by Pakistan after the insurgency had taken off wore the cloak of Islamic jihad as they waged their campaign against the Indian state.

Daniel Byman writes, "The proliferation of groups is in part a deliberate move on the part of Pakistan, which has tried to 'segment' the militant market to attract different types of support for the movements and to ensure its control. . . . All the leading Kashmiri militant groups fighting New Delhi had bases in Pakistan. . . . This haven allowed these groups to recruit, train, plan, proselytize, and enjoy a respite from Indian counterinsurgency efforts" (Byman 2005, 164). The existence of militant camps on the Pakistani side of Kashmir is something other authors on Kashmir have also talked about. Wajahat Habibullah writes that the Kashmiri disillusionment was "carefully nurtured and led by the ubiquitous ISI, [which] led to an outflow of young men to Pakistan's Kashmir and Afghanistan for training in the use of weapons—many seized from the retreating Soviet armies. . . . The migration of youths exposed grave weaknesses in the Indian defenses patrolling the LoC. In September 1988, the first group of Pakistan-trained

10. For an authoritative account of the 1971 war, see Sisson and Rose (1991).

youths was arrested by the Kashmir police; they were by no means the first to have crossed over the LoC" (Habibullah 2008, 67).

Many accounts have suggested that four factors encouraged Pakistan to indulge in a low-intensity war of this kind in the late 1980s and early 1990s:

1. It wanted to take advantage of the political turmoil and discontent in the Kashmir Valley during these years.

2. By the late-1980s, Pakistan had become nuclear weapon capable (able to assemble nuclear weapons on short notice), which gave it the confidence that India, fearing escalation, would not attack in retaliation (Kampani 2002).[11]

3. The Pakistan-trained fighters who had just defeated the Soviet Union in Afghanistan and were immersed in the fervor of jihad were jobless and, therefore, available to be shifted to the Kashmir front.

4. Pakistan wished to avenge the inability to achieve its objectives in the wars of 1947–48 and 1965 and its outright defeat in 1971 (Bhattacharjea 1994).

Had Pakistan not played the supporting role it did in the 1980s, the nature of the Kashmir insurgency would have been very different. If Pakistan had not given political, diplomatic, and military support to the Kashmiri youth who had turned against India, militancy in Kashmir may not have survived much beyond its start. Specifically, without the support from the Pakistani state, it would have been impossible for the Kashmiri militants to acquire sophisticated weapons, get adequate training, and have a base within the Indian part of J&K. Moreover, as mentioned, Pakistan contributed hundreds of non-Kashmiri mercenaries to the cause.

The Pakistani involvement in aiding the Kashmiri insurgency is undeniable. But this does not imply the conclusion often made by those holding the statist view in India: that Pakistan was ultimately responsible for causing the insurgency. Quite the contrary: The domestic political aspects of the problem outweigh the external factors in explaining the root causes of the insurgency. Pakistan can most accurately be seen as an active aider and abettor and sustainer of the insurgency, but not as its creator. In other words, Pakistan armed and trained a resistance movement that the Kashmiris began in response to New Delhi's misdeeds and blunders. The resent-

11. For a contrarian view of this argument, see Rajagopalan (2006).

ment, agitation, disillusionment, and rebellion that Kashmiris showed in the latter half of the 1980s did not stem from Pakistan's influence.

The 1989 insurgency, then, was not a Pakistani plan, even though the decision to support it in every possible way and to sustain it militarily was a well-orchestrated strategy. As Byman accurately argues, "Pakistan's role in creating the violence that escalated after 1989 was limited, but it quickly exploited the strife and made it far harder for the Indian government to defeat the insurgents" (Byman 2005, 167). Counterfactually, the acute resentment and mobilization in the Valley in the 1980s suggests that the insurgency would still have erupted without Pakistan, although it may not have lasted very long or been as intense, and the timing of its eruption could also have been different. On the other hand, without New Delhi's failure to give J&K its promised constitutional autonomy and fundamental democratic rights, no amount of Pakistani instigation would have led to the events of 1989.

Conclusion

The historically fractious relationship between New Delhi and the J&K state has been the single most important driver of the insurgency in Kashmir. This is a tale of a federal relationship that went terribly wrong. Specifically, the historical roots of the Kashmir conflict lie in (a) the dilution of J&K's special status (enshrined in Article 370 of the Indian constitution) over the years by the central governments in New Delhi; (b) the high-handed manner in which New Delhi has made a mockery of the democratic processes in the state of J&K; and, to a lesser extent, (c) Pakistan's armed support and training of the Kashmiri insurgents in the late 1980s.

In *Peacebuilding as Politics,* editors Elizabeth Cousens and Chetan Kumar put political processes and their stability at the center of external peacebuilding efforts. By focusing on the political distortions as a key driver of violence, this chapter has underscored New Delhi's inability to allow Kashmiris the opportunity to build their "political capacity to manage conflict without violence" (Cousens and Kumar 2001, 12). In fact, since Kashmiris saw New Delhi as the "external" actor, the central government actively undermined the possibility of transforming "intergroup relations into viable political processes" and, thus, became a cause of violence (Cousens and Kumar 2001, 187). The center instituted a constitutional provision for a special status for J&K, made numerous offers and attempts at dialogue, and, until the 1980s, kept up the pretense of wanting to restore Article 370 in letter and spirit. It nonetheless failed to prove its sincerity.

The Kashmir insurgency raged throughout the 1990s, causing tremendous loss of human life and property and further alienating the Kashmiris. Over time, however, the Kashmiri youth began to withdraw from the insurgency, which came to be increasingly dominated by Pakistan-sponsored foreign Islamist mercenaries. A lot more nonviolent conflict management came into the mix after the mid-1990s and especially in the early 2000s, as New Delhi sought to revive the democratic process and initiate dialogue with a number of dissident Kashmiri factions. In the rest of India, too, the debate on Kashmir has changed drastically. The country's mainstream discourse has switched from solely blaming Pakistan to a growing awareness of the nuances to the Kashmir problem and of the follies the Indian state has committed there. There is an understanding of the pervasive sense of alienation among Kashmiris and a growing realization that anti-India protests are not necessarily pro-Pakistan. There is also appreciation of the fact that the problem in Kashmir demands a political solution. All this has led to an unprecedented process of political reconciliation between New Delhi and Kashmiris in recent years. The logical conclusion of such a process is to correct the historical wrongs committed in Kashmir. The process in this regard is ongoing, but it needs to move at a faster pace and to continue being informed by the clear lessons of history.

References

Badhwar, Inderjit. 1987. "A Tarnished Triumph." *India Today,* Apr. 15.

Bhattacharjea, Ajit. 1994. *Kashmir: The Wounded Valley.* New Delhi: UBS.

Byman, Daniel. 2005. *Deadly Connections: States that Sponsor Terrorism.* Cambridge, UK: Cambridge Univ. Press.

Chari, P. R., Pervaiz I. Cheema, and Stephen P. Cohen. 2007. *Four Crises and a Peace Process: American Engagement in South Asia.* Washington, DC: Brookings Institution Press.

Chowdhary, Rekha. 1998. "The Muslim Identity and the Politics of Fundamentalism in Kashmir." QEH Working Paper no. 19, Queen Elizabeth House, Univ. of Oxford. www3.qeh.ox.ac.uk/pdf/qehwp/qehwps19.pdf.

Chowdhary, Rekha, and V. Nagendra Rao. 2004. "National Conference of Jammu and Kashmir: From Hegemonic to Competitive Politics." *Economic and Political Weekly* 39 (14/15): 1521–27.

Cousens, Elizabeth, and Chetan Kumar, with Karin Wermester, eds. 2001. *Peacebuilding as Politics: Cultivating Peace in Fragile Societies.* Boulder, CO: Rienner.

Dasgupta, Chandrashekhar. 2002. *War and Diplomacy in Kashmir 1947–48.* New Delhi: Sage.

Davis, R. A. 1991. "Kashmir in the Balance." *International Defense Review* 24 (4): 301–04.

Evans, Alexander. 1999. “Kashmir: The Past Ten Years.” *Asian Affairs* 30 (1): 21–34.

Frontline. 2002. “A Voice from Kashmir.” Aug. 3–16. www.frontline.in/navigation/?type=static&page=flonnet&rdurl=fl1916/19160200.htm.

Ganguly, Sumit. 1996. “Explaining the Kashmir Insurgency: Political Mobilization and Institutional Decay.” *International Security* 21 (2): 76–107.

———. 1997. *The Crisis in Kashmir: Portents of War, Hopes of Peace.* Cambridge, UK: Cambridge Univ. Press.

Habibullah, Wajahat. 2008. *My Kashmir: Conflict and the Prospects of Enduring Peace.* Washington, DC: U.S. Institute of Peace Press.

Hagerty, Devin T. 1998. *The Consequences of Nuclear Proliferation: Lessons from South Asia.* Cambridge, MA: MIT Press.

Hassan, Ishfaq-ul. 2010. “BJP Brings Up Issue of Revoking Article 370.” *dna,* Dec. 24. www.dnaindia.com/india/1485385/report-bjp-brings-up-issue-of-revoking-article-370.

Hussain, Ijaz. 1998. *Kashmir Dispute: An International Law Perspective.* Islamabad: Quaid-i-Azam Univ.

Indiacourts. 2012. *Khazan Chand etc. vs. State of Jammu and Kashmir and Others.* www.indiacourts.in/KHAZAN-CHAND-ETC.-Vs.-STATE-OF-JAMMU-AND-KASHMIR-AND-OTHERS_f8fdcfec-68a3-4309-90d7-4521b0aed3dd.

Indian Express. 2012. “Repeal of Article 370 Remains BJP’s Core Agenda: Advani.” July 10. www.indianexpress.com/news/repeal-of-article-370-remains-bjp-s-core-agenda-advani/972443/.

Jammu & Kashmir. 1947. “Instrument of Accession.” www.jammu-kashmir.com/documents/instrument_of_accession.html.

Kampani, Gaurav. 2002. “Placing the Indo-Pakistani Standoff in Perspective.” Center for Nonproliferation Studies. http://cns.miis.edu/reports/pdfs/indopak.pdf.

Koithara, Verghese. 2004. *Crafting Peace in Kashmir: Through a Realist Lens.* New Delhi: Sage.

Korbel, Josef. 1954. *Danger in Kashmir.* Princeton, NJ: Princeton Univ. Press.

Kumar, Radha, Dileep Padgaonkar, and M. M. Ansari. n.d. “A New Compact with the People of Jammu and Kashmir.” Report of the Group of Interlocutors for J&K. http://mha.nic.in/pdfs/J&K-InterlocatorsRpt-0512.pdf.

Maini, K. D. 2010. "Rajouri and Poonch: Identifying Early Warning Signals and Addressing New Challenges." IPCS Issue Brief no. 148, Apr. www.ipcs.org/pdf_file/issue/IB148-BPCR-Maini.pdf.

Marcus, Jonathan. 2000. "Analysis: The World's Most Dangerous Place?" *BBC News,* Mar. 23. http://news.bbc.co.uk/2/hi/south_asia/687021.stm.

Ministry of External Affairs (MEA). 2013. "Simla Agreement July 2, 1972." www.mea.gov.in/bilateral-documents.htm?dtl/5541/Simla+Agreement.

Ministry of Home Affairs, Govt. of India (MHA). 2013. "Jammu and Kashmir Division." http://mha.nic.in/uniquepage.asp?id_pk=306.

Morup, Tashi. 2010. "Understanding the Transformation in Ladakh: Issues, Threats and Early Warnings." IPCS Issue Brief no. 151, May. www.ipcs.org/pdf_file/issue/IB151-BPCR-Tashi.pdf.

Pandit, Kashinath. 2013. "J&K: The Deep Divide Within." Apr. 7. www.ipcs.org/article/india/jk-the-deep-divide-within-3875.html.

Puri, Balraj. 2000. "The Farooq Doctrine: Kashmir's Relations with New Delhi." *Economic and Political Weekly* 35 (26): 2218–19.

———. 2008. *Kashmir: Insurgency and After.* New Delhi: Orient Longman.

Rajagopalan, Rajesh. 2006. "What Stability-Instability Paradox? Subnational Conflicts and the Nuclear Risk in South Asia." SASSU Research Paper no. 4, Feb. www.sassu.org.uk/pdfs/R_Rajagopalan.pdf.

Schofield, Victoria. 2000. *Kashmir in Conflict: India, Pakistan and the Unending War.* London: I. B. Tauris.

Sehgal, Narendar. n.d. *Converted Kashmir: Memorial of Mistakes.* Chapter 20, "Kashmir Conspiracy Case." www.kashmir-information.com/ConvertedKashmir/Chapter20.html.

Shah, Mubarak K. H., ed. 1964. *The Kashmir Conspiracy Case, Report.* Srinagar: Legal Defence Committee.

Sisson, Richard, and Leo E. Rose. 1991. *War and Secession: Pakistan, India, and the Creation of Bangladesh.* Berkeley, CA: Univ. of California Press.

South Asia Forum for Human Rights (SAFHR). 2012. "Kashmir Chronology of Key Events—Page 11." www.safhr.org/index.php?option=com_content&view=article&id=72&Itemid=358.

South Asia Terrorism Portal (SATP). 2001a. "Article 370 of the Constitution of India." www.satp.org/satporgtp/countries/india/states/jandk/documents/actsandordinances/article_370_constitution_india.htm.

———. 2001b. "Sheikh-Indira Accord, 1975: Agreed Conclusions." www.satp.org/satporgtp/countries/india/states/jandk/documents/papers/sheikh_indira_accord_1975.htm.

Tremblay, Reeta Chowdhari. 1996. "Nation, Identity and the Intervening Role of the State: A Study of the Secessionist Movement in Kashmir." *Pacific Affairs* 69 (4): 471–97.

United Nations Charter. 2013. "Chapter VI: Pacific Settlement of Disputes." www.un.org/en/documents/charter/chapter6.shtml.

Verghese, B. G. 2010. *A J&K Primer: From Myth to Reality*. New Delhi: India Research Press.

Widmalm, Sten. 1997. "The Rise and Fall of Democracy in Jammu and Kashmir." *Asian Survey* 37 (11): 1005–30.

2

India's Response to the Kashmir Insurgency

A Holistic Perspective

Rekha Chowdhary

The Kashmir insurgency, as it manifested in 1989, was not an isolated political phenomenon but was very much rooted in the troubled history of the state of J&K, which can be traced back to the partition of the Indian subcontinent in 1947. It is a protracted conflict, having acquired complexity not only through the competing claims of India and Pakistan on the one hand and of the Kashmiris on the other but also through the interplay of its external and internal dimensions. The external dimensions are defined by the ongoing hostility between India and Pakistan over the question of Kashmir and its internationalization, whereas the internal dimensions are defined by the Kashmiris' deep sense of alienation from the Indian state.

Although the external and internal dimensions became meshed in Kashmir starting in 1989, the immediate context of insurgency stemmed from internal factors, especially the political events in J&K in the years immediately preceding the insurgency's outbreak. Both the armed militancy and the popular insurgency that shook the Kashmir Valley in 1989 were local responses to the situation. But once the local responses erupted, the external dimension also came into play and soon got intertwined.

Three distinct developments during 1989–90 marked the beginning of the present (post-1989) phase of conflict. First, armed militancy started making its impact through selective targeting of security forces, government officials, political activists belonging to mainstream political parties, and others perceived as sympathetic to the Indian state. Second, a popular upsurge, resounding with slogans of *azadi* (freedom), manifested in massive demonstrations on the streets of the Valley. Third, the political order collapsed. With people openly defying the state, the government had difficulty enforcing its writ.

Armed militancy came to capture the political imagination of Kashmiris immediately after the 1987 J&K state elections, which people perceived as heavily rigged. The election was a contest primarily between an Indian National Congress-NC alliance and the MUF. The NC had been Kashmir's most popular party since 1947 and traditionally operated as J&K's chief interlocutor with the successive central governments in New Delhi.[1] The party was led by Sheikh Mohammed Abdullah, the charismatic leader of Kashmir, until his son, Farooq Abdullah, succeeded him as the party president months before the sheikh's death in 1982. The NC lost popularity after Farooq Abdullah entered into an alliance with the Congress Party in 1986 and openly acknowledged that he had made his decision to sustain himself and his party in power. The Rajiv Gandhi-Farooq Abdullah Accord, as this alliance was termed, was hugely unpopular among Kashmiris, who felt that it was merely a ploy to bring Congress to power in the state through the back door. This development opened space for new political forces, which organized under the banner of MUF and sought to articulate popular resentment against the NC and the Congress. MUF, formed in 1986, was a conglomerate of a number of religious and political organizations.[2] Though led by Jama'at-e-Islami, which had only a limited popular base in rural Kashmir, MUF "could now fill in the political void created by the alliance especially in the anti-Congress and anti-center political constituency of Kashmir. This constituency was represented by the NC during the 1975–86 period through its politics of Kashmiri identity. The new conglomerate sought to represent it through a different kind of identity—a Kashmiri identity that was essentially Islamic" (Chowdhary 1998).

The MUF contested the 1987 elections but failed to win as many seats as it had expected. There was widespread belief that the NC-Congress combine had rigged the elections. This ultimately became the spark for the Kashmiris' deep-rooted resentment to boil over. Many of those associated

1. For a discussion on the NC, see Chowdhary and Rao (2004).

2. Before the formation of the MUF, a conglomerate under the name of United Muslim Front (UMF) formed at the initiative of Jama'at-e-Islami. But UMF was banned after a few months, and MUF was formed. Jama'at-e-Islami, Ummat-e-Islami, and Anjuman-e-Ittehad-ul-Musalmeen were the prominent parties that formed the MUF.

with the MUF were to form the leadership and cadre of the first generation of Kashmiri militants (Hewitt 1995).

Soon after the elections, a number of young people crossed the LoC, the de facto border dividing the former princely state of Jammu and Kashmir between India and Pakistan, in search of arms, training, and funding for waging a violent struggle in Kashmir.[3] Systematically trained in the camps established by Pakistan in PAK, the armed militants began the era of militancy in 1989 through their attacks on security forces, political workers, and government officials.[4]

Although most of the groups that combined to form the MUF (and People's Conference, which had remained out of MUF during 1986–87 but had a formidable presence in north Kashmir) formed their own militant wings, it was the JKLF that emerged as the major militant organization early on.[5] The JKLF was established much earlier but became involved in militancy only in 1989. Pakistan supported it at first but abandoned it in favor of Hizbul-Mujahideen (or Hizb). Hizb, like the JKLF, was manned by local Kashmiri youth, but its ultimate objectives were quite different from JKLF's. While the JKLF aimed at complete independence of the former princely state of Jammu and Kashmir (as it was before October 1947), the Hizb aimed at the state's merger with Pakistan. Quoting Amanullah Khan, chairman of the JKLF, Desmond notes that from spring 1990, Pakistan's premier intelligence agency, "the ISI (Inter-Services Intelligence) mounted pressure on the JKLF, harassing its leadership, hijacking recruits, and inducing or coercing JKLF members to join Hizbul-Mujahideen, or any of the many smaller, pro-accession, Islamic groups" (Desmond 1995, 5–16). Al-Umar Mujahideen and Ikhwan-ul-Muslimeen were two such pro-Pakistan factions that had come out of the JKLF in 1991 (Bose 2005).

Devoid of financial and other kinds of support from Pakistan and facing elimination of its cadre by the Hizb, JKLF was forced to declare a cease-fire in 1994 and, thereafter, operated as a political rather than militant group. By this time, militancy in Kashmir had acquired a more violent and brutal

3. Among those first to cross over to Pakistan for armed training was Mohammad Yusuf Shah, a candidate for one of the assembly seats in the city of Srinagar. He later assumed the name Syed Salahuddin and has since headed the Hizbul-Mujahideen. Others included Yasin Malik, chief of the JKLF, Abdul Hamid Sheikh, Ashfaq Majid Wani, and Javed Ahmad Mir. Known as the HAJI group, they were to form the core of JKLF.

4. Among the first assassination targets were Yusuf Halwai, the NC leader; Tikka Lal Taploo, the BJP leader; Neel Kath Ganjoo, the retired judge who had delivered the death sentence to JKLF founder Maqbool Bhatt; Lassa Kaul, director of Doordarshan, the Kashmir-based national television channel; H. L. Khera, general manager of HMT, an Indian watch manufacturing company; and Mushir-ul-Haq, vice chancellor of Kashmir University. But apart from these high-profile killings, what brought the militancy into the limelight was the JKLF's kidnapping of Rubaiya Sayeed, daughter of Mufti Mohammad Sayeed, the Indian home minister. In exchange for Rubaiya's release, the government released five JKLF members.

5. These included Al Barq, Al Fateh, Al Jehad, Allah's Tigers, and others.

form. In the name of Islamic jihad, groups manned by mercenaries from Afghanistan, Pakistan, and other countries started operating there. The three major organizations operating through foreign jihadi elements were Harkat-ul Mujahideen (HuM), Lashkar-e-Taiba (LeT), and Jaish-e-Mohammed (JeM).[6] Many smaller groups were also active. Most of these groups either were associated with the larger groups or were front organizations, floated in the wake of government bans imposed on some of the prominent organizations. Although the years 1990–95 can be seen as the peak period of the militancy, militants remained active in Kashmir throughout the 1990s and the early years of the new millennium (Srivastva 2009, 12).[7]

Although the city of Srinagar was the focus of the first militant attacks, violence reached the rural areas of Kashmir in early 1990. By the middle of the decade, it had proliferated to the Jammu region, especially in Doda district, adjoining Kashmir Valley, and the bordering districts of Poonch and Rajouri. Later years saw a substantial decrease in the number of militants. By 2008, the official estimate of militants active in the state was eight hundred, including three hundred foreigners (Srivastva 2009, 12).

In 2004, India's Ministry of Home Affairs recorded "a perceptible decline in the number of (militant) incidents and also, in the number of civilians, security forces personnel and terrorists killed" (MHA 2005, 1).[8] There has been a substantial further decline in militancy since 2004 (MHA 2011, 6).[9]

Pakistan had a significant role in sustaining militancy in Kashmir. Involved in the insurgency from the very beginning, it provided direct support, both politically and militarily. Portraying the militants as "freedom fighters," Benazir Bhutto, then prime minister of Pakistan, pledged to them

---

6. HuM started working in Kashmir in 1993. It was initially named Harkat-ul-Ansar. Harkat, based first in Pakistan and then in Afghanistan, was established in the mid-1980s. It was active in terrorist operations in Burma, Tajikistan, and Bosnia. JeM is a more recent organization, formed in 2000 by Pakistani cleric Maulana Masood Azhar.

7. We can get some idea of the number of militants active during this period from the number killed by security forces. 2,213 militants were killed between 1990 and 1992; 1,310 in 1993; and 1,596 in 1994 (Bose 2005, 128). According to the Indian Home Ministry, 976 militants were killed in 2004, 917 in 2005, 591 in 2006, 472 in 2007, 339 in 2008, 239 in 2009, and 232 in 2010 (MHA 2011, 6).

8. The Ministry of Home Affairs recorded a much lower number of incidents of militant violence in 2004 than in 2003, and fewer civilians and security forces killed. There were 3,401 incidents in 2003; that number shrank to 2,565 in 2004. 795 civilians and 314 security forces were killed in 2003; 707 civilians and 281 security forces were killed in 2004. In 2003, 1,494 militants were killed; this number declined to 976 in 2004 (MHA 2005, 1).

9. According to official figures made available in March 2011, 13,215 civilians, including 698 political leaders, were killed from 1990 to February 25, 2011. The highest number of civilians killed in one year (1,275) was in 1996.The total numbers of civilians killed during the past few years are 707 in 2004, 557 in 2005, 389 in 2006, 158 in 2007, 91 in 2008, 78 in 2009, and 47 in 2010 (MHA 2011, 6).

Pakistan's full "moral and diplomatic" support in 1990 (Schofield 2003, 149). Meanwhile, the ISI got deeply involved in militancy, providing arms and financial backing to militants, establishing training camps, and even sending the trained militants to Afghanistan to acquire practical training (Bose 2005). Desmond notes that as the "young Kashmiri men began to cross into Pakistan by the hundreds in search of weapons and training, the Pakistan military and intelligence services quickly woke up to the opportunities at hand. Jama'at-e-Islami (JI), which has very close ties with the ISI, played an instrumental role in pushing for a policy of direct support for the rebels" (Desmond 1995, 8). In its efforts to control the militancy directly, the ISI not only strengthened Hizb but also encouraged "zealot Islamic groups based in Pakistan, such as Harkat-ul-Ansar, to enter the Kashmir war" (Bose 2005, 127).

Since its onset in 1989, the political insurgency continued to change its form in response to developments from both within and from outside the insurgency. The popular legitimization of violence that characterized the early phase of insurgency, for instance, was not to be seen in the later period. Rejecting violence of all kinds, including armed militancy, the popular response came to be articulated more in favor of political means and dialogue. But well before the shift in popular discourse actually took place, Kashmiris felt the need to give the militancy a political face. The All Parties Hurriyat Conference (APHC) was formed in 1993, with Mirwaiz Umar Farooq as its chairman. The APHC was an amalgam of about twenty-six political and militant organizations following different ideological paths, ranging from those with pro-independence inclinations to those with the goal of merging with Pakistan. For some of these organizations, religion was at the center of conflict, and Kashmir was part of a global jihad, which was in the headlines at the time because of the decade-long "jihad" against the Soviet occupation of Afghanistan during the 1980s. But other organizations felt that the conflict was indigenous and political in nature. Despite the differences within its ranks, the "Hurriyat Conference gave the militants a united political platform through which they could voice their grievances" (Schofield 2003, 160).[10]

The Indian state's response to the insurgency has been changing according to the shift in the nature of insurgency and the interpretation of the re-

10. The Hurriyat Conference is a broad-based organization whose support remains linked with the separatist politics of Kashmir. The support base of each of its component groups is limited to a few pockets. The JKLF, for instance, is Srinagar based, with the locality of Maisuma as its stronghold; the Awami Action Committee, led by Mirwaiz Umar Farooq, has its base in downtown Srinagar; the People's Conference, founded by Abdul Ghani Lone, was based in north Kashmir, particularly Kupwara district; Jama'at-e-Islami, led by Syed Ali Shah Geelani, is based in Sopore and Baramulla. Rather than representing any specific constituency, the Hurriyat Conference represents the separatist sentiment.

ality on the ground by successive political regimes. But it took a long time to reach a stage where the possibility of peacebuilding could truly be explored. The first problem that the Indian state faced was to restore its authority and have some semblance of political order. As the state's authority was asserted, the state agencies, particularly the central political leadership in New Delhi, started looking for ways and means to build peace in a more sustained manner. The approach to peacebuilding that evolved over the period included three elements. First, even while the militaristic response was considered indispensable, the Indian government recognized that the long-term approach had to be political. Second, India also recognized that the problem had a complex character of intertwining external and internal dimensions. Therefore, it began to understand the need to address both dimensions holistically. Third, India also acknowledged that long-term peace could not come about until the people's confidence in the state had been restored and that institutionalized democratic mechanisms were vital to achieving this.

This chapter analyzes the response of the Indian state during six phases of insurgency. Each stage involved both military and political responses, although the political aspects of counterinsurgency became progressively more important. The first section deals with the response during the initial phase of insurgency (1989–92), when the state faced not only the armed militancy but also popular defiance. During this period, the state approached the problems at hand using purely coercive mechanisms. By 1993, as the state began to reestablish its writ, it sought to extend its strategies in other directions—the focus of the second section. The third section examines the role of surrendered militants in suppressing militancy and is an introduction of the "political processes" after 1995. The fourth section deals with the external dimension of the problem, especially the tensions and engagement with Pakistan. The fifth section discusses the Indian state's reticent approach toward internal dialogue (until 2000), and the sixth section deals with the comprehensive peace process as India's strategy for dealing with the insurgency in Kashmir (2002 onward). The concluding section presents an assessment of the current situation and thoughts on the way forward.

Insurgency and Political Upsurge: The Initial Phase

Although the 1989 outbreak of armed militancy, backed by Pakistan, resulted from the Kashmiris' widespread political discontent, the Indian state initially responded mainly to the militancy, not to its source. All its strategies, therefore, were geared toward vigorously tackling militancy, which it saw as a "proxy war" waged by Pakistan. Popular resentment, which was explicitly manifesting through massive protest demonstrations, was merely a "law and order situation" to be handled in an administrative manner or through the coercive apparatus of the state. In any case, the state did not have the political wherewithal to deal with the situation in 1989–90. It lost the political initiative mainly because the situation in the Valley was aggravated thanks to excessive political manipulation by the Congress, the center's ruling party during 1984–89. Moreover, Kashmir was experiencing a political vacuum created by the local political elite's eroding credibility. The ruling alliance, especially the NC, was ill equipped to deal with the situation, because it had grown too distant from the people, while the rest of the Kashmiri political leadership had joined the ranks of separatists and militants.

Historically, India has privileged Kashmir's strategic, security, and territorial aspects over political aspects. The situation, as it was evolving in 1989–90, was seen in this strategic context: armed militancy challenging the sovereignty of the Indian state and endangering the security of its citizens and its boundaries.

Even though there were ample warning signs throughout 1987–89, the situation seemed to have taken the Indian government by surprise. The best strategy that could be imagined at that time was to hand J&K over to an efficient administrator who could deal with the growing "law and order problem." Jagmohan Malhotra, who had earlier served the state as governor, was brought back to deal with the situation. But after his arrival, any available minimal political mechanisms were grounded. While the NC-Congress government, formed after the controversial 1987 Assembly election and led by Farooq Abdullah, resigned in protest, the Legislative Assembly was dissolved to make way for governor's rule (later converted to presidential rule). This started a prolonged period of administrative governance under the supervision of the central government in New Delhi.

According to Puri, bringing in Jagmohan as governor of the state was a tactical mistake that "brought New Delhi into direct confrontation with the Kashmir rebels. The dissolution of the State assembly by the Governor . . . further removed whatever vestige of a buffer was left. . . . The Kashmir problem thereafter acquired a new complexion—India versus Kashmir, with corresponding psychological change on either side" (Puri 1993, 60). Jagmohan saw the situation in black and white and did not recognize the local base of the popular unrest. As Schofield notes, he "saw the insurgency as a movement, abetted by Pakistan, which had to be brutally crushed" (Schofield 2003, 150). In his understanding, a tough approach was needed to deal with "inner and outer forces of terrorism," which had "conspired to subvert the Union and to seize the power" (Jagmohan 1991, 21).

In many ways, the Indian state's stance toward the armed militancy in Kashmir was influenced by its approach toward the terrorism it had confronted in the northwestern state of Punjab during the 1980s. By the time the political upsurge in Kashmir started, the armed militancy in the Punjab had receded. However, it had generated a discourse around the need for a "strong state" to maintain the unity and integrity of an India threatened by terrorism perpetrated by external forces. Though Kashmir represented an altogether different case—where militancy was supplemented by massive popular response never experienced in the Punjab—the state saw the crisis here simply as terrorism. The popular upsurge was played down, in fact, since the armed militancy was seen as challenging the unity, integrity, and sovereignty of the state. The fear of being perceived as a "soft state" was a self-imposed pressure that called for a militaristic response from India.

The complete breakdown of civil authority in Kashmir further impelled the Indian state to respond in a militaristic manner. The situation in Kashmir during 1989–90 was quite precarious. The popular response against the state was so intense that it was difficult to enforce authority of any kind. Mass demonstrations occurred almost daily. People came out in the thousands and, a few times, in the hundreds of thousands, joining the long marches and openly chanting the slogans of azadi. There was no way to contain the mass response. People openly defied curfews. On the other hand, to show their utter disregard for the authority of the state, they strictly observed the call of "civil curfew" by any militant group. The local government was totally ineffective in dealing with the situation.

Bringing in a large number of security forces and giving them extraordinary powers to deal with the situation was part of the Indian state's militarized strategy. The police were incapable of dealing with the situation and, therefore, were replaced by paramilitary forces stationed in large numbers throughout Kashmir. The Central Reserve Police Force (CRPF) was the first such force brought to the Valley. This unit was charged not only with maintaining law and order but also with countering the insurgency. But after a few years, responsibility for counterinsurgency operations was given to the Border Security Forces (BSF).

To give the security forces absolute authority in their counterinsurgency operations, several laws had to be extended to J&K. The local Public Safety Act (1978), which had the provision of keeping people in detention without charge—up to a year in cases of threat to public order and two years in cases of threat to security of the state—was amended and made more stringent in 1990. Later, the Armed Forces Special Powers Act (1990) and the Disturbed Area Act (1997) were introduced, giving the army officials sweeping powers and immunity from prosecution for "anything done or purported to be done in the exercise of the powers conferred by this Act."[11] Authorities invoked several additional laws over the course of the insurgency.[12] Apart from the security forces, the intelligence service was also involved.

It was also during this time that restrictions were placed on the press. While foreign correspondents had restricted entry into the Valley, local correspondents' mobility was constrained by the curfews. The central government, meanwhile, encouraged a self-imposed censorship in "national interest" (Puri 1993).

This one-track militaristic approach, while helping bring down the level and intensity of militant violence and restoring order, became counterproductive and intensified separatist sentiments. By the end of 1990, mass protests and demonstrations ceased as the writ of the state came to be enforced. But this came at the cost of further alienating the masses. The massive use of force affected not only militant operations but also the lives of ordinary people. Apart from the day-to-day harassment during the crackdowns, house-to-house searches, and body searches at any public place, there were frequent cases of arbitrary arrest, torture in custody, and disappearances. There were also a large number of killings of civilians caught in crossfires, in extrajudicial custody, and during protest demonstrations. In particular, indiscriminate firing on people participating in protests generated much public anger and legitimized the armed militancy in the eyes of common Kashmiris. In aggravating the situation in Kashmir, two specific incidents of indiscriminate firing on protest marches proved critical. These included the protest march against security forces' crackdown in Gaukadal in January 1990 and the funeral procession of Mirwaiz Maulvi Farooq, the spiritual leader of the Muslims of the Kashmir Valley and a prominent politician, in May 1990. These incidents have become permanently etched in the Kashmiris' collective memory as manifestations of the repressive nature of the Indian state (Navlakha 1993).[13]

This perception of the repressive attitude of the state was exacerbated by the reality that the security forces tasked to bring order were not trained to

11. Armed Forces (Jammu and Kashmir) Special Powers Act (AFSPA), 1990, Clause 7; Gazette of India Extraordinary, Part II, Section 1. The AFSPA gives army officers, even at the very junior level, discretionary powers, including giving the order to shoot and kill if, in the officer's opinion, this is required to maintain public order; to destroy any shelter from which there is a possibility of armed attack or that militants can use as a hideout. The Act also allows arrest without warrant, and use of force for that purpose on grounds of suspicion.

12. These included the National Security Act (1980), the Prevention of Terrorism Act (2002), and the Enemy Agents Ordinance (2005).

13. Navlakha notes that by January 1993, eighty-seven probes by the Government of J&K had been ordered into cases of transgression by the security forces. A large number of militants were killed, but the number of custodial deaths was not known. Around four thousand people were detained under the national preventive detention law, TADA. Also, there were a large number of missing persons (Navlakha 1993, 2442).

deal with a situation like Kashmir's. The local police were sidelined by these forces and did not play a role in the first year of the insurgency. This near-total absence of a local enforcement element estranged the people, and the political element was also missing. The state was placed under president's rule and was directly administered by the governor and his advisers. The governors who succeeded Jagmohan were from intelligence and army backgrounds and did not have much political acumen. Therefore, even the normality and order they managed to create had limitations. This new "order," imposed by the coercive arm of the state, changed the overall social climate of Kashmir. This resulted not only from the increased physical visibility of the armed forces—with bunkers in the streets and large army camps in the rural areas—but also from the security presence in the local administrative systems. The number of companies of security forces deployed in the state had increased substantially, from 36 companies in 1989, to 300 companies and one entire division of the army by 1993 (Navlakha 1993).

By the beginning of 1990, the presence of the security forces was quite marked in the city of Srinagar, J&K's summer capital. Paramilitary forces routinely patrolled the main streets and guarded strategic locales, such as government buildings, banks, and hotels. Meanwhile, bunkers were set up all over, including in the narrow lanes of the old city's interior. People were frisked at the soldiers' whim, areas were cordoned off, and anyone passing by or relaxing in the city's open places was subject to search. The security forces had been "successful in establishing themselves as a dominant and quasi-permanent institution," ensuring "the daily functioning of the society, overseeing the safety of the roads, keeping the tourist spots open and even manning the Hindu Temples" (Tremblay 2001, 571).

Second Phase: From "Law and Order" to Political Possibilities

As the Indian state managed to establish public order in the Valley, it sought to extend its strategies to deal with the insurgency. By 1993, it also sought to respond to the pressure of international human rights organizations, such as Amnesty International, which had been taking note of, and reacting to, the cases of human rights violations. Although the state continued with its insensitivity to the human rights discourse, perceiving it as detrimental to the national interest, it also felt the need to go beyond purely coercive mechanisms. While still not allowing international human rights organizations to visit Kashmir, the state made its first efforts toward internal legal measures. It introduced the Protection of Human Rights Bill (1993), which became the basis for establishing a National Human Rights Commission (1993). The state now also felt the need to address the Kashmiris and take on the responsibility of respecting their rights. But the coercive mechanisms in place and the almost complete dependence on security forces made it difficult for the state to stand by its own commitments. Nevertheless, the component of human rights sensitization came to be introduced in the training of army and paramilitary forces.

Meanwhile, the state also started exploring the political possibilities more seriously. The Narasimha Rao-led government of the Congress Party in New Delhi took some political measures concerning Kashmir in 1993. A cabinet committee was formed to find ways of opening "dialogue" on Kashmir, and the internal affairs minister, Rajesh Pilot, was sent to Kashmir on a goodwill mission. Even though these measures did not change the ground situation, they did suggest an acknowledgment that purely military means were becoming counterproductive and that the government needed to supplement these with political initiatives.

Again, much of the state's response was defined by the ground situation in Kashmir, which, after 1993, was largely under the control of security forces. The level of militant violence had been brought down, and a large number of militants killed. JKLF, the indigenous organization that had initiated armed militancy in Kashmir, had come under massive pressure from the Hizb, which sought to establish its supremacy there. The internal struggle for domination came as an opportunity for the Indian security forces. The hardcore element of JKLF was eliminated, and the organization was forced to declare a unilateral cease-fire. Shibli notes, "By 1994, almost all the insurgent groups in Kashmir were in disarray; the JKLF had surrendered and its chief called for peaceful struggle. Other groups like Al-Jihad, Muslim Janbaz Force, Al-Umar and Jamiat-ul-Mujahedeen had entirely vanished leaving the Hizb as the only Kashmiri insurgent group with any presence of credibility" (Shibli 2009, 25).

An opening was also seen in the Kashmiris' changed orientation toward militancy. Although they still identified with the cause of the militants, they were feeling the brunt of the violence in many ways. Puri notes, "The militants lost some of their original élan due to a number of reasons: a continuous proliferation of groups, confusion and division in their ranks, regarding their ultimate objective, and Pakistan's changing policy towards different groups of militants" (Puri 1993, 78). Then some fundamentalist organizations sought to intervene and change the social and cultural patterns of society. Their dictates led to the closure of cinema halls and beauty parlors. But Kashmiri society did not approve of many of their interventions. Specifically, the attempts to restrict the freedom of mobility and education of women met with forceful, though silent, resistance from the women themselves. Fundamentalism, in any case, was alien to Kashmir, which had a rich philosophical tradition and was attuned to cultural openness. Islam, popularized by the Sufi Order, was rooted in the humanist traditions.[14]

Another cause of militancy's decline was common criminality. Many of the new recruits to the insurgency, who were not necessarily as ideologically committed as the original militants, indulged in intimidation and extortion. As a result, the kinship that the masses had originally felt with the militants was gradually lost. The entry of the jihadis also affected the relationship between the people and insurgents. The jihadis were initially welcomed as "guest militants," but their lack of sensitivity to local cultural and religious practices soon alienated them from society. However, what disenchanted the people most was the intensity of the violence and its implications for Kashmiri society. The ascendancy of gun culture over everything else had taken a toll on society, not only in the number of people killed but also in other ways. With the fear of the gun being clear and present, and dissenting voices facing the threat of death, the society had become muted. Along with this sense of abiding fear came the psychological trauma linked to prolonged violence. As time passed, there came a growing sense of fatigue and disillusionment with militancy and violence.

It was in this context that the central government started talking about restoring the political process in Kashmir. During 1994, there were frequent references to "political process" and "normalization" in the Indian government's political discourse in the context of J&K (Schofield 2003). In fact, during Prime Minister Narasimha Rao's formal address to the nation on August 15, he announced that a political process would begin in J&K. To show that it was serious, the government also released from detention several top separatist leaders, including Shabir Shah, Syed Ali Shah Geelani, and Abdul Ghani Lone. (Yasin Malik had earlier been released on bail.)

During this phase, then, the political element entered the policy discourse. But the fundamental strategy still remained wedded to applying coercive mechanisms in response to what was popularly seen as the proxy war being waged by Pakistan. Even within counterinsurgency operations, however, there was greater professionalism in the way the security forces operated. The operations of the various forces on the ground were now coordinated under a unified command, which was established in 1993 (Schofield 2003, 169). With the chief minister as chairman, and the general

14. Islam came to Kashmir as the Hindu social order was overburdened by the weight of rituals, superstitions, and sectarian divides. Islam formed the basis of a liberating, resurgence movement, with its own popular cultural form. This popularized religious humanism and drew upon eclectic influences, including Hindu Shaivism. The Rishi order played an important role in popularizing this cultural form of Islam in Kashmir. This order was established by Sheikh Noor ud Din, a local Sufi mystic who was influenced by the spiritual ideas of a female Hindu mystic poet, Lalleshwari, who had rebelled against the dogmatic traditions of Brahmanism and was spreading the message of humanism (Chowdhary 1998, 5).

officers commanding of the Fifteenth and Sixteenth Corps as security advisers, the unified command comprised the army, BSF, CRPF, and state police. The same year, Rashtriya Rifles, an elite unit of the army specializing in counterinsurgency operations, was also created. In 1994, the local police were activated. In the police, the Special Operations Group was also set up and would assume a major role in the counterinsurgency operations after the mid-1990s.

Third Phase: The "Renegades," Counterinsurgency, and a Political Process

What became the most crucial strategy for dealing with the insurgency was the involvement of former militants, also known as renegades. Many of the militants who had been captured by the security forces were "rehabilitated" and integrated into counterinsurgency operations by the security forces.

Many militants chose to surrender because of pressure put on them by security forces and also because of the changed nature of militancy. While many of those who surrendered lacked political commitment or still had criminal links, most of them had initially been drawn to militancy by an ideological commitment to their vision of azadi (Bose 2005). They subsequently became disillusioned by the violence and by Pakistan's role in the conflict. One militant who chose to surrender said, "After the first few years of militancy, by 1992–93 or so, I had come to realize the futility and destructiveness of armed struggle as a means to achieving our ends in Kashmir. I had also seen through Pakistan's game, which was to exploit us for its own ends" (Syed 2000). Bose notes that many among those who surrendered were the "front-ranking militants" of pro-Pakistan groups, who were "genuinely disillusioned by what they perceived as Pakistan's corrupting influence on the struggle and the willingness of the pro-Pakistan hard core to perpetrate violence against those among their own people who did not agree with them" (Bose 2005, 133). Explaining this point, he refers to the attacks by Hizb not only on JKLF but also on other, smaller militant groups: "Many of these ex-guerrillas, and their relatives and friends, sought protection, or vengeance, or money—or all three—through collaboration with the Indian counterinsurgency campaign" (Bose 2003, 133–34).

Many young people had joined the insurgency with the expectation that it would lead to a definite result of liberating Kashmir from India. Faced with the might of the Indian state, they could understand the futility of violence as the strategy for attaining this goal. Firdous Syed, who was among the most prominent militants, explains: "In reality, people as well as the militant and separatist leaders were carried away by the popular euphoria [that] overestimated the strength of their movement and underestimated power of a state and its capability of resorting to violence. The ill-prepared throng of militants who lacked proper planning and prospective thinking, proved utterly insufficient in the face of vast resources of an all powerful modern state" (Syed 2007).

Many others had joined the insurgency in the post 1989–90 period, not for ideological reasons but for the power and money involved. While their presence changed the very character of militancy and contributed to the disillusionment of the first-generation militants, they could not sustain themselves as militants and either were killed or chose to surrender. Syed notes:

> In "Pindi Chalo" (let's go to Rawalpindi) syndrome, thousands flocked for militant training across the border without even knowing the ABC of militancy. And the worst irony is that a student, a layman, a "Khar," "Najjar," "Gilkar," "Thantur" and "Zamindar" (ironsmith, carpenter, mason, coppersmith and farmer) all were turned into militants and militant commanders after simple seven-days dry training and sent back to get consumed as cannon fodder while facing the second largest Army of the world. Bereft of any ideology, conceptually and technically weak crowd of militants stimulated the proliferation of many scores of militant organizations, turning the whole scene into a battle of "free for all." Group hegemony, criminalization and pursuits for vested interest became the order of the day. (Syed 2007)

Ethnic divides also played a role in weakening the militant ranks. As Schofield notes, many of the militants who had surrendered were ethnically non-Kashmiris and not as ideologically committed as the Kashmiri militants: "That many of them were reported to be Gujars who had not traditionally supported the militancy, reflected the dynamics of an insurgency which, in reality, had not engendered widespread support from amongst the non-Kashmiri speakers of the Valley" (Schofield 2003, 198–99).

Militants who surrendered and joined the security forces contributed a lot in weakening the armed militancy in Kashmir. While many of them were absorbed into the police, many others were encouraged to float their own organizations (Ghate 2002). Of these, Kukka Parrey, initially associated with the Jammu Kashmir Student Liberation Front, emerged as the powerful pro-India militant who formed Ikhwan-ul-Muslimeen. Muslim Liberation Army, Muslim Mujahideen, and Al Ikhwan were other organizations launched by the surrendered militants. The targets of these organizations were the cadres of Hizb and other Pakistan-supported militant groups active in Kashmir.

The Ikhwani counterinsurgents, as these surrendered militants came to be known, provided not only the missing local element in the counterinsurgency operations but also, more importantly, the crucial insider element. Having been part of the insurgency, they were the best source of intelligence. Now, armed with the patronage of the security forces, they could break the back of the insurgency.

The effectiveness of the strategy of involving the former militants in the counterinsurgency operations could be gauged through New Delhi's confidence about the possibility of holding elections in J&K in 1996. Despite the general sense of fatigue associated with the militancy, holding elections without enlisting the ex-militants would have been quite a far-fetched idea in the given situation. Significantly, there was the problem of a political vacuum. During the prolonged violence, not only had the mainstream political parties and processes gone under, but even the separatist political forces represented under the banner of the APHC were no longer in command. The growing weariness of violence was now causing a shift toward the political course of action. But the space that was being created definitely did not have much room yet for mainstream politics. For one, mainstream politics, delegitimized since 1987, was seen as opposed to the separatist movement, and those participating in it were seen as betraying the cause that underlay the movement (Chowdhary and Rao 2003). There was also the practical problem of holding elections. Not only was there a fear of delegitimizing the electoral process—the people might boycott the election, thereby reducing it to a farce—but there was also concern about gun-wielding militants who would not allow such a process to go smoothly. Then there was the issue of the unavailability of a political party ready to take on the political mantle. Most of the political parties, including the dominant NC, faced with the resentment of the people on the one hand and threat of death at the hands of militants on the other, had gone to ground. A sudden return to the political scene to contest elections was, thus, not an easy process.

Aware of the considerable challenge involved in restoring political governance, the government of India sought to create suitable conditions. To send a signal to Kashmir about a change of its strategy, it released a number of political prisoners who had been in detention for a long time. At the same time, the government also brought the alienation of the Kashmiris into focus. By the mid-1990s, there was a clear feeling within political circles that the government had mishandled the situation and that the militaristic approach had its limitations and needed to be supplemented with some kind of political symbolism. The feeling was much stronger than in phase two. Now the sense was that concrete actions were needed. It was during this time that Narasimha Rao talked of delivering autonomy to the Kashmiris, saying "only the sky is the limit" (Ahmad 2000). Emphasis was placed on autonomy as a substitute for azadi, with the United Front government in New Delhi committing to give "maximum autonomy" to J&K (Ahmad 2000). In preparation for elections in J&K, Mulayam Singh Yadav, who was holding the portfolio of defense minister under the United Front government in New Delhi, visited Kashmir in

June 1996 and promised that the people's aspirations would be met and autonomy would be restored (Navlakha, Manchanda, and Bose 1996). Later, the NC was persuaded to contest elections on the grounds that the central government would give a sympathetic ear to its long-standing demand for restoration of autonomy.

By the time the elections were announced in March 1996, the surrendered militants had become a force unto themselves and, therefore, could facilitate the electoral process. By breaking the hold of militants in many areas, especially in northern Kashmir, these surrendered militants could create a situation in which elections could actually take place. Apart from countering the guns of the militants, the surrendered militants also formed their own political parties and put up candidates. Among the parties floated by them were the Awami League of Kukka Parrey and the Awami Conference of Hilal Haider.

The resulting 1996 Assembly elections were a success for the Indian state. By holding elections, it was able to install the NC government and bring about a change from administrative to political governance. The central government continued to face the challenge of legitimacy, however. The 1996 elections were still held under the supervision of the security forces—a fact that led to widespread allegations of coercion. Moreover, even if the armed militancy was contained to a large extent, the popular separatist sentiment challenged the state's ability to regain mainstream political space. This challenge was even more problematic because the ground situation for the people had not changed much. The militaristic approach to dealing with insurgency was intact even when a civil authority was in place.

Moreover, there was also a downside to using the surrendered militants: Their extralegal power and lack of accountability added to the people's woes. This introduced another dimension of violence to the already violence-fatigued society. Backed by the security forces yet left totally free to indulge in acts of violence, the counterinsurgents further alienated the people from the state. Like the surrendered militants, the Special Operations Group within the local police also added to the general discontent. Although it became more professional and modernized and succeeded in containing militancy via its local intelligence network, it used coercive and arbitrary methods to achieve this end.

The above problems notwithstanding, the somewhat broader strategies used by the state in the third phase proved effective not only in tackling the armed militancy but also in creating a situation in which the political vacuum, existing since the onset of militancy, could be filled. Restoring the political character of local administration and governance was an important step forward in the process of tackling the insurgency. And the political space so reclaimed, while very much contested, could later expand and generate processes that had the potential for democratizing governance.

Interestingly, political initiatives such as the release of prisoners also helped generate political space within the separatist sphere so far dominated by the armed militants. This was so because their release and reentry into the political arena signaled the distinction that the Indian state drew between armed militants and separatists following political mechanisms. This not only brought an element of negotiability to the conflict but also changed the local discourse with the militants. The militants who had already come under physical pressure built up by the security forces now also felt political pressure. With the diminishing popular support for militancy, the militants were forced to retreat from many areas, change their tactics, limit their level of operations, and reassess their targets to avoid public displeasure.

With the political government in place, attempts were also made to give the Kashmiris economic incentives. From the very beginning, the conflict had constricted economic development of the state, making it dependent on subsidies and loans from the center (Planning Commission 2003). The State Development Report of the Planning Commission reported:

> The trend in the development of Jammu and Kashmir was not encouraging. It was lagging behind most of the states in regard to the growth of Net State Domestic Product (NSDP) at current prices. The average annual growth of Net State Domestic Product at current prices during 1980–81 to 1999-2000 was 12.45 per cent for Jammu and Kashmir as against 15.01 per cent, 14.28 per cent, 13.83 per cent and 14.3 per cent for Andhra Pradesh, Gujarat, West Bengal and Kerala respectively. In the case of the growth of Per Capita Net State Domestic Product at current prices also, the state of Jammu and Kashmir was lagging behind most Indian states. The average annual growth of Per Capita Net State Domestic Product at current prices during 1980–2000 was estimated as 9.63 per cent for Jammu and Kashmir against 12.9 per cent, 11.63 per cent, 11.63 per cent, and 12.86 per cent for Andhra Pradesh, Gujarat, West Bengal and Kerala respectively. (Planning Commission 2003, xxv)

With only marginal industrial development, the employment situation, especially for educated youth, was dismal. Soon after the formation of the government, the NC promised government jobs, and in 1997–98, a package of twenty-six thousand jobs was announced (Planning Commission 2003). Even before this, in 1996, the state was given an economic package that also included a major rail link between Udhampur and Baramulla. Both the central and state governments also offered various other special packages for youth.[15] To create employment opportunities through indus-

15. These included Jammu and Kashmir Self-Employment Scheme, Prime Minister's Rozgar Yojana, Swarna Jayanti Shahari Rozgar Yojana, and Swarna Jayanti Gram Swarozgar Yojana.

trialization, the New Industrial Policy of 1998 was also announced (Planning Commission 2003).

That the situation was improving was clear. And yet, despite all these efforts, the overwhelming emphasis on the militaristic strategy—and its role in the Kashmiris' continued lack of confidence—was equally obvious. The gun culture that people found themselves trapped in (now by three different sources of violence: militants, security forces, and surrendered militants) continued to generate a sense of deep antipathy, and the brutality of the local police further alienated the people.

Fourth Phase: Engaging Pakistan

New Delhi still attributed the primary responsibility for the insurgency to Pakistan, but it had no direct engagement with Islamabad on the issue of Kashmir. The general refrain since the beginning of militancy had to do with keeping "the military option" against Pakistan open. In view of the armed training camps in PAK and the continued supply of arms to the militants, the Indian discourse dwelt on the need for remaining in a state of preparedness for war with Pakistan. Although the United Nations and other international forums provided space for the prime ministers and foreign ministers of both countries to meet, nothing came of these meetings. In 1992, diplomatic relations grew so strained that both countries expelled each other's diplomats. India's aggressive posturing manifested clearly in 1994 when Prime Minister Narasimha Rao claimed India's rights over PAK (Dahlburg 1994).[16]

In 1997, under the United Front government led by I. K. Gujral, India took the initiative of engaging Pakistan. It was under his leadership and vision for India's foreign policy, formulated as the Gujral Doctrine, that a composite dialogue began with Islamabad. New Delhi made some efforts to get past the traditional position of blaming Pakistan for aiding and abetting the armed militancy in Kashmir and agreed to discuss all outstanding issues, including Kashmir, with Pakistan. In a joint statement in May 1997, Gujral and his Pakistani counterpart, Nawaz Sharif, committed to address all issues including J&K (Lyon 2008). But despite engagement between India and Pakistan at the level of foreign secretaries and prime ministers, the peace process initiated during Gujral's time could not be sustained. With the change of government after the 1998 parliamentary elections in

16. Narasimha Rao responded to a statement made by Benazir Bhutto, then prime minister of Pakistan, that Pakistan would not stop its support for Kashmiris in their fight against security forces, since Kashmir was a part of the unfinished agenda of partition of India. Referring to this statement, in his Independence Day address to the nation, Rao said, "The one unfinished task is that Pakistan vacate its occupation of those areas of Kashmir which are under its control and should form part of India" (Dahlburg 1994).

India, the Indian position toward Pakistan started hardening once again. The BJP, which came to the helm, had a different approach toward Pakistan and Kashmir. L. K. Advani, India's new home minister, saw the problems in Kashmir mainly as "terrorism," to be resolved through a tough stance toward Pakistan.

This was a period of immense unpredictability in relations between India and Pakistan. Nuclear tests by both countries in May 1998 raised tensions. Some opening in the relationship could be seen during Indian Prime Minister Vajpayee's visit to Lahore in 1999. During this visit, both prime ministers signed the Lahore Declaration. Also, the foreign secretaries of the two countries signed a memorandum of understanding. The declaration resulted in intensified efforts to resolve the two nations' issues, including J&K. But soon after Vajpayee's visit to Lahore, the Pakistan army instigated the Kargil War, and relations hit a new low.[17] Fresh efforts were made to ease tensions between the two countries after the war, but an attack on the Indian Parliament in December 2001, allegedly conducted by Pakistan-based militants, brought the two countries to the verge of war again (Ganguly and Kapur 2012, 54).

Despite all these hostilities, there was an underlying force pushing India and Pakistan toward fresh initiatives to engage diplomatically. Externally, Pakistan's newly acquired nuclear status had placed their mutual tensions in the international glare; therefore, the pressure to resolve outstanding issues was intense. Internal forces were also driving both sides toward reconciliation despite the continuing frictions and both countries' official and declared positions. Pakistan was facing internal crises on the political, security, and economic fronts, making it difficult to continue the militaristic engagement in Kashmir. For India, its emerging economic status had redefined not only its trade- and finance-related ambitions in the international arena but also its political ambitions. Seeking its place in the emerging international order, it needed to resolve its internal conflicts and have a more congenial relationship with its neighbors.

Then there were reasons internal to Kashmir. Holding on to Kashmir through the coercive power of security forces was not the best scenario for India. New Delhi was realizing that beyond a certain point, repressive methods were counterproductive. Along with increasing alienation of the Kashmiris, the central government's methods were inviting international censure. From within the army itself, voices were being raised for resolving

17. The Kargil War was triggered in the spring of 1999 by some two thousand infiltrators from Pakistan who crossed the LoC and captured Indian army posts in the Kargil-Drass area of Kashmir. The infiltrators included Pakistan army regulars and militants. India retaliated, but the war remained largely contained and ended swiftly without growing into a full-scale conflict across international borders (Schofield 2003, 207–08). For a more detailed account of the Kargil War, see Lavoy (2009).

Kashmir politically. In 2000, the retiring army chief, Gen. V. P. Malik, had clearly taken a position that the Kashmir issue could not be resolved through militaristic methods. Acknowledging the alienation of the local people, he stressed the need for political initiatives to counter this feeling. Moreover, this perspective was not merely his personal view, but a general feeling within the army, as is clear from the statement of his successor, General Padmanabhan: "In the history of mankind no insurgency has been solved by any army" (Noorani 2000). Within political circles as well, a strong feeling was emerging for a more aggressive political initiative on Kashmir. Not only were the people feeling a strong urge for peace and normality, but the separatist leaders were also showing flexibility and offering to engage in dialogue with the government of India. With the exception of some hardliners, such as Syed Ali Shah Geelani, most of the separatist leaders could feel that the movement had gone astray. Many of them, including Abdul Ghani Lone, felt that the presence of foreign militants was a hindrance to resolving the Kashmir issue. It was not just a case of censuring the foreign-based militancy from within, however, but an overall sense of dissatisfaction with the armed militancy that had grown progressively across the four phases of the insurgency thus far.

Fifth Phase: Moving toward Formal Dialogue

By 2000, voices in favor of political resolution to the Kashmir issue were growing louder. There were many more references to dialogue with Kashmiris. But even now the Indian state remained quite hesitant. Though it had opened back channels with the separatists, it did not openly acknowledge the need for dialogue. At best, there was ambivalence about the political discourse. Much of this ambivalence resulted from the ideological position of the BJP, which favored a hard-line stance on Kashmir and against Pakistan. In 1999, the Vajpayee government turned down the demand for autonomy that the NC-led state government in J&K had formalized after winning the 1996 state election. The J&K government's State Autonomy Committee had strongly recommended restoring the state's pre-1953 constitutional status.[18] On this recommendation, the state assembly had also passed an autonomy resolution, which demanded effective steps by both the central and state governments for implementing the report. The cabinet in

18. The terms of reference of the State Autonomy Committee were "to examine and recommend measures for the restoration of autonomy of the state of Jammu and Kashmir consistent with the Instrument of Accession, the Constitution Application Order, and the Delhi Agreement of 1952"; "to examine and recommend safeguards that be regarded necessary for incorporation in the Union/State Constitution to ensure that the Constitutional arrangement that is finally evolved in pursuance of the recommendations of this Committee is inviolable"; and "to also examine and recommend measures to ensure a harmonious relationship for the future between the State and the Union" (*Report of the State Autonomy Committee* 1999, 5–6).

New Delhi summarily dismissed the resolution without even a discussion (Chowdhary 2000).

The NC and its autonomy slogan were important resources that the state agencies could have used meaningfully in their fight against insurgency, especially in a situation where there was growing disillusionment with armed militancy and an urge for normality. True, there were not many takers for the NC's autonomy slogan during the 1996 assembly elections. But that was mainly because of the NC's lack of credibility and its track record of subordinating the interest of the people to its own ambitions. Still, the mood had shifted enough that the autonomy slogan could have generated some positive response. This would also have given the NC a much-needed sense of legitimacy. After all, the party was still the most important indigenous political organization, with roots in Kashmiri history and cadres all the way down to the village level. Given a chance, it could have re-created a space for itself even within the overall support for the azadi sentiment. The two were not necessarily in opposition to each other and, given the right context, could even act in alliance.

The central government, for its part, had frittered away another important opportunity to tackle the insurgency politically: the cease-fire offer by Hizb. In July 2000, Hizbul-Mujahideen, the most active indigenous militant organization, which had earlier enjoyed mass support in Kashmir, announced a unilateral cease-fire for three months.[19] It had hinted at a further extension of the cease-fire if India responded positively to its demands, which included suspension of the state's repressive approach and initiation of dialogue with Pakistani and Kashmiri separatists (Noorani 2000). The BJP-led National Democratic Alliance government in New Delhi had been offering to talk to the militant organizations if they shunned the path of violence, and it had initially welcomed the cease-fire, but even so, it couldn't muster the flexibility required to respond to the offer. Making a clear distinction between Hizb as "our own people who may have strayed towards the path of militancy" and Pakistan, which was responsible for "cross-border terrorism," it promptly rejected the idea of engaging Pakistan. Nor did it offer Hizb much political space for negotiation.

In assessing New Delhi's response during this period, it is worth noting that India's acknowledgment of the need to shift the strategy from militaristic to political efforts certainly helped create an environment that emphasized dialogue over dependence on violent methods. The cease-fire initiative by Hizb, therefore, was the high point for this new strategy by the Indian state.

---

19. The Hizb cease-fire was a well-developed plan involving both India and Pakistan. Noorani notes, "It was not a sudden move. Neither India nor Pakistan nor the United States was taken by surprise. Nor were the leading figures of the All Party Hurriyat Conference (APHC); except perhaps, by the timing of the announcement" (Noorani 2000, 3949).

But the strategy was not properly worked out, and without the needed political will, New Delhi couldn't make the most of the opportunity. Stuck in the "security paradigm," it had too little confidence in dialogue as a process.

On the positive side, having brought the militancy down to a manageable level, the Indian state could now divert its energies to tackling the popular alienation. After replacing administrative with political governance, it made fresh attempts to bring a shift in the popular response. One of these involved goodwill projects by the army itself. In 1998, the army's Northern Command launched Operation Sadbhavana, aimed at positive interventions in Kashmir's socioeconomic life. Activities included rebuilding educational infrastructure damaged during the period of militancy, running goodwill schools, opening vocational training centers for women, providing medical care through primary health centers, and opening community development centers.

The government also introduced sizable economic packages in 2002 and 2003. The largest one, however, came in 2004, when Prime Minister Vajpayee pledged twenty-four thousand crore rupees for the state's economic development.[20] A major chunk of the package was to be spent on building hydroelectric projects in J&K.

Sixth Phase: The Comprehensive Peace Process

A major shift in India's approach to tackling the insurgency in Kashmir took place in 2003, when Prime Minister Vajpayee initiated the Comprehensive Peace Process. It was not until he came out boldly in favor of the peace process that the political aspects of New Delhi's strategy really became less tentative. Aimed at resolving all outstanding issues between India and Pakistan on the one hand and addressing the internal context of discontent and alienation among the Kashmiris on the other, this process was formalized during the South Asian Association for Regional Cooperation meeting in January 2004. The composite dialogue, as the process came to be known, represented a major shift in India's approach to tackling the insurgency in Kashmir. It formally recognized the complexity underlying the Kashmir problem. This new approach was peculiar in its willingness to tackle all issues through a process of dialogue—a process that would take place at both the India-Pakistan and India-Kashmir levels. Until now, India had not officially recognized either the centrality of Kashmir as the major point of tension between India and Pakistan or the need to engage Pakistan on this issue. Now for the first time, Prime Minister Vajpayee was taking the initiative to engage Pakistan on various tension points between the two countries. These included disputed territorial issues, such as Siachen and Sir

20. One crore = 10,000,000.

Creek, and other concerns, such as terrorism, drug trafficking, and economic exchanges. The issue of J&K was also included in this list (Ghosh 2009, 1).

Even before the comprehensive peace process was formalized, Vajpayee had already started giving indications of the Indian government's changed approach toward Kashmir. He had been taking a position quite different from New Delhi's traditional position. One could get a glimpse of it during his address to the nation on Independence Day 2002. Rather than merely repeating the usual rhetoric on Kashmir, he spoke of the people's suffering and of healing their wounds. During the same address, he also mentioned the Kashmiris' "trust deficit" regarding the Indian state. Acknowledging the Kashmiris' distrust of the electoral process, he promised "free and fair" elections. But most significantly, he owned up to the Indian state's mistakes in Kashmir and promised to make amends (*Times of India* 2002).

Vajpayee paved a new beginning for the Kashmir issue by going beyond the territorial approach. He tried to see the problem from the perspective of the Kashmiri people and sought to win their hearts and minds. His commitment to free and fair elections was aimed at winning the confidence of common Kashmiris. It was in pursuance of this commitment that the 2002 general elections took place under the eye of the international community and were generally perceived to be fair. Significantly, the security forces were kept away from the electoral process, and consequently, there were no allegations of coercion. What satisfied the people most, however, was the absence of electoral manipulation from New Delhi. After a long history of rigged elections, the people felt a sense of gratification that a government was voted out of power in J&K by the common people rather than through manipulation by the center.

The shift in the Indian state's approach to Kashmir became more visible during the spring of 2003. Visiting the Valley, Vajpayee was categorical in stating that problems could not be resolved through the barrel of the gun. All issues, "whether internal or external," could be solved only by talks. "It may take time but no blood will be spilt. Humanity has to be the bottom line" (Jaleel 2003). Making dialogue his central point, he said that there was no problem that could not be resolved peacefully and democratically and hinted that dialogue with the separatists would begin. Significantly, Vajpayee put considerable emphasis on the denial of democracy in Kashmir and the Indian state's role and responsibility in it: "Today, our sincere commitment to bring peace and normalcy to Jammu and Kashmir makes me admit that we have often faltered in our journey towards this goal. It was sometimes forgotten that democracy is too delicate a plant to be subjected to manipulation and mishandling. We must learn from these mistakes and resolve not to repeat them" (Tareen 2005, 98).

Laying out the new approach, he extended "a hand of friendship" to Pakistan, adding, "We have everything which makes us want to have good relations" (Bukhari 2003; Jaleel 2003).

The formal initiation of the Indo-Pakistan peace process took place in January 2004 when the two heads of state, in a joint statement, laid down the basis for normalizing relations. While President Musharraf assured Prime Minister Vajpayee that he "will not permit any territory under Pakistan's control to be used to support terrorism in any manner," both agreed to start the process of a composite dialogue "for peaceful settlement of all bilateral issues, including Jammu and Kashmir" (SATP 2004).

The composite dialogue had significant implications for Kashmir. Until then, India had maintained that Kashmir was an internal issue and that nothing related to it could be discussed with Pakistan (except, of course, the issue of PAK's return to India). But now, for the first time since the beginning of the insurgency, the Kashmir dispute's centrality to Indo-Pakistani friction was acknowledged and brought into the bilateral sphere.

In opening dialogue channels with the separatists, the Indian government held two rounds of talks with the moderate faction of the Hurriyat Conference, led by Mirwaiz Umar Farooq, before the 2004 general elections. The initiation of this dialogue generated much excitement in Kashmir. It acknowledged the Kashmiris as the main party in the conflict and provided them a role in the process of its resolution. Even though the talks revolved around general issues, such as calling for "an end to all forms of violence at all levels" and agreeing to a "step by step approach" to resolve all outstanding disputes related to J&K, they signaled the beginning of a new approach to the resolution of conflict—an approach that was more open, participatory, and attuned to the realities on the ground (*Indian Express* 2004).[21]

Along with dialogue with the separatists, the peace initiatives for Kashmir included major confidence-building measures (CBMs). Opening bus service and trade across a few points on the LoC has been, by far, the most important CBM. This was a major development since, up to this point, the LoC had divided the former state of J&K between India and Pakistan and was militarized and sealed by the two countries. This division made it virtually impossible for people on the two sides to have any interaction with each other. Based on the concept of "fluidity" or "irrelevance" of borders, this CBM has made the movement of the people across the LoC possible,

21. The mood of Hurriyat after its first meeting with Vajpayee on March 23, 2004, is reflected in Mirwaiz Umar Farooq's statement: "The Hurriyat believes that a new era of peace is beginning in the sub-continent. We have a firm belief in Vajpayee's vision and Musharraf's realism which will herald a new atmosphere where disputes like Jammu and Kashmir will be resolved amicably and peacefully" (*Indian Express* 2004).

thereby helping thousands of divided families get together. It also ignited hope for this landlocked state to have a better economic future by becoming a major hub of trade activity between India and Pakistan.

The impact of this CBM goes beyond material gains. The concept of fluid borders for Kashmiris has redefined the process of conflict resolution. Through this initiative, it has been possible to move the conflict away from its past intractability. The maximalist and mutually exclusive territorial claims of India, Pakistan, and Kashmiris had made the problem complex and virtually impossible to resolve. The new concept defused the territoriality of the problem and introduced a more people-oriented approach, enabling progress beyond the status quo. And it has given Kashmiris a basis for the "notional unity" of the state of J&K as it stood before its division in 1947 and has given them a very important point of exit from the conflict.[22] Indeed, after a protracted conflict leading to huge losses for the Kashmiris, they cannot exit without achieving something tangible and substantial. The concept of irrelevance of borders opens many possibilities for them.

With the political approach now central in the state's response to dealing with insurgency, the people felt for the first time that some progress toward conflict resolution was afoot. The marked change in the state's discourse, reflected in terms such as "healing touch" and "confidence-building measures," helped generate a sense of genuine expectation. The post-2002 period saw not only the decline of militancy but also a decline in the influence of the separatist leadership. The most productive result of the political approach was the extension of the democratic space and the people's increasing involvement in the mainstream political processes. The democratic space actually became quite vibrant in the post-2002 period since the two competing Kashmir-based political parties, the NC and the People's Democratic Party, brought almost every issue related to the conflict into the mainstream political sphere, which helped legitimize the role of even those political actors not associated with the separatist organizations.

The extension of democratic space had not completely healed the feelings of alienation and the trust deficit that had accumulated over six decades. But it did create grounds for the state to work further toward winning the people's confidence. Despite these positive developments, this phase was not free of problematic government policies. And yet again, the state failed to

22. The discursive shift away from the physical and geographical unity of J&K was implied in Musharraf's "regional" formula. Rather than looking for a single solution for the problem of the whole of J&K, he suggested identifying some regions on both sides of the LoC by their local culture and demographic composition, gradually demilitarize them, and eventually change their political status. Musharraf suggested seven regions and later settled on five. "Azad Kashmir" and Gilgit Baltistan were on the PAK side, and Jammu, Kashmir, and Ladakh were on the Indian side. It is from this regional formulation that he developed his later formulations of "demilitarization," "self-rule," and "joint control."

make the best use of this potential. Even though militancy had declined to the lowest level since its onset, the militaristic aspect of the state's strategy did not disappear. Despite the explicit demand of the separatist leaders and mainstream politicians that the demilitarization process in J&K begin, New Delhi made little effort in this direction.

One of the reasons for this could be the lack of confidence within the Indian security establishment about Pakistan's intentions. Positive engagement between the two nations notwithstanding, a lurking apprehension remained about Pakistan's commitment to end material support for the militancy in Kashmir. Moreover, given the security forces' massive involvement in the area, the reversal of militarization was never going to be an easy process.

The state agencies could not appreciate that insurgency in Kashmir was acquiring a postmilitancy character, defined more by popular protests than by armed militancy. By 2000, even as militancy declined, the politics of resistance continued to manifest through mass protests. Since the popular separatist sentiments initially inspired by armed militancy remained unaddressed, these feelings persisted even after the militancy abated. The start of the India-Pakistan peace process had raised hopes that the conflict would be resolved and normality restored. The unprecedented success of the peace process during 2003–07, when a mood of cooperation and understanding grew between India and Pakistan and they made significant progress on a number of issues including J&K, made the Kashmiris even more hopeful. However, the rather abrupt stalling of the peace process, at both the external and internal levels, generated a feeling of restlessness in Kashmir.

The loss of momentum in the peace process was a result of a combination of unfortunate dynamics. Internally, the initiative taken by the Vajpayee-led National Democratic Alliance could not be pursued with the same zeal under the new United Progressive Alliance government. After initial attempts, Prime Minister Manmohan Singh ultimately abandoned direct talks with the separatists and started a new process of dialogue under the banner of roundtable conferences on Kashmir. These conferences brought together an assortment of political groups in a formal dialogue that the separatists refused to join. The process continued until 2007, when it slowed down due to internal political turbulence in Pakistan, eventually breaking down after the November 2008 Mumbai terrorist attacks orchestrated by the Pakistan-based LeT. By 2007, mass protests had returned as the major means for expressing discontent in Kashmir. The frequency and intensity of the politics of protest increased as the internal and external peace processes slowed down and stalled.

One of the reasons for reversal in the process of dialogue with the separatists can be attributed to the multiplicity of factions within the separatist groups. The APHC, which the Indian government had started a dialogue with, underwent a major split after the 2002 state assembly elections. The result was not only the formation of two major Hurriyat Conferences, one led by Mirwaiz Umar Farooq and the other by Syed Ali Shah Geelani, but also the withdrawal of the JKLF, led by Yasin Malik, and the People's Conference, led by Sajjad Lone, from the APHC altogether. Despite multiple efforts, unity has continued to elude the separatists. Meanwhile, multiple pressures on the separatists have resulted in the loss of dynamism in their politics. Since 2007, when popular protests started becoming the order of the day again, the separatists have lost initiative. Rather than providing leadership, they have been following the public mood and adjusting their political agendas accordingly. It is this context and failure of the separatist leaders to grasp the opportunity to direct the masses that is rendering them somewhat irrelevant and allowing radical elements to monopolize the political space. That explains the increasing stature of the hardline Syed Ali Shah Geelani in Kashmir's politics during the past few years.

While there have been frequent protests in various parts of the Valley since the beginning of 2007, it was the massive protest demonstration during the summer of 2008, over the Amarnath land issue, that brought to the surface the people's increasing discontent over the lack of movement in the dialogues with the Kashmiris and Pakistan. The agitation took place in June 2008, against an order of the state government of J&K that allocated Kashmir forestland to the Shri Amarnath Shrine Board, to construct temporary structures for people making the annual Amarnath pilgrimage. The locals suspected a grand design behind the order, aiming to change the "demographic character" of this Muslim-dominated part of Kashmir. After massive protests, the order was ultimately revoked.[23]

In 2009, Kashmir erupted many times over the issue of the rape and murder of two women in Shopian. The summer of 2010 witnessed a massive outbreak of protests over the issue of a "fake encounter"—an encounter that never really took place even though the police claimed it did—between civilians and security forces in the Machail sector of Kupwara district. The protests were so intense that they persistently disrupted normal life for five months (Chowdhary 2010, 10).[24]

Aware of the consequences of the popular upsurge, the state once again started making an effort to bring the strategy of political dialogue (mainly at the internal level) to the fore. To soothe Kashmiris' anger over the large number of killings of protesting civilians and over the neglect of the dia-

23. For press coverage of the Amarnath row as it progressed in 2008, see *Rediff News* (2008).

24. The state's inability to control the fury of protesting youth was evident in the 112 deaths, mostly of the stone-throwing youth, during this period, which has been compared to the early 1990s, when massive popular protests against the Indian state were the order of the day.

logue process, New Delhi sent an all-party delegation to Kashmir. It also appointed three interlocutors who were assigned the task of starting a dialogue with different contesting groups, including separatists. Other groups representing Indian civil society, as well as political parties and groups at the national level, were also present. In December 2010, a ten-member delegation of parliamentarians and civil society activists, including members of the Communist Party of India, Lok Jan Shakti Party, Telugu Desam Party, and Janata Dal (Secular), visited Kashmir and interacted with the people, including the separatists. In April 2011, the Centre for Policy Analysis, New Delhi, brought a ten-member delegation of prominent Indians to Kashmir. The BJP's study team, headed by former BJP president Rajnath Singh, also visited Kashmir in the early months of 2011. Later on, the Kashmir Committee, headed by Ram Jethmalani, the BJP leader and Rajya Sabha member, was also activated. All these engagements reflected another round of positive overtures toward Kashmir.

Although the situation in Kashmir has been quite normal, with no major popular upsurge in 2011 or 2012, not much has been achieved in the direction of political dialogue. The interlocutors appointed by the Indian government never managed to create confidence during their prolonged process of interaction with various political actors within J&K, and their findings report has met with little enthusiasm. Meanwhile, the demand for repeal or amendment of the Armed Forces Special Powers Act has also remained unaddressed. The Indian state did, however, make an effort to start removing bunkers from the city of Srinagar. According to G. K. Pillai, the Indian home secretary, out of a total forty-one bunkers in Srinagar city, twenty-nine had been removed by 2011. Twelve battalions of troops had also been withdrawn since 2010 (*Tribune* 2011). Meanwhile, special attention also went into humanizing police response. To avoid a repeat of the incidents of the summer of 2010, when many protesting youth were killed during police action, the state police and the paramilitary CRPF were trained in 2011 in nonlethal methods of mob control.

Militancy, on the whole, is on the decline. In February 2011, Lt. Gen. A. K. Choudhary said, "The security situation in Jammu and Kashmir has come to a satisfactory level. The number of militants operating in Jammu and Kashmir has decreased to 400 from 800–900 in the past few years" (*Indian Express* 2011). The number of terrorism-related casualties has also been quite low. According to the defense minister, only thirteen civilian casualties and fifty-eight terrorist casualties were recorded during January–October 2012. This was half the casualties of civilians and terrorists in 2011 (Security-Risks.com 2012). Meanwhile, the popular response toward militancy has also undergone tremendous change, thanks in part to two developments. One is the killing of Maulana Showkat Ahmad Shah, the president of Jamiat Ahl-e-Hadith, by an improvised explosive device in April 2011. Popular resentment against this killing by militants manifested in a complete shutdown in the Valley. Separatists of every stripe also criticized the killing (*Greater Kashmir* 2011). The other development is the Panchayat elections, which showed the enthusiasm of the people, with an average of 70 to 89 percent coming out to vote despite threats issued by militant groups.

But notwithstanding the people's changing response toward armed militancy, the general feeling of resentment toward the central government continues in Kashmir. This feeling stems not only from the perception that the dialogue process initiated by Vajpayee has come to a dead end but also from the occasional human rights violations by police and security forces. Since 2010, calm has generally prevailed in Kashmir, and no prolonged protest has surfaced. This is mainly due to sheer exhaustion, not only from the violence but also from the frequent disruptions in normal life. Gauging the mood of the people, the separatist organizations and leaders, whether the Hurriyat faction led by Geelani or the one led by Mirwaiz (or Yasin Malik's JKLF), are also lying low. But without a political process of engaging the Kashmiris, the calm at the surface can be disturbed at any moment.

Conclusion

The Indian state's response to the political insurgency in Kashmir during the past two decades has gone through several stages. During that time, New Delhi's response to the insurgency has moved from a heavy-handed approach, mostly lacking in nonviolent means, to an active search for dialogue and broader peaceful interventions. As the situation has moved from stable peace, before the troubles of the 1980s, to war and back toward crisis and unstable peace along the conflict curve, an increasing emphasis has been placed on peacebuilding approaches aimed at bringing about sustainable peace and harmony. And yet the Indian state's actions have not fully moved away from militarism, which continues to impede a faster transformation to a normalized situation.[25]

Maturing from a purely militaristic response, India's approach has come to acquire more nuanced militaristic-cum-political aspects. It has also evolved from a simplistic assessment of the Kashmir problem as a proxy war waged by Pakistan to a more complex understanding of the internal and external dimensions. And yet the state's approach never truly became "politics led." And thus, resentment lingers and manifests

25. For a discussion of conflict curves and their conceptual relevance to this volume, see the introductory chapter.

periodically in the form of mass protests. Sustained peace has remained an elusive goal.

The heavy cost of the coercive mechanism is well understood in New Delhi. This is what led the central government to focus on the political mechanism of dialogue, despite a lack of political consensus on dialogue with the separatists and with Pakistan. And yet the policy has lacked consistency, and the state has continued to dither in its approach. This lack of consistency can be damaging to Indian interests, as was recently proved by the summer upsurge of 2010, which breathed new life into separatism and passed it on to the next generation of Kashmiris. Even though the state has come a long way since the early 1990s to bring sustainable peace to Kashmir, more must be done on the strategy's political front. Nonviolent peacebuilding approaches will have to dictate the move toward permanent stability.

References

Ahmad, Aijaz. 2000. "Kashmir Conundrum." *Frontline* 17 (15). www.hindu.com/fline/fl1715/17151090.htm.

Bose, Sumantra. 2005. *Kashmir: Roots of Conflict, Paths to Peace*. Delhi: Lancer.

Bukhari, Shujaat. 2003. "PM Extends 'Hand of Friendship' to Pakistan." *Hindu,* Apr. 19. www.hindu.com/thehindu/thscrip/print.pl?file=2003041905500100.htm&date=2003/04/19/&prd=th&.

Chowdhary, Rekha. 1998. "The Muslim Identity and the Politics of Fundamentalism in Kashmir." QEH Working Paper no. 19, Queen Elizabeth House, Univ. of Oxford. www3.qeh.ox.ac.uk/pdf/qehwp/qehwps19.pdf.

———. 2000. "Autonomy Demand." *Economic and Political Weekly* 35 (30): 2599–2603.

———. 2010. "The Second Uprising." *Economic and Political Weekly* 45 (39): 10–13.

Chowdhary, Rekha, and Nagendra Rao. 2003. "Kashmir: Elections 2002: Implications for Politics of Separatism." *Economic and Political Weekly* 38 (1): 15–21.

———. 2004. "National Conference of Jammu and Kashmir." *Economic and Political Weekly* 39 (14–15): 1521–27.

Dahlburg, John-Thor. 1994. "India, Pakistan Exchange Harsh Words on Kashmir: Asia: At Separate Independence Ceremonies, Leaders Give Little Sign of Compromise on Territorial Dispute." *Los Angeles Times,* Aug. 16. http://articles.latimes.com/1994-08-16/news/mn-27741_1_independence-day.

Desmond, Edward. 1995. "The Insurgency in Kashmir (1989–1991)." *Contemporary South Asia* 4 (1): 5–16.

Ganguly, Sumit, and S. Paul Kapur. 2012. *India, Pakistan, and the Bomb: Debating Nuclear Stability in South Asia.* New York: Columbia Univ. Press.

Ghate, Prabhu. 2002. "Kashmir: The Dirty War." *Economic and Political Weekly* 37 (4): 313–22.

Ghosh, Samarjit. 2009. "Indo-Pak Composition Dialogue—2008." Institute of Peace and Conflict Studies Special Report no. 65, Feb. http://ipcs.org/pdf_file/issue/SR65-Samarjit-Final.pdf.

Greater Kashmir. 2011. "Maulana's Killing Shocks Separatists, Religious Leaders, Traders." Apr. 9. http://greaterkashmir.com/news/2011/Apr/9/moulana-s-killing-shocks-separatists-religious-leaders-traders-55.asp.

Hewitt, Vernon. 1995. *Reclaiming the Past? The Search for Political and Cultural Unity in Contemporary Jammu and Kashmir.* London: Portland Books.

Indian Express. 2004. "We Should Talk, Not the Gun." Jan. 22. www.indianexpress.com/storyOld.php?storyId=39737.

Indian Express. 2011. "Fall in Presence of Militants in J-K: Army." Feb. 15. www.indianexpress.com/news/fall-in-presence-of-militants-in-jk-army/750200.

Jagmohan. 1991. *My Frozen Turbulence in Kashmir.* New Delhi: Allied Publishers.

Jaleel, Muzamil. 2003. "Dialogue Recurs in Poem for Kashmir." *Indian Express,* Apr. 19.

Lavoy, Peter R., ed. 2009. *Asymmetric Warfare in South Asia: The Causes and Consequences of the Kargil Conflict.* New York: Cambridge Univ. Press.

Lyon, Peter. 2008. *Conflict between India and Pakistan: An Encyclopedia.* Santa Barbara, CA: ABC CLIO.

Ministry of Home Affairs, Govt. of India (MHA). 2005. "Annual Report: 2004–2005." www.mha.nic.in/pdfs/ar0405-Eng.pdf.

———. 2011. "Annual Report: 2010–11." www.mha.nic.in/pdfs/AR%28E%291011.pdf.

Navlakha, Gautam. 1993. "Kashmir: Time for Rethinking." *Economic and Political Weekly* 28 (45): 2441–43.

Navlakha, Gautam, Rita Manchanda, and Tapan Bose. 1996. "Political Situation in Kashmir: Duped by Media and Government." *Economic and Political Weekly* 31 (29): 1927–31.

Noorani, A. G. 2000. "Questions about the Kashmir Ceasefire." *Economic and Political Weekly* 35 (45): 3949–58.

Planning Commission, Government of India. 2003. "Executive Summary, Jammu and Kashmir: Development Scenario." http://planningcommission.nic.in/plans/stateplan/sdr_jandk/sdr_jkexecutive.pdf.

Puri, Balraj. 1993. *Kashmir: Towards Insurgency*. New Delhi: Orient Longman.

Rediff News. 2008. "Amarnath Row Rocks Jammu & Kashmir." www.rediff.com/news/amarnath08.html.

Report of the State Autonomy Committee. 1999. Jammu, Jammu and Kashmir.

Schofield, Victoria. 2003. *Kashmir in Conflict: India, Pakistan and the Unending War*. London: I. B. Tauris.

Security-Risks.com. 2012. "Security Trends South Asia." Nov. 27. www.security-risks.com/security-trends-south-asia/jammu-kashmir/situation-in-j-&-k-under-control-1766.html.

Shibli, Murtaza. 2009. "Kashmir: Islam, Identity and Insurgency (With Case Study: Hizbul Mujahideen)." *Kashmir Affairs*, Jan.

South Asia Terrorism Portal (SATP). 2004. "India-Pakistan Joint Press Statement, Islamabad, January 6, 2004." www.satp.org/satporgtp/countries/india/document/papers/indo_pak-6jan04.htm.

Srivastva, Devyani. 2009. "Terrorism and Armed Violence in India: An Analysis of Events in 2008." Institute of Peace and Conflict Studies Special Report no. 71, May. www.ipcs.org/pdf_file/issue/SR71-Final.pdf.

Syed, Firdous. 2000. "Sharing Dreams." *Seminar* 496, Dec. www.india-seminar.com/2000/496/496%20firdous%20syed.htm.

———. 2007. "Straight Lines: Real Feelings, False Expressions?" *Countercurrents*, Sept. 9. www.countercurrents.org/syed090907.htm.

Tareen, Jalees A. K. 2005. *Fire under Snowflakes: The Return of Kashmir University*. New Delhi: Mittal.

Tribune. 2011. "Join Talks or Get Isolated, Centre Tells Separatists." Apr. 11. www.tribuneindia.com/2011/20110411/j&k.htm#3.

Times of India. 2002. "Full Text of Prime Minister's Independence Day Speech." Aug. 15. http://articles.timesofindia.indiatimes.com/2002-08-15/india/27294480_1_cross-border-terrorism-jammu-and-kashmir-freedom-struggle.

Tremblay, Reeta Chowdhari. 2001. "Kashmir Conflict: Secessionist Movement, Mobilization and Political Institutions." *Pacific Affairs* 74 (4): 569–77.

3

Peace Process with India

A Pakistani Perspective

Khalid Mahmood

After fighting three wars over the disputed territory of J&K, Pakistan and India were finally pushed to find peaceful ways to resolve the issue. The result has been the "composite dialogue process," initiated in 2004. This period represents a unique time when both nations realized the vital need for dialogue and negotiations in sorting out this intractable dispute. For India, the process addressed one of the two major aspects of the Kashmir problem that it had faced for over five decades—the second being the internal resentment that Kashmiris have felt toward New Delhi ever since the independence of British India in 1947. Seen through a conflict resolution lens, the composite dialogue process has brought some positive developments.

Pakistan's relations with India have been burdened with suspicion and mistrust and pose a serious challenge to peace and stability in South Asia. As argued by former Pakistani foreign minister Khurshid Mahmud Kasuri, the heart of this mistrust lies in unresolved disputes, especially that of Kashmir, "that not only threaten regional peace and security but also hinder economic development and efforts to eradicate poverty, illiteracy, and disease in the two countries" (Kasuri 2011). These disputes have prevented both countries from realizing their full potential. Among the negative ramifications has been Pakistan's inability to tackle an active insurgency and terrorism raging within its borders for a decade.

In the words of Indian prime minister Manmohan Singh, "If there is cooperation between Pakistan and India and not conflict, vast opportunities will open up for trade, travel and development that will create prosperity in both countries. . . . It is impossible for any Government in India to work towards full normalization of relations with Pakistan unless the Government of Pakistan fulfills, in letter and spirit, its commitment not to allow its territory to be used in any manner for terrorist activities against India. . . The people of India expect these assurances to be honored and this Government recognizes that as the national consensus" (*Outlook India* 2009).

For such cooperation to take place, in the Pakistani view, there must be a negotiated settlement on Kashmir that is acceptable to Pakistan, India, and the Kashmiri people. Such a move would also be critical to Pakistan's efforts to control extremism and terrorism at home.

India and Pakistan have been in conflict over Kashmir since 1947 because of the former princely state's disputed accession to India upon the partition of British India. To recount the milestones is to recognize the Kashmiri people's sufferings through four wars and many more skirmishes over the issue. Over the years, the cease-fire line, which originated in 1949 after the first Kashmir war between India and Pakistan, was slightly altered during the 1965 and 1971 wars and renamed the LoC in July 1972.[1] After the Kargil War in July 1999, the two sides agreed that respecting the LoC as a temporary boundary was vital for peace in South Asia.

In 1989—a year of change in the world inspired by movements for freedom—Islamic freedom fighters who had succeeded in driving the Soviets out of Afghanistan turned their attention to Kashmir. As Strobe Talbott notes, "They did so with the support of the Pakistani Intelligence Services" (Talbott 2004, 20). India had just manipulated Kashmir's state elections, and the jihadi organizations, who had the public's sympathy at the time and were emboldened by their success in Afghanistan, stepped up their activities in Indian-administered Kashmir.

Before 1989, India and Pakistan fought over Kashmir. Since then, it is the Kashmiris who have done much of the fighting and, as a result, suffered huge casualities. Pakistan's support to the insurgency lessened after 9/11 changed the global outlook on violent "freedom fights," but the struggle in Indian-administered Kashmir continues. From the insurgency's onset in 1989 until June 30, 2010, 93,274 Kashmiris have been killed (Siddiqi 2010). The situation remains troubled. The summer of 2010 saw the biggest protests against Indian control in Kashmir since the early 1990s, when unarmed youth threw stones while calling for azadi from the curfews and killings under the shadow of Indian security forces. After 112 people died, the unrest subsided in September, when the Indian government took mea-

1. For a detailed history and background of the Kashmir dispute since its onset, see Schofield (2000); Wirsing (2003).

sures to defuse the crisis and offered compensation to the bereaved families (Gopalan 2011; Freedom House 2012). One major difference from the early years of the Kashmir dispute, however, is that such resentment against New Delhi no longer translates into support for Pakistan per se.

The Simla Agreement of 1972—concluded in the wake of Pakistan's loss in the 1971 India-Pakistan war—slightly altered the cease-fire line in Kashmir to the present-day LoC but did not alter the status of J&K as an outstanding dispute (A. Sattar 2010, 154). Looking back over the years, it is noteworthy that since the signing of Simla, various governments in both countries took steps to create peaceful conditions in South Asia. This has been especially true over the past fifteen years or so, as reflected in confidence-building agreements and statements such as the Lahore Declaration of February 21, 1999, the Indo-Pak Joint Press Statement of January 6, 2004, and the joint statement of April 18, 2005.[2] None of these, however, managed to truly transform Pakistan-India relations or the dispute over Kashmir.

Considering that regional peace in South Asia hinges on a solution to the dispute, Kashmir's importance increases multifold. From Pakistan's perspective, resolution of Kashmir would reduce tensions with India, strengthen civilian control over the military, and enable Pakistan to focus fully on the militancy within its own borders. Such a development would also affect the situation in Afghanistan, since India's and Pakistan's divergent interests there may hold up progress toward a sustainable settlement before the 2014 drawdown of U.S. and other NATO troops from Afghanistan. Peace in Afghanistan, then, depends in no small part on how Pakistan views and reacts to India's presence there (Hanauer and Chalk 2012; Yusuf and Lynch 2012). U.S. president-elect Obama had perceived this connection clearly when he told NBC's *Meet the Press* in December 2008, "We can't continue to look at Afghanistan in isolation. We have to see it as a part of a regional problem that includes Pakistan, includes India, includes Kashmir, includes Iran" (Obama 2008). Understanding this regional link is key to appreciating the connection in the mutual polices of Islamabad, New Delhi, and Kabul; promoting a regional détente; and building a promising future free from violence and terrorism.

This chapter examines the process of improving Pakistan-India relations, facilitated by the United States, and the move toward dialogue in 2003. The formula for resolving Kashmir was negotiated by back-channel diplomacy.

2. The Lahore Declaration was signed by Indian prime minister Atal Bihari Vajpayee and Pakistani prime minister Nawaz Sharif during Vajpayee's visit to Lahore. The 2004 joint press statement was issued by Prime Minister Vajpayee and Pakistani president Pervez Musharraf at the conclusion of the twelfth South Asian Association for Regional Cooperation (SAARC) summit in Islamabad. The 2005 statement was signed by President Musharraf and Indian prime minister Manmohan Singh during Musharraf's visit to India.

This analysis covers the key points, including self-governance, demilitarization, and the joint mechanism. It also investigates why the two governments, after making substantial progress, ultimately failed to reach a final settlement to this six-decade-old dispute.

Reviewing the Past: Buildup to the Peace Process

Over the years, after India reneged on its commitment to hold a plebiscite in Kashmir, Pakistan realized that the plebiscite option was not feasible.[3] But it was not prepared to accept the status quo. So the two countries held talks, the most noteworthy being the six rounds of Zulfiqar Ali Bhutto-Swaran Singh negotiations in 1963. In the fifth round of these talks, Pakistani foreign minister Bhutto offered the concept of condominium—joint sovereignty, with autonomy in domestic affairs and joint Indian-Pakistani control over foreign affairs and defense—but India refused the offer (Schaffer 2009, 80–91).

After failing to achieve progress in Kashmir through the UN process; through coercive tactics, such as infiltrating its troops into Indian-administered Kashmir; and through peace agreements, such as Simla; the Pakistani military-dominated decision-making establishment decided to support a proxy war against India. Finding an opening via an indigenous uprising in Indian-administered Kashmir in 1989, the security establishment used militant Islamist jihadi groups in the 1990s as an active instrument of its policy in Kashmir. Pakistan began by supporting the pro-independence militant group JKLF at the onset of the insurgency but quickly dumped it in favor of groups such as the Hizbul-Mujahideen and LeT, which were created to support the Kashmiri uprising and backed Indian-administered Kashmir's incorporation into Pakistan (Desmond 1995).[4] This started a new game. A disturbing account now details how various militant organizations engaged in a bloody shadow war for control of Kashmir and how these organizations were financed and received training and arms for the militants (Jamal 2009). In Pakistan during the 1980s, there was also a "mushroom growth of sectarian and ethnic militant organizations under the state patronage" (Khosa 2013). The support for jihadi organizations in Kashmir and the growth of militant outfits within Pakistan is haunting the country today through widespread internal violence.

---

3. For details of UN involvement in Kashmir, the makings of the plebiscite option, and Indian and Pakistani reactions, see Korbel (1954, 97–197).

4. Hizbul-Mujahideen, founded in 1989, was the largest and best-armed of the Kashmiri militant organizations. It began an "Islamization" drive in the Kashmir Valley in Indian-administered Kashmir in the early 1990s.

This is the direct legacy of Pakistan's tactical use of Islamist militants as policy tools, which began during the 1980s (Z. Hussain 2007; M. Hussain 2012; ICG 2009).

Notwithstanding the impasse in relations resulting from Pakistan's role in the insurgency in Indian-administered Kashmir throughout the 1990s, in 1997, Pakistani prime minister Nawaz Sharif pursued initiatives to resume bilateral talks with his Indian counterpart, I. K. Gujral, in an effort to resolve the two countries' outstanding issues, including Kashmir. Sharif's approach to relations was colored by his business background and his desire to have greater trade and economic ties with his eastern neighbor. Through this initiative, the two countries agreed on the format for a composite dialogue and held three rounds of foreign secretary-level talks. The agreed eight-item agenda included peace and security (including CBMs), J&K, Siachen, Sir Creek, terrorism and drug trafficking, the Wullar Barrage/Tulbul project, economic and commercial cooperation, and promotion of friendly exchanges in various fields. But they made little progress on Kashmir during this period.

India's and Pakistan's nuclear tests in 1998 provided fresh impetus—a compulsion, some would argue—to talk further and ease the international community's concerns over the security situation in the region. In response to the invitation from Pakistani prime minister Sharif, Indian prime minister Vajpayee visited Pakistan on February 20–21, 1999, during which they signed the Lahore Declaration. This agreement once again committed the two countries to intensify efforts to resolve all outstanding bilateral issues, including Kashmir. It also obliged both sides to strengthen the regional interaction through the otherwise subdued South Asian Association for Regional Cooperation (SAARC) process, combat terrorism in all its forms and manifestations, promote and respect human rights, and refrain from interfering in each other's internal affairs. A memorandum of understanding signed at the Lahore summit also listed eight CBMs in nuclear and conventional fields, including consultation on security concepts and doctrine (*Dawn* 1999). Details of most of these CBMs were ironed out between the two countries during the 2003–07 peace process.

This period of warming ties was also short-lived. Relations between Pakistan and India reverted to high tension soon thereafter. From 1999 to 2002, tension was high because of several factors: the Pakistani army-instigated Kargil War in May 1999, in which Pakistani infiltrators captured unprotected territory inside Indian-administered Kashmir; a military coup in Pakistan, in which army chief Pervez Musharraf took power; the inconclusive "Agra summit" in July 2001, where the leaders of the two sides aimed at rebuilding ties; the attack on the Indian Parliament in December

2001 by a Pakistan-based militant group; and the subsequent mobilization of a million troops along both sides of the international border.[5]

The Kargil episode, the border confrontation in 2001–02, and the world's reaction to both proved consequential for Pakistan's approach to India. Kargil was an obvious manifestation of Pakistan's troubled civil-military relationship. Deep-rooted tensions between the civilian governments and security establishment have marred Pakistan's democratic history, and there is vigorous debate on just how much the prime minister knew (Musharraf 2006, 95–98; Siddique 2006, 38–39). There is great controversy in Pakistan over who approved this operation and when. General Pervez Musharraf claims in his memoirs that he "briefed the PM in Skardu on January 29, 1999 and various subsequent occasions," although the prime minister has denied knowledge of the Kargil operation, which was carried out on the heights of the Kargil sector across the LoC. Musharraf has claimed success in one of the other objectives of the operations besides securing territory: to internationalize the conflict. Each of the Pakistani incursions was intended to recast the conflict and give fresh impetus to diplomatic efforts (Jamal 2009). Musharraf argues, "Whatever movement has taken place so far in the direction of finding a solution to Kashmir is due considerably to the Kargil conflict" (Musharraf 2006, 98). For most observers, however, Kargil failed to focus attention on the need to resolve the Kashmir question. In fact, Pakistan was embarrassed and diplomatically chastised by the whole world (Fair 2009, 248–56).

Washington asked Pakistan to withdraw its forces and restore the status quo ante (Talbott 2004, 162–69). Even Pakistan's staunchest allies, including China, refrained from supporting its position outright (Singh 1999). The international sentiment was crystallized by U.S. president Bill Clinton during his brief visit to Pakistan on March 25, 2000. He stated, "This era does not reward people who struggle in vain to redraw borders with blood. It belongs to those with the vision to look beyond borders, for partners and commerce and trade" (FAS 2000). Nawaz states that Pakistani officials were treated as liars and that whatever they said subsequently was seen as suspect (Nawaz 2008, 524).

5. The Kargil conflict resulted from a surprise Pakistani incursion into Indian-administered Kashmir in the spring of 1999, which led to an Indian retaliation in May–June of that year. The conflict remained limited and ended with Pakistan being forced to withdraw its forces. The Agra summit was a two-day meeting held in July 2001 as President Musharraf and Prime Minister Vajpayee tried and failed to break the impasse and resolve outstanding issues. Disagreement over Kashmir and questions of terrorism led to a breakdown. The Indian Parliament attack on December 13, 2001, was carried out by five gunmen allegedly belonging to a Pakistan-based militant organization. Four were later put on trial in December 2002, and one received the death penalty. The attack led to military mobilization by India, countermobilization by Pakistan, and a ten-month border standoff. For detailed studies on Kargil and the 2001–02 crisis, see respectively Lavoy (2009) and Davis (2011).

In the wake of the 9/11 attacks on the United States and the December 13, 2001, attack on the Indian Parliament, India unleashed a diplomatic campaign to project itself as a longstanding victim of terrorism from Pakistan and to convince the world of links between Osama bin Laden, the Afghan Taliban, and the militant struggle in Indian-administered Kashmir (Jaspal 2011, 59–61; Ganguly 2002; Sood and Sawhney 2003, 21–26). Quite abruptly, the Kashmir freedom struggle was now seen internationally in a very different—and negative—light. Pakistan's official stance until then, that the Kashmir freedom struggle was indigenous and that Pakistan extended only political, diplomatic, and moral support to the "freedom fighters"—read *insurgents*—was no longer acceptable to the United States and the European Union (EU) in closed-door diplomatic encounters. After 9/11, Pakistan's closest friends began advising the government to think of an alternative way to achieve its objectives in Kashmir. It was becoming clear to Islamabad that while maintaining its position of principle on the issue of Kashmir, it had to adopt a different strategy for settling the dispute (Kasuri 2009).

Changing Tactics: Soul-Searching in Pakistan

The year 2002 was a time for soul-searching and a change of mind-set that had already begun in Pakistan's Foreign Office and in some sections of its security establishment. Many representatives of Pakistani civil society also came to the conclusion that normalization of relations was in the best interest of both countries. People increasingly felt that an attempt at peace with India on a mutually acceptable basis was needed. A number of causes led to this conclusion. First, in the backdrop of 9/11, it was clear that militancy was no longer an acceptable means of pursuing national strategic objectives. Second, Pakistan's nuclear tests had given the state a sense of security and given the government a sense it could achieve compromise on Kashmir without undermining Pakistan's territorial integrity. Third, the success of regional organizations, such as the Association of Southeast Asian Nations and the EU, was beginning to resonate among some officials. Also, Pakistan's friends abroad conveyed through diplomatic channels that they supported a policy of normalization between Pakistan and India.

It is noteworthy that after the 2001–02 Indian military mobilization in response to the terrorist attack on the Parliament, Pakistan did not yield to an Indian show of military might (Davis 2011). Perhaps nuclear weapons had indeed made all-out war obsolete and given Pakistan the confidence to stand up to the Indian threat of aggression. Ultimately, New Delhi pulled back. First of all, it seems to have concluded that heightened tensions with Pakistan would hurt the Indian economy (Chari, Cheema, and Cohen 2007, 170–71; Friedman 2002). Second, no country in the world wanted a confrontation between the two nuclear powers, and all were advising them accordingly. Third, a popular sentiment in favor of peace was also emerging in both countries. Indeed, leaders on both sides began to talk openly about changing mind-sets and the need for a lasting solution to the Kashmir problem as efforts at rapprochement began at the tail end of the 2001–02 crisis. Finally and perhaps most importantly, India realized the need to settle its differences with Pakistan over Kashmir—and thereby incentivize a reversal of Pakistani support to the insurgents—if it was ever to put a permanent end to the violence in Indian-administered Kashmir.

Following the realization of this new reality, it became possible for both sides to take the road less traveled. Accordingly, on April 18, 2003, Prime Minister Vajpayee offered, in his own words, “a hand of friendship” to Pakistan, and India reversed various punitive unilateral measures taken after the attack on Parliament in December 2001. These reversals included resumption of overflights, return of high commissioners to Islamabad and New Delhi, and restoration of cricketing links, along with various other CBMs.

Pakistan’s prime minister, Mir Zafarullah Khan Jamali, welcomed the announcement of his Indian counterpart and invited him to visit Pakistan. On May 6, 2003, he offered resumption of train and bus services between India and Pakistan, restoration of air links, immediate release of all Indian fishermen detained by Pakistan, resumption of sporting ties between the two countries (beginning with cricket and field hockey), and restoration of the full strength of diplomatic missions in the two capitals (*Times of India* 2003; *Economic Times* 2003). This started the process of confidence building that gradually restored mutual understanding and resulted in improved relations.

A vital CBM by Pakistan—a unilateral cease-fire by Pakistani forces along the LoC, in effect from Eid al-Fitr on November 26, 2003—was well received in India and has been generally observed to date.[6] Prime Minister Vajpayee responded and told his party’s parliamentary committee that talks with Pakistan would resume because infiltration across the LoC had decreased considerably. Also, Pakistan’s policy of restraint and image of responsibility were beginning to come across internationally as positive and constructive.

These positive developments occurred in time for Prime Minister Vajpayee’s visit to Pakistan in January 2004, when the two countries decided to resume serious talks on Kashmir and all other outstanding issues.

6. While the cease-fire has held, there have been many incidents of violation across the LoC. Perhaps the highest-profile and most disturbing incident took place in January 2013. Both sides allegedly ended up killing each other’s soldiers, and there were also accusations of beheadings of Indian soldiers—a charge that Pakistan denied. Fortunately, after a week of mudslinging and a public blame game, both sides agreed to curb tensions surrounding the issue. See *Express Tribune* (2013); *Nation* (2013). Tensions flared up again in August 2013, when five Indian soldiers were killed on the Indian side of the LoC, but again, they were quickly curtailed.

The joint statement made during Vajpayee's 2004 visit formally initiated the Indo-Pak peace process. It was significant in that it reflected a spirit of compromise that had arisen after the 2001–02 crisis involving military mobilization was over. The public mood between the two countries had also changed quickly during 2003, thanks to the various CBMs that the two nations undertook immediately after the crisis ended. This shift allowed both countries to make headway during Vajpayee's January 2004 visit. A three-track process began in February 2004. Both sides made various proposals for working toward normalization of relations. These steps culminated in the start of the composite talks in February 2004.

It is interesting that a Pakistani general, the reputed architect of the Kargil War, and India's hard-liner BJP should engage in an effort toward détente. To be sure, external patrons helped the process along. Most obviously, the Bush administration in the United States played an active role in nudging India and Pakistan toward a dialogue in 2003, focusing on the issue of cross-border infiltration with Pakistan and intervening strongly with India on the need to respond positively when Pakistan clamped down on cross-LoC infiltration. Washington seemed convinced that an end to the infiltration would be a prelude to the resumption of dialogue. The behind-the-scenes engagement of Secretary of State Colin Powell, Deputy Secretary Richard Armitage, and Powell's successor, Condoleezza Rice, with the foreign ministers and leaders of the two countries enabled Washington to nudge, facilitate, and move the peace process forward. While the Americans played a major role, other countries also supported the peace process. Pakistan, engaging with the world proactively, also kept the EU, China, and other major powers fully briefed on developments. India thus felt pressure to ease tensions over Kashmir. There was also a pervasive feeling at the time that the two countries were in a political and strategic balance—a stalemate—and that the only way forward was through dialogue.[7]

Review in the Pakistani Foreign Office and the "Back Channel"

As the debate in civil society and the media ensued, a formal review of relations with India took place at the Pakistan Foreign Office in July 2003. Select envoys and diplomats were invited to participate.[8] Pakistani diplomats held the view that Pakistan, while maintaining its principled position, should explore options for easier interaction between Kashmiris across the LoC. Some felt that the primary objective should be a meaningful reduction

7. The information about third-party roles at the time comes from my position as head of the Foreign Minister's Office, where I was privy to these developments.

8. I attended several of these meetings and remained privy to sensitive foreign-policy matters during 2002–07.

of Indian government repression in Kashmir through significant withdrawal of Indian armed forces and an end to human rights violations on the Indian-administered side. It was proposed that Pakistan should obtain political space for all Kashmiri leaders to hold meetings and rallies freely—something that India traditionally had not allowed. Interestingly, nearly everyone agreed that Pakistan's political differences should not stand in the way of trade and economic relations with India, if those relations were to Pakistan's advantage. This implied a need to review Pakistan's long-standing policy of holding back on trade and transit relations with India in the absence of progress on Kashmir.

Some diplomats felt that continuing support to militant groups would further harm the Kashmiri struggle and Pakistan's internal dynamics. They recommended that in return for Pakistani restraint on the LoC, India must end its repression and human rights violations and enter into meaningful bilateral discussions on the dispute.

At the same time, the Foreign Office did a review of models of conflict resolution and other peace processes. This was based on the experience of previous bilateral negotiations, proposals put out by the Kashmir Study Group—a U.S.-based group led by influential Kashmiris (Kashmir Study Group 1998)—and other models, including the Good Friday Agreement in Northern Ireland. President Musharraf's subsequent four-point proposal—start the dialogue; accept the centrality of Kashmir; eliminate whatever is not acceptable to Pakistan, India, and the people of Kashmir; and arrive at a solution that is acceptable to all three—had its underpinnings in the work of the Pakistani Foreign Office and eventually remained the guiding spirit of the evolving bilateral negotiations.

During this period, President Musharraf convened meetings periodically to review the conduct of back-channel diplomacy and guide it toward a meaningful outcome. Those in attendance included General Ashfaq Kayani (then director general of ISI), Foreign Minister Khurshid Kasuri, and Foreign Secretary Riaz Mohammad Khan. These meetings served as brainstorming sessions during which various issues were discussed exhaustively. They also served as the platform to decide the brief and the talking points for bilateral back-channel diplomacy.

The back-channel discussions, which were the principal forum for working out details of a Kashmir formula with India, started in 2003 and began to take concrete shape with a growing degree of focus after 2004. Tariq Aziz, secretary of the National Security Council and a close aide of the president, represented Pakistan at the back-channel talks. The Indian prime minister's principal secretary, Brajesh Mishra; National Security Adviser J. N. Dixit; and Ambassador Satinder Lambah successively represented the

Indian side. Nearly two dozen meetings were held in Dubai, London, and Bangkok from 2004 to 2007.[9]

Product of the Peace Process: The Kashmir Formula

The nonpaper, without names and signatures but still a basis for a possible agreement, exchanged in early 2007 between the two sides reflected the output of the protracted back-channel efforts aimed at putting together elements of a solution to the Kashmir issue. What the back-channel talks achieved has been revealed through various interviews over time. The two sides agreed that two "units" would cover the entire area of the former state of J&K. The focus, however, was mostly on Pakistani Kashmir, the Kashmir Valley, and Jammu. The Pakistani Northern Areas of Gilgit-Baltistan and the Ladakh region in Indian-administered Kashmir, while part of the former princely state, have always been considered somewhat less contentious. At least from the Pakistani side, the status quo over Gilgit-Baltistan—under Pakistani control and fairly disconnected from the Kashmir dispute—was nonnegotiable.

The progress made in the dialogue with India has now been accurately recorded in open-source information. Giving details in a July 2009 interview with prominent Indian journalist Karan Thapar, Musharraf said that the two countries were close to an agreement on three issues: Kashmir, Siachen, and Sir Creek. He added that the agreement on Kashmir was based on three principles: demilitarization, self-governance, and a joint mechanism. He said, "We should carry out demilitarization on the Line of Control and also within held [Indian-administered] Kashmir. And on our side, [take] reciprocal action. I was suggesting that the military, the Indian military, should move out of two or three cities like Srinagar, Baramulla" (Musharraf 2009). He noted that while there was an agreement in principle to carry out demilitarization on the LoC and also within both sides of Kashmir, the two countries had not worked out the schedule and timeline for doing so.

On self-governance, he said, "This would have meant giving maximum governance to the people of Kashmir on both sides—on the Indian side as well as the Pakistan side" (Musharraf 2009). He added that there was a common understanding on the devolution of power to both Srinagar and Muzaffarabad; both sides needed to give maximum power to the people of Kashmir so that they could have a feeling of governing themselves. The joint mechanism, according to him, was meant to "have been an overwatch on whatever we have decided. . . . The problem was the Line of Control. . . .

9. For a more general discussion, see also Coll (2009).

The idea was to make the Line of Control irrelevant. . . . when you have free passage of people and free passage of goods trade"—essentially, by removing all the obstacles to facilitating this movement (Musharraf 2009).

Musharraf further said that the joint mechanism would oversee self-governance and the implementation of what had been devolved to the people of Kashmir. This was to be done through a body formed with representation of Kashmiris on both sides. The idea was to share sovereignty and give comfort to the people of Kashmir with the approval of the governments of Pakistan and India. The LoC would become "like borders in the European Community today, which exist on paper but people can freely cross" (Musharraf 2009).

The two countries agreed to inter-Kashmir trade and economic interaction and to address tariff and nontariff barriers affecting locally produced goods. Liberalized arrangements would also be put in place for a freer flow of investment and services between the two units of Kashmir. It was further agreed that the defense of each of the two units would continue to be the responsibility of the two countries in accordance with existing positions. And finally, India and Pakistan would reach an agreement on the reduction of military forces in the region, including across the LoC. It was also thought that the joint administrative mechanism would facilitate cooperation in other fields, such as hydroelectric power, which has great potential in Kashmir.

As a result of the peace process, the two countries agreed in principle to establish conditions conducive for peaceful coexistence. Conditions in Kashmir were to be addressed through agreed protocols and structures to give the region's people a life of dignity, prosperity, and peace, in which they could enjoy fundamental freedoms and rights. Moreover, there was to be complete cessation of terrorism, violence, and hostility. A Monitoring and Review Agreement was also envisioned, under which the foreign ministers from both countries would meet to monitor progress, and the agreement itself would be subject to review after fifteen years.

Along with Kashmir, substantial progress was also made on other outstanding disputes, chief among them being the Sir Creek maritime boundary and Siachen, a glacier that has seen Indian and Pakistani military skirmishes since 1984.[10]

Steve Coll aptly sums up what the efforts at rapprochement amounted to: "At issue, they believed, was not just a settlement in Kashmir itself but an end to their debilitating covert wars and, eventually, their paranoiac mutual

10. The Sir Creek dispute has lingered since partition, concerning interpretation of the maritime boundary in a specific zone between Pakistani Sindh and Indian Gujarat. The Siachen glacier dispute was triggered in 1984 when the Indian military occupied this territory in Kashmir. Both sides claim it and have since militarized the glacier, making it the world's highest battleground.

suspicions. They hoped to develop a new regime of free trade and political cooperation in the region, from Central Asia to Bangladesh" (Coll 2009). This would have become a "cleansing peace" and would have fundamentally transformed relations between Pakistan and India.

Shaping the Broader Environment

This back-channel peace process was not taking place in a vacuum. Rather, there was an overall mood among the peoples on both sides and an acknowledgement and mutual appreciation by the two countries' governments. The joint statement of January 2004 captured the sentiment just as the peace bid was getting under way: "The resumption of the Composite Dialogue will lead to peaceful settlement of all bilateral issues, including Jammu and Kashmir, to the satisfaction of both sides" (*Dawn* 2004).

The leaders on both sides continued to reinforce each other. The joint statement by the leaders of the two countries on April 18, 2005, during President Musharraf's visit to New Delhi—that "the peace process was now irreversible" and that acts of terrorism should not derail it—was an important decision that made the overall process and back-channel diplomacy sustainable (*Outlook India* 2005). The two leaders agreed to set up a joint business council to improve trade and increase the frequency of bus travel across divided Kashmir. While seemingly banal to those not familiar with the India-Pakistan context, it was such an important development that UN secretary-general Kofi Annan formally welcomed the joint statement.

Even Indian views, as expressed behind closed doors to Pakistani interlocutors, were encouraging. During a 2005 visit to Pakistan, Indian opposition leader L. K. Advani stated that the government and people of India wanted to continue the current peace and that all Indian political parties supported it. He added that the BJP, the major right leaning party in Parliament, had a special responsibility to make the hostility and tension between the two countries "a thing of the past."[11] This represented a consensus at the time, and the feeling was shared in Pakistan.

A broad awareness of the problem and a need for positive movement had become common through public debates and the interest of think tanks and media. Think tanks arranged discussions on models for resolution of disputes with a focus on Kashmir. These discussions became more frequent especially after President Musharraf initiated in October 2004 a public debate on various options for Kashmir's resolution. Public celebration of the new mood manifested in cricket matches, with the Indian team visiting Pakistan in 2004, and the Pakistani team reciprocating in 2005. Further,

11. L.K. Advani, in meeting attended by the author, June 2005, Islamabad.

since both countries were doing well economically, it provided a helpful background for continuing the dialogue process.

A critical test, which both countries passed, was the July 11, 2006, Mumbai train attacks, which left over two hundred people dead and were blamed on Pakistan-based LeT and the Students Islamic Movement of India (SIMI). These attacks caused a temporary chill in relations but did not lead to a complete break. After a brief hiatus, the president of Pakistan and the prime minister of India signed a landmark "Joint Anti-Terrorism Mechanism" at the Non-Aligned Movement summit in Havana in September 2006, and the dialogue resumed (Fayyaz 2009).

The positive ambience of the peace process and progress in back-channel talks facilitated the Kashmiri leadership's association with these developments. Islamabad had started a dialogue with the Kashmiri leadership after the India-Pakistan composite dialogue began in 2004. India agreed to the Pakistani proposal that the leadership of the APHC—an amalgam of several Kashmiri political groups largely opposed to New Delhi's control over Indian-administered Kashmir—should be associated with the peace process. The top Kashmiri leaders were divided, however. Syed Ali Shah Geelani, a hard-line APHC leader, was opposed even to the proposal of starting a bus service between Muzaffarabad and Srinagar (Lakshman 2005). He criticized President Musharraf's four points and his softer position on the UN Security Council's resolutions on Kashmir and was against showing any flexibility whatsoever. Other Kashmiri leaders recognized the need for unity but were unwilling to go along with Geelani's approach. Most viewed militancy as counterproductive. Notwithstanding the division between the Ali Geelani, Mirwaiz Umar Farooq, and Yasin Malik groups within APHC, Pakistan was so keen to promote endorsement of the idea of the dialogue process that it maintained contacts and held consultations with all the major Kashmiri leaders on both sides of the LoC.

India allowed Kashmiri leaders representing the APHC—including Mirwaiz Umar Farooq, Professor Abdul Ghani Bhatt, Moulana Abbas Ansari, Bilal Ghani Lone, Yasin Malik, and others—to come to Muzaffarabad, Pakistani Kashmir's capital, in early June 2005 on an unprecedented visit to Pakistani Kashmir and Pakistan (Mustafa 2005; Ul Haque 2005). They met with the leadership in Muzaffarabad and Islamabad. The visit gave Kashmiri leaders from both sides of the LoC a unique opportunity to discuss ways and means of finding a solution to the Kashmir dispute by taking the dialogue process forward.

A number of Kashmir-related CBMs that had been discussed in the Pakistan-India talks were now being put in place. These included the bus service (without India's previous conditions regarding passports), trade and trucking services along the LoC, meeting points for divided families on the LoC, and greater interaction among the Kashmiri leadership on both sides of the LoC (Yusuf 2009, 1). A Pugwash Conferences on Science and World Affairs meeting in Islamabad in 2006, involving Kashmiri leaders from both sides, helped garner support for Musharraf's proposal of demilitarization and self-governance among pro-Indian Kashmiris. Prominent leaders from Indian-administered Kashmir, such as Omar Abdullah and Mehbooba Mufti, were present at the meeting and started entertaining the idea. As a result of their association, the Kashmiri leaders' comfort level with the four-point formula increased, and the dialogue and the way forward being discussed via back channels gave rise to growing support. Kashmiri politicians were keen to hold political rallies to explain the evolving situation to the people of the Kashmir Valley in Indian-administered Kashmir. Pakistan, for its part, continued to explain the moves as a means of improving the human rights situation in Indian-administered Kashmir. Perhaps it was also Pakistan's desire that pro-Pakistan sentiment in Kashmir—whatever remained of it—should somehow remain alive.

As the dialogue between India and Pakistan gained momentum and progressed on various issues, the APHC leaders visited Pakistan again in January 2006. During the visit, Mirwaiz Umar Farooq stated that there could be no military solution to the Kashmir issue and that the Kashmiri people must be involved in any dialogue process aimed at resolving the dispute. Later, Mirwaiz was quoted as having told people in Pakistan that the time to end armed struggle in Kashmir had come because violence had not "achieved anything other than creating more graveyards" (Wani 2007). Positive public comments supportive of the Kashmir peace process started appearing regularly when Syed Salahuddin, the hard-line chairman of the United Jihad Council, who was actively involved in the Kashmir insurgency during the 1990s, endorsed the formula on Kashmir in February 2007, declaring it the first step in the right direction. After this significant comment, in March, Mirwaiz declared that the APHC would soon strengthen its public contact program to make people aware of the four-point formula on Kashmir.

Why the Peace Process Did Not Deliver

It would be disingenuous to take credit away from the Pakistani, Indian, and Kashmiri leaderships for pushing ahead with the bid for peace in Kashmir and promoting an overall environment favoring reconciliation and normalization. And yet the fact remains that the peace process ultimately failed to deliver a sustainable solution simply because the net was not cast wide enough to bring all those who mattered on board with the effort. In retrospect, the efforts were laudable but insufficient.

In the view of Pakistani political leaders, the political dispensation headed by a military ruler proved to be the biggest drawback. Despite

Musharraf's efforts to create buy-in, mainstream opposition political parties never supported the effort wholeheartedly, because they maintained that Musharraf was an unconstitutional leader. Indeed, the present civilian government has all but discounted Musharraf's four-point formula and insists that the process will have to be restarted virtually from square one; to own up to prior efforts under a military ruler is seen as politically damaging (*Times of India* 2010).

On one end of the political spectrum, the right-wing parties criticized Musharraf for having taken an abrupt U-turn on Kashmir and for giving up Pakistan's traditional position of resolving Kashmir based strictly on UN Security Council resolutions calling for a plebiscite. Critics also said that Pakistan was offering concessions on various issues without any quid pro quo from India. As for the mainstream political parties, their soured relationship with Musharraf and his allies meant that they were not briefed on various aspects of the negotiations with India. In the absence of a consensus through a parliamentary session, politicians dare not come out in support of the peace process, especially since major opposition voices were arguing that the Musharraf government had no constitutional mandate to negotiate a settlement on Kashmir. Also, for Pakistan's mainstream political parties and leaders, animosity toward Musharraf was personal because he had manipulated the political system to keep former prime ministers Nawaz Sharif and Benazir Bhutto, heads of the two largest political parties, out of politics. In the final outcome, this fact and the inherent question mark on Musharraf's legitimacy prevented a true political consensus from emerging in Pakistan. To pull off such a monumental transformation in Pakistan's traditional stance on Kashmir, he ultimately needed the political parties on board. To be fair to Musharraf and his team, however, they failed on the Kashmir initiative not because they ignored this reality but because they simply could not overcome it.

Many in Pakistan believe that India, too, missed an opportunity. Had it responded boldly, agreements on Siachen and Sir Creek could have been signed in 2006. On both counts, the broad contours of the settlement were known for some time, but the political will to go through with the solutions wasn't there. On Siachen, for instance, Pakistan has for some time maintained that the Indian military has blocked settlement, arguing that demilitarization would undermine the many sacrifices it has made on the glacier over the years (*Express Tribune* 2011; M. Sattar 2011). Moving ahead on Siachen (and Sir Creek) would have given the peace process a major boost since groundwork had already been made through increased people-to-people contacts, friendly exchanges, increased trade and economic ties, nuclear CBMs, and cross-LoC CBMs. Cross-LoC infiltration was also down dramatically, as India has publicly acknowledged.

The final blow to the peace process was the judicial crisis in Pakistan, which began in March 2007 when Musharraf sacked the country's chief justice, triggering nationwide agitation.[12] This distracted the government completely. Prime Minister Manmohan Singh, while recounting his government's achievements, said on May 2, 2009, "General Musharraf and I had nearly reached an Agreement, a non-territorial solution to all problems" (Noorani 2009). However, after the chief justice debacle in Pakistan, the process came to a halt.

Each country's position subsequently hardened, and contact between them was limited. Although dialogue has resumed, the post-Musharraf civilian setup in Pakistan has been reluctant to start the process where it left off. Also, India has continued to fall back on its "address terrorism first" stance. All this has happened as both civilian governments have struggled with coalition politics and with being perceived as internally weak. They also faced criticism over poor governance performance, which adversely affected their ability to pursue these initiatives.

At one level, the situation seems to be reverting back to India's stubborn stance on terrorism. The external affairs minister, S. M. Krishna, on the eve of his visit to Pakistan in September 2012, called for an "expeditious and successful conclusion of the trial in Pakistan relating to those involved with the Mumbai terrorist attacks." He mentioned Prime Minister Manmohan Singh as saying that action in this regard would bridge the trust deficit and help build public support in India for the kind of relationship India would like to see between the two countries (*Express Tribune* 2012). Pakistan, for its part, seems to be growing increasingly frustrated with India. According to a report based on knowledgeable sources, Pakistani officials conveyed to their Indian counterparts during S. M. Krishna's three-day trip that "while Islamabad had shown flexibility in its approach to normalization it has not yet found a matching response from Delhi, whose 'mindset' does not seem to have changed on core issues." In fact, "even on disputes where agreement in principle was reached in the past, like Siachen, they remain unimplemented and had given way to a hardening in Delhi's position. Similarly on water issues, information that India is obliged to provide under treaty commitments to the Indus Waters Commission had not been forthcoming" (Lodhi 2012).

The good news is that the realization that the way forward entails returning to the progress made during the peace process remains intact on both sides. Before arriving in Pakistan in September 2012, Krishna also acknowledged, "The period between 2004–2008 saw the most fruitful and productive discussions ever between India and Pakistan, including on the

12. Musharraf's act triggered the "lawyers' movement," which many credit for ultimately bringing his rule to an end. For a chronology of the movement, see Tanveer (2008).

issue of Jammu and Kashmir. These discussions were based on the common understanding that while boundaries could not be redrawn, we could work towards making them irrelevant by enabling people on both sides of the Line of Control to move freely and trade with each other. We need to carry those discussions forward and build on them" (*Express Tribune* 2012).

The Way Forward in the Peace Process

The period of developments recounted here is unprecedented in the history of India-Pakistan relations. Violence and coercion were shunned for private and public dialogue, for CBMs that would alter the lives of Kashmiris, and for a sincere attempt to find a sustainable solution to the Kashmir issue, which has underpinned the acrimony that both countries have felt toward each other since 1947. The conflict resolution mode that New Delhi and Islamabad adopted was one of quiet diplomacy and sought to build bridges of peace while transforming their mind-sets regarding the way forward on specific outstanding issues and on the overall relationship.

The most prudent way forward is for both countries to pick up the pieces from where they fell in 2007. Many in policymaking circles believe that uninterrupted dialogue will promote a narrative of the relationship that will take into account the new realities and challenges, including recognition of terrorism as a common enemy (Dixit 2004). Moving forward, lessons must be learned from the past peace efforts, and future interaction should be modified to capitalize on the positives and minimize the pitfalls experienced before. Both governments have to own the process, and they must make a much broader effort to convince people in India, Pakistan, and Kashmir of its merits. This effort has to include the parliaments, the military establishments, and the media. It is only when all stakeholders are taken into confidence that such a major initiative can enjoy the support of the people.

Other countries, including the United States, should also show an understanding of Pakistan's rivalry with India and its difficult relations with Afghanistan, which result in regional insecurity, and should undertake quiet dialogue to promote "a different future by making long-term commitments—on both sides of the Durand Line" (Crocker 2010). The United States must see a direct interest in helping India and Pakistan make progress. Although this is not always fully comprehended in Washington, Afghanistan will not become peaceful unless India and Pakistan normalize their relations. Pakistan has vital stakes in Afghanistan, and India has steady influence in Kabul. Given the history of Pakistan and Afghanistan offering sanctuary to each other's opponents, noninterference in the internal affairs of Afghanistan by its neighbors, including Pakistan, is imperative. The expectation is that Afghanistan, likewise, will not allow its territory to be used for acts of terrorism against Pakistan.

The point here is not to digress into the Indo-Pak competition over Afghanistan. It is only to suggest that such competition could easily spill over and affect the bilateral relationship between the two sides—ultimately holding back progress on key issues such as Kashmir. Cooperation between India and Pakistan on the situation in Afghanistan would also facilitate overall regional peace and cooperation.

Hard work and diplomacy lie ahead. Pakistan and India should work toward a results-oriented dialogue through back channels and early agreement on outstanding issues, taking into account the detailed and comprehensive diplomatic work done during 2004–07. Meanwhile, potential distractions, such as Afghanistan, must be worked out so that they do not hinder progress. Only then will Pakistan find the space to address its militancy challenge wholeheartedly. This will also be when anti-India terrorism from Pakistani soil becomes history.

References

Chari, P. R., Pervaiz Iqbal Cheema, and Stephen P. Cohen. 2007. *Four Crises and a Peace Process: American Engagement in South Asia*. Washington, DC: Brookings Institution Press.

Coll, Steve. 2009. "The Back Channel." *New Yorker*, Mar. 2.

Crocker, Ryan. 2010. "Pakistan Is Not America's Enemy." *Wall Street Journal*, Oct. 12.

Davis, Zachary S., ed. 2011. *The India-Pakistan Military Standoff: Crisis and Escalation in South Asia*. New York: Palgrave Macmillan.

Dawn. 1999. "Lahore Declaration." Feb. 22. www.pakistani.org/pakistan/lahore_declaration.html.

———. 2004. "Pakistan, India Joint Statement." Jan. 6. http://archives.dawn.com/2004/01/07/top2.htm.

Desmond, Edward. 1995. "The Insurgency in Kashmir (1989–1991)." *Contemporary South Asia* 4 (1): 5–16.

Dixit, Jyotindra, N. 2004. *Makers of India's Foreign Policy*. New Delhi: Harper Collins.

Economic Times. 2003. "Pak Announces Series of Reciprocal Steps." May 6. http://articles.economictimes.indiatimes.com/2003-05-06/news/27530239_1_core-issue-mir-zafarullah-khan-jamali-indian-fishermen.

Express Tribune. 2011. "Siachen Dispute: Pakistani Official Blames India for Collapse of Talks." June 6. http://tribune.com.pk/story/183301/siachen-dispute-pakistani-official-blames-india-for-collapse-of-talks/.

———. 2012. "I Bring a Message of Goodwill: Krishna." Sept. 7. http:// tribune.com.pk/story/432857/3-day-visit-i-bring-a-message-of-goodwill-krishna/.

———. 2013. "Indian Army Kills Pakistani Soldier Who 'Inadvertently' Crossed LoC." Feb. 15. http://tribune.com.pk/story/507722/india-kills-pakistani-soldier-who-crossed-loc-report/.

Fair, C. Christine. 2009. "Militants in the Kargil Conflict: Myths, Realities, and Impacts." In *Asymmetric Warfare in South Asia: The Causes and Consequences of the Kargil Conflict,* ed. Peter R. Lavoy. New York: Cambridge Univ. Press.

Federation of American Scientists (FAS). 2000. "Remarks by the President in Greeting to the People of Pakistan." Mar. 25. www.fas.org/news/pakistan/2000/000325-pak-wh2.htm.

Fayyaz, Shabana. 2009. "Indo-Pak Joint Anti-Terrorism Mechanism: Perspectives from Pakistan." Institute of Peace and Conflict Studies. IPCS Issue Brief 126, Sept. www.ipcs.org/pdf_file/issue/IB126-Ploughshares-Shabhana.pdf.

Friedman, Thomas L. 2002. "India, Pakistan and GE." *New York Times,* Aug. 11, sec. 4, 13.

Freedom House. 2012. "Indian Kashmir: Freedom in the World 2012." Report. www.freedomhouse.org/report/freedom-world/2012/indian-kashmir.

Ganguly, Sumit. 2002. "Continuing Challenges." Securing South Asia: A Symposium on Advancing Peace in the Subcontinent, no. 517, Sept. www.india-seminar.com/.

Gopalan, Divya. 2011. "Kashmir: Before and After the Politicians." *Al Jazeera,* Aug. 5. www.aljazeera.com/indepth/spotlight/kashmirtheforgottenconflict/2011/08/20118411402506865.html.

Hanauer, Larry, and Peter Chalk. 2012. "India's and Pakistan's Strategies in Afghanistan: Implications for the United States and the Region." Occasional paper, RAND Center for Asia Pacific Policy. www.rand.org/content/dam/rand/pubs/ occasional_papers/2012/RAND_OP387.pdf.

Hussain, Mujahid. 2012. *Punjabi Taliban: Driving Extremism in Pakistan.* New Delhi: Pentagon Press.

Hussain, Zahid. 2007. *Frontline Pakistan: The Struggle with Militant Islam.* New York: Columbia Univ. Press.

International Crisis Group (ICG). 2009. "Pakistan: The Militant Jihadi Challenge." Asia Report no. 164, Mar. 13. www.crisisgroup.org/en/regions/asia/south-asia/pakistan/164-pakistan-the-militant-jihadi-challenge.aspx.

Jamal, Arif. 2009. *Shadow War: The Untold Story of Jihad in Kashmir.* New York: Melville House.

Jaspal, Zafar N. 2011. "Understanding the Political-Military Context of the 2002 Military Standoff—A Pakistani Perspective." In *The India-Pakistan Military Standoff: Crisis and Escalation in South Asia,* ed. Zachary S. Davis. New York: Palgrave Macmillan.

Kashmir Study Group. 1998. "Kashmir: A Way Forward." Dec. 1. www.kashmirstudygroup.net/awayforward/proposal.html.

Kasuri, Khurshid Mahmud. 2009. "Address on Pak-India Relations: Security Dynamics and Future Scenario," excerpted in *Policy Perspectives* 6 (1), Institute of Policy Studies (Islamabad). www.ips.org.pk/pakistanaffairs/security-a-foreign-policy/1056-pak-india-relations-security-dynamics-and-future-scenario.pdf.

———. 2011. "Address at the Asian College of Journalism." http://hindu.com/thehindu/nic/acjkasuri.pdf.

Khosa, Tariq. 2013. "Frail State, Not a Failed One." *The News,* Mar. 8.

Korbel, Josef. 1954. *Danger in Kashmir.* Princeton, NJ: Princeton Univ. Press.

Lakshman, Kanchan. 2005. "A Bus-Ride to Uncertainty." *Kashmir Herald* 4, no. 7 (May). www.kashmirherald.com/opinions/busridetouncertainty-prn.html.

Lavoy, Peter R., ed. 2009. *Asymmetric Warfare in South Asia: The Causes and Consequences of the Kargil Conflict.* New York: Cambridge Univ. Press.

Lodhi, Maleeha. 2012. "More Process than Outcome." *The News,* Sept. 18. www.thenews.com.pk/Todays-News-9-132550-More-process-than-outcome.

Musharraf, Pervez. 2006. *In the Line of Fire: A Memoir.* New York: Free Press.

———. 2009. "India, Pak were Close to Kashmir Deal: Musharraf." *Devil's Advocate,* July 20. CNN-IBN interview. http://ibnlive.in.com/videos/97374/india-pak-were-close-to-kashmir-deal-musharraf.html.

Mustafa, Zubeida. 2005. "APHC's Message to Pakistan." zubeidamustafa.com, June 15. www.zubeidamustafa.com/aphcs-message-to-pakistan.

Nation. 2013. "India, Pakistan Resume Border Links as Tensions Ease." Jan. 28. www.nation.com.pk/pakistan-news-newspaper-daily-english-online/national/28-Jan-2013/trade-bus-services-resume-across-loc-as-tensions-ebb.

Nawaz, Shuja. 2008. *Crossed Swords: Pakistan, Its Army, and the Wars Within.* Karachi: Oxford Univ. Press.

Noorani, A.G. 2009. "The Four-Point Formula." *Dawn,* Aug. 1.

Obama, Barack. 2008. Interview with Tom Brokaw on NBC's *Meet the Press,* Dec. 7. American Presidency Project. www.presidency.ucsb.edu/ws/?pid=85042.

Outlook India. 2005. "The Peace Process Is Now Irreversible." Apr. 18. www.outlookindia.com/article.aspx?227150.

———. 2009. "No Dilution of Our Position." July 29. www.outlookindia.com/article.aspx?261042.

Sattar, Abdul. 2010. *Pakistan's Foreign Policy 1947–2009.* Karachi: Oxford Univ. Press.

Sattar, Madiha. 2011. "Indian Army Hurdle in Way of Siachen Solution." *Dawn,* June 2. http://dawn.com/2011/06/02/indian-army-hurdle-in-way-of-siachen-solution/.

Schaffer, Howard B. 2009. *The Limits of Influence: America's Role in Kashmir.* Washington, DC: Brookings Institution Press.

Schofield, Victoria. 2000. *Kashmir in Conflict: India, Pakistan and the Unfinished War.* London: I. B. Tauris.

Siddiqi, Shahid R. 2010. "Kashmir: The New Wave of Uprising." *Dawn,* Aug. 1. http://archives.dawn.com/archives/67516.

Siddique, Tahir. 2006. "Interview with Nawaz Sharif." *Herald (Karachi),* June, 38–39.

Singh, Swaran. 1999. "The Kargil Conflict: Why and How of China's Neutrality." *Strategic Analysis* 23 (7): 1083-94.

Sood, V. K., and Pravin Sawhney. 2003. *Operation Parakram: The War Unfinished.* New Delhi: Sage.

Talbott, Strobe. 2004. *Engaging India: Diplomacy, Democracy, and the Bomb.* Washington, DC: Brookings Institution Press.

Tankel, Stephen. 2011. *Storming the World Stage: The Story of Lashkar-e-Taiba.* New York: Columbia Univ. Press.

Tanveer, Rana. 2008. "A Chronology of the Lawyers' Movement." *Daily Times,* Nov. 3. www.dailytimes.com.pk/default.asp?page=2008\11\03\story_3-11-2008_pg7_40.

Times of India. 2003. "Pak Announces Resumption of Air, Bus, Rail Links with India." May 6. http://articles.timesofindia.indiatimes.com/2003-05-06/pakistan/27274010_1_air-links-core-issue-kashmir-issue.

———. 2010. "Pak Trashes Musharraf's 4-Point Kashmir Formula." June 30. http://articles.timesofindia.indiatimes.com/2010-06-30/pakistan/28302692_1_kashmir-issue-foreign-minister-india-and-pakistan.

Ul Haque, Ihtasham. 2005. "APHC Visit to Help Resolve Issue: PM." *Dawn,* June 22, http://archives.dawn.com/2005/06/23/top2.htm.

Wani, Riyaz. 2007. "End Armed Struggle, Says Mirwaiz, It Has Achieved." *Indian Express,* Jan. 21. www.indianexpress.com/news/end-armed-struggle-says-mirwaiz-it-has-achieved/21405/.

Wirsing, Robert G. 2003. *Kashmir in the Shadow of War: Regional Rivalries in a Nuclear Age.* New York: M.E. Sharpe.

Yusuf, Moeed. 2009. "Promoting Cross-LoC Trade in Kashmir: An Analysis of the Joint Chamber." U.S. Institute of Peace Special Report no. 230, Aug. www.usip.org/publications/promoting-cross-loc-trade-in-kashmir.

Yusuf, Moeed, and Thomas Lynch. 2012. "India-Pakistan Dynamic Holds Key to Afghanistan's Future." *CNN World,* Nov. 29. http://globalpublicsquare.blogs.cnn.com/2012/11/29/india-pakistan-dynamic-holds-key-to-afghanistans-future/.

II
Pakistan

Map 2. Pakistan Administrative Regions

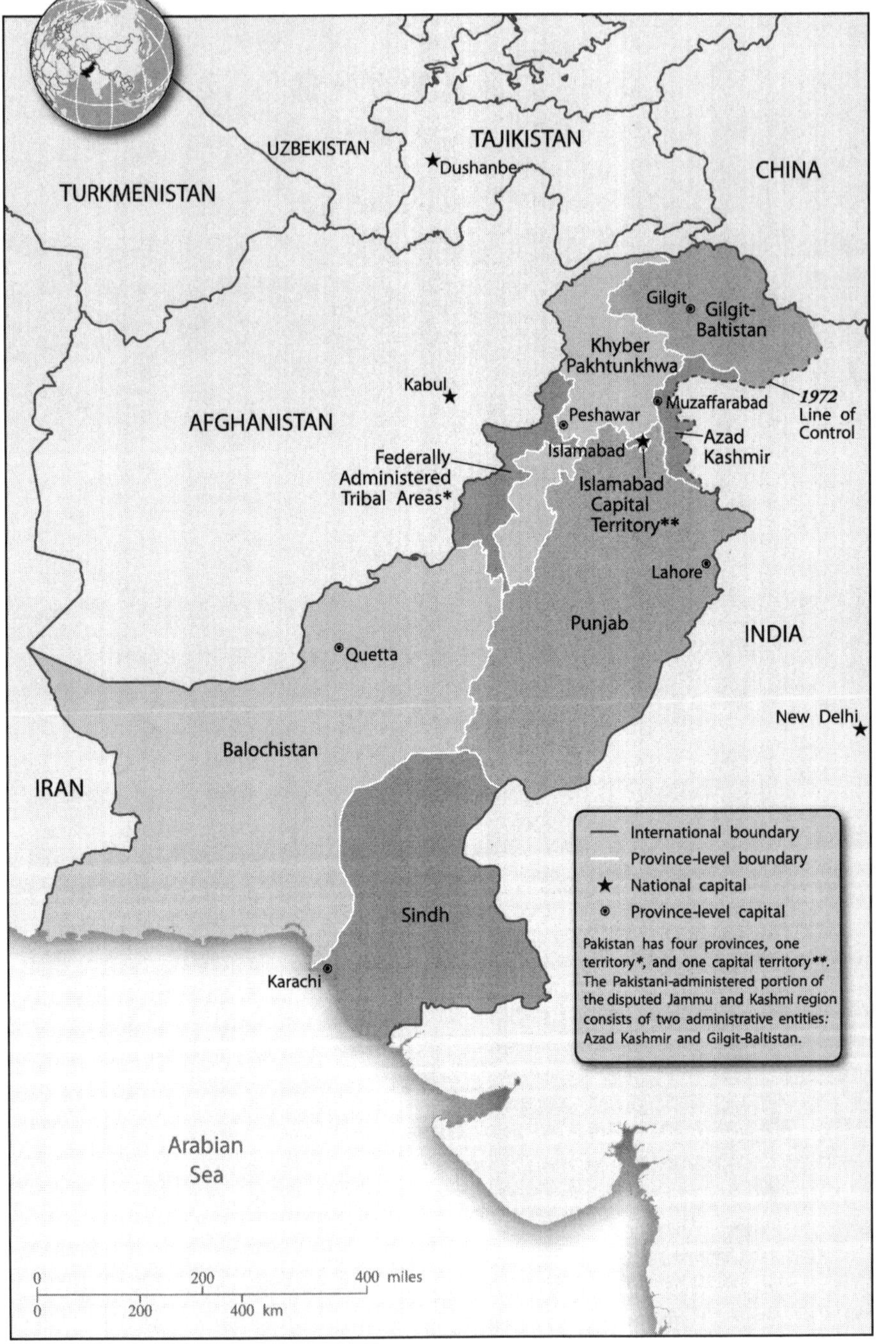

Map 3. KPK and FATA

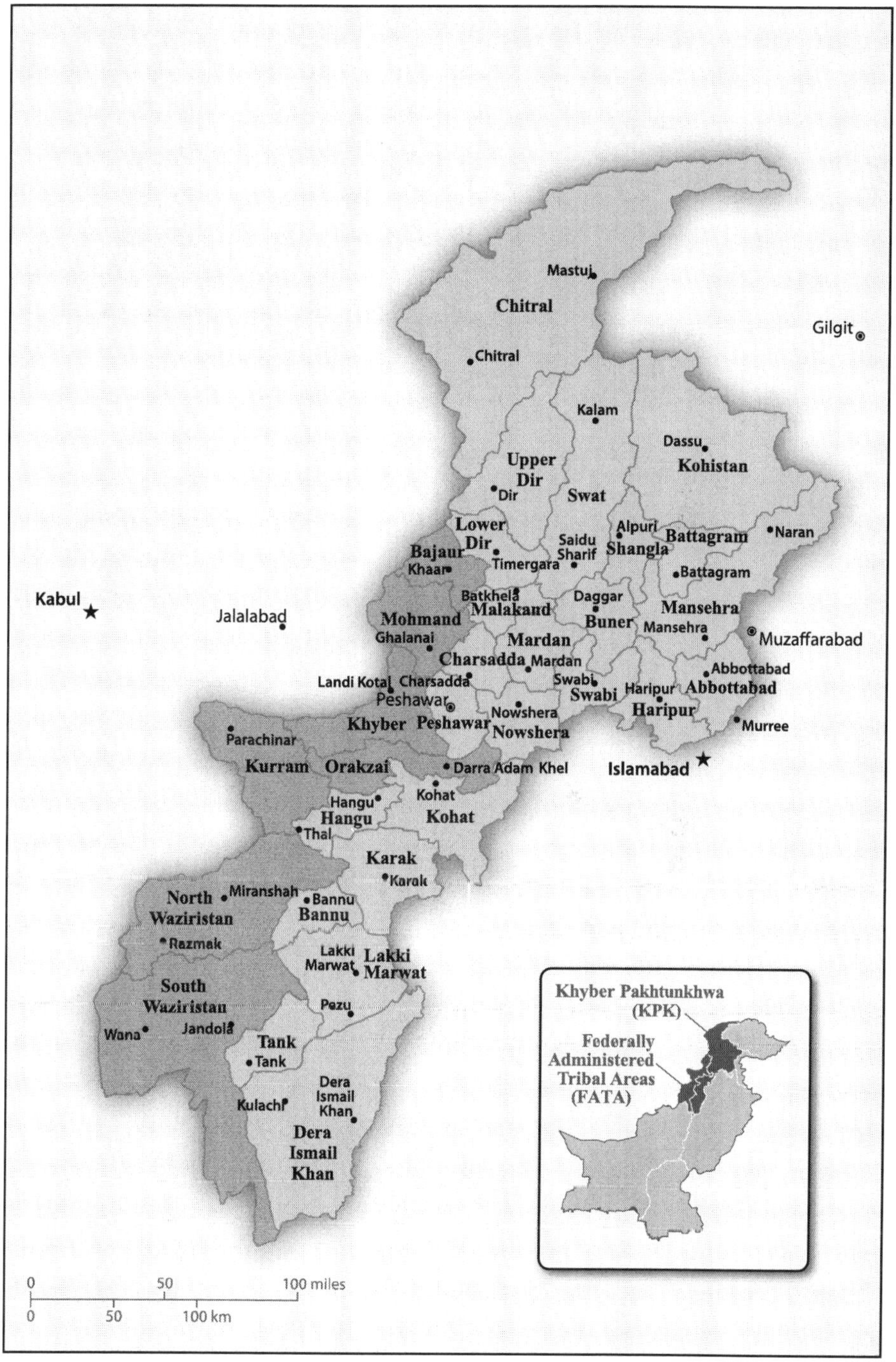

Pakistan: Timeline of Events

1947

Creation of Pakistan.

1950–79

Tehrikul Mujahideen, the political activist group of Syed Ahmed Barelvi, develops into a Wahhabi preaching group.

1979

December Soviet occupation of Afghanistan begins.

1980s

With U.S. support, Pakistan promotes Islamist resistance groups fighting Soviet occupation in Afghanistan. Tehrikul Mujahideen establishes ties with insurgents in Afghanistan and facilitates bases for Salafi jihad in the region.

1980

Maulana Irshad Ahmed establishes first jihad training camp in Pakistan in Wana, South Waziristan Agency of FATA. Later, Darul Islam base camp in FATA emerges as a jihad hub for madrassa students and Afghan, Pakistani, and foreign mujahideen involved in anti-Soviet struggle in Afghanistan.

1984

Future al-Qaeda chief Osama bin Laden first visits Pakistan's tribal areas, seeks to develop separate base camp for Arab militants in 1985.

1989

May Soviet withdrawal from Afghanistan.

2001

September 11 Al-Qaeda carries out attacks on U.S. homeland.

October U.S. invades Afghanistan in response to the 9/11 attacks. Taliban and al-Qaeda militants take refuge in Pakistan's FATA region.

2002–07

Over fifty militant religious groups, including al-Qaeda and Afghan Taliban fighters, flood into FATA or arise there. Pakistan military increases its presence in tribal areas through intermittent military operations, but militant organizations continue to grow.

2002

August The first jirga is held in South Waziristan, encouraged by Islamabad as a way to isolate foreign militants and al-Qaeda operatives from the local tribes.

2003–04

Targeted killing of tribal elders, the traditional power brokers in FATA, by militants opposing the elders' support of Pakistan military presence in the region. Clerics begin to fill the power vacuum. Start of Pakistani Taliban insurrection(s) targeting the state, ostensibly because Pakistani military supports U.S. occupation of Afghanistan. Pakistani forces begin concerted operations against militants in tribal areas.

2004

March Militant leader Nek Muhammad and Pakistani military strike a peace deal, the Shakai Agreement, in South Waziristan. Pakistan military agrees to pardon five militants in exchange for their peaceful coexistence. This unwritten agreement fails to materialize, because militants and Pakistani officials disagree over several of its terms.

April Pakistani army wages another operation in South Waziristan. In response, militants carry out massive campaign against the army and get local clerics to declare Pakistan *darul harb* (a territory of war) to legitimize their campaign.

June Nek Muhammad, Pashtun military leader of the Wazir tribe and veteran of the anti-Soviet war, is killed in U.S. drone strike in South Waziristan. Commander Mualvi Nazir succeeds him.

2005

February Baitullah Mehsud, the emerging militant leader, reaches an agreement with Pakistan government: He may enforce sharia in South Waziristan in exchange for not sending his militants to Afghanistan.

2007

Pakistani militants formally unite under the banner of TTP. Baitullah Mehsud heads the group.

July Militants occupy the Lal Masjid (Red Mosque) in Islamabad. After negotiations fail, Pakistan army's Special Service Group storms the compound. In the confrontation, 154 die inside the mosque compound. Militants declare all peace agreements null and void.

September	Al-Qaeda declares Pakistan its "number one" enemy. Swat Valley chapter of the TTP coalesces under leadership of Maulana Fazlullah and rallies to al-Qaeda's call for support.

2008

May	Swat peace deal with TTP: Pakistani government agrees to implement sharia law and accept TTP demands. Emboldened, al-Qaeda increases its presence in Swat and South Waziristan.

2009

April	TTP takes control of Swat and enters adjacent Buner. News headlines declare it "60 miles from Islamabad." Pakistan military operations begin in Swat and South Waziristan.
June	Pakistani army clears Swat Valley in its first major military success since the insurrection began in 2004.
August	Baitullah Mehsud is killed in U.S. drone strike in South Waziristan.
September	Military operations begin in South Waziristan.
October	TTP-led attack on General Headquarters of Pakistani army in Rawalpindi amplifies the threat TTP poses to the Pakistani state.
December	TTP militants' attack on Rawalpindi mosque kills 40 people, including high-ranking military officers.

2010

	Swat Valley has a functioning administration again, though it is largely receiving instructions from the military.

2010–12

	Several military operations are launched in FATA to clear out strongholds of TTP and affiliates. Military succeeds in part as TTP takes heavy losses and retreats to North Waziristan and to pockets in other FATA areas.

2011–12

	Fears of TTP resurgence return as the group begins attacking Pakistani security forces in FATA from sanctuaries across the border in Afghanistan. High-profile urban terrorism incidents resume in Pakistan.

2013

May	Pakistan holds general elections, which are marred by excessive violence attributed to the TTP.
August–September	The new Pakistani government expresses willingness to negotiate with the TTP, but violence continues.

4

Taliban Insurgency in FATA

Evolution and Prospects

Muhammad Amir Rana

Pakistan's Federally Administered Tribal Areas (FATA) are the epicenter of the insurgency that has been raging in the country in recent years. Situated in northwestern Pakistan along the Afghan border, FATA consists of seven agencies, each administered independently under legal regimes specific to the area. The agencies have a combined population of three million and are inhabited by ethnic Pashtuns, divided into various tribes. Bajaur and Mohmand agencies are inhabited predominantly by the Mohmand tribe, Khyber Agency by the Afridi, Orakzai by the Orakzai tribe, Kurram by a mix of Sunni and Shia tribes, and North and South Waziristan by the Wazir and Mehsud tribes respectively. To the east of FATA is KPK, previously known as the Northwest Frontier Province, one of Pakistan's four provinces (see map 2).

The following factors have contributed to the emergence and expansion of the insurgency in FATA and its spillover into parts of KPK:

1. the warrior culture of local tribesmen

2. the proliferation of a "culture of jihad" after the 1979 Soviet invasion of Afghanistan

3. the crystallization of the Taliban regime in the 1990s civil war in Afghanistan following the Soviet withdrawal

---

This chapter draws in part on the Pakistan Institute for Peace Studies report "Dynamics of Taliban Insurgency in FATA" (Rana et al 2009).

4. the civil war's cascading effects in FATA

5. the post-9/11 "war on terror" and the resultant concentration of Pakistani and transnational militant networks in FATA

Although many Pashtun tribesmen residing in the FATA may have joined the war against the Soviets in the 1980s due to their ethnic and religious affinity with the Afghans, many non-Pashtun Pakistani individuals and groups also took up arms because they deemed Islam to be under threat in Afghanistan. Pakistan, acting in its own geopolitical interests, encouraged and facilitated the expansion of these networks. Pakistan partnered with the United States, which was the driving force behind the agenda to weaken the Soviet Union. Also included in the coalition were a number of Western and Middle Eastern countries that fought the decisive Cold War struggle in Afghanistan together.

While acknowledging the complex interests of regional and international players in the war and their devastating consequences for Afghanistan, this analysis narrows its focus on these policies to their impact on Pakistan in general and on FATA and KPK in particular. The emphasis, therefore, is on tracing the evolution of the militant groups and their linkages with regional and local terrorist groups that have shaped the contours of the insurgency on Pakistan's western borders. The chapter also highlights the shortcomings of the state, especially its failure to prevent the situation from moving closer to the undesirable crisis and war stages on the conflict curve *before* an active counterinsurgency strategy—including use of military force—became unavoidable. Pakistan's case is somewhat anomalous in that the party with the highest stake in maintaining peace—the state apparatus—pursued for decades a policy that actively stoked the flames of militancy and, combined with unrelated episodes such as 9/11, ultimately led to the insurgency that Pakistan is confronting today.

Growth of Militancy in FATA and KPK: A Historical Perspective

In addition to the militant organizations whose presence in FATA and KPK preceded the 9/11 attacks, over sixty local Taliban groups emerged in the region during 2002–10. Initially, around forty Taliban groups were part of the TTP alliance, and the number continues to rise.[1] As many as fourteen Taliban groups are part of the Waziri alliance, led by Maulvi Nazir (killed in a January 2, 2013, drone strike) and Commander Hafiz Gul Bahadur. There are many other small Taliban groups in the settled districts of

1. The TTP is an alliance of Taliban groups, operating in different areas of FATA and KPK, that came together under the TTP umbrella in 2007, largely by the efforts of Baitullah Mehsud, a militant leader from the Mehsud tribe in the South Waziristan region of FATA.

KPK, such as Karak, Lakki Marwat, Bannu, Kohat, Peshawar, Mardan, Dera Ismail Khan, Nowshera, and Dir (Rana, Basit, and Sial 2009).[2] For locations of the various districts of both KPK and FATA, see map 3.

The local tribes in FATA put up strong resistance to the British in the eighteenth century, providing the core for the radical movements of Syed Ahmed Shaheed in British India. Syed Ahmed's armed movement against Sikh rule in Punjab was aimed at establishing an Islamic state according to the principles enunciated by Sheikh Abdul Wahhab Najdi—founder of the Wahhabi movement—and it gained remarkable traction in the tribal areas.[3] The struggle later became a movement against British colonial rule, and it remained active until Pakistan gained independence in 1947. Bajaur, Khyber, and Mohmand tribal agencies in FATA were the strongholds of Syed Ahmed's movement at the time, with the group's headquarters located in Chamerqand, Bajaur Agency (Rana 2003).

Tehrikul Mujahideen, the political party of Syed Ahmed, continued to operate under this name until 1979, with the organization's fundamental character going through many changes over the decades. For example, in 1948, the group issued the first fatwa supporting jihad against the Indian occupation of Kashmir, after which thousands of tribesmen poured into Kashmir and played a pivotal role in wresting a large part of the state Kashmir from Indian rule. From 1950 to 1979, Tehrikul Mujahideen acted as a Wahhabi preaching group, establishing links with Wahhabi insurgent groups in Afghanistan during the Afghan-Soviet war, thereby facilitating bases for Salafi jihad in the region (Rana 2003).

Continuation of Jihad: From Soviet Afghanistan to the "War on Terror"

The Taliban, both in Afghanistan and Pakistan, have sought to appeal to the tribesmen by claiming that their movement is a continuation of the same legacy. The wider pro-jihad environment in Pakistan has also played into the hands of the militants.

Before 9/11, 104 suprasectarian and 82 sectarian militant groups of varying strengths operated in Pakistan, all of them coming into being in the 1980s and 1990s (Rana 2003). Pakistani state policy during the 1980s, which favored Sunnis over Shias, and Deobandis within the Sunni sect, was a key factor in nurturing these groups. Other key factors helping these groups were the Soviet-Afghan war and the Pakistani state's support for the insurgency in Indian Kashmir during the 1990s. These groups had ties with

2. For an excellent discussion and analysis of the militant landscape in this region, see Fishman (2010).

3. The Wahhabi movement began in Saudi Arabia with Muhammad ibn Abd-al-Wahhab (1703–87). The movement inspired South Asian theologians, who then began their own Wahhabi-oriented reform initiatives.

regional and international terrorist organizations, and they shared an array of agendas and ideologies. Shortly after 9/11, the number of these organizations decreased in Pakistan and Kashmir to twenty-one suprasectarian and thirty-nine sectarian groups.[4] This was mainly due to the Pakistani government's U-turn on its promilitancy stance and its subsequent incursions into the tribal areas to target militants. However, at the same time, these groups grew in number in FATA, where more than fifty local Taliban groups and many other militant religious groups formed between 2002 and 2007. This surge in Pakistani militant groups grew from the rush to join the al-Qaeda and Afghan Taliban fighters who had concentrated in the Pakistani tribal areas to oppose the U.S. invasion of Afghanistan that began in 2001. As many as forty groups joined the TTP, headed by Baitullah Mehsud, the successor to Nek Muhammad, a Wazir and a veteran of the anti-Soviet jihad who can aptly be described as the first Taliban commander in FATA.[5] Other major groups who are still keeping a separate identity are Lashkar-e-Islam in Khyber Agency—a group led by Hafiz Gul Bahadur in North Waziristan—the Maulvi Nazir group in South Waziristan, the Dr. Ismail group in Bajaur, and local militant groups in Darra Adam Khel in KPK.[6]

Many of these organizations already had networks in the tribal areas, and as the Pakistani Taliban movement emerged, members of many of these groups joined its ranks. The splintering of militant groups, some of which were under state patronage and control, has created one of the most underestimated challenges for the Pakistani state apparatus since 9/11. In 2009, Maulana Masood Azhar, the head of the banned, traditionally anti-India militant organization JeM, echoed the view of many who believe that splits in militant groups are a direct consequence of Islamabad banning jihadi groups. During the TTP insurgency in Swat, KPK, in 2009, he wrote in a weekly publication: "Many (Taliban) commanders fighting in Swat today were once affiliated with the faithful, spiritual and ethical system of Jaish-e-Muhammad and they were not allowed to hurt any Muslims but when the government banned Jaish these individuals parted ways with the

4. The statistics are based on the data collected by Pak Institute for Peace Studies (PIPS) from field and media reports. PIPS maintains an active database of these statistics, which can be made available upon request.

5. For more on Nek Muhammad, see Yusufzai (2004).

6. Lashkar-e-Islam, established in 2005 by Mangal Bagh, vowed to eliminate "social vices" in Khyber Agency in FATA. Gul Bahadur, who had fought against Soviet troops in Afghanistan, is considered a close aide of leaders of the Haqqani Network in Afghanistan. Mullah Nazir, a South Waziristan-based militant commander, had links with the Afghan Taliban and engaged in guerrilla operations in Afghanistan. Initially, he was part of the Wazir and Mehsud militant alliance and became the key Wazir involved in jihad after Nek Muhammad's death. Nazir was wooed away by the Pakistani state in 2008 when Baitullah Mehsud chose to expand terrorist attacks inside Pakistan. Dr. Ismail, who had fought against Soviet troops in Afghanistan under the banner of Hizb-e-Islami, formed his own militant group in 2005.

organization and became local and regional militant commanders. That was the fallout of banning the jihad groups in Pakistan" (Saddi 2009).

Thus many militant groups, several of which were previously part of Pakistan's foreign policy adventures in Afghanistan or Indian Kashmir, turned against the state after Islamabad joined the international alliance aimed at fighting the militants based in Afghanistan and in the Pak-Afghan border areas. Militant groups quickly began to project themselves as saviors of the Muslim Ummah against the Western "occupation" of Afghanistan and built support for their new jihad. Neither the government of then-president Pervez Musharraf nor the United States realized at the time that their strategies, instead of defeating al-Qaeda and the Afghan Taliban, would spur fresh militancy in the region. After the U.S. invasion of Afghanistan, Pakistan's focus was mainly to capture al-Qaeda militants, and it overlooked addressing the domestic sources of militancy.[7] Moreover, since 2003, when the United States invaded Iraq, Afghanistan has become a secondary concern for Washington. These factors gave militants a major opportunity to strengthen their networks in FATA.

The Formative Phase: Key Players and the Developing Nexus

Deobandi, a South Asian movement following an orthodox interpretation of Islam, remained the dominant school of thought for jihadis throughout the Soviet-Afghan war, even though Pakistan is predominantly Barelvi—a more tolerant Sufi mystical interpretation of Islamic tenets. During the 1980s, the conservative Jama'at-e-Islami political party and its affiliated groups—mainly Hizb-e-Islami of Gulbuddin Hekmatyar, one of the major Afghan mujahideen groups—developed their own discourse while casting a covetous eye toward Kabul.

When Soviet troops left Afghanistan and power-sharing disputes erupted among the Afghan mujahideen, the major Deobandi groups supported Ahmed Shah Masood, a Tajik commander, because he subscribed to the same school of religious thought. Hizb-e-Islami won the support of Pakistan, and this was instrumental in allowing the group to secure a major share of power in Afghanistan after the Soviet pullout. Deobandis first tasted power in 1995, when the Taliban captured 87 percent of Afghanistan—interestingly enough, in opposition to Ahmed Shah Masood. Both Deobandi mujahideen groups and the Jama'at-e-Islami found allies among Arab volunteers who had come to Afghanistan to take part in the anti-Soviet jihad. The majority were Salafis, for whom even Deobandis were not orthodox enough, and they came up with new ultraconservative political

7. From 2002 to May 2006, Pakistan arrested more than one thousand al-Qaeda suspects and handed most of them over to the United States (Rana and Bukhari 2007).

and religious ideas that were much more amenable to violence. This subsequently influenced the militant groups and led to the expansion of their agendas.

The current insurgency in FATA is mainly dominated by Deobandi-cum-Salafi groups. Pakistani Deobandis joined Afghans in the war against the Soviet Union mainly through fatwas (religious edicts) in favor of the Afghan jihad, issued by leaders such as Maulana Mufti Mehmood, head of the largest Deobandi religious political party in Pakistan; Maulana Abdul Haq of the Darul Uloom Haqqania madrassa at Akora Khattak; and Maulana Yousaf Binori, principal of the Darul Uloom Islamia Binori Town madrassa in Karachi. These orders were pivotal in encouraging Deobandi madrassa students in Pakistan to join the anti-Soviet jihad in Afghanistan.

A key development was the establishment of a base in northwest Pakistan from which future militants could be ideologically indoctrinated and trained. On February 18, 1980, a number of students from Darul Uloom Islamia Binori Town, Karachi, including Maulana Irshad Ahmed, Qari Saifullah Akhtar, and Maulana Abdul Samad Sial, crossed the border into Afghanistan with the aim of fighting the Soviets (Rana and Gunaratna 2007). Before entering Afghanistan, they visited Peshawar and joined the Harkatul Inqilab-e-Islami of Maulana Nasrullah Mansoor, partly due to their shared Deobandi beliefs.[8] After spending four months in Afghanistan, Maulana Irshad returned to Pakistan in order to prepare more seminary students for holy war in Afghanistan (*Al-Irshad* 1994). A few months later, Maulana Noor Muhammad, a cleric from South Waziristan, persuaded Maulana Irshad and his associates to set up a training camp in Wana, the headquarters of South Waziristan Agency in FATA.[9] Eventually, they established a base camp in Wana called Darul Islam (abode of Islam), which soon emerged as the most prominent jihad hub for Pakistani madrassa students (Rana and Bukhari 2007, 15).

This space proved integral to the consolidation of militant groups in Pakistan. During the early 1980s, Darul Islam served as the launching pad for mujahideen groups involved in the struggle against the Soviets across the border. Wana became a town swarming with agents of the U.S. Central Intelligence Agency (CIA) and the Pakistani ISI, who, along with Afghan and Pakistani jihad organizations, recruited and trained the tribal youth, arranged supplies, and planned attacks against Soviet troops. Meanwhile,

8. Harkatul Inqilab-e-Islami Afghanistan was one of seven Afghan guerrilla groups supported by the United States and other Western nations in waging war against the Soviet Union during the 1980s. In 1996, the Taliban toppled the guerrilla government.

9. Maulana Noor Muhammad was killed in a suicide attack in Wana, South Waziristan, on August 22, 2010. Media reports hinted that his opposition to the presence of Uzbek militants in South Waziristan may have been the reason for his assassination.

Arab militants also built concrete bunkers in the Shakai and Nawai Ada areas near Wana. Around this time, mosques and seminaries from the Persian Gulf countries began channeling millions of rupees in donations to these fighters, leading to a phenomenal proliferation of madrassas, mostly Deobandi, across Pakistan.[10] These factors led to the emergence of a new generation of ideologically indoctrinated and well-trained mujahideen, who relied mainly on networks and resources in Pakistan for their struggle next door in Afghanistan.

Role of Pakistani Organizations in the Afghan Jihad

Pakistani madrassas were integral to the growth of the Afghan jihad, providing steady supplies of militants and financial resources. The Darul Uloom Haqqania madrassa, also known as Jamia Haqqania, is located along the main Islamabad-Peshawar Road in Akora Khattak, in Nowshera district of KPK. It has always been an important madrassa for Deobandi students from KPK and Afghanistan. When the political crisis in Afghanistan in 1972 led to the ouster of King Abdul Zahir's government and the induction of the pro-Soviet and reformist prime minister Muhammad Musa Sadiq, it annoyed the right-wing Afghan parties, who resented the Soviet Communist influence in the country. Jamia Haqqania was an important center from which to gauge Afghan political sentiments at the time because a large number of Afghan students were studying there since its principal, Maulana Abdul Haq, had close ties with influential politicians in Afghanistan. When Soviet troops invaded Afghanistan, Maulana Haq was the first religious scholar from Pakistan to issue a fatwa declaring the fight against the Soviets to be jihad. He also persuaded some of his Afghan students to engage in the war (Rana and Gunaratna 2007, 23).

Meanwhile, Maulvi Younis Khalis, a student of Maulana Abdul Haq, started guerrilla activities in eastern Afghanistan from Hizb-e-Islami's platform.[11] Soon, another accomplished student of Jamia Haqqania, Jalaluddin Haqqani, joined Khalis, and the two stepped up guerrilla operations in the Afghan province of Khost. Khalis asked his mentor, Maulana Abdul Haq, for weapons and fighters, and Haq tried to persuade Jamia Binori Town students group Harkatul Jihad-e-Islami (HuJI) to help. This group was already engaged in militant activities in Afghanistan in collaboration with Harkatul Inqilab-e-Islami.

10. The statistics are based on the data collected by PIPS from field and media reports.

11. Hizb-e-Islami was led by Maulvi Younis Khalis, who parted ways with his former colleague, Gulbuddin Hekmatyar, in 1979. Although seventy years old, Khalis was actively involved in the anti-Soviet operations. He viewed the Afghan resistance movement as a struggle between Islam and nonbelievers. Khalis maintained close ties with Burhanuddin Rabbani of Jamiat-e-Islami. He died on July 22, 2006, in Afghanistan.

Afghan jihad organizations in the early 1980s were competing to win the support of Pakistani jihad volunteers, not only to boost the numbers of their fighters but also to fill their coffers, since the volunteers could collect substantial donations from their native regions in the name of the Afghan jihad. The HuJI was one of the most important Pakistani organizations because of its ability to raise funds on a large scale. Nasrullah Mansoor, HuJI's chief, was not ready to curtail his group's expenditure, but he promised HuJI that he would send the maximum number of his mujahideen fighters to the front lines. He also allowed HuJI to set up a training camp in Afghanistan. The HuJI became the first Pakistani group with two training camps: one in Wana and another in Afghanistan (*Al-Irshad* 1994).

A small group led by Maulana Masud Alvi, who had studied at the Jamia Khairul Uloom madrassa in Multan, Pakistan, fought independently against Soviet troops in Afghanistan with help from various local Afghan groups. Maulana Abdul Haq invited Alvi to join Haqqani. Alvi accepted the invitation mainly because of ideological differences with his partner Afghan groups. Alvi and Maulana Fazlur Rehman Khalil, a skilled fighter who had worked with HuJI, formed an independent organization called Harkat-ul-Mujahideen (HuM). The HuM managed to win the support of a number of prominent Pakistani seminaries, including Jamia Binori in Karachi, Jamia Khairul Uloom in Multan, Jamia Qasim ul Uloom in Multan, and Jamia Ashraffia in Lahore. This support not only helped the HuM in fund-raising across Pakistan but also facilitated its links with Saudi Arabia and other Persian Gulf states in generating resources (Jamatul Mujahideen 1996).

Maulana Khalil soon managed to recruit around three thousand militants from Pakistani Kashmir, the KPK, and southern Punjab. The HuM, with the help of Maulana Abdul Haq, set up its base in Miranshah, the headquarters of North Waziristan Agency in FATA, and two more camps in towns along the Afghan border in Pakistan's tribal areas. Surrounded by the Dragg Mountains, the HuM headquarters looked like a massive fortress. The group set up a training facility in a small valley near the River Shamil, just a few kilometers from its headquarters. Meanwhile, across the River Shamil in Khost, Arab militants received combat training at Jalaluddin Haqqani's camps. The camps of Gulbuddin Hekmatyar, Maulana Abdul Rab Sayyaf, and other Afghan jihad leaders were also nearby (Rana and Gunaratna 2007, 24).

The HuM established links with jihad leaders and Arab militants in the nearby camps to the extent that HuM militants from Miranshah would cross the Afghan border and report at Kochi-I, the camp run by Haqqani. Meanwhile, the area's strategic location had appealed to Osama bin Laden, later to become al-Qaeda's chief, when he visited in 1984. In 1985, he decided to develop the area as a separate base camp for Arab militants in 1985 (Rana and Gunaratna 2007, 15–20). Haqqani soon won the ISI's support and started providing training facilities to bin Laden's Arab volunteers. Celebrated as "the noble savage" by preachers in Saudi Arabia's wealthy urban mosques, Haqqani became a hero to adherents of Wahhabism, the dominant Muslim sect in Saudi Arabia. He maintained fund-raising offices in the Persian Gulf and trained young Arab jihad volunteers in the tribal areas.

Because of Haqqani's patronage, the Pakistani region bordering Afghanistan soon became a hub of Pakistani intelligence officers, Arab volunteers, and Wahhabi seminaries. Haqqani also became a close collaborator of the Pakistani and Saudi intelligence agents during the last years of the Soviet-Afghan war. Many foreign intelligence agencies regarded him as the most impressive Pashtun battlefield commander during the war (Coll 2004).

Haqqani, HuM leader Maulana Khalil, and Osama bin Laden developed high levels of coordination. The HuM took the initiative in the tribal areas by recruiting tribesmen for jihad and used bin Laden's money to gain the support of the tribal elders. Over time, because of bin Laden's patronage and encouragement, eleven major Islamic charities started operating in the area. These stood intact on the eve of 9/11. Eventually, the entire Waziristan region came under bin Laden's influence, and the Arabs considered it their second home, even marrying local women in a bid to strengthen their ties with the local tribes.[12]

Impact of the Afghan Taliban's Rise on Pakistani Tribal Areas

The Pakistani security establishment, specifically the ISI, helped the hitherto little-known Afghan Taliban's rise to power in Afghanistan. The group's consolidation of power in the mid-1990s affected Pakistani tribal areas in two ways. First, the ethnic and religious affinity of the tribes with the Taliban augmented the latter's support base, and the influence of Deobandi militant organizations and madrassas increased in the region. During the Taliban regime in Afghanistan, attempts to establish a similar system in the tribal areas had already begun. For example, Mullah Abdul Raheem, a cleric from Orakzai Agency, launched his own Taliban movement in Orakzai in 1997 and tried to impose sharia by force.

Second, the Pakistani state failed to visualize the implications of these developments. The above developments should have made clear how the jihad industry could spread its tentacles not only across Pakistan but also internationally. That the fervor of jihad and its instrumental use might be-

12. Maulana Yousaf Shah (secretary of the Jamiat Ulema-e-Islam [Sami group]), interview by the author, Akora Khattak, Aug. 2005.

come a monster that would haunt even its former patrons never occurred to those who should have seen it coming.

Instead, throughout the crucial decades of the Soviet-Afghan war and the subsequent Afghan civil war in the 1990s, Islamabad's whole emphasis was on safeguarding its strategic interests in Afghanistan. Pakistan's decision to support the Afghan Islamist resistance groups in the 1970s and 1980s was swayed by strategic, not ideological, considerations. Islamabad was essentially trying to install a friendly government in Kabul to counter the Indian influence there and secure economic and strategic ties with Central Asian states.[13] The Afghan Taliban was a last-resort option for the Pakistani establishment, but Islamabad failed to take into account the influence of the Taliban's allies, including Arab fighters. Also, in spite of common regional goals, Pakistani militant groups had different ideological tendencies from the Pakistani state's, and while their interests converged on the issue of the Kashmir dispute with India, they had a vision that was not necessarily in line with the strategic and political ambitions of their patron, the Pakistani security establishment.[14] This proved to be a fatal error. The groundwork that had been laid over two decades was overturned after 9/11, and the key militant actors started challenging the Pakistani state as soon as it declared an alliance with the United States against the jihadi outfits in Pakistan's northwest.

FATA: Fertile Ground for Jihad

To understand the success of the militants in the tribal areas, it is important to consider societal structures in FATA and the failures of the FATA governance system. The Pakistani state's longstanding legal, administrative, and economic neglect of FATA is today seen as a major compounding factor enabling the militancy. One in five people living in FATA attributes religious extremism in the region to poor governance (Haider 2009).

After independence, FATA's tribesmen acceded to Pakistan as enshrined in Article 1 of the Pakistani Constitution. However, this was on the condition that the Pakistani state not interfere with the FATA tribes' autonomy. This quickly turned into neglect, which resulted in FATA becoming one of Pakistan's most economically backward areas, with 60 percent of its people living below the poverty line (International Crisis Group 2006).

The stagnation in Pakistan's northwest has been not only economic but also political. FATA has had extremely limited participation in the political system of Pakistan; indeed, FATA representatives do not have the right to

---

13. Afghanistan also provoked and supported the Pashtun and Baloch nationalist and separatist movements in Pakistan during the 1970s. It also strengthened its relations with New Delhi, especially when pro-Soviet governments took control of Kabul.

14. For details of Pakistan's role in the Afghan Taliban's rise to power, and the security establishment's thinking at the time, see Coll (2004) and Rashid (2000).

legislate matters pertaining to FATA itself. Until 1997, most of the representatives from FATA were handpicked by tribal elders (*maliks*). Only very recently has the Pakistan Political Parties Act been extended to the FATA, providing for party-based elections as in the rest of the country (Nawaz 2009). FATA's governance is a legacy of British colonial governing strategies aimed at keeping the tribes under control. The "three pillars" of FATA governance—the political agents (PAs), maliks, and the 1901 Frontier Crimes Regulation (FCR)—which may have functioned to serve this colonial interest, could not withstand the spread of militancy in the post-9/11 period. And today they have been overridden by the influence of militant groups and their conflicting interests.

The malik system that traditionally held FATA's governance structure together in collaboration with the PAs (the state's administrative representative in each of the FATA agencies) has experienced fissures for several reasons. For one, tribal clerics, who previously lacked political authority, have become key drivers of radical ideology. After 1979, a huge inflow of funds during the anti-Soviet jihad made clerics less dependent on maliks for survival. After the Soviets' departure, the clerics were further empowered by an influx of funds and weapons into FATA. They adopted a "Kalashnikov culture" and led militias in the name of enforcing a strict Deobandi Sunni interpretation of Islam. After 9/11, as Pakistani Taliban militants perpetrated violence internally, the maliks were principal targets; their killings created a fresh vacuum that allowed the clerics unprecedented powers. In total, over six hundred maliks were killed by militias during 2004–08 (Aziz 2008). Also, demographic changes confined to specific regions have eroded tribal systems. For instance, in Waziristan, Taliban members have taken advantage of the growing tensions between influential tribal elders (*mashars*) and younger men belonging to less influential lineages (*kashars*). Kashars, frustrated with the rampant poverty and seeking to contest the tribal hierarchy dominated by mashars and the PAs, have gone to the Taliban. In sum, not only have these dynamics overturned the malik system but they have displaced tribal customs and codes that were once a mix of religiocultural norms. The result is a narrower, more hegemonic definition of Islam (Aziz 2008).

The lack of an effective legal system in FATA has aggravated the local people's frustration with the state's inability to administer justice. The FCR is a legal system based on British civil and criminal laws but adapted to include Pathan tribal code, or Pakhtunwali, and customary laws (*riwaj*), such as the trial procedure of the jirga (tribal elders' council). Although this code attempted to take into account existing forms of administration and justice, in modern times, the FCR is widely known to obfuscate justice by retaining harsh British-era penalties, such as the power to blockade hostile or unfriendly tribes (Section 21); demolition and restriction of construction of hamlets, villages, or towns on the frontier (Section 31); and the removal of persons from their places of residence (Section 36) (Haider 2009,6).[15] This has only increased the appeal of groups, such as the Taliban, who claim that in imposing rigid Islamic laws, they are restoring and dispensing speedy justice to the people. Indeed, as many of the tribal jirgas lose their credibility (with people perceiving them as heavily manipulated by the state), the militant enclave presents a viable alternative that can administer "speedy and cheap justice." They have established courts in various agencies, with a large number of tribesmen visiting them daily (Khan 2008).

Finally, there are also areas in FATA that remain simply ungoverned. This is because the terrain is perceived as too inhospitable for the state to maintain a solid presence and because governing these areas has historically never been a priority. This lack of governance has resulted in enclaves of militancy and drug smuggling, aided by the porous border that Pakistan shares with Afghanistan. Militant groups, such as Lashkar-e-Islam in Khyber Agency, have allegedly formed in response to the need to implement an agenda for social reform and to curb gambling, drug smuggling, and kidnappings (MEMRI 2008).

The Post-9/11 Scenario

When the Afghan Taliban rule collapsed in Kabul and al-Qaeda was dislodged from Afghanistan after the U.S. invasion in October 2001, Taliban and al-Qaeda operatives sneaked across the border and into Pakistan's tribal areas. Initially concentrated in South Waziristan Agency, they had connections going back to the 1980s and ethnic linkages among the local tribes—a support base that they expanded through ideology and by marrying into local families (*Mashriq* 2005). The Taliban received an outpouring of sympathy from the local population, who saw them as having been ousted by an invading power. Using this support, between 2002 and 2004, these Afghan groups organized scattered militants, linked up with local tribesmen, and waged extensive guerrilla operations against coalition forces in Afghanistan until Pakistani forces began concerted operations against them in February 2004.

Islamabad tried to resolve the conflict in the tribal areas through traditional mechanisms, such as holding jirgas and forming tribal *lashkars* (private militias) against the militants. This effort turned out to be a major policy error that later intensified the conflict. The primary focus of the state was to isolate al-Qaeda from the Taliban, but distinguishing between them

15. For more on the FCR and its discontents, see HRCP (2005).

proved to be a tricky affair since both groups faced challenges to their survival. This common purpose united the two, at least momentarily.

The issue that led to the initial tension between the tribes and the state was the presence of foreign militants in the region. The first jirga in South Waziristan was held in August 2002, and the first armed lashkar, or community militia, to expel foreign militants was raised in October the same year (Rana and Gunaratna 2007, 55). But the tribes made these attempts halfheartedly, with the goal of protecting their narrow financial and political interests. They were generally inclined toward the militants and perceived them as holy warriors, fighting against the infidel forces in Afghanistan. When all else failed to achieve the desired results, the government imposed economic sanctions on the tribes. The Pakistani militants based in FATA responded to the sanctions by expanding their operations to settled areas of KPK, launching several attacks in Peshawar and Bannu districts in 2003 and 2004.

When the militants intensified their activities in the tribal areas it became clear that military operations against them had not yielded the desired results. The government tried other strategies to resolve the issue, and at one point in 2004, it was even willing to let foreign militants remain in the area if they agreed to register with the authorities. The political administration and Pakistani army searched for rapprochement with the militants and struck several deals. The tribes agreed to conciliatory measures because the government's economic sanctions had begun to bite (Rana, Basit, and Sial 2009, 81). One agreement, between the tribal chiefs and the Pakistani army on March 27, 2004, established that the houses and property of any person giving refuge to a foreigner (Afghans were not included in the category of "foreigners") would be destroyed (Rana, Basit, and Sial 2009). Also, the Pakistani army and the political administration of the tribal areas settled all issues with tribal militants by paying them huge amounts of money (Rana, Basit, and Sial 2009, 93).

But jirgas, lashkars, economic sanctions, plans to register foreign militants, monetary inducements, use of force, and even peace deals failed to resolve the matter. The writ of the state was challenged and found wanting as the FATA political administration failed to curtail either the militants' access to resources or their mobility. The Afghan Taliban exploited the situation. But more worrisome from the Pakistani perspective, because of this situation and the general mood of resentment over the state's military operations, was when Pakistani FATA-based militants began to band together and call for direct attacks against the Pakistani army. The TTP has become Pakistan's principal challenge today. It has forged links with other Pakistan- and Kashmir-based anti-India jihad groups, such as

JeM and HuM, and has established strongholds in the Bajaur, Waziristan, Mohmand, Khyber, and Orakzai tribal agencies in FATA, as well as in Swat, Darra Adam Khel, Tank, Bannu, Mardan, Lakki Marwat, and Dera Ismail Khan in KPK. Ironically, the leadership of the tribal Taliban groups that fought against the Soviet troops in the 1980s remained engaged with Pakistani intelligence agencies. The same is true of Kashmir-based militant groups who operated as state assets for years. And although their principal emphasis was on liberating the Muslims of Kashmir, Afghanistan, and elsewhere in the world from "tyrannical" rule, their secondary focus was always sectarian and bent on achieving an ultraorthodox theocracy in Pakistan. As mentioned earlier, after 9/11 many splinter groups broke away from these militant outfits. Incensed by the Pakistani state's U-turn, militants in splinter groups focused on their parent organizations' "secondary agenda"—targeting the Pakistani state—and started to pursue it through violent means. Apart from this key factor, other structural and dynamic factors that were already present or had evolved during this time—particularly in FATA's political, social, ethnic, religious, administrative, and economic milieus—provided further impetus to the growth of militancy.

Birth of an Insurgency

Once the confrontation between the tribes and the state began, foreign militants encouraged the local tribes to form groups to wage jihad in Afghanistan and against anyone who opposed the jihad. This was their way of maintaining and preserving their presence. Local militants began to coalesce and come together, even if their ideological motives were suspect and even though many were energized by narrower political and power motives.

In any case, very little suggested that the local militant movement in the tribal areas had the potential to become a full-fledged insurgency. This changed on March 27, 2004, when militant leader Nek Muhammad and the Pakistan military struck a peace deal, known as the Shakai agreement, in South Waziristan (Khattak 2012). The deal empowered the local militants, later to coalesce into the TTP, to enforce their writ in the area, including imposing sharia. The government had agreed to pull its troops out of the tribal areas and to release all those arrested during operations. In return, it received the assurance that the tribes would never allow the use of their territory for militant activities in any other country—mainly against NATO forces in Afghanistan (Rana, Basit, and Sial 2009, 86–95). In his address on the occasion of the agreement, Nek Muhammad declared that the militants were not willing to challenge the writ of the state but would use their weapons against it if they were persecuted (Rana, Basit, and Sial 2009, 75).

Ample evidence suggests that the Taliban was not keen to impose sharia in the tribal areas. Rather, its primary purpose was to use the slogan of jihad to recruit fighters and collect donations to fight the foreign occupation in Afghanistan (Nazir 2007). The pronouncements in militant literature, whether in the form of publications, *shabnamas* (night letters), pamphlets, or CDs and DVDs, produced by the TTP or its affiliates in Pakistan during 2002–04, corroborate this intention. Inside Pakistan, their strategy against Pakistani troops was defensive (PIPS 2010). It was only with the passage of time that their agendas expanded, and in 2007, different local militant factions came together under the banner of the TTP. The TTP adopted orthodox extremist tendencies of *takfir* (declaring other Muslim sects and groups as non-Muslim) and called for the "Islamization" of the Pakistani state.

As mentioned, until 2004, the main focus of the Pakistani Taliban was to protect foreign militants, recruit and train fighters for the war in Afghanistan, and secure its position against security operations. What transformed the group into a major player in FATA was a tactical change in its operations: From 2004 onward, the TTP began kidnapping security personnel and state officials. Although suicide attacks on security forces started in 2006 and played a role in demoralizing them, the kidnapping strategy elevated the TTP to a position that compelled the state to negotiate on the TTP's terms, and the TTP began to bargain for the release of arrested militants as well. Over time, this became one of the Taliban's most lucrative strategies. Independent sources estimate that the Taliban kidnapped more than one thousand security personnel and state officials in 2007, with over five hundred militants being released in return (PIPS 2010, 89–95).

Neither side honored the Shakai agreement, and the breakdown resulted in another military operation in April 2004. This was the first time that the militants waged a massive campaign against the army in South Waziristan, and it inspired local clerics to issue fatwas declaring Pakistan to be darul harb (literally, a territory of war)—a land where Muslims could not live with personal security or religious freedom (PIPS 2010, 79). Economic sanctions against tribes further fueled antistate sentiment and paved the way for militants to develop parallel systems in areas under their sway.

Baitullah Mehsud, who united the tribal Taliban groups under the TTP banner in 2007 and was killed in a U.S. drone strike in August 2009, had first shaped the contours of his own system in the tribal areas when he made the Sararogha agreement with the government on February 22, 2005, in South Waziristan (Khattak 2012). He had gotten the government's guarantee that he would be allowed to enforce sharia in the area in exchange for not sending his militants to Afghanistan. Not only did he not keep his end of the deal, but the pact also helped the Taliban consolidate its grip on the area. Other militant groups followed in Baitullah's footsteps (Rana 2013).

Baitullah formulated a four-point strategy to gain control over the area. His militants took steps against criminals, started collecting "taxes" to speed up their operations, killed or forced out influential tribal elders who might challenge their authority, and created a parallel justice system to resolve disputes promptly.[16] In Bajaur Agency alone, a single Taliban court had registered fourteen hundred cases before August 2008 and had decided one thousand of them (Ali and Afridi 2008). They organized their parallel administration and appointed their trusted men to key positions (Aziz 2008). Anyone who posed any ideological or tactical challenge to Taliban rule was treated harshly, especially nongovernmental organizations (NGOs) and formal and modern educational institutions. Taliban groups banned NGOs, targeted CD shops, and attacked educational institutions, especially girls' schools. In 2009, forty-eight educational institutions, including fourteen girls' schools, were targeted in FATA (PIPS 2009, 9).[17] These local insurgent groups also provided welfare services to gain the local population's sympathies. For instance, in June 2008, the TTP established a fund to help the victims of the military operation in South Waziristan and distributed fifteen million rupees among them (*Ummat* 2008).

The Taliban also shrewdly exploited tribal, ethnic, and religious sentiments. As stated earlier, flaws in FATA's political and administrative setup allowed militants to weaken and gradually replace the system with their own, in the name of providing adequate security and prompt justice to the aggrieved. The Taliban also offered financial incentives to the tribesmen and recruited unemployed youth into their cadres (Rana, Basit, and Sial 2009, 153). There was also plenty of outright coercion and intimidation in the mix.

The process of Talibanization in the tribal areas was gradual. The militants eventually managed to establish parallel justice and administrative systems in virtually all areas they controlled. Taliban leaders' statements suggested that their agenda was to enforce their system not only in FATA and the KPK but also across the entire country. The Taliban had matured into a full-fledged insurgent movement in Pakistan within four to five years. And as the state, in its dealings with militants, continued to waver between peace agreements and military operations, it failed to contain the march of Talibanization. By 2008, the TTP not only partially controlled large areas of FATA, but its branches also reached settled areas in KPK. The most high profile of these was the Swat Valley, adjacent to FATA, which was overrun by the TTP's Swat chapter. This region subsequently

16. In August 2008, Baitullah reorganized the Taliban judicial system and brought all the courts under a "supreme court" with Rais Mehsud as its chief justice.

17. This information is drawn from the PIPS database. The statistics are based on monitoring of media reports.

became the site of the first full-scale counterinsurgency operation in which the Pakistani army decisively pushed back the TTP. The TTP also forged strong alliances with Punjab-based militant groups, some of whom fought the jihad in Indian Kashmir during the 1990s. Others were sectarian in their orientation, and yet others had sprung up in the wake of the burgeoning demand for militants after 9/11.

Factors That Aided the Insurgency after 9/11

Several disparate factors contributed to the rise of the Pakistani Taliban. But it is their combined effect that ultimately enabled the violent insurrection to coalesce into the feared insurgency it has become today.

Pakistani Taliban Rhetoric

At the core, the Pakistani Taliban espouses Deobandi sectarian teachings. This commonality allows it to function under a single umbrella, even though its political interpretation of Deobandi principles is at times not monolithic. As a group, the TTP maintains a dogmatic stance by espousing an interpretation that is intolerant of all other Muslim sects. This stance ought to isolate the Taliban from most Pakistanis, who adhere to less severe Barelvi traditions. But it was only partially the case when the insurgency took off, because the TTP crafted a narrative around its movement that found sympathy across the sectarian divide. It strove to portray its struggle as a move to drive out foreign occupation forces from Afghanistan in the short run and all "infidel" forces from Muslim lands in the long run (Rana 2012).

In doing this, they not only tied in to transnational jihadist groups materially but also presented themselves as ideologically similar. Since the rhetoric of anti-imperialism and fighting against subjugation of Muslims appeals to many across the Muslim world—Pakistan being no exception—Pakistani religious political parties, Islamic scholars, and even average citizens found themselves confused about the true nature of the Taliban movement. Many mistook it to be a revolutionary movement responding only to the state's excesses, which thus allowed the TTP to coalesce without much popular opposition.

Astonishingly—and this is perhaps an indication of just how powerful the Taliban's messaging was—even the Pakistani army was not immune to this rhetoric. The Pakistani armed forces, otherwise trained to fight conventional battles against "Hindu India," lacked a firm resolve to fight fellow Pakistanis using Islam as their raison d'être— historically, a rallying mechanism used by the Pakistani army itself. Indeed, the Pakistani army fought under great psychological duress during the time when the antistate elements were coming together and had not yet emerged as a full-fledged insurgency. Moreover, when the Taliban movement first emerged in the tribal areas, the state continued to pretend it was not a major issue, dismissing the possibility that a "small violent group" could undermine or challenge its authority. The upshot is that the state gave the Taliban precious space and time to strengthen its ranks.

Even more tangibly, the TTP leadership—especially its first chief, Baitullah Mehsud—tried to portray the TTP as an operation under Mullah Omar's Afghan Taliban. Every militant faction that wished to join the TTP had to take an oath to commit to enforcing sharia and to be loyal to Mullah Omar.[18] In doing this, Baitullah Mehsud hoped to gain more legitimacy and further portray his struggle as justifiable and Afghanistan-focused. Baitullah knew that existing as an anti-Pakistan group openly targeting the Pakistani state would quickly generate widespread opposition. Therefore, he used the TTP's ideological, ethnic, and sociopolitical ties with the Afghan Taliban to stress a natural cohesion between the two groups' operations and goals. This strategy was also instrumental in attracting other sectarian groups, such as Lashkar-e-Jhangvi and splinters of Kashmir-oriented groups, to work closely with the TTP (Rana 2012).

Financial Sustainability

External links with groups such as al-Qaeda have been a key financial resource for the TTP. But this ought not to overshadow the TTP's ability to raise domestic finances on its own. The TTP has required all affiliated groups to contribute half their income (through "taxes" and donations) to a major "jihad fund" (Rana 2009). The fund is used to sustain Taliban activities in the tribal areas and in Afghanistan.[19] These small groups—which mainly operate in Mohmand and Orakzai agencies in FATA and Tank, Bannu, and other settled areas of KPK—engage in crimes, especially murder, kidnapping for ransom, and extorting "protection" money from ordinary people involved in transport and trade. As with his predecessor, Baitullah Mehsud, the slain TTP chief Hakimullah Mehsud's opponents—both within and outside Taliban circles—feared his increasing influence and proved to be too weak to challenge him effectively. Even the political administration and tribal elders could not deny his authority in North and South Waziristan. The Taliban enjoys similar power in almost all other agencies of FATA. Such a sudden rise in the status and power of militants has been a major sociological attraction to militancy for disenfranchised young men.

---

18. This information is drawn from the author's interviews with unattributable sources in the tribal areas since 2007.

19. KPK Governor Owais Ahmed Ghani claimed that by 2008, Baitullah was spending around three billion rupees (US$3 million) annually on procuring weapons, equipment, and vehicles; treating wounded militants; and supporting families of killed militants.

FATA's Unique Administrative and Political Environment

The political structure, the administrative bureaucracy, the police, and the armed forces are the key instruments for controlling an insurgency. The Taliban took advantage of the lack of political mainstreaming and the weak and often ruthless administration in FATA. In the absence of political consensus and will, the police and local security forces, such as Khasadars, Levies, and Frontier Constabulary, failed to evolve a security mechanism and an effective administrative system. The lack of security coverage by the local police makes the armed forces' job difficult, and most of their energies are consumed in developing an alternative security apparatus in the insurgency-hit areas. This is why, at the outset, the state applied the traditional local tactics of jirgas, lashkars, selective operations, and peace agreements. Ultimately, however, these measures strengthened the Taliban's hand and further undermined the writ of the state. The state has also used a divide-and-rule strategy of supporting some Taliban groups while targeting others, such as those led by Mullah Nazir and Hafiz Gul Bahadur in South Waziristan. But even this strategy was based on a questionable rationale, especially since the state has often been manipulated by these very groups.

The Geostrategic Milieu

The presence of external actors in Afghanistan, combined with Pakistan's ambivalence regarding the Afghan Taliban, greatly complicated the quest to eliminate the Pakistani Taliban. While the insurgents focused on raising the costs of war for the state, state policy wavered as Pakistan remained both unsure of the United States' strategy and end goal in Afghanistan and insecure over the presence of other external actors with the potential to roil Pakistan's already troubled waters.

Regionally, the Pakistani state was aware of the potential fallout from tackling all militants on its soil. According to Barnett Rubin and Ahmed Rashid, "The Pakistani security establishment believes that it faces a US-Indian-Afghan alliance and a separate Iranian-Russian alliance, each aimed at undermining Pakistani influence in Afghanistan and even dismembering the Pakistani state. Some, but not all, in the establishment see armed militants within Pakistan as a threat but they largely consider it one that is ultimately controllable" (Rubin and Rashid 2008, 36–37).

This view colored the Pakistani approach, so it often failed to see the militant threat posed by the TTP for what it was. Often, issues were confounded and the blame was directed toward outside meddling rather than focusing wholeheartedly on the threat. Moreover, even though Pakistan and the United States partnered closely on a wide array of targets, when it came to the Taliban, they did not see eye to eye. While Pakistan did not engage the Afghan Taliban with as much vigor as the United States, the United States also maintained its focus on al-Qaeda and the Afghan insurgents and did not necessarily support Pakistan's fight against the TTP and its affiliates. This position was especially true until it became obvious that the insurgency within Pakistan threatened to challenge the state's writ in the regions bordering Afghanistan, and, in turn, its ability to support the U.S. campaign in Afghanistan.

External Support for the TTP

Confusion in distinguishing the enemy from partners was not an issue for the insurgents—not only did the TTP have a well-defined ideological base, but also the geostrategic milieu worked in its favor. The Pakistani Taliban has strong connections with nonstate actors, which allow it to thrive despite opposition from the Pakistani state. It has connections with smugglers and mafias in the border regions of Afghanistan and Pakistan and support from international terrorist networks, including al-Qaeda. The Pakistani state's belief that the Afghanistan conflict was upsetting the regional power balance in favor of its adversaries, coupled with its concerns that the theater was entertaining covert wars of international and regional spy agencies and players, diluted and distracted its counterinsurgency focus.

Baitullah Mehsud's successor as TTP chief, Hakimullah Mehsud, also recognized the benefits to associating himself with global terrorism rings and used these associations to enhance his and his organization's stature. For instance, his 2009 appearance in a video with a Jordanian suicide bomber—who later killed several CIA agents in the Afghan province of Khost—put his name on the list of high-value militant targets for the United States. Thus, the Taliban endorsed his stature as a worthy successor to Baitullah (Rana 2012). Similarly, TTP fingerprints on the failed Times Square bombing attempt by Pakistani-born Faisal Shehzad in May 2010 elevated the TTP's stature as a group that could directly threaten the U.S. homeland.

The Future

While this chapter has focused on FATA and the spillover of the insurgency into KPK, the challenge for the Pakistani state is complex, with dire implications for the country's internal security. Al-Qaeda, the TTP, and militant groups in Punjab, Karachi, and elsewhere have developed a nexus. Splinter groups of banned militant organizations or emerging groups have been involved in terrorism in the heartland of Pakistan. These groups, labeled the "Punjabi Taliban," are the product of a narrative of destruction fostered within the country over the past three decades.[20]

20. For an excellent analysis of the Punjabi Taliban, see Hussain (2012).

Their agendas revolve around Islamization and sectarianism. Al-Qaeda has enhanced their operational capabilities by providing training and logistics, and the Pakistani Taliban has offered them safe sanctuaries. Breaking these links between al-Qaeda, the Taliban, and heartland militant groups is no easy task, especially when the state continues to lack the vision to build a comprehensive counterterrorism strategy and the capacity for effective implementation (Rana 2012).

Apart from the internal security implications, Pakistani militants' connections offer them increasing international scope. As a result, the TTP has furthered al-Qaeda's global operations while demonstrating its ability to launch attacks in the West. The Times Square bombing attempt in New York City was not the first time that the TTP or its constituent organizations aided and abetted in an act of international terrorism. TTP spokesman Maulvi Umer notes that the London bombings of July 7, 2005, "one of the most devastating terrorist attacks since 9/11, were planned from Bajaur Agency in FATA. Similarly, the foiled terrorist attacks in Barcelona, Spain, in January 2008 were also traced back to the Al Qaeda-TTP nexus in the FATA" (Iqbal 2010).

The Pakistani state striving to pacify this existential threat is, ironically, the same one whose policies since the 1980s permitted the insurgency to take off in the first place. The state's ambivalence is what created space for FATA to become a de facto hub for jihad and, moreover, made it virtually impossible for the security establishment to tackle the Pakistani Taliban effectively when the TTP was still in its infancy. The state's inability to defeat the group militarily, combined with its concern over even greater backlash from the Taliban groups, led it to cut peace deals that backfired and provided further impetus to the insurgent movement. Whether the state would have prevailed had it persisted with a wholehearted military operation during 2003–07 must remain an open question. And even if it had succeeded, what would be the cost in innocent civilian lives and overall resentment among the tribal population?

The state's obvious failing was to remain complacent about the potential for the culture of jihad in FATA to create the kind of backlash that the Pakistani state and citizens are facing today. The time to prevent this mayhem was perhaps even before the forced U-turn of Pakistani policy in the wake of the 9/11 attacks. The state needed a holistic policy with a focus on deradicalization, opposition to the use of FATA as a hub for radical ideology, improvement in FATA's socioeconomic well-being, and legislation to mainstream FATA into the rest of Pakistan. In retrospect, once the state had been forced to intervene militarily in FATA, it was always going to be an uphill battle to stop the trajectory from moving swiftly up the conflict curve.

References

Al-Irshad. 1994. [Monthly] May, Islamabad.

Ali, Yousaf, and Javed Afridi. 2008. "People Throng Shariat Court to Get Disputes Resolved." *The News,* Aug. 4.

Aziz, Khalid. 2008. "The Impact of 9/11 War on Tribal Society." *The News,* June 1, Islamabad.

Coll, Steve. 2004. *Ghost Wars: The Secret History of the CIA, Afghanistan, and Bin Laden, from the Soviet Invasion to September 10, 2001.* New York: Penguin.

Fishman, Brian. 2010. "The Battle for Pakistan: Militancy and Conflict Across the FATA and NWFP." New America Foundation Counterterrorism Strategy Initiative Policy Paper, Apr. http://counterterrorism.newamerica.net/sites/newamerica.net/files/policydocs/fishman.pdf.

Haider, Ziad. 2009. "Mainstreaming Pakistan's Tribal Belt: A Human Rights and Security Imperative." Belfer Center Student Paper Series, Harvard University. http://belfercenter.ksg.harvard.edu/files/xstandard/Student%20discussion%20paper%200901.pdf.

Human Rights Commission of Pakistan (HRCP). 2005. *FCR: A Bad Law Nobody Can Defend.* Peshawar: HRCP.

Hussain, Mujahid. 2012. *Punjabi Taliban: Driving Extremism in Pakistan.* New Delhi: Pentagon.

International Crisis Group. 2006. "Pakistan's Tribal Areas: Appeasing the Militants." Asia Report no. 125, Dec. 11. www.crisisgroup.org/en/regions/asia/south-asia/pakistan/125-pakistans-tribal-areas-appeasing-the-militants.aspx.

Iqbal, Khuram. 2010. "Tehrik-e-Taliban Pakistan: A Global Threat." *Conflict and Peace Studies* 3 (4): 1–13. www.san-pips.com/download.php?f=162.pdf.

Jamatul Mujahideen. 1996. *Al-Masood* (official publication of Pakistani militant group Jamatul Mujahideen), Sept.

Khan, Anwarullah. 2008. "Taliban Set Up Sharia Courts in Bajaur Agency." *Dawn,* July 7. http://archives.dawn.com/2008/07/07/top5.htm.

Khattak, Daud. 2012. "Reviewing Pakistan's Peace Deals with the Taliban." Combating Terrorism Center, Sept. 26. www.ctc.usma.edu/posts/reviewing-pakistans-peace-deals-with-the-taliban.

Mashriq. 2005. Feb. 7, Peshawar.

Middle East Media Research Institute (MEMRI). 2008. "Pakistan-Based Militant Group Laskhar-e-Islam Vows 'To Spread Islam across the World,'" Apr. 23. http://memri.org/bin/latestnews.cgi?ID=SD190608#_edn2.

Nawaz, Shuja. 2009. *FATA—A Most Dangerous Place*. Washington, DC: Center for Strategic and International Studies.

Nazir, Mullah. 2007. Interview by Jamshed Baghwan. *Daily Express*, May 13, Peshawar.

Pak Institute for Peace Studies (PIPS). 2010. *Pakistan Security Report 2009*. Islamabad: PIPS.

———. 2010. *Understanding the Militants' Media in Pakistan: Outreach and Impact*. Islamabad: PIPS.

Rana, Muhammad Amir. 2003. *Jihad aur Jihadi*. Lahore: Mashal Books.

———. 2009. "Taliban Insurgency: A Counterinsurgency Perspective," *PIPS Research Journal, Conflict and Peace Studies* 2 (2): 9–31.

———. 2012. "Why Pakistani Taliban Matter." *Dawn*, June 30.

———. 2013. "Chemistry of Dialogue." *Dawn*, June 24. www.dawn.com/news/1020265/chemistry-of-dialogue.

Rana, Muhammad Amir, Abdul Basit, and Safdar Sial. 2009. *Dynamics of Taliban Insurgency in FATA*. Islamabad: PIPS.

Rana, Muhammad Amir, and Mubashi Bukhari. 2007. *Arabs in Afghan Jihad*. Islamabad: PIPS.

Rana, Muhammad Amir, and Rohan Gunaratna. 2008. *Al-Qaeda Fights Back: Inside Pakistani Tribal Areas*. Islamabad: PIPS.

Rashid, Ahmed. 2000. *Taliban: Militant Islam, Oil and Fundamentalism in Central Asia*. New Haven, CT: Yale Univ. Press.

Rubin, Barnett R., and Ahmed Rashid. 2008. "From Great Game to Grand Bargain." *Foreign Affairs* 87 (6): 30–44

Saddi [Masood Azhar]. 2009. *Al-Qalam Online*, Peshawar, May 22–28. www.alqalamonline.com/rangonoorold.htm.

Ummat. 2008. June 7, Karachi.

Yusufzai, Rahimullah. 2004. "Profile: Nek Mohammed." *BBC News*, June 18. http://news.bbc.co.uk/2/hi/south_asia/3819871.stm.

5

The State's Response to the Pakistani Taliban Onslaught

Shaukat Qadir

In recent years, the Pakistani state has been in the grip of an armed Islamist insurgency. It began with localized resistance against the Pakistani army's incursions into the semiautonomous FATA, bordering Afghanistan in the country's northwest. From there, the resistance coalesced into a full-fledged insurgency of international notoriety and managed to undermine the state's control, not only in large swaths of FATA but also in parts of the adjacent settled districts of KPK. This period lasted from 2002–03 to 2009, at which point the Pakistani Taliban, or TTP, as the conglomerate spearheading the insurgency came to be known after 2007, had made maximum gains against the state. In April 2009, the TTP had taken full control of the tourist hub of Swat in KPK and encroached into neighboring Buner. News headlines around the world famously spoke of the Pakistani Taliban as being "60 miles from Islamabad," Pakistan's capital city (Constable 2009). Since then, the Pakistani state has made significant inroads, thanks to successful military operations. While TTP's capacity to physically take over territory in settled areas of KPK has been suppressed for now, it can still periodically challenge the state's writ in parts of FATA. Moreover, from time to time, it continues to perpetrate individual acts of terrorism in the northwest and across the country.

I wish to thank Moeed Yusuf for his extensive support in finalizing this chapter as it went through its various iterations.

The spirit of armed struggle in the name of Islam—or jihad—in FATA can be traced back decades. In contemporary times, it was most notably harnessed when the tribal belt became the launching pad for Afghan mujahideen, backed by the "free world," to fight the Soviet occupation of Afghanistan during the 1980s (Coll 2004). The Pakistani state continued to back Islamist elements as part of its support for the insurgency in Indian Kashmir that took off after 1989. Islamabad was also instrumental in backing the Afghan Taliban's rise to power in Afghanistan in the mid-1990s (Rashid 2000). Part of what incited the pro-jihad lobby in FATA to turn against the Pakistani state was the abrupt U-turn in Pakistan's policy of support to the Afghan Taliban.

The simultaneous terrorist attacks on the World Trade Center and the Pentagon on September 11, 2001, stunned the entire world and led to the "war on terror." With the focus on al-Qaeda and the Afghan Taliban next door, Pakistan came under the spotlight. U.S. deputy secretary of state Richard Armitage's blunt threat to bomb Pakistan "back to the Stone Age" in the event of its noncooperation proved sufficient to get the Pakistani military establishment—in charge of the country at the time—to oblige (Musharraf 2006, 201). It almost goes without saying that Pakistan should independently have changed its policy toward the Afghan Taliban and Islamist elements fighting in Indian Kashmir during the 1990s. But since Pakistan had not yet done so, President Musharraf's decision to agree to support the U.S. military campaign in Afghanistan must have given an unexpected jolt to Pakistan's relationship with the Afghan Taliban and its many sympathizers in the FATA region.

Musharraf's decision to back the United States did not go unopposed (Musharraf 2006, 201–07). There were die-hard pro-Taliban supporters in the military at the time. Some, even in the higher ranks, still adhered to former army chief Gen. Mirza Aslam Beg's concept of "strategic depth." Though not necessarily pro-Taliban, they felt that the Taliban might be Pakistan's only hope for a pro-Pakistan dispensation in Afghanistan. Interestingly, Musharraf also remained unconvinced of the merits of this complete reversal of policy and was well aware that the U.S. ultimatum had forced him to his knees. Domestically, throughout his tenure, Musharraf conveyed the impression that Pakistan had been forced into fighting the United States' war even as, internationally, he repeatedly stressed that the war was Pakistan's own (Yusuf 2009a, 23–24). Pakistan continued to suffer from a lack of clarity and commitment regarding the counterinsurgency. While this changed after Musharraf's departure in 2008, the situation seems to be drifting back to the point where the state's lack of a unified stance against the insurgency is once again becoming all too apparent.

Proponents of counterinsurgency often assert that the response to an insurgent challenge is not really a military function but one of governance. Therefore, any meaningful strategy dealing with counterinsurgency, even if it involves the use of force, must be holistic in nature. Ultimately, this discussion focuses disproportionately on the military aspects of the state's response. This is indicative of the conspicuous absence of a broad-based, holistic counterinsurgency strategy by the Pakistani state over the past decade.

Why an Insurrection?

To understand Pakistan's response to the insurgency, it is important to appreciate how the state and society viewed the developments that led to the insurrection and the threat it posed. To be sure, this is a contested battleground. Mainstream Pakistani and Western perspectives differ greatly on why the insurgency managed to coalesce successfully and why the Pakistani state remained ineffectual in the early years when it would arguably have had an easier time dealing with those seeking to challenge its writ. But what matters here is the Pakistani mind-set, since this perspective, and not how outsiders perceived the situation, ultimately determined the state's strategy.

FATA lies in the northwestern part of Pakistan and is inhabited by ethnically Pashtun tribes with affinities both to Pakistani and to Afghan Pashtuns. It is a mostly barren land, sparsely populated by a deprived, politically and socially isolated people living in an antiquated culture. FATA comprises seven agencies, each independently administered. Of the seven, only Orakzai does not share a border with Afghanistan. In 2009, at the height of the TTP's power, it held sway over not only most of FATA but also some adjacent settled districts of KPK Province.

While various FATA tribes had experienced brief periods of unrest, they had remained loyal to the state. Except for the 1962 revolt in Dir Bajaur (Bajaur being the northernmost tribal agency, and Dir an adjacent settled area), little had happened to threaten the integrity of the Pakistani state. Naturally, then, the question arises: Why an insurrection in the post-9/11 context?

In 2001, as the war clouds gathered before the U.S. invasion of Afghanistan, many members of these tribes not only welcomed the U.S. intervention but also were prepared to help the coalition forces. The Afghan Taliban's dogmatic and totalitarian ways may have brought an end to the lawlessness that marked the Afghan civil war of the 1990s, but over time they also alienated the people. The Afghan Taliban was defeated just as it had conquered: without much resistance. The Afghans had had their fill of the Taliban.

This capitulation, however, did not accurately represent the sentiments that were soon to emerge in FATA. For many locals, the U.S. presence had a similar tinge to the Soviet occupation of the 1980s. Fervor for jihad, fomented by local clerics, once again took center stage, and a number of Pakistani jihadi groups and clerics even crossed over with their bands of followers to join the fight against the American presence (Qazi 2011, 578). In the eyes of the locals, another Afghan freedom struggle had begun against the foreign occupation, and the Pashtun tribes straddling the Durand Line were taking up arms to help their Afghan brethren. Some even saw the U.S. operation in Afghanistan as a war against Pashtuns per se (Z. Hussain 2011, 7).

The reverse flow began almost instantly. The al-Qaeda and Afghan Taliban cadres started crossing over into FATA, where they not only received protection but also began to recruit for the fight against the United States (Behuria 2007; Qazi 2011, 578). There was one major difference between the 1980s and 2001–02, however: This time the desire to fight the U.S.-led occupation of Afghanistan was opposed by Pakistan's government and, at the state's behest, even by the traditional tribal leadership. The revolt, therefore, took on a dimension beyond a fight against the United States. But it is essential to understand that both levels of the revolt—against the foreign presence in Afghanistan and, later, against the Pakistani state—centered on the tribes' desire to aid the Afghan resistance against foreign occupation. Take that away, and the cause célèbre disappears. The reasoning of those in revolt is best explained in the words of Nek Muhammad, a Wazir tribesman who can be considered the first Pakistani Taliban commander in FATA after 9/11. A month before his death from a U.S. drone strike in June 2004, addressing a jirga also attended by senior Pakistani army commanders, he said, "Fifteen years ago, it was jihad, sanctioned by the Pakistan and Saudi governments and supported by the USA, to kill the pale-faced infidel who had occupied Afghanistan by force. Why is it that today, when we have another pale-faced infidel occupying Afghanistan, we are being asked to kiss his boot when he kicks us, instead of killing him for it?"[1]

A Slow Start: Pakistan's Nonresponse to the Growing Insurrection

Until at least 2008, the Pakistani state's response to the armed resistance progressively challenging its writ in FATA and adjoining areas was ad hoc. It combined a mix of military and nonmilitary tools but was inconsistent and left substantive political and socioeconomic aspects out of the mix.

During the early stages of the resistance against the Pakistani state, until perhaps 2003–04, the use of force could and should have been avoided. This

1. Quote was provided during author's personal discussions with senior military officers (Aug. 14, 2004, Rawalpindi) and Waziri elders (July 2004, Islamabad) who were present at the jirga.

part of the country had long been neglected and treated as an appendage—indeed, FATA is popularly known in Pakistan as *ilaqa-e-ghair* (foreign land)—and its people had every reason to resent the administrative system and socioeconomic deprivation thrust on them.[2] And yet they had remained content. Since the immediate cause for the insurrection was the desire to help those Afghans (and other foreigner jihadis) fighting against the U.S.-led presence and not to challenge the Pakistani state per se, the resistance, in its early stage, was an occasion for true peacebuilding, not brute force. The state should have used interlocutors and tribal elders to launch a concerted campaign explaining why support to the insurgency in Afghanistan was counterproductive for the FATA tribes and for the Pakistani state. At that point, the state might have made a case for how the Pakistani government could use peaceful means to effect the foreigners' withdrawal from Afghanistan over time. But given the abrupt U-turn of Pakistani policy and the visibly jittery decision-making enclave in Islamabad, no one at the time attempted to respond to Nek Muhammad's very pertinent question.

As with all counterfactuals, the argument that peacebuilding would have worked is unprovable. And yet it has merit grounded in the history of the Pashtun tribes that straddle the Durand Line. Under the traditional system of collective responsibility and deference to the decisions of the tribal jirgas, in all likelihood, peer pressure from the vast and silent majority of each tribe would have achieved the aim of the Pakistani state: preventing these tribes from joining the insurgency in Afghanistan. Admittedly, the more committed elements would still have moved across the Durand Line to fight the international forces, but they would have been far fewer in number. Simultaneously, there should have been an immediate effort, with a clearly laid out medium- to long-term vision, to bring these tribes within the mainstream sociopolitical ambit of the state and give them a larger stake in Pakistan. This effort would have emphasized the advantages they would gain as equal citizens of Pakistan—something they have been deprived of since the nation's beginnings.

Instead, Musharraf, bowing to tremendous international pressure, ordered the Pakistani army to deploy in FATA. FATA has been semi-autonomous ever since Pakistan's independence; its tribes joined Pakistan on the very condition of autonomy in their domestic affairs. For this

2. Under the constitution, there are two types of tribal agencies/regions: FATA, administered by the president of Pakistan, and the Provincially Administered Tribal Areas (PATA), mostly adjacent to FATA and administered by the provincial governor of KPK. FATA and PATA enjoy special "privileges," among them exemption from legal jurisdiction of the courts. However, due to the myriad problems resulting from this and other special arrangements, these areas remain backward and underdeveloped.

reason, not since 1947 had the state ordered the army to deploy in FATA (Nawaz 2009, 9). Also, it is important to understand the intensely independent nature of the Pashtun tribes. It was this fierce independence and resistance to any form of outside interference that ultimately forced the British colonial authorities to leave FATA and its surroundings alone as a largely autonomous region (Z. Hussain 2010, 16; FATA n.d.). The Pakistani state was well aware of this but felt compelled by international pressure to go in.

When the military did go in, it went with no clear objective or vision. The initial scope of the military engagement was to target "foreign" militants who had escaped from Afghanistan and found sanctuary in FATA. Afghans were not necessarily considered foreign. But even military action against Arab, Uzbek, and other militants met with disapproval. Initially, the state merely sought to deal with rebellious tribes—in particular, the Mehsuds, who led the resistance against the Pakistan army and the Wazirs—as and when the need arose. Over time, as the armed opposition grew, the army employed a still ad hoc mix of forceful action and customary tools involving negotiations with the tribal elders, community pressure, and—most importantly and controversially—peace deals that would force foreign fighters out of the region while exempting locals and Afghans. Collectively, these peace deals only allowed the Pakistani Taliban to gain further strength, traction, and confidence. In return, they did not even keep their side of the deal: cessation of action against the Pakistan army; expulsion of, or guarantee of good behavior by, the foreign militants; and cessation of support for cross-border attacks in Afghanistan.[3]

If, during this period, there was one game-changing event that provided the spark needed for the insurrection to transform into a full-fledged insurgency, it was Nek Muhammad's death. Even though it is now known that he was killed by a U.S. drone, the Pakistani state took credit for his death to protect its public stance that the United States had not been allowed any direct activity using Pakistani ground or airspace.[4] In any case, Nek Muhammad became an instant martyr and a hero for all tribes. Hundreds of thousands thronged to his funeral, shown live on the national media, and "not a single tribal elder of any tribe, dared be

3. For a discussion of the peace deals and the Pakistani state's oscillation between military operations and peace deals at the time, see ICG (2006).

4. It has now been acknowledged that the killing of Nek Muhammed was the first U.S. drone strike in Pakistan and that it was probably carried out at the request of the Musharraf-led government. See Mazetti (2013). Pakistan had given the United States considerable counterterrorism support, including a logistical lifeline, an air base, and other intelligence and counterterrorism support. Musharraf also recently acknowledged that he had a secret deal on U.S. drone strikes within Pakistan (Musharraf 2006, 205–07; *Dawn* 2013).

absent."[5] The die was cast, and the insurgency had begun targeting the Pakistani army presence in FATA—not just sporadically, as had been the case until then, but regularly.

During 2002–08, the initial military efforts having failed, the Pakistani state continued to waver between the use of force and negotiations. At no stage was a holistic strategic response visible. As each successive effort to negotiate with the various chapters of the TTP came to naught, the army launched military forays intermittently. It carried out a large number of small- and medium-sized operations. For the most part, however, these were halfhearted attempts that used excessive force, largely to appease the United States and other allies who wanted to see evidence of Pakistan's seriousness about dealing with those elements that perpetrated violence in Afghanistan and fanned the flames of militancy at home. Consequently, military successes were few and isolated, while failures continued to increase. This development only emboldened the TTP. The International Crisis Group (ICG) aptly summarized the problem with the state's strategy, arguing that use of force to deny "al-Qaeda and Taliban safe haven and curb cross-border militancy failed, largely due to an approach alternating between excessive force and appeasement" (ICG 2006, 3).

Explaining Pakistan's "Nonresponse"

Just as the Pakistani state faltered, the Pakistani Taliban grew by leaps and bounds. A number of factors were responsible for the state's inability to curb the militants' growth during the first five years or so of the armed resistance.

The rise of the cleric and the militant in FATA. Foremost, the Pakistani state underestimated the challenge. It never considered that its own citizens would turn against it so fiercely and in so short a time. Its miscalculations suggest that it had not paid due attention to the changing nature of the tribal society over the two decades preceding 9/11.

Over many years, the Pashtun tribes evolved their own system of what can best be referred to as the "blue-blooded" families. These are not necessarily the wealthiest, but only their scions can be invited to assume the role of elder and be eligible to become a member of the jirga. During the struggle against the Soviet occupation of Afghanistan, the voluntary fighters did not include tribal elders or their scions. Consequently, non–blue-blooded leaders emerged from within to assume leadership of these volunteers in each tribe. Nek Muhammad was one of these leaders. Within each tribe, it

5. Muhammed Talib Orakzai, an Orakzai tribal elder, in a personal conversation with the author after Nek Muhammad's death, Sept. 2004, Hangu, Orakzai Agency.

was these non–blue-blooded warlords who led their bands of fellow veterans, with better weapons (acquired during the anti-Soviet struggle) than other members of the tribe had, to launch the insurrection. The traditional tribal leadership that supported the Pakistan government in seeking an ouster of al-Qaeda and other foreign militants was helpless in the face of this onslaught. The Taliban systematically eliminated the tribal leadership to remove any opposition to its rise and its quest to dominate the FATA strongholds (Qazi 2011, 582). From 2004 to 2007, nearly five hundred elders of the insurrectionist tribes were killed, and over six hundred have been killed during the past decade (Nawaz 2009, 7).[6]

The vacuum was filled by the cleric and the militant. Even though the process happened gradually, the difference this time was that the traditional elders were completely displaced (Nawaz 2009). This shift was significant because, without upending the customary norms and behavior patterns of the Pashtun tribes in FATA, it would have been impossible for an anti-Pakistan insurgency to take root. Indeed, in the traditional tribal hierarchy, the cleric is so far down the social ladder that a Pashto saying, in which a tribal elder is addressing a cleric, roughly translates thus: "I will not treat you less than a menial, but don't ever dare look upward." Nonetheless, it was this segment and its ideology that would lead the ideological and physical campaign against the Pakistani state.

Expansion of the Taliban conglomerate. The Pakistani Taliban also used the state's ad hoc policy to good effect. Not only did it make the most of the peace deals, but it also established links with a number of other Pakistani and foreign militant groups. Al-Qaeda became TTP's chief patron over time (Siddiqa 2011). Also, splinters of several traditionally anti-India and sectarian militant groups joined the TTP's militant nexus. The splinters originated from developments on the India-Pakistan front after 9/11 and in the broader context of the U.S. presence in Afghanistan. Pakistan was under tremendous pressure to reverse its support for the insurgency festering in Indian Kashmir since 1990. After a near-war crisis with India in 2001–02, Musharraf agreed to back off and, from 2002 onward, tried to curtail infiltration of militants into Indian Kashmir from Pakistani soil. This effort irked the anti-India groups who, until this point, were backed by the Pakistani intelligence apparatus, primarily the ISI, which had enabled them to set up an extensive presence in Pakistani Kashmir, FATA, and southern Punjab. The most disgruntled of these groups split off, and a whole host of them developed linkages with the TTP–al-Qaeda combine in the coming

---

6. The figure of over five hundred during 2004– 07 is the author's own compilation based on primary source information and news reports.

years (Abbas 2009a; M. Hussain 2012). Traditionally sectarian groups also came to support this conglomerate, though without losing sight of their principally sectarian agendas. A whole new category of militants, the Punjabi Taliban, has emerged as a result of these developments. These are mostly splinter groups based in the Pakistani heartland of Punjab that not only target the Pakistani state independently but have also, over time, become active in Afghanistan.[7] They have also provided a large number of suicide bombers to the TTP in recent years (Ahmed 2013). Even as the Pakistani state remained ambivalent about the threat then, the Pakistani Taliban was growing into a conglomerate bigger than anyone in the Pakistani decision-making enclave—or, for that matter, in the United States, from where the pressure for the initial forays into FATA came—could ever have imagined.

Genius of the Taliban narrative. The rise of the ideological warriors in FATA notwithstanding, at the core, the Pashtun tribes of FATA remain patriotic, and despite the tremendous neglect they have faced over the years, there has been little doubt of their allegiance to the Pakistani state. While the pervasive anti-American sentiment did generate widespread support for the fight in Afghanistan, the tribesmen did not accept en masse the Pakistani Taliban's attitude toward the Pakistani state. In fact, although they could do little against the Taliban's violent onslaught, the tribesmen, especially from those tribes not in the insurrection, remained opposed to the Taliban's systematic targeting of tribal elders and jirgas—the symbols of Pashtun culture.

The Pakistani Taliban leadership knew that it would find few takers for any designs to overthrow the Pakistani state. Even the Afghan Taliban, from Mullah Omar to its current spokesman, Abdul Mannan, despite its established al-Qaeda connections, has repeatedly stated that it is not Pakistan's enemy and that it will not fight Pakistan's armed forces.[8] Moreover, even though Pakistani groups established links with al-Qaeda, a number of them continued to work independently without openly rallying to al-Qaeda's every call. Two Pakistani Taliban chapters that did, however, were those of Baitullah Mehsud (the now slain TTP chief who emerged as the key Taliban leader after Nek Muhammad's death), in South Waziristan, and Maulana Fazlullah, in Swat. Fazlullah's motives are understandable, since his

7. For an in-depth examination of the Punjabi Taliban, see M. Hussain (2012).

8. Mullah Omar and his group have always maintained that their purpose is to free Afghanistan of foreign occupation. In January 2012, in a statement typical of his stance, Omar was quoted as saying, "Convey my message to the Pakistani Taliban that you have forgotten the real purpose, which is to fight the invading forces in Afghanistan and liberate it from their occupation" (Siddiqi 2012).

following in Swat, a settled region in KPK, was very small. He was perhaps the most dependent on foreign support, including warriors. Baitullah Mehsud was stronger and had a local following of fighters within the Mehsud tribe. But even there, as soon as Baitullah turned inward to target Pakistan, he lost support from the bulk of his own tribe and was increasingly forced to rely on foreigners and suicide bombers recruited from southern Punjab with the help of the Punjabi Taliban groups. At their peak, at some point during 2006–09, Pashtun Taliban members in FATA numbered forty thousand, and by 2010, they numbered less than twenty-five thousand (Qazi 2011, 588). This number compares with an estimated population of four hundred thousand Mehsuds—only one of the insurrectionist tribes.

And yet the Pakistani Taliban very shrewdly created a public narrative conflating the many objectives in play. The group desperately and constantly tried to portray its struggle as Afghan-centric and pledged its allegiance to Mullah Omar (even as Mullah Omar sought to maintain an arm's-length distance). Throughout, the Pakistani Taliban's public narrative was focused on fighting the foreign occupation in Afghanistan, and whenever targeting the Pakistani state was justified it was done through the same logic: Since the Pakistani army was fighting in FATA to prevent the jihad in Afghanistan, it had to be targeted as a last resort (Yusuf 2009a, 2009b). Without this deliberate conflation, the TTP did not stand a chance of getting any support in FATA, let alone elsewhere in Pakistan.

The narrative worked to a great extent. It conflated the pervasive anti-American sentiment and the Afghan Taliban's goals with those of the Pakistani Taliban. Throughout this phase, the Pakistani populace remained ambivalent about the threat that the Pakistani Taliban really posed. Thus, the people failed to fully back the state in taking decisive action against the insurrection even when it was clear, after Nek Muhammad's death, that the time for pure peacebuilding had passed.

Lack of unity in the state's stance. Finally, lack of clarity and conviction in the state's response was also a product of Pakistan's anomalous civil-military relations and the specific context in which they played out during the period under discussion. Pakistan's military has always been the strongest pillar of the state. After 9/11, it was even stronger given that Musharraf, a general, was leading the country since his military coup in 1999.[9] In 2002, General Musharraf's regime held elections that brought a right-wing alliance of religious political parties to power in KPK.[10] This

9. For Musharraf's version of the coup, see Musharraf (2006), 101–42.

10. The Muttahida Majlis-e-Amal (MMA), as the alliance was called, consisted of six religious political parties, some of which had close links to the Afghan Taliban. The alliance rose to power largely because of the anti-American sentiment in KPK at the time.

alliance created an interesting mix that only made Pakistan's counterinsurgency task more complicated.

On the one hand, the military has always had an overbearing influence on security policy, and FATA is ruled directly by the central government in Islamabad. This influence meant that the military devised the strategies in the initial years of the insurrection with little input from civilian quarters. On the other hand, when the TTP made serious inroads into KPK after 2006, it was within the provincial government's purview to decide how to handle the situation. Here, the religious political alliance, most of whose component units depended on constituencies sympathetic to the Afghan Taliban and viciously opposed to the United States, created roadblocks impeding the central government's ability to apply consistent pressure on the likes of Fazlullah, even when it was clear that he had become strong enough to capture settled areas in KPK (Cheema 2008, 25–26).[11] As the Taliban expanded, the provincial government dragged its feet, not allowing a popular consensus to develop on tackling the Pakistani Taliban decisively. This hamstrung the military until fresh elections led to new developments after 2008.

The situation even affected the junior military officers and the rank and file of the army, which also remained ambivalent, believing that it was fighting "America's war" against its own citizens. This belief had disastrous consequences for the morale and commitment of those actually engaged in conducting operations.

Turning the Page: Counterinsurgency Takes Off

The lack of unity in the Pakistani state's message to its people, combined with the Taliban's genius in conflating its own objectives with those of the Afghan Taliban, meant that the Pakistani public was not truly convinced that the military was fighting its own war. It is safe to say that by 2007, the Taliban was winning the war of narratives, with the majority of Pakistanis not seeing the Taliban as a critical threat.[12] Support for military operations dwindled.

The 2007 Lal Masjid episode, whereby Musharraf ordered paramilitary action against militants holed up in a mosque compound in the heart of Islamabad, proved to be the final blow.[13] The operation ended up killing nearly one hundred people—a number of them allegedly children hailing from Swat and other parts of KPK—who were students of the seminary

11. For MMA's linkage with the Afghan Taliban, see Norell (2007).

12. According to the World Public Opinion poll in September 2007, only 34 percent of Pakistanis saw "activities of Islamist militants and local Taliban in FATA and settled areas" as a critical threat (Ramsay et al. 2009, 4).

13. For details and a timeline of the Lal Masjid episode, see Haq (2007) and Pardesi (2008).

adjacent to the mosque (Raza 2009). The insurgency that had so far fought the Pakistani military in the northwest was now to unleash a wave of terrorism, including an astronomical increase in the frequency of suicide attacks across Pakistan's major metropolises.[14] It was also the beginning of a more assertive campaign by the Taliban in the northwest. By 2008, Maulana Fazlullah had all but taken over Swat.

This period was also the time when Pakistan's general elections brought a left-leaning, secular Awami National Party (ANP) into power in KPK and a broad coalition government led by another left-of-center group, the Pakistan People's Party (PPP), into office at the center. Musharraf was on his way out—forcibly so.[15] Ironically, the ANP, despite its deep ideological differences with the Taliban, kept an eye on the street's sentiments. Within a year of taking office, the party, backed by the newly elected president of Pakistan, Asif Zardari—also head of the PPP—negotiated a peace deal with the Taliban in Swat. The Pakistani government agreed to impose sharia and accepted a number of other demands by the TTP.[16] Many neutral observers saw the deal as capitulation by the Pakistani state (Koelbl 2009). To be fair to the ANP and Zardari, they were under tremendous pressure: Pakistan Muslim League–Nawaz (PML-N), the largest opposition party, had been sloganeering in favor of negotiating with the Taliban, and the newly influential media had also thrown its weight behind negotiations (*Business Recorder* 2009). Analysts on daily talk shows responded to loaded questions and agreed with the anchors or faced their wrath. Moreover, people were getting tired of seeing their cities blown up regularly by suicide attacks and wanted to try peaceful means. The new government could not but succumb to this public sentiment.

In hindsight, the deal turned out to be a blessing in disguise. Within a month of the deal in February 2009, the Taliban showed the people how it would rule. It proudly made its inhumane cruelty available for all viewers on national and regional television channels.[17] For the first time, the Taliban also came out publicly, proclaiming that it had no regard for the Pakistani constitution or the laws of the land (Roggio 2009a). Strangely, this was also the first time that the Pakistani public got an opportunity to see through the conflation of the Taliban's narrative. Until then, the ambivalence had

---

14. There were four suicide attacks in Pakistan in 2005, nine in 2006, fifty-seven in 2007, and sixty-one in 2008. They peaked at ninety in 2009. See Pakistan Body Count (2013).

15. After getting embattled in a tussle with the judiciary, which led to widespread protests against him, Musharraf first gave up his position as army chief in October 2007. He was then threatened with impeachment proceedings by the newly elected parliament, whereupon he resigned from his second post, that of president, in August 2008.

16. The text of the "Nizam-e-Adl" deal in Swat is available at *Daily Times* (2009).

17. The game changer proved to be the Taliban's public flogging of a woman in Swat in April 2009, which was carried by TV channels the world over (Walsh 2009).

only grown, as evidenced by the general mood favoring talks going into the Swat deal. As soon as the TTP consolidated its hold over Swat, it also demonstrated that it had no intention of being confined to that small territory but, to the contrary, had expansionist designs. Moreover, some media personnel were attacked. Suddenly, the threat was palpably close to home for the elite Pakistani sitting in Islamabad.

By April 2009, the mood had changed rather abruptly, but tangibly, and the nation stood united in its resolve to support military action. The same fickle media personalities who had been screaming for a peace deal turned anti-Taliban, roundly condemning the same people they had earlier portrayed as being merely misunderstood. Few could have imagined such a quick turnaround in sentiment when the Swat peace deal was being inked. Within two months, two of the key reasons for the state's lackluster response thus far had been corrected: The Taliban's narrative had been exposed, and the state and society stood united to take on the TTP.

The Major Military Thrust

President Musharraf's 2007–08 exit from the political and, more importantly, the military scene heralded a new era for the military. Fortunately, in his successor, General Kayani, the military found just the right kind of commander. Fully aware of the threat, Kayani knew that the military had virtually no chance of success without popular support for its actions. When he took command of the army, the military was seriously demoralized by its many failures in the initial years and by the conflation of narratives that it, like the society at large, had bought into. Kiyani gradually created space to infuse new life into this demoralized army. What really made the difference, however, was that the nation was now determined to back the military as long as the military was willing to make a concerted effort against the Taliban onslaught.

Swat was the first test. The Pakistan army had to beat the guerrilla warriors of the TTP at their own game. The army had thrice before entered the Swat Valley to get rid of Fazlullah during 2007–09.[18] In 2007, after capturing almost the entire valley, the government aborted the operation and reneged on its assurance of a permanent military presence in Swat. The lack of consensus among the central and provincial authorities was at the fore of this decision. Fazlullah returned again to exact bloody vengeance on those who had celebrated his exit. Again in early 2009, military operations had just begun when the Swat peace deal was struck.

18. The army had launched three operations: Rah-e-Haq I, II, and III in November 2007, July 2008, and January 2009, respectively.

Determined to succeed even though Fazlullah was reputed to have the support of three thousand battle-savvy Tajiks and Uzbeks, General Kayani planned his battle.[19] What is most remarkable is that he had, in such a short while, understood the strategic and tactical nuances for achieving success against guerrilla warriors. Strategically, they must be surrounded, with no escape routes left, to force them into joining battle. Tactically, small groups of ground forces must be made logistically independent and given the initiative to operate independently of orders. As military operations began to look inevitable, in late April 2009, the vast majority of Swat's non-Taliban residents escaped to avoid the mayhem. Swat is an oblong valley, running northeast to southwest, with numerous entrances. The major ones are through Lower Dir in the west, Buner to the southeast, another opening to the east, and Malakand to the southwest. There are also other less well-known entrances from Upper Dir to the northwest and two from the east (see map 4).

The military began by first clearing all entrances to the Swat Valley, Buner, Malakand, and Dir (lower and upper). It then planned to enter the Valley from all three directions—south, west, and east. To cover the remaining escape route over the mountains in the northwest, two battalions were air-dropped into these remote heights. Closing all exits was the finest aspect of the army's strategic plan. The Taliban had retreated before the advancing military but had prepared Mingora, the city center, for an entrenched battle. Urban warfare against an entrenched enemy is a soldier's nightmare. Moreover, the collateral damage in human lives and destruction of the city would have been horrific. However, discovering the extent of the encirclement, the Taliban, in typical guerrilla fashion, vacated Mingora and sought escape routes in small groups along less well-known routes. Fazlullah and some of his deputies escaped, but most foreigners were killed or captured in the attempt.

The tactical change was in the creation of small fighting groups, logistically independent and trained in the German concept of *Auftragstaktik* (mission-oriented tactics), a concept that features loose orders relating to the ultimate mission, leaving room for subordinate commanders to exercise initiative in how to achieve the mission, depending on the ground situation. Without such liberty of action, subordinate commanders get tied down to the letter of the orders and are unlikely to succeed against guerrilla warriors. By mid-June 2009, within four weeks of the military campaign's commencement, Swat was cleared.

---

19. The number is the official estimate provided to the author by the Pakistani military. The author's own conversations with locals from Swat in IDP camps in 2009 suggest that the number may be closer to four thousand to five thousand.

Map 4. Swat District, Khyber Pakhtunkhwa

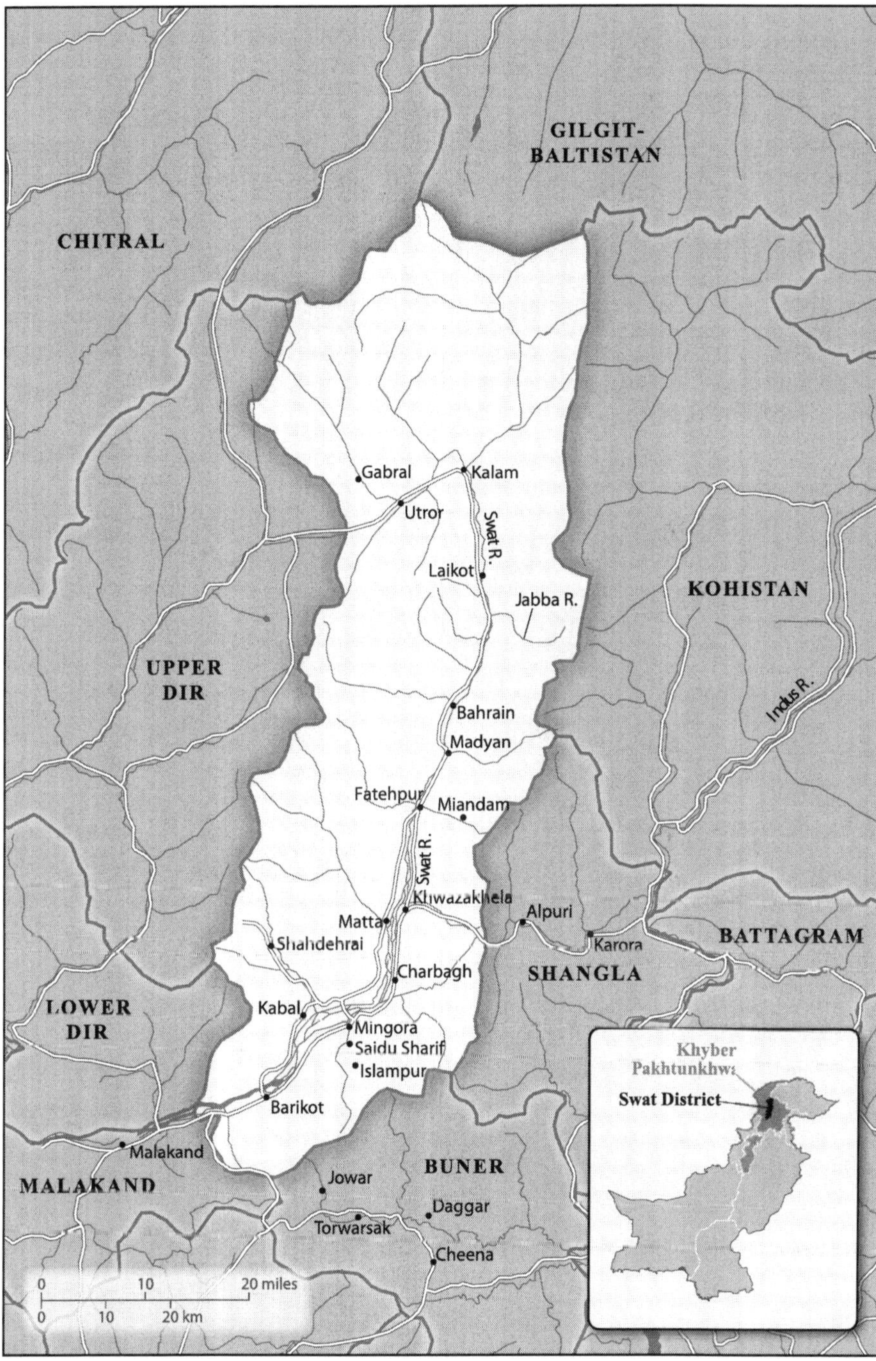

The next major operation was in South Waziristan, the real base of operations for all factions of the TTP. Here, the ground situation was different because of the agency's long and porous border with Afghanistan. And just as military operations were about to begin in South Waziristan in September 2009, the United States vacated more than a half-dozen posts along the border on the Afghan side (Akhlaque 2009). Logically, the United States should have massively reinforced this border to seal it effectively, thus playing the anvil to the Pakistan military's hammer. While reasons are complex and underpinned by the reality that these two sides were fighting two different wars by this time—Pakistan against the TTP and the United States against the Afghan Taliban and its affiliates—with some overlap, the end result was that the move allowed a large number of Pakistani Taliban to escape. Significantly, even though the U.S. pullback provided a golden opportunity to do so, the Afghan Taliban gave no reinforcements to the Pakistani Taliban—keeping its word that they would not target the Pakistani state. In fact, even the Mehsuds across the Durand Line refused to aid the Taliban fighters. They found no help until they reached the caves of Tora Bora, where al-Qaeda continued to maintain a presence.[20]

The military launched various other operations in FATA and adjoining areas of KPK during this time.[21] The Swat and South Waziristan operations, however, were the ones that hit the TTP at its center. The state was quick to declare victory and claim that the TTP's back was broken. Since the TTP had lost the capability to do a reprise of 2008 in Swat—or, for that matter, completely eliminate the state's writ from FATA—the claim had merit. Swat is now clear and all but normalized, and the state's writ across KPK is largely restored. The Taliban, while continuing to perpetrate terrorism, has been unable to conduct large-scale attacks in the Pakistani heartland as frequently as it did in 2008 and 2009. However, the group is still operational and has continued to challenge the army repeatedly in various agencies of FATA. Its ability to tie down a significant number of military troops in prolonged battles by occupying remote areas in the tribal belt is very much intact. The Mehsud faction of the TTP, led by the organization's overall chief, Hakimullah (Baitullah's successor), once again infiltrated FATA to occupy Orakzai Agency. The infiltration was through the Khyber and Kurram agencies, since Orakzai shares no borders with Afghanistan. In Khyber, Mangal Bagh Afridi's Lashkar-e-Islam faction, another local

20. Tora Bora is an area of over two hundred square miles of caves. Most of them are interlinked, but not even all the locals know the intricate network inside. Al-Qaeda has maintained a presence in the area since 2001.

21. According to official figures, there were a total of 140 "major" and 263 "minor" operations during 2007–10.

militant group, supported Hakimullah's group (Shinwari 2013). In the spring of 2013, the army had to launch a fresh operation after the Taliban and its affiliates took control of the Tirah Valley in this agency—incidentally the location of the military's first forays into FATA after 9/11 (Sherazi 2013). For a variety of reasons, the army has also not been able to secure Kurram, which is why the operations in Orakzai and Khyber have gone on for over two years with little success.

Then there is North Waziristan. This agency has made the headlines repeatedly in the Western press in recent years because it is home to a number of militant groups—Pakistani, Afghan, and others. The Haqqani Network, one of the two main groups fighting the insurgency in Afghanistan, also finds haven there (Dressler 2012). The TTP, after being forced out of South Waziristan, also shifted its command center to North Waziristan and is now geographically colocated with the Haqqanis. The Pakistani military has claimed for over three years that it will go into North Waziristan at a time of its own choosing (*Express Tribune* 2012). In reality, with the pending 2014 exit of the U.S. and NATO forces from Afghanistan, and the Haqqanis being wooed as part of the Afghan reconciliation talks, the army sees little reason to antagonize the network at this stage.[22] But the absence of a concerted military effort in North Waziristan implies that the TTP also continues to exist and use the territory as a launching pad for its insurgent operations and terrorist attacks across Pakistan. Since 2011, the TTP has also found sanctuaries across the Durand Line in Afghanistan (Khan 2012).

The Broader Horizon: Counterinsurgency Performance beyond Military Might

The period since 2009 has seen more clarity in the Pakistani state's purpose and drive to take on the Pakistani Taliban. As discussed, the results were also significantly different. However, in counterinsurgency operations, the military can win only battles. The war has to be won through broader law enforcement, political, and socioeconomic means. The following discussion looks at some of the broader aspects of counterinsurgency and their role in the state's performance since 2009.

---

22. The Afghan Zadran tribe is considered to be the largest of the Afghan Pashtun tribes. It is the majority in most provinces along the Durand Line from South Waziristan to Mohmand in Pakistan, virtually encircles Kabul, and is "kissing cousins" to the Wazirs in North Waziristan. Its most well-known scion is Jalaluddin Haqqani. While the Pakistan army has many reasons for its reluctance to enter North Waziristan, one officially unstated fact is that the Wazirs and Zadrans, including the Haqqanis, were never considered to pose a direct threat to Pakistan.

Law Enforcement and Intelligence

The military can clear and temporarily hold on to areas. However, it is ultimately the civilian administration and law enforcement that must take over. Moreover, in contexts such as Pakistan's, where the insurgent also uses terrorism in urban metropolises as a pain-inflicting mechanism, civilian law enforcement becomes even more crucial.

The Pakistani track record for instituting an overarching, coordinated infrastructure to tackle the insurgency-cum-terrorism threat has been dismal. A step in the right direction was the envisioning of a National Counterterrorism Authority (NACTA) in 2009. The body was to coordinate the country's efforts against the threat coming from militant quarters. For petty political reasons, which included personality clashes, the body has turned out to be toothless. Only in March 2013 was it given constitutional cover (T. Hussain 2013; Z. Hussain 2012).

NACTA's failings notwithstanding, civilian law enforcement has seen considerable progress in recent years. The improvement in the law enforcement–intelligence combine can be credited for the appreciable decline in the number of major Taliban-orchestrated attacks in urban metropolises since 2011. The Pakistani police have traditionally enjoyed unquestioned authority while being underpaid, untrained, corrupt, and despised by the public. They had no incentives to improve their image. Until late 2008, some months after the army assumed responsibility for the training of the Elite Police Force, the country's police services had no sharpshooters or handgun experts, and most of the rank and file, equipped with only the most basic weapons training, could not be trusted with weapons and ammunition. The existing bomb squad was one in name only, with no modern training in defusing bombs with multiple detonation devices and cutoffs. Even when the police began to be an increasingly attractive choice for aspiring young bureaucrats, producing an increasing number of inquisitive, intelligent, young officers who sought to lead their force by example, there was no real effort to train the rank and file or to improve their criminal investigation, forensic, and weapons-handling abilities.[23] The state officially sought training assistance from the FBI and other foreign agencies in 2005 (*Daily Times* 2005). Although, even after this intervention, police services could not be called efficient, their performance did begin to improve.

Since then, the Pakistani military has assumed responsibility for training the police services. Having realized the need to let the police lead the counterinsurgency campaign, the military has stepped in to train the police to handle weapons and respond rapidly and actively. The police are also benefiting from on-the-job training, which is apparent in the fact that police

23. For an analysis of the challenges facing the Pakistani police, see Abbas (2009b, 2011, 2012).

personnel have begun to spot individuals acting suspiciously and have, on some occasions, as in the attempted attack on the Naval Headquarters in Islamabad on December 2, 2009, prevented major disasters (Roggio 2009b).

More significantly, an increasing number of police personnel are risking their lives—and, indeed, losing them—to protect ordinary civilians. As a consequence, Pakistani citizens are seeing them with respect and sympathy. To be sure, the police have been a weak link in Pakistan's counterinsurgency efforts, and the civil-military collaboration in tackling this threat holistically still leaves much to be desired. But the realization that quashing the insurgency-cum-terrorism will ultimately require a synergic civil-military partnership has begun to set in.

The intelligence apparatus has undergone significant improvement in recent years as well. The ISI, the country's premier intelligence agency, is constitutionally answerable to the prime minister even though, in reality, it is a military-dominated institution. The ISI's pre-9/11 close links to the Afghan Taliban tainted the agency and impaired its ability for rational analysis of the emerging threat. In 2003, Musharraf finally decided to replace General Mahmood, the all-powerful and ideologically motivated ISI chief, with General Ehsan ul-Haq, with instructions to purge the ISI of its pro-Taliban elements. Since 2004, the ISI refocused on the threat from the Afghan Taliban and al-Qaeda, but resistance continued. After all, the same agency had nurtured and assisted the Taliban—how had the Taliban suddenly become its principal enemy? The ISI continued to consider other possibilities of where such a threat could emanate from: India, the traditional enemy; Israel; and even the United States. It would take years for the intelligence apparatus to realize its mistake. While halfhearted attempts to infiltrate various Taliban chapters began in 2006, it was not until al-Qaeda's 2007 announcement that Pakistan had replaced the United States as al-Qaeda's principal enemy that the ISI acknowledged the Pakistani Taliban–al-Qaeda combination as a real threat to the Pakistani state.[24]

By this time, the Intelligence Bureau (IB), responsible for intelligence at the provincial levels, had also begun to be more active domestically and develop its own sources. Together, the ISI and IB exhibited tremendous improvement. Even though the resurgence of the Taliban in parts of FATA suggests that there are still significant gaps, at least in matters of urban terrorism, the intelligence has been fairly accurate in predictions of possible terrorist attacks. We now know that high-profile attacks—such as the ones on the Sri Lankan cricket team in Lahore in March 2009, the police

24. A senior ISI official, who had been dealing with the Taliban and was ousted in the purge ordered by General Ehsan ul-Haq, admitted this in a private conversation with the author in early 2008.

training school in Manawan the same month, General Headquarters in October 2009, and even the Rawalpindi mosque in December 2009—had all been predicted, though without precise locations or dates.[25] In short, despite the frequent accusations leveled at the intelligence services, improved intelligence has been a significant factor in tackling the insurgents' capability to carry out successful attacks since the major military operations concluded in Swat and South Waziristan.

The Narrative Question: Political Consensus, Public Opinion, and the Media

Perhaps the most crucial shift in the state's favor from 2009 onward was the open questioning—and, indeed, discrediting—of the Pakistani Taliban's narrative. The TTP's actions after the Swat peace deal exposed the group for what it was. Also, the political elites got over their ambivalence and lack of consensus, for the first time coming out with an unequivocal call to deal decisively with the Pakistani Taliban. Parties that had earlier backed the Swat peace deal now recanted (*Business Recorder* 2009). But the crucial role in swinging the narrative in favor of the state apparatus, and in supporting the military operations in Swat and South Waziristan, was the media's.

The media's outlook was quite interesting. After 9/11, it started off with a feeling that yes, Musharraf had given in tamely to U.S. demands but that he had little choice in the matter. By around 2006, however, the media grew increasingly critical of Musharraf's policies. On the one hand, the fallout from Musharraf's contention that "we are fighting America's war" was telling in the military's performance. On the other hand, coupled with Musharraf's visibly vacillating one-step-forward, two-steps-back policy, the media began to question the wisdom of fighting this war and its costs to Pakistan. So did the public. The religious political parties and the right-of-center mainstream PML-N had been consistently opposed to military means to resolve the insurgency and favored a negotiated peace. By 2007, the media had decisively begun to reflect this sentiment and actively called for peace talks with the Taliban.

When incidents of soldiers surrendering to Taliban forces proliferated, Musharraf finally realized that he had lost control of the army, not to mention public support. However, after the abrupt change in the post–Swat deal scenario, the media, backed by public opinion, aided the military's cause tremendously. For one, when the military operations were about to begin in Swat, the media announced the fact. This announcement resulted in a mass exodus of the Swat population. Although the flight should have been ex-

25. For brief descriptions of these and other major terrorist attacks in Pakistan in 2009, see SATP (2009).

pected—and, indeed, the military had warned the government—the important point to note is that the migration was not orchestrated by any act of government or military. Rather, it was a direct outcome of the media informing the public of the imminent military operation. This exodus of noncombatants saved thousands of lives in potential collateral damage.

Before undertaking the operation in South Waziristan in September 2009, the military decided to orchestrate the same campaign of public information, this time deliberately. Apart from the media's announcements of impending military operations, millions of leaflets were airdropped throughout the length and breadth of South Waziristan. In Urdu and Pashto, they stated that the Pakistan military was not at war with the Mehsud tribe. The pamphlets emphasized Mehsud loyalty to the country and acknowledged that Mehsud blood had been shed while defending Pakistan. The war was defined as directed against those few misled Mehsuds who killed innocent men, women, and children. People were asked to vacate the area and seek shelter in camps set up for them in surrounding localities.[26] This move by the army again saved thousands of innocent lives since, otherwise, the bulk of the Mehsud tribe would have believed that the military had clubbed the entire tribe as being an extension of Baitullah's Taliban.

During the past two years or so, the debate among the intelligentsia on the role of the media is back. Some point to the media's right-wing tendencies and see a move back toward the ambivalence that characterized its outlook before 2009. Although this observation has some merit, the fact remains that the Taliban's narrative, once dented, is not easily reparable. The Pakistani people have again started to tire of military operations, but they would be loath to let the Taliban again take control of Pakistani territory unopposed.

Governance and Political-Administrative Response

The Pakistani state's improved performance in tackling the insurgency since 2009 has come about despite, not because of, its emphasis on a governance and political-administrative response. In fact, the state's insistence on such a response will likely cause it to lose some of the ground gained after 2009.

This critical aspect of counterinsurgency merits elaboration, and the Swat operation provides a perfect example. When the TTP took over Swat as a result of the peace deal, all state functionaries steadily withdrew, led by the local police. But as military operations to clear Swat began in April 2009, political-administrative support could have been in place to immediately fill the vacuum left by the TTP's expulsion if a comprehensive

26. I read some of these leaflets.

counterinsurgency response had been planned in advance. Sadly, this was not the case. Even after the military had recaptured the entire Swat Valley, government administrative functionaries and police officials were reluctant to take over from the army. It was not until late 2009 and early 2010 that some police personnel, led by the more intrepid young police officers, ventured into Swat. Administrative functionaries followed a few months later. By mid-2010, the police forces in and around Swat were functioning, although the administration still preferred that the police receive instructions from the military (*Express Tribune* 2011). Moreover, virtually all administrative support functions, including medical assistance and provision of rations, stayed with the army. Even members of the TTP captured by the military in Swat have not been taken over by the provincial government for prosecution. By all legal and human rights standards, they remained in illegal custody of the army (Amnesty International 2011).

But even before the return to normality in Swat, something unknown to most counterinsurgency efforts saved the day for the Pakistani state. The military tactics in Swat, though they proved effective, did have a major downside: They created the largest number of internally displaced persons (IDPs) since the Rwandan genocide in 1994. The exodus of over half a million families from Swat was to be expected, but the provincial government made only token attempts to prepare for them and was caught flat-footed. Some tent villages were set up, extending from Buner to Nowshera in KPK, but these locations were barely sufficient for a quarter of the IDPs.[27] Compounding the difficulties, the IDPs' credentials had to be verified to prevent Taliban infiltration. It frequently took days, sometimes weeks, to complete the verification and provide accommodations.

Had it not been for the astoundingly generous response of the local Pashtun communities, the IDP tragedy would have been far more serious. The response was unexpectedly kind, and while it cannot find its way into counterinsurgency manuals, it does highlight just how much the local culture and context matter in preventing any further breakdown of order in conflict environments. Locals threw open their houses to the refugees. Four-bedroom houses frequently housed three IDP families (sometimes as many as twenty individuals). In this way, the householders shared in the hardship—an outcome of entertaining so many "guests" with no expectation of return. The Pashtuns lived up to their traditional reputation of hospitality and generosity—something that had not been apparent for several years. Perhaps it was a collective feeling of guilt for having imposed the "peace deal" on the hapless citizens of Swat. Whatever the reason, human suffering on a

27. Given the lack of space, many of these IDPs ended up in major cities such as Rawalpindi and Islamabad, causing worries about overcrowding. See *Dawn* (2009).

monumental scale—and, quite possibly, a buildup of fresh resentment and attraction to the Taliban's antistate message among the IDPs—was averted by the collective generosity of many thousands of Pashtun families. In the wake of the South Waziristan operation, too, residents of Bannu, Kohat, Karak, and even Tank—traditional enemies of the Mehsud and Wazir tribes—bridged the gap and accommodated as many IDPs as possible.

Nonetheless, the lack of a coordinated political response in the state's overall counterinsurgency strategy overstrained the army. Leaving an administrative vacuum that the army must then contrive to fill could only result in reducing its efficiency. There are many examples of this problem. It has been mentioned earlier that terrorists captured by the army continue to languish in army custody since no government institution dare take them over and prosecute them. Nor can the army turn them loose. The civilian authorities' reluctance is driven largely by Pakistan's broken criminal justice system, which has meant an excessive acquittal rate for militants known to be involved in armed insurgent and terrorist violence against the state.[28] Much has been said and written about it, but there has been little political will to address this vitally important area.

On the positive side, one major development for which President Zardari's PPP government does deserve credit is the passage of the FATA reforms package (*Daily Times* 2011). Most notably, the reforms include an amendment to the more than a century-old Frontier Crimes Regulation—which imposes laws in direct contravention of human rights fundamentals—and the provision for political parties to operate in FATA as in the rest of the country. Before this, the FATA representatives in the assembly could not compete from party platforms. These changes have already taken effect, and the 2013 general elections were held on a party basis in FATA. With a stronger voice for FATA representatives, space for political parties, and modernized laws, the region's political economy can only improve. FATA's mainstreaming, toward which the reforms package is only a first step, may also, over time, take some burden off the military.

Thus far, a large number of development programs in the tribal belt are being envisioned, planned, organized, assisted, or run by the army. Even the development programs initiated by foreign donors, with NGOs as their implementing partners, need military support, not merely for security, which would be quite understandable, but also to sell these programs to locals. Moreover, the funders have no oversight to speak of, given that they are prohibited from venturing into FATA because of security concerns. Although the FATA Secretariat housed in Peshawar manages development in FATA and liaisons with the donors, the participation of provincial or

28. For an excellent analysis of the problems in Pakistan's criminal justice system, see ICG (2010).

central governments often remains confined to approving and funding projects for socioeconomic development of the region. In some instances, even governmental supervision of projects they have funded is lacking.

The political leadership's voluntary cession of governmental functions to the army only serves to reinforce the domestic and international impression that the army actually calls all the shots. The virtual absence of a holistic governance response to the counterinsurgency strategy leaves a vacuum that, if left unfilled, will doom the state's efforts to pacify militants permanently. The longer the army fills this vacuum, the more politicized it will become, and the tougher it will be to fight future military battles.

The Way Ahead

Pakistan's Taliban challenge is far from over. The insurgency has been dented but not eliminated. In fact, since 2012, the TTP seems to be raising its head again in FATA and has challenged the army by taking over remote locations across FATA and engaging it in battle. A holistic counterinsurgency policy is still lacking despite much debate and political discourse on the issue. Moreover, the Taliban conglomerate—perhaps more bloated than ever before given the increased support from the Punjabi Taliban and sectarian groups—has also shown continuous capacity to strike urban targets through small improvised attacks. This is vastly better than the regular, headline-making events of 2008 and 2009, but it suggests that the state has a long way to go in permanently taming the menace.

Perhaps most worrisome are indications that the national consensus against the Taliban may be dwindling again. In the run-up to the 2013 elections, there was a clear division within the political ranks as virtually all parties sought to reinitiate talks with the Taliban. Ironically, the ANP, which has been a constant target of the TTP ever since the Swat operation of 2009, called the first All-Party Conference in February 2013 to discuss the outreach (Muhammad 2013). The right-wing Jamiat Ulema-e-Islam followed soon thereafter (*Express Tribune* 2013). The initiative went nowhere because the military was strongly opposed to it and because the Taliban upped its attacks on election-related targets. (Pakistan's general elections were held in May 2013.) Also, it was never clear what the agenda for the talks with Hakimullah Mehsud and his lieutenants was going to be, since they remain defiant and in no mood to give up their fight. Even more worrisome, mainstream parties, such as PML-N, allegedly worked out seat adjustments with militant groups in southern Punjab (not contesting against these groups' candidates in certain constituencies in return for their support elsewhere) as part of their election strategy (Mir 2013). Also, there was a conspicuous absence of any sincere condemnation by the right-of-center parties of Taliban attacks specifically targeting left-of-center parties, such as the ANP, PPP, and the Muttahida Qaumi Movement, in the run-up to the May 2013 elections.

If Pakistan is to slide back down the conflict curve to a state of stable peace—durable peace would be too much to ask for at this stage—and make this move permanent, it needs to do a lot more. Moreover, most of the work has to be in the nonmilitary sphere. Keeping public opinion and the national political consensus on the state's side is one obvious aspect. Even more broadly, however, the vision of the FATA reforms package needs to be implemented. And the state must proactively pursue further measures to make the people of the tribal belt *want* to stay within the union of the state by providing good governance and a better quality of life. Specifically, it will be necessary to develop a fresh socioeconomic structure for the entire region—one that seeks economic betterment based on local resources and equal opportunities for the future, including education. FATA requires a "Marshall Plan" to revitalize its social and economic makeup (Qadir 2008). In essence, a comprehensive policy that includes short-, intermediate-, and long-term plans to improve education, health, economic opportunities, justice, and equal opportunities for the future is essential. Politically, with traditional tribal leadership gone and ongoing military operations to remove the insurgents, this is the ideal opportunity in many ways to absorb FATA constitutionally into mainstream Pakistan. Among other alternatives, it could conceivably be made part of KPK, with each tribal agency a division of the province.

While the focus of this chapter is on FATA, it would be incomplete without reemphasizing the importance of Punjabi groups that have become equal partners of the TTP's FATA-based chapters over the past couple of years. Although still dependent for training on the Pashtun chapters, they have found refuge in the southern portion of North Waziristan. These Punjabi Taliban are far more lethal, committed, and intrepid than the TTP in planning and executing terrorist attacks, and they are also focused on fanning the flames of sectarianism by targeting Shias as well.

Finally, Pakistani policy also needs to address the issue of religious extremism that is growing by the day. This is the real breeding ground for terrorists, and it lies in the Punjab. Due to territorial constraints, it is unlikely that a terrorist command, control, communication, or training facility could be built in the Punjab. But as long as minds are corrupted there, they are willing recruits for training by terrorists in the tribal areas. If any meaningful headway is to be made to prevent religious extremism, it will have to be through absorbing the clergy into the mainstream of socioeconomic life. No tangible progress is visible on this count yet.

References

Abbas, Hassan. 2009a. "Defining the Punjabi Taliban Network." Combating Terrorism Center, Apr. 15. www.ctc.usma.edu/posts/defining-the-punjabi-taliban-network.

———. 2009b. "*Police and Law Enforcement Reform in Pakistan: Crucial for Counterinsurgency and Counterterrorism Success.*" Institute for Social Policy and Understanding, Apr. http://belfercenter.hks.harvard.edu/publication/18976/police_law_enforcement_reform_in_pakistan.html.

———. 2011. "Reforming Pakistan's Police and Law Enforcement Infrastructure: Is It Too Flawed to Fix?" U.S. Institute of Peace Special Report no. 266, Feb. www.usip.org/files/resources/sr266.pdf.

———, ed. 2012. *Stabilizing Pakistan through Police Reform.* New York: Asia Society.

Ahmed, Khalid. 2013. "Punjab: Driver of Terrorism in Pakistan." *Viewpoint,* Apr. 26. www.viewpointonline.net.

Akhlaque, Qudssia. 2009. "On Whose Side Is US Anyway?" *The News,* Oct. 19. www.thenews.com.pk/TodaysPrintDetail.aspx?ID=25079&Cat=13&dt=10/19/2009.

Amnesty International. 2011. *Annual Report 2011.* London: Amnesty International.

Behuria, Ashok K. 2007. "Fighting the Taliban: Pakistan at War with Itself." *Australian Journal of International Affairs* 61 (4): 529–43.

Business Recorder. 2009. "PML-N Retracts from Support to Peace Deal with Swat Taliban." Apr. 23. http://epaper.brecorder.com/2009/04/23/17-page/75240-news.html.

Cheema, Pervaiz I. 2008. "Challenges Facing a Counter-Militant Campaign in Pakistan's FATA." *NBR Analysis* 19, no.3 (Aug.). www.nbr.org/publications/nbranalysis/pdf/vol19no3.pdf.

Coll, Steve. 2004. *Ghost Wars: The Secret History of the CIA, Afghanistan, and Bin Laden from the Soviet Invasion to September 10, 2001.* New York: Penguin.

Constable, Pamela. 2009. "Defiant Taliban Forces Advance to within 60 Miles of Islamabad." *Washington Post,* Apr. 24. www.washingtonpost.com/wp-dyn/content/article/2009/04/22/AR2009042200863.html.

Daily Times. 2005. "FBI Training Law Enforcement Officials." Feb. 23. www.dailytimes.com.pk/default.asp?page=story_23-2-2005_pg7_34.

———. 2009. "Text of the Nizam-e-Adl Regulation 2009." Apr. 15. www.dailytimes.com.pk/default.asp?page=2009%5C04%5C15%5Cstory_15-4-2009_pg7_51.

———. 2011. "Political Activities Allowed in FATA." Aug. 13. www.dailytimes.com.pk/default.asp?page=2011%5C08%5C13%5Cstory_13-8-2011_pg1_1.

Dawn. 2009. "Fresh Waves of IDPs to Further Strain Pindi, Islamabad." May 9. http://archives.dawn.com/archives/133415.

———. 2013. "Musharraf Admits to Secret Drone Deal with US." Apr. 12. http://dawn.com/2013/04/12/musharraf-admits-to-secret-deal-with-us-on-drone-strikes/.

Dressler, Jeffrey. 2012. "The Haqqani Network: A Strategic Threat." Institute for the Study of War, Afghanistan Report 9, March. www.understandingwar.org/sites/default/files/Haqqani_StrategicThreatweb_29MAR_0.pdf.

Express Tribune. 2011. "Slow Government Development Threatens Swat Military Gains." Apr. 15. http://tribune.com.pk/story/150037/slow-government-development-threatens-swat-military-gains/.

———. 2012. "Government Deliberating Military Operation in N Waziristan: Rehman Malik." Oct. 12. http://tribune.com.pk/story/450683/government-deliberating-military-operation-in-n-waziristan-rehman-malik/.

———. 2013. "Immediate Talks with Taliban, Urges APC." Feb. 28. http://tribune.com.pk/story/513809/immediate-talks-with-the-taliban-urged-at-the-apc/.

Federally Administered Tribal Areas (FATA). n.d. "History of FATA." http://fata.gov.pk/index.php?option=com_content&view=article&id=85&Itemid=83.

Haq, Noor ul, ed. 2007. "Lal Masjid Crisis." Islamabad Policy Research Institute, Oct. 4. http://ipripak.org/factfiles/ff90.pdf.

Hussain, Mujahid. 2012. *Punjabi Taliban: Driving Extremism in Pakistan*. New Delhi: Pentagon Press.

Hussain, Tayyab. 2013. "Senate Passes NACTA, Electoral Laws Amendment Bills." *Pakistan Today*, Mar. 13. www.pakistantoday.com.pk/2013/03/13/news/national/senate-passes-nacta-electoral-laws-amendment-bills/.

Hussain, Zahid. 2010. *The Scorpion's Tail: The Relentless Rise of Islamic Militants in Pakistan—And How It Threatens America*. New York: Free Press.

———. 2011. "Sources of Tension in Afghanistan and Pakistan: A Regional Perspective." CIDOB Policy Research Paper, Dec. www.cidob.org/en/ publications/stap rp/policy_research_papers/sources_of_tension_in_afghanistan_and_pakistan_a_regional_perspective.

———. 2012. "Nacta: A Non-Starter." *Dawn*, Dec. 4. http://dawn.com/2012/12/04/nacta-a-non-starter/.

International Crisis Group (ICG). 2006. "Pakistan's Tribal Areas: Appeasing the Militants." Asia Report no. 125, Dec. 11. www.crisisgroup.org/~/media/Files/

asia/south-asia/pakistan/125_pakistans_tribal_areas___appeasing_the_militants.

———. 2010. "Reforming Pakistan's Criminal Justice System." Asia Report no. 196, Dec. 6. www.crisisgroup.org/en/regions/asia/south-asia/pakistan/196-reforming-pakistans-criminal-justice-system.aspx.

Khan, Tahir. 2012. "TTP Admits to Having Safe Haven in Afghanistan." *Express Tribune,* June 26.

Koelbl, Susanne. 2009. "Islamists Triumph in Swat Valley: Bowing Down to the Taliban." *Der Spiegel,* Aug. 9. www.spiegel.de/international/world/islamists-triumph-in-swat-valley-bowing-down-to-the-taliban-a-609575.html.

Lieven, Anatol. 2011. *Pakistan: A Hard Country.* New York: Public Affairs.

Mazetti, Mark. 2013. "A Secret Deal on Drones, Sealed in Blood." *New York Times,* Apr. 6. www.nytimes.com/2013/04/07/world/asia/origins-of-cias-not-so-secret-drone-war-in-pakistan.html?pagewanted=all.

Mir, Amir. 2013. "Punjab Govt May Not Act Against LeJ PML-N Has Seat Adjustment with Defunct SSP." *The News,* Feb. 22. www.thenews.com.pk/Todays-News-13-21114-Punjab-govt-may-not-act-against-LeJ-PML-N-has-seat-adjustments-with-defunct-SSP.

Muhammad, Peer. 2013. "ANP Sponsored Moot: Two Dozen Parties Endorse Peace Talks with Taliban." *Express Tribune,* Feb. 15. http://tribune.com.pk/story/507628/anp-sponsored-moot-two-dozen-parties-endorse-peace-talks-with-taliban/.

Musharraf, Pervez. 2006. *In the Line of Fire: A Memoir.* New York: Free Press.

Nawaz, Shuja. 2009. *FATA—A Most Dangerous Place.* Washington, DC: Center for Strategic and International Studies.

Norell, Magnus. 2007. "The Taliban and the Muttahida Majlis-e-Amal." *China and Eurasia Forum Quarterly* 5 (3): 61–82.

Pakistan Body Count. 2013. "Suicide Bombing Incidents in Pakistan 1995–2011." http://pakistanbodycount.org/analytics.

Pardesi, Manjeet. 2008. "The Battle for the Soul of Pakistan at Islamabad's Red Mosque." In *Treading on Hallowed Ground: Counterinsurgency Operations in Sacred Spaces,* ed. C. Christine Fair and Sumit Ganguly. New York: Oxford Univ. Press.

Qadir, Shaukat. 2008. "Marshall Plan for FATA." *Daily Times,* Aug. 2. www.dailytimes.com.pk/default.asp?page=2008%5C08%5C02%5Cstory_2-8-2008_pg3_6.

Qazi, Shehzad H. 2011. "Rebels of the Frontier: Origins, Organization, and Recruitment of the Pakistani Taliban." *Small Wars and Insurgencies* 22 (4): 574–602.

Ramsay, Clay, Steven Kull, Stephen Weber, and Evan Lewis. 2009. "Pakistani Public Opinion on the Swat Conflict, Afghanistan, and the US." World Public Opinion.org, July 1. www.worldpublicopinion.org/pipa/pdf/jul09/WPO_Pakistan_Jul09_rpt.pdf.

Rashid, Ahmed. 2000. *Taliban: Militant Islam, Oil and Fundamentalism in Central Asia.* New Haven: Yale Univ. Press.

Raza, Syed Irfan. 2009. "Revenge Attacks in Swat for Lal Masjid: Cleric." *Dawn,* May 4. http://archives.dawn.com/archives/79064.

Roggio, Bill. 2009a. "Sufi Muhammed 'Hates Democracy' and Calls for Global Islamic Rule." *Long War Journal,* Feb. 18. www.longwarjournal.org/archives/2009/02/sufi_mohammed_hates_democracy_and_calls_for_global_islamic_rule.php.

———. 2009b. "Suicide Bomber Strikes outside Pakistani Naval Headquarters." *Long War Journal,* Dec. 2. www.longwarjournal.org/archives/2009/12/suicide_bomber_strik_4.php.

Sherazi, Zahir Shah. 2013. "Tirah Valley Operation Intensifies, 23 Soldiers Killed." *Dawn,* Apr. 7. http://dawn.com/2013/04/07/tirah-valley-operation-intensifies-23-soldiers-killed/.

Shinwari, Ibrahim. 2013. "Mengal Bagh Becomes LI, Taliban Supremo in Khyber." *Dawn,* Apr. 10. http://dawn.com/2013/04/10/mangal-bagh-becomes-li-taliban-supremo-in-khyber/.

Siddiqa, Ayesha. 2011. "Pakistan's Counterterrorism Strategy: Separating Friends from Enemies." *Washington Quarterly* 34 (1): 149–62.

Siddiqi, Tanvir. 2012. "5-Member Body Pledges to Fight Foreign Forces: Ceases Activities Against Pak, Afghan Nationals." *Pakistan Observer,* Jan. 3. http://pakobserver.net/detailnews.asp?id=133351.

South Asia Terrorism Portal (SATP). 2009. "Major Incidents of Terrorism-Related Violence in Pakistan, 2009." www.satp.org/satporgtp/countries/pakistan/database/majorinci2009.htm.

Walsh, Declan. 2009. "Video of Girl's Flogging as Taliban Hand Out Justice." *Guardian,* Apr. 2. www.guardian.co.uk/world/2009/apr/02/taliban-pakistan-justice-women-flogging.

Yusuf, Moeed. 2009a. "Rational Institutional Design, Perverse Incentives, and the US-Pakistan Partnership in Post-9/11." *Defense against Terrorism Review* 2 (1): 15–30.

———. 2009b. "Taliban Have Been Fooling Us All Along." *Friday Times* 21 (12).

III
Nepal

Map 5. Nepal Borders, Development Regions, Districts, and Administrative Zones

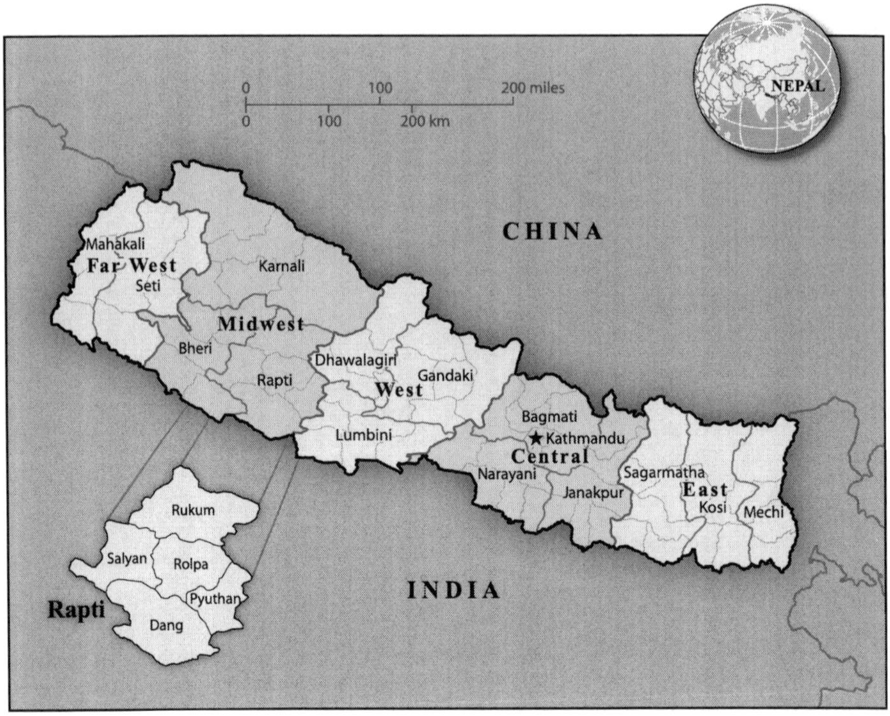

Nepal: Timeline of Events

1767

Kingdom of Nepal is formed.

1864

September Kot massacre leads to eclipse of the monarchy, under the dominance of hereditary Rana prime ministers.

1947

Communist Party of Nepal joins with the centrist Nepali Congress Party against Rana rule.

1950–51

People's resistance against Rana prime ministers, led by King Tribhuvan, ends Rana rule and establishes constitutional monarchy.

1955

March King Mahendra accedes to throne.

1960

December King Mahendra dismisses the elected parliament and representative government.

1962

December New constitution introduces the panchayat system as a means to keep political forces loyal to king.

1972

January King Mahendra dies and is succeeded by King Birendra.

1989–90

Jan Andolan (People's Movement) succeeds in removing the panchayat system. King Birendra is forced to restore multiparty democracy, but constitutional monarchy is kept intact.

1991

May First parliamentary elections. Maoists compete and acquire nine seats in Parliament.

1994

Faction of Maoists splits off and establishes new party, later named Communist Party of Nepal (Maoist).

November Nepali Congress Party–led government falls.

1995

November	Police conduct Operation Romeo against Maoists.

1996

February	Maoists issue 40-point charter of demands in response to state repression. Even before the 10-day ultimatum for government response expires, Maoists begin violent resistance, launching their "people's war" with six concurrent attacks on government and police outposts in midwestern Nepal. Insurgency begins in full force.

1997

April	Dhami Commission studies ways to resolve the insurgency, primarily by advocating political solutions that are never implemented.

2000

March	Girija Prasad Koirala, Nepal's first democratically elected prime minister, becomes prime minister again, heading 9th government in 10 years.

2001

January	Government forms Armed Police Force, a paramilitary unit intended to fight the Maoists.
June	Royal massacre, perpetrated by Crown Prince Dipendra, kills King Birendra and seven other members of royal family. King's brother Gyanendra accedes to throne.
July	Cease-fire is announced concurrently with swearing in of Prime Minister Sher Bahadur Deuba.
August	First round of peace talks begins between government and Maoists.
November	Peace talks collapse with withdrawal of Maoists. Government declares state of emergency after over 100 people are killed within 4 days.
December	U.S. declares Maoists a terrorist organization.

2002

May	Code of conduct is agreed between Nepal government and Maoists, but King Gyanendra dismisses Parliament.

2003

January	Second cease-fire begins, and new peace talks begin between government and Maoists.

August	Renewed violence between activists and Nepalese police as Maoists pull out of cease-fire.

2004

December	15,000 people hold peace rally in Kathmandu.

2005

February	Gyanendra assumes all executive powers in military-backed coup, leading all political parties to unite against him.
April	Under international pressure, Gyanendra lifts state of emergency.
September	Under "united front" strategy, Maoists declare three-month cease-fire.
November	Seven Party Alliance (SPA), a conglomerate of political parties, and the Maoists reach 12-Point Understanding to end royal rule.

2006

April–May	SPA and Maoists lead Jan Andolan-II, 19 days of peaceful protests.
May	May 18 Act passes, stripping King Gyanendra of many of his assumed powers. Date is referred to as Democracy Day.
November 21	Comprehensive Peace Accord is signed by Prime Minister Koirala and Maoist leader Prachanda, ending civil war that killed some 13,000 people.

2007

January	Interim constitution declares Nepal a federal republic.
April	Maoists join the government.
September	Maoists quit interim government, demand abolition of monarchy.
December	Parliament approves abolition of monarchy to persuade Maoists to rejoin government.

2008

April	Maoists win largest bloc of seats in Constituent Assembly, though not a majority.
May	Nepal officially abolishes monarchy and becomes a republic.

2009

May	Prime Minister Prachanda resigns after political impasse with President Yadav over Prachanda's desire to remove army chief.

2010

May	Deadline for Constituent Assembly to draft new constitution is extended to May 2011.

2011

February	Jhala Nath Khanal is elected prime minister after seven-month gridlock during which no one receives enough votes to be elected.
May	Constituent Assembly fails to meet extension deadline for new constitution.
August	Khanal resigns as political gridlock continues.

2012

May	Constituent Assembly misses another deadline for consensus on new constitution to complete the country's peace process. Prime Minister Bhattarai dissolves Constituent Assembly and calls for new elections in November.
November	Parliamentary elections are delayed until mid-April or mid-May 2013.

2013

March	President Yadav passes ordinance establishing Truth and Reconciliation Commission called for in 2006 peace accords.
April	Yadav swears in Chief Justice Khil Raj Regmi as head of interim government.
July	Supreme Court blocks establishment of Truth and Reconciliation Commission, citing concerns over possible granting of amnesties for wartime offenses.
	Parliamentary elections are delayed again until November.

6

Anatomy of a South Asian Revolt

Nepal's Maoist Insurgency in Perspective*

S. D. Muni

If we were to identify South Asia's single most important political transition in the first decade of the twenty-first century, it would be the mainstreaming of Nepal's Maoist insurgency. This insurgency succeeded in dethroning the nation's nearly 250-year-old monarchy and has transformed itself from a revolutionary movement into a conventional national political formation. Its evolution and transition, within the span of a decade and a half, presents a fascinating study of an ideologically driven violent and extremist movement in South Asia. The insurgency arose out of the mix of deprivation and discrimination built into the Nepalese state structure and the state's inability to correct these deep-rooted anomalies. Such a correction could have stopped the progression along the conflict curve, from a state of unstable peace to one of war. But before we look at the reasons behind the rise and redefinition of the Maoist movement in Nepal, we need some understanding of the Nepali monarchy that this movement was so stridently pitted against.

Characteristics of the Nepalese Monarchy

Nepal was established by King Prithvi Narayan Shah, who, by 1767, had succeeded in integrating several small feudal principalities scattered in the Himalayan region into one compact kingdom. Since then, Nepal has been governed by monarchical order until only recently. But monarchy as an institution has played a rather insignificant role in the building of the Nepali state and society. Only three kings, Prithvi Narayan Shah, Tribhuvan, and his son Mahendra, may be considered exceptions to the otherwise inglorious history of Nepalese monarchy. For nearly a century, from 1864 to 1950, the monarchy was eclipsed under the rule of Nepal's Rana prime ministers.[1] After 1972, King Mahendra's successors not only failed to preserve the panchayat system—innovated and imposed by him to legitimize the monarchy's assertive role in Nepali politics—but also led to the monarchy's complete elimination.

The panchayat is a political institution common in South Asia, featuring grassroots-level governance with local norms and traditions. King Mahendra introduced this system at the national level in Nepal under the 1962 Constitution, promulgated following his abolition of the elected parliamentary system in 1960. The Nepali panchayat system included legislative councils from the village to the national level (Khadka 1986). The councils at the top level drew their authority from the king. The panchayat system was abolished as a result of Nepal's first People's Movement (known in Nepali as the Jan Andolan-I), led by the Nepali Congress and other political parties in 1989–90. In 2008, Nepal's first popularly elected Constituent Assembly abolished the monarchy, as a result of the second People's Movement (known in Nepali as Jan Andolan-II) in 2006 (Upreti 2009). The Maoist insurgency spearheaded the assault on the institution of the monarchy.

King Tribhuvan of Nepal is identified as an icon of democracy for leading the people's resistance in 1950–51 against the anachronistic regime of the Ranas. But democratic aspirations unleashed as a result of this change could not be institutionalized. His son, King Mahendra, reversed the gradual process, initiated in 1951, of establishing a constitutional monarchy. Instead, he established an assertive monarchy by dismissing an elected parliament and representative government in December 1960. King Birendra, who succeeded King Mahendra in 1972, had to succumb to democratic resistance, first in 1980, by softening the "partyless" panchayat system, and again in 1990, by restoring multiparty democracy. His successor and brother, King Gyanendra, tried to revive the assertive monarchy of his father, Mahendra, in the face of a determined Maoist insurgency. In the process, however, he ended up creating the circumstances—by alienating all the major political forces, democratic and extremist alike—that eliminated the monarchy altogether.

1. The Ranas assumed power as prime ministers following the Kot palace massacre in 1846. They reduced the king to a mere rubber stamp and established a political order wherein the succession of the Rana prime ministers became hereditary (Lohani 1969).

The Maoist insurgency is generally condemned for its resort to violence, but violence has been endemic to the political evolution of Nepal from the beginning. King Prithvi Narayan Shah's establishment of the Kingdom of Nepal was the result of his many ruthless wars with a number of feudal principalities. Violence has been a characteristic feature of Nepal's major political transitions at the apex level and also of resistance against the autocratic state at the grassroots level. Two landmark events at the apex level changed the face of monarchy in Nepal. The first was the Kot massacre of 1846, which led to the eclipse of monarchy under the system of hereditary Rana prime ministers.[2] The second was the palace massacre of June 2001, resulting in the brutal deaths of King Birendra and all his family. The monarchy was eventually eliminated in 2008, following the success of the People's Movement (Jan Andolan-II) in 2006.

At the level of resistance to the state, the creator of Nepal, King Prithvi Narayan Shah, while still in the process of consolidating his new kingdom, was confronted by the ethnic groups of eastern Nepal—the Rais, Limbus and Murmis—concerning the preservation of their autonomy. They even sought the help of the Chinese in this quest (Regmi 1999). These groups, along with others—including the Gurungs, Magars, and Kiratis—constantly raised the flag of resistance against the Nepali monarchy for over 150 years from 1793 to 1950 (Gurung 2004). It is worth noting that these tribal groups provided the mainstay of support to the Maoist insurgency. In 1951, when King Tribhuvan led the movement of democracy—which also meant liberation of the monarchy from the dominance of autocratic Rana rule—he was, in fact, lending his support to the struggle for democracy that had been brewing in Nepal since 1935. From the late 1940s on, this movement also included armed resistance by the Nepali Congress (NC) and the Communist Party of Nepal. These parties were seeking to establish a democratic order under constitutional monarchy. The Ranas were overthrown, and the monarchy regained its lost glory, but democracy moved forward only partially. In the messy transition of 1951–55, various Nepali groups took up arms against the weak and unstable Nepali regimes (Thapa and Sijapati 2005).

The next round of armed resistance against the state occurred during the early 1960s. This resistance was triggered when King Mahendra unceremoniously dismissed Nepal's first elected parliament and representative government barely eighteen months into its term. The NC and other banned mainstream political parties continued their struggle for the restoration of democracy, with occasional use of armed resistance, until at least 1980, when a national referendum restored the freedom to function to the political

2. For a more thorough discussion of the Kot massacre, see Adhikari (1977).

parties under the panchayat system. But the referendum failed to replace this system with the desired parliamentary democracy under a constitutional monarchy. King Birendra finally had to abolish the panchayat system in response to a brief struggle for more substantial democratic processes (i.e., a parliamentary system) during 1989–90. The violent struggle of the Maoists lasted for a decade, from 1996 to 2006.

Emergence of the Maoists

The Maoists emerged from the communist movement of Nepal, which has had a checkered history. Established by Pushpa Lal Shrestha in 1947, the Communist Party of Nepal joined hands with the NC, a centrist party, to remove the Rana rule. Its performance in Nepal's first popular elections was dismal, and while still fighting against King Mahendra, it suffered upheaval resulting from the Sino-Soviet ideological split in the international communist movement. The king co-opted the pro-Soviet section to isolate the NC. The long, drawn-out struggle for democracy in Nepal further fragmented the communist movement, so that by the end of the 1980s, according to some estimates, there were nearly twenty communist groups. These groups did not launch any major armed struggle. Indeed, many of them were described in Nepali and international media as the "king's communists," for their encouragement to counter the NC. Some of these communist groups were also Maoists, who were radical precursors of the current Maoists. During 1970–85, they encouraged the ethnic peasant groups of eastern Nepal to take up arms in what is known as the Jhapali revolt.[3] The ruthless suppression of this revolt induced an ideological churning among the Maoist groups over the strategy for taking their struggle forward. The younger groups of Maoists, led by Mohan Baidya, Pushpa Kamal Dahal, and Baburam Bhattarai, challenged such senior leaders as Mohan Bikram Singh and Nirmal Lama on ideological issues. They also lobbied to place the struggle within the wider international context by linking up with similar groups in Peru, India (Naxalites), and elsewhere. While Mohan Bikram Singh continued to toe the traditional Maoist line, Nirmal Lama followed Deng Xiaoping's ideological lineage. In 1994–95, the younger groups, led by Baidya, Dahal, and Bhattarai, joined hands to regroup themselves as the Communist Party of Nepal (Maoist). The name changed later to the Unified Communist Party of Nepal (Maoist) (UCPN [M]) (Mikesell 1999; Karki and Seddon 2003; Thapa and Sijapati 2005).

The ideological issues of the "mass struggle" and the "people's war," as well as the power struggles for leadership and dominance, were often at the

---

3. Jhapa is a district town in eastern Nepal. Because the Maoist revolt began there, it is called the Jhapali revolt or uprising.

root of splits and mergers among the Maoists. Both during the student protests in 1979–80, which led to the national referendum on the partyless panchayat system, and during the first Jan Andolan (People's Movement) of 1989–90, which removed the panchayat system and restored parliamentary democracy under constitutional monarchy, the Maoists joined the other mainstream parties to advance the cause of the "mass struggle." The Maoists were not happy, however, with the outcome of these movements. During 1989–90, they were asking for an elected Constituent Assembly to draft a "people's" democratic constitution. The simultaneous use of "mass struggle" and the "people's war" was justified under their strategy of the "two-line struggle." Accordingly, while joining the other mainstream parties for the "mass struggle," the Maoists continued to prepare for the "people's war" (Hutt 2004; Lawoti and Pahari 2009). Disappointment with the outcome of the first Jan Andolan led the Maoists to wholeheartedly launch their "people's war" in 1996.

Socioeconomic and Political Context as a Root Cause

In a very significant way, the Maoist insurgency of Nepal was a product of the country's socioeconomic and political context. Nepal is a poor agricultural country where land has been controlled by the feudal vested interests thriving under the monarchy. In 1951, when the Ranas' rule fell, 85 percent of employment and income was generated by the agricultural sector, and literacy was less than 25 percent. The monarchy was content using the state for rentier purposes without devoting any serious attention to economic and social development. For thirty years, from King Mahendra's takeover of the elected government in December 1960 until the restoration of the parliamentary democracy in 1990, Nepal's gross domestic product grew at an annual rate of 1.5 percent (Shakya 2009). This slow growth added to the country's poverty, forcing people to migrate to India and other countries for livelihood. The status quo suited the feudal regime because, were the unemployed and restive youth to remain within the country, they would give teeth to the "mass struggle" against the regime, thereby making it more radical and effective (Bhattarai 2003). Landownership remained archaic, reinforcing feudal dominance. Nepal's huge potential in hydropower and tourism remained unharnessed. Industrialization was avoided under the fear that it would turn landless agricultural laborers into radicalized factory workers. Hopes for development-oriented politics, aroused during the first people's movement in 1990, were frustrated by the disappointing role of the political parties' leadership, which also followed the king in using the state as an instrument for personal and partisan gain. This continued to reinforce and perpetuate social fault lines dividing the dominant castes (Brahmins, Chettries, and Newars) and the marginalized tribal and ethnic groups

(Gurung 2004; P. Sharma 2008). Even today, another social divide persists between the dominant hill people (Paharis) and the flatland dwellers (Terai/Madhesh people).[4] The Terai dwellers claim that despite representing half or more of Nepal's population, they are discriminated against, as reflected in their meager share in the country's army, business, higher bureaucracy, governance, and political leadership (Gaige 1975; ICG 2007b; Miklian 2009; Singh 2011).

A closer look at Nepal's midwest region—comprising Rukum, Rolpa, Jajarkot, Salyan, Sindhuli, and Gorkha districts of the Rapti Administrative Zone—makes the nexus between Nepal's socioeconomic underdevelopment and its feudal political context, on the one hand, and the rise of Maoist insurgency, on the other, quite obvious. (King Mahendra divided Nepal into fourteen north-south zones for administrative purposes, as shown on map 5.) In 1996, the Maoists first launched the "people's war" in this region, in the districts of Rukum and Rolpa, which have traditionally remained strongholds of the communists in Nepal. Historically, these districts have been not only extremely underdeveloped but also difficult to reach. Only 10 percent of the land is arable, and the first road in the region was built as recently as 2003. The economy of these districts was based on migration for employment in the Indian and British armies and also on hashish, which grew in abundance in the area's hilly terrain. In 1976, the government of Nepal, under King Birendra, banned the production, distribution, and sale of hashish, resulting in further economic hardship for the people of these districts (Gersony 2004).

The resentment of the poor and marginalized ethnic groups of these districts against the royal decision was reinforced as the local feudal lords of Rukum and Rolpa thrived and prospered from matrimonial ties with the Kathmandu royals. These local feudal lords could easily have persuaded the Nepali royal regime to initiate developmental projects in these areas but chose not to do so. Even the foreign-funded development projects undertaken in the neighboring districts—such as the $50 million Rapti Integrated Development Project, run by the U.S. Agency for International Development—had no positive impact on Rukum and Rolpa, since these districts were inaccessible due to lack of roads and communication infrastructure (Gersony 2004). The intense sense of neglect and discrimination felt by the residents of these districts made them easy targets as a social base for the Maoists, and their inaccessible geography made them a fortress of the "people's war."

---

4. Topographically, Nepal is divided into three zones: the sparsely populated region of northern high mountains, the moderately populated middle zone of rugged hills (Pahar), and the densely populated southern region of flatland, called Terai.

This region's role became even more pronounced because most residents of Rolpa and Rukum were Magars—members of Nepal's largest minority ethnic group, accounting for 7 percent of the country's total population. Their alienation from the state of Nepal stemmed from their differentiated identity and their sense of being neglected and left ungoverned by Kathmandu. The Magars living in these districts speak the Kham language, which is quite different even from the Magar mainstream language, and they traditionally looked for employment outside Nepal. They never fully submitted themselves to Nepal's founder, King Prithvi Narayan Shah, and their desire for autonomy put them at the forefront of the resistance against him (Gersony 2004). The influence of Christianity in these districts also distanced the Magars from the traditionally Hindu character of the Nepali monarchical state (Gersony 2004; Ramirez 1997).

When deciding to make midwestern Nepal a base of their revolutionary operations, the Maoists had carefully studied the political economy as well as the topography. The party documents adopted at the Third Plenum of the Central Committee in March 1995, describing the "strategy and tactics of armed struggle in Nepal," clearly took note of the "conscious peasant class struggle developed in the western hill districts, particularly Rolpa and Rukum, that represented the high level of anti-feudal and anti-imperialist revolutionary struggle. That struggle has given birth to some new tendencies in the Nepali communist movement which have inspired us to be more serious about the business of armed struggle" (Karki and Seddon 2003, 18).

Later, in 1999, the Maoist chief Pushpa Kamal Dahal, alias Prachanda, spoke in an interview to Li Onesto of *Revolutionary Worker*:

> The west is historically, geographically and culturally the core of the revolution. It is the main starting point for the revolution—the people here are more oppressed by the ruling classes and the government in Kathmandu is very far from here . . . masses of the Western region were not so much under the control of the ruling government, and they did not care what the government did or did not do . . . in Western Nepal there are the Mongoloid ethnic groups . . . These nationalities are so sincere and such brave fighters—historically they have had this kind of culture. Upper caste chauvinism and feudal ties do not prevail among these nationalities. (Prachanda 1999)

But the question of underdevelopment and deprivation in Nepal goes well beyond Rolpa and Rukum. There are a number of marginalized minority ethnic groups—including Tamangs, Gurungs, Limbus, Kiratis, Rais, Tharus, and Dalits (untouchables)—spread across the country's hills and plains. All these groups have been excluded from mainstream national life and its political and economic opportunities. The most numerous are the Madheshis, inhabitants of the Terai (Nepal's southern flatland). Along with the tribal minorities (called Janjatis), they constitute more than 70 percent of Nepal's population. The Madheshis have been clamoring for their rights and respect since the 1930s and have always actively participated in the struggles for democracy in the hope that democratic governance will help them achieve their aspirations. Linking such aspirations with the Maoists' goals, Baburam Bhattarai wrote in 2003, "The principle objective and rationale of 'people's war' in Nepal is thus to develop the social productive forces and create a higher form of society through continuous revolution of the base and the super structure by putting 'politics in command'" (Karki and Seddon 2003, 164).

A strong link was obvious between the Maoists' insistence on assuming power and their agenda for Nepal's socioeconomic transformation. They wanted to create a "new Nepal," based on the communist concept of "new democracy." They wanted to depose the monarchy and establish a "people's republic" through an elected Constituent Assembly, in keeping with the demand they had voiced since 1990. In their "new Nepal," the state was envisioned to be secular and devoid of any discrimination according to caste, religion, ethnicity, or gender. It was also to be fully democratic in its functioning, with a federal structure in which autonomous regions, keeping their specific identities, governed their own affairs in harmony with each other and with the central authority. The Maoists wanted a radical restructuring of the army, wherein a "people's militia" was accorded a significant place under the overall leadership of the political party. A small country like Nepal could maintain a small standing army and mobilize the "people's militia" in times of internal or external emergency. There was flexibility in their proposed economic structure, based on an appropriate balance between private, united, and joint ownership within a broader framework of "socially induced national capitalist development." This goal could not be achieved without rapid industrialization and workers' participation at every level of industry (Muni 2003, 90–110). Many of these goals have since been defined and redefined to suit evolving political dynamics as the Maoists, as the head of coalition governments, have shaped economic and social priorities.[5] The Maoists' insistence on a secular, federal, and democratic constitution through an elected Constituent Assembly has remained constant, however.

Role of the Maoist Leadership in the Struggle

Before we look at the rise of insurgency and its violent approach, a brief understanding of the leadership that carried out the Maoists' ideological

5. The objectives of the Maoist movement and its strategic principles were spelled out in a seventy-five-point party document on united policy and program. This document was formally adopted by the party in its United Revolutionary People's Council, held in September 2001 in Western Nepal. See Hutt (2004), Thapa (2004), and S. Sharma (2004).

struggle may be in order. People, even when disenfranchised and aggrieved, need leaders to mobilize them for political action. Maoist chief Prachanda has noted that by 1985, the group had a clear idea of how to pursue the struggle on the foundations of Marxist-Leninist-Maoist ideas. In the Maoist party, as it was established in 1994, there were three distinct leadership streams, one each headed by Prachanda, Baburam Bhattarai, and Mohan Baidya. All three leaders were relatively well educated, but Prachanda and Bhattarai had special qualifications, Prachanda being an agricultural science graduate and Bhattarai holding a PhD from India's prestigious Jawaharlal Nehru University. The theme of Bhattarai's dissertation was the regional socioeconomic development of Nepal. These two men's intellectual agility and exposure to the wider world enabled them to evolve a realistic and resilient approach to their movement based on a variety of ideological and institutional inputs from both within and outside Nepal.

The vision of Nepal's Maoist leadership was shaped and sharpened considerably by Prachanda's and Bhattarai's international contacts and exposure. As founding members of the Revolutionary International Movement, an international communist organization looking to impose a Marxist-Leninist-Maoist version of communism, they came in contact with a number of other radical groups, including the Peruvian Communist Party and the Revolutionary Communist Party of America. Their first ideological exposure, before they had even clarified their own ideas, was to the vision of the Indian Naxalite Maoists. These contacts, begun in the early 1970s, continued, and in 2004, Prachanda was even believed to have played a role in bridging the differences between India's People's War Group and the Maoist Communist Centre. However, the Nepalese Maoists always strongly denied any operational liaison or organizational linkages between their struggle and that of the Indian movement. Nepalese Maoists also took the initiative in aligning the political platform of South Asian Maoists by establishing a Coordination Committee of Maoist Parties and Organizations of South Asia. Prachanda underscores the usefulness of these external contacts:

> [There] was consistent international involvement. First and foremost, there was the RIM (Revolutionary International Movement) Committee. . . . From the RIM Committee, we gained the experience of the PCP (Communist Party of Peru) and of the two-line struggle there, and also we shared experience in Turkey, in Iran, in the Philippines. We learned from the experience in Bangladesh and from some of the experience in Sri Lanka. There was a South Asian Conference in which we participated. At the same time we were also having direct and continuous debate with the Indian communists, mainly the People's War (PW) and the Maoist Communist Centre (MCC) groups. All of this helped in one way or another; it helped us to understand the whole process of People's War (Prachanda 1999).

While keeping their links with the international Maoist groups, the Nepalese Maoists constantly kept in mind international and regional developments. In their attempts to distinguish themselves from terrorist groups, particularly following 9/11, they tried to reach out to the United Nations and the heads of state in the United States, Europe, and India (Muni 2012). In India, the Maoists also reached out to various political parties, intellectuals, media persons, and civil society groups while preparing to launch Nepal's second People's Movement, Jan Andolan-II, in 2005–06.

Taking advantage of their international exposure and contacts, the Maoist leadership of Nepal carefully analyzed the failure of the communist movement all over the world and, learning from these failures, tried to cast their movement in the specific Nepali context. They also analyzed their own failures and learned from them. Explaining the praxis of their "people's war," Prachanda said, "[We] must also learn war by waging war. The intellectuals' instinctive tendency is that we have to learn all these things, we should read everything and then we can make war. These kinds of tendencies were there right from the beginning. But we said, no, this is not Maoism. This is not Marxism. This is not dialectical materialism. . . . The issue is of learning war through war itself" (Prachanda 1999).

Later, in 2001, while still in this experience of learning war through war, he added, "In our opinion, the real key to rapid development of the people's war is the fusion between the science of proletarian revolution on the one hand and the needs and fighting spirit of the Nepalese people on the other" (RIM 2001).

Prachanda had earlier called his approach the "Prachanda Path," perhaps influenced by the Peruvian left movement and its ideology of "Shining Path." What is clear is his ideological resilience and pragmatism in the Prachanda Path's claim to go beyond the Marxist-Leninist-Maoist straitjacket. In his 1999 interview with Li Onesto, Prachanda described it as "enrichment of Marxism-Leninism-Maoism" and "a new example of creative Marxism, opposed to both, the right revisionists and sectarian dogmatists." Though using his own name to describe the body of thoughts is typical of Prachanda's acutely self-conscious personality, it nonetheless synergized the Marxist/Maoist ideology with Nepali nationalism and added a typical popular appeal to the movement. The ideological resilience and pragmatism also enabled the movement to utilize Marxist concepts, such as "united front" and "two-line struggle," for forging alliances and tactical equations with all sorts of contradictory forces, ranging from the monarchy to proponents of a multiparty system.

The Maoist leaders never really considered consistency an ideological virtue, and for this, they were criticized as being opportunist and "revisionist." But the strength of this approach was evident in the Maoists' success at bringing together diverse marginalized social groups and securing support even from their known adversaries (however tactical and short-lived that support might prove to be). A significant success of their pragmatic approach was the involvement of women in the struggle. Almost 30 percent of the Maoist cadres were women, and this inclusion strengthened the movement in several respects—for one, by bringing gender equality to the forefront of the "new Nepal's" political agenda (Karki and Seddon 2003; Yami 2010; Manchanda 2004).

On the downside, the resilience and pragmatism of the Maoist leadership hurt its internal harmony and coherence. There were instances of acute tensions and rivalries among the top three leadership streams within the party. These tensions arose on issues of ideology, tactics and strategy, identification of allies and adversaries, the movement's short- and long-term goals, and so on (ICG 2005, 2007a). Needless to say, these ideological tensions have not been free from intense clashes of personalities and power ambitions. And such clashes remained and even intensified as a result of the Maoists' sharing power and leading the government in 2007, 2008, and 2011–13. Both Bhattarai and Baidya periodically clashed on ideological and personality issues, with Prachanda playing a balancing role not only to take the goals of the movement forward but also to preserve his leadership position within the party. While Prachanda pushed for Bhattarai's ideological line in taking the agenda of building a "new Nepal" forward, tactically he leaned toward the Baidya faction to keep the party together and his own leadership within the party unchallenged. The trio avoided a formal split in the party until June 2012, when, after a protracted internal struggle, Baidya walked away from the parent party with his supporters, leaving Prachanda and Bhattarai leading the majority of the Maoists (Shah 2012; SATP 2012).

From Ballots to Bullets: Unfolding of the Insurgency

Outside Nepal, it is not widely known that Nepal's Maoists did not jump directly into the "people's war." Rather, they were almost pushed into it by the nature of the power struggle under parliamentary politics. As noted earlier, Maoist groups under different names and shades actively participated in the first People's Movement of Nepal, which overthrew the panchayat system and restored multiparty democracy in 1990. Since they preferred an elected constituent assembly rather than a parliament, they did not fully endorse the outcome of that movement. But they participated in the first parliamentary elections in 1991, under their "two-line struggle" theory. And they performed fairly well, taking third place—with nine seats in Parliament—behind the two mainstream parties, the NC and the CPN (UML). Simultaneously, under their strategy of mass struggle, the Maoists mobilized civil servants, professional groups, and rural masses to agitate against the government's policies. These agitations were put down vigorously as the two major parties, the NC and the UML, despite their rivalries, united in curbing the Maoists both within and outside Parliament (Thapa 2002). Nonetheless, the NC-led government fell in 1994, and fresh elections were ordered.

The Maoist groups also underwent splits and regroupings, and the Maoist Party emerged in 1994, led by Prachanda and Bhattarai, as noted earlier. This group decided to recontest elections while other Maoists boycotted them. However, the Election Commission did not recognize the Prachanda-Bhattarai group as the successor party and disallowed its candidacy. The group went to court against the Election Commission's orders and won the case, but the elections were long over by then. This experience reinforced the Maoist group's alienation from the prevailing system and its resolve to take the extremist course of "people's war."

It would be unrealistic to assume that this group would have abandoned the violent and extremist course altogether had they been allowed to participate in the elections. It is possible, however, that if the other mainstream groups had encouraged and facilitated their participation in parliamentary politics, Nepali politics might have taken a different course. This outcome was at least a possibility since, at that time, an intense debate was raging among the Maoists on strategy, tactics, and timing of the "people's war." With the dominant segment of the Maoist groups—the one led by Prachanda and Bhattarai—participating in the elections, the debate would have deepened. With the mainstream parties giving them their due political space, this could have strengthened the argument within the Maoists that politics of mass mobilization within a parliamentary framework could be a viable alternative and deserved serious exploration before any "people's war" ideas were pursued practically.

Instead, the mainstream political parties and the government continued with their strong-arm methods against the Maoists. Ruthless police operations against the Maoist cadres during 1994–95—particularly the 1995 operation code-named Romeo—provoked a reactive response and reinforced the Maoists' resolve to launch the "people's war." In their way, these police operations facilitated and hastened the launch of the insurgency as the Maoist ranks swelled with the innocent victims. Many young people were now willing to fight the state under the Maoists' leadership, and there was widespread sympathy and support for such a fight in the areas affected by the police actions. Commenting on Operation Romeo in Rolpa, Bhattarai said in a 1995 press interview, "There has been indiscriminate ransacking and looting of properties of common people by the ruling party hoodlums under the protection of the police force. More than 10,000 rural youth out of a population of 200,000 for the whole district have been forced to flee their homes and take shelter in remote jungles" (Thapa 2002, 84–85).

In February 1996, the Maoists submitted a forty-point charter of demands to the government in reaction to the Nepali state's repressive approach. This charter of demands came with an ultimatum to respond within ten days, but internal pressures within the party caused the "people's war" to erupt even earlier. The state reacted with full force. In 1998, it unleashed yet another ruthless police operation, code-named Kilo Sierra II, in eighteen Maoist-leaning districts. This reaction boosted the Maoists' recruitment drive, and by 2001, the insurgency had spread to forty-five of Nepal's seventy-five districts.

The Maoist insurgency unfolded in two broad stages: from 1996 to 2001 and from 2001 to 2006. In the first phase, the Maoists were confronted by the state police force, augmented by the Armed Police Force, raised under Girija Prasad Koirala's prime ministership in February 2001.[6] The Maoists fought with rudimentary weapons, using a guerrilla warfare strategy. In the course of their fighting, they expanded their cadres and areas of operations, strengthened their organization, established base areas, and developed some institutions of governance, such as "kangaroo courts."[7]

The Maoists described this stage of their "people's war" as being the outcome of six strategic plans, namely "decentralized actions within centralized plan and command; balance between political and military offensives against the enemy; political justification of military action and military justification of political action; utilization of the contradictions amongst the enemies to isolate the main enemy; organization and mobilization of the masses in the quickest and best possible way" (RIM 2001). The main targets of the Maoists' violence were the party governments of the NC and the UML, police stations, and the active cadres of the ruling parties. Property of ruling party cadres was forcibly taken and their lands distributed among the Maoists' cadres, supporters, and sympathizers.

The government repression unleashed against the Maoists could have been far bloodier had the army been deployed. However, King Birendra did

6. Prime Minister Koirala raised the Armed Police Force because the king had refused to let the army be used in operations against the Maoists and because Koirala saw the existing police force as completely inadequate to meet the Maoist challenge. Initially, there were plans to build a joint military and police force, but the army refused to be part of any such paramilitary outfit. Establishing the Armed Police Force allegedly doubled police expenditures for arms and recruitment (Hachhethu 2004).

7. Kangaroo courts were one of the hallmarks of the Maoists' parallel governance structure, whereby they set up their own judicial system that expeditiously handed out verdicts and punishments. In 2007, upon signing the Comprehensive Peace Accord, the Maoists agreed to dismantle these courts, but the leadership in Nepal's southeastern city of Biratnagar reneged by resuming their operation (*Times of India* 2007).

not let this happen. Known for his comparatively liberal views, Birendra emphasized a political approach instead. He established clandestine contacts with the Maoists through his younger brother Dhirendra and even arranged to have direct talks with them. The Maoist leader Prachanda disclosed this engagement years later, in 2010: "Birendra's youngest brother Dhirendra was in touch with us, and we were to start direct talks with him (King Birendra) within a month with the request to abdicate his throne and become the country's first president. He was killed in this backdrop" (Parashar 2010). Analysts in Nepal also see King Birendra's reluctance to deploy the army against the Maoists as a reflection of his frustration with the way the political parties were managing the insurgency. Also, the possibility of his maneuvering the Maoist insurgency to weaken and discredit the political parties cannot be ruled out. The Maoists considered King Birendra an ally. They never criticized him during the first phase of the "people's war," and they deeply lamented the royal massacre that killed him and his family on June 1, 2001. On the sixth day after the royal massacre, the Maoist leader Bhattarai said this in an open letter published in the local Nepali newspaper *Kantipur:*

> Whatever your political ideology might be, one thing every honest Nepali nationalist has to agree with is this: King Birendra's liberal political ideology and his patriotism were seen as his weaknesses and had become a crime in the eyes of the expansionist and imperialist powers . . . his unwillingness to mobilize the army—which has a tradition of loyalty towards the King—to curb the People's revolution taking place under the leadership of the Nepal Communist Party (Maoist) became his biggest crime. . . . Some Marxist pundits, based on this, called us a pro-monarchist party, and we can now say that we—UNCP (Maoist) and King Birendra—had similar views on many national issues and this had created in fact an informal alliance between us. (Bhattarai 2001)

The mutually supportive relationship between the monarchy and the Maoists was drastically altered after the royal massacre, which also marked the onset of the second phase of the insurgency and a radical shift in the character of the Nepali monarchy. The new king, Gyanendra, fast acquired more powers at the cost of representative institutions. In May 2002, less than a year after his crowning following the massacre of his brother's entire family, Gyanendra dismissed Parliament. After three years, in February 2005, he subsumed all executive powers under his direct control. Hoping to exploit the post-9/11 international mood against terrorism, he set aside his predecessor's considerations and deployed the army to deal with the Maoists. He succeeded in mobilizing military support from India, the United States, and the UK but could not dent the spirit of the Maoists. The army was ill prepared to fight a guerrilla war against a determined enemy, but the extent and intensity of violence on both sides significantly escalated as a result of the army's deployment. Independent estimates by the Informal Sector Service Centre, a Kathmandu-based NGO, calculated more than thirteen thousand people killed in the conflict between February 13, 1996, and April 24, 2006. Two-thirds of the killings were attributed to the Royal Nepal Army (RNA), and one-third to the Maoists (Conflict Study Centre 2006).[8] The brutality of this conflict has left a legacy of bitterness in the issues to be resolved in the post-2006 political and social reconstruction, including those related to truth and reconciliation and to integration of the Maoist cadres into the Nepal army.

It was this use of the army in crushing the Maoist insurgency that made the RNA and the Maoists enemies. There are no indications of hostility between them until the end of King Birendra's regime in 2001. The army's introduction into the conflict did not lead to the defeat of the Maoists. At best, it created a stalemate, in which the army could defend its cantonments but could not move out and take the fight to the Maoists in rural or urban areas.

The RNA's inability to deal with the Maoists paralleled the overall structural weaknesses of the Nepali state. The state was primarily feudal, with the institutions of parliamentary democracy reduced to a mere facade. From this emanated the contradictions between the monarchy and the state's representative component (i.e., the political parties). The unrealistic distribution of power between the two, being skewed heavily in favor of the monarchy, allowed the insurgency to grow. The king's unspecified patronage of the Maoists during the initial years and the dispute between the king and Prime Minister Koirala over using the army against the Maoists further widened the divide. Then, after the palace massacre of June 2001, which altered the character of the monarchy and made it unpopular, the Nepali state's difficulties grew.[9] King Gynanedra's moves to push the state toward authoritarianism isolated the monarchy from the political parties and the people. The king also isolated himself from the international community, particularly India and the United States, by his persistent refusal to take the political parties along in the fight against the Maoists. In his authoritarian zeal, he wrongly assumed that the international community would simply endorse his actions in the name of fighting terrorism. While doing so, he overlooked the fact that his army—indeed, the state's entire security struc-

8. The estimates of total deaths during the insurgency have since been revised, raising the figure to eighteen thousand (*Economist* 2011). There are no reliable estimates of the numbers killed by the Maoist insurgents versus by the state's security forces.

9. In the June 2001 palace massacre, King Birendra, his crown prince, and most other family members were killed. This brought to the throne his brother Gyanendra, a hard-liner who wanted to restore the assertive character of the monarchy, as his father, King Mahendra, had done in 1960 (Lecomte-Tilouine and Gellner 2004).

ture—was incapable of facing the insurgency, due to the lack of training, equipment, and experience. To cover its failures (even after increasing its size), the RNA indulged in ruthless and indiscriminate use of force, inviting charges of human rights violations. These charges further isolated the king and his state from the Nepali people, in turn strengthening the Maoists and the popular resistance against him. It also resulted in facilitating the ordinary people's and the political parties' endorsement of the Maoists' demands to restructure the RNA and integrate the People's Liberation Army cadres into the state security structure. This situation created new and extreme concerns about the state of civil-military relations in Republican Nepal.

The second phase of the insurgency, which began in 2001, was significant in two respects. While it isolated the monarchy and exposed the limits of the army's capacity to deal with the Maoists, it also brought about a shift in the Maoists' "people's war" strategy. By 2002–03, the Maoists had realized that they had reached a strategic balance with the RNA but could not achieve total victory. To exploit the emerging conflict between King Gyanendra's growing power and the political parties, the Maoists initiated their "united front" strategy with the parties. Under this strategy, the Maoists projected their movement to India and the international community as a genuine effort to transform Nepal socioeconomically, with the ultimate goal of removing the monarchy. King Gyanendra's coup and assumption of direct power in February 2005 greatly facilitated this strategy. It also gave rise to the Twelve-Point Understanding signed between the Maoists and the mainstream political parties, which had come together as the SPA.[10] In this understanding, the Maoists abandoned their "people's war," and the political parties agreed to create a "new Nepal" based on inclusive democracy.[11] Nepal's Jan Andolan-II, a peaceful nineteen-day people's struggle led by the Maoists and the mainstream parties in April 2006, was the result of this Twelve-Point Understanding. The monarchy was finally eliminated by the popularly elected Constituent Assembly through an amendment in the Interim Constitution in 2008.

Conclusion

Insurgencies grow from the fertile ground of socioeconomic deprivation and discrimination, though not all such injustice leads to rebellion. Political catalysts and forces of history intervene to transform social misery into

10. The SPA formed in 2005, after the King's coup in February 2005, to resist monarchy's autocratic actions. The parties included were the Nepali Congress, Nepali Congress (Democratic), UML, Nepal Workers and Peasants Party, Nepal Sadbhavana [Goodwill] Party, United Left Front, and Jan Morcha [People's Front].

11. Author's interviews with a number of leaders of the Maoists, the Nepali Congress, and the UML during 2005–06 and later.

popular turbulence and uprising. In Nepal, the Maoists played the role of political catalyst. They emerged because the feudal state had become an impediment to the rising aspirations of the Nepalese people and because the political parties, which had promised to steer socioeconomic change and transformation following the revival of democracy in 1990, proved insincere and inadequate to the challenge. The state also remained engaged in political manipulation in its quest to maintain the status quo. The immediate triggers for the insurgency were the political alienation of the Maoists in the 1994 elections and repressive actions against them thereafter. To be sure, the Maoists' "two-line struggle" may have led them to a people's movement regardless, but the state's behavior, at the very least, hastened the outcome.

The Maoists have projected a vision of a "new Nepal" and demonstrated the political will to translate this vision into reality, but they have not yet managed to shed convincingly their dependence on extremist methods or their outdated notions about political and social structures' capacity to cope with and sustain the desired transformation. The Maoists' emergence has seriously disturbed the prevailing power structure in Nepal. The deepening wedge between the Maoists and the political parties has paralyzed the post–Jan Andolan-II peace process, without which neither stability nor lasting peace can occur, nor can the vision of a new Nepal take any concrete shape.

Will the Maoists go back to the jungle and revive their "people's war" to bring their frustrated revolution about? This possibility is highly unlikely even though the new Maoist wing headed by Baidya has kept the option of reviving the "people's war" open. The Maoists recognize that they have made real gains, both political and ideological, even though these gains fall short of their ideals. There is also the realization that neither Nepal and its people nor the international community wants another "people's war" to get off the ground. The new party program endorsed by Prachanda and Bhattarai's Unified Communist Party of Nepal in February 2013, after Baidya and his hard-line supporters split, amply reflects this realization.[12] The only way this may change and lead Baidya to take up arms against his former party and disrupt peace and stability in Nepal will be if the already seriously disrupted constitution-making process breaks down completely.[13] Barring that possibility, there is reason for cautious optimism.

12. During February 6–8, 2013, the Maoists led by Prachanda and Bhattarai held the seventh General Convention of their party after a gap of twenty-one years, in the town of Hetauda. At the convention, the Maoists reiterated their faith in democracy and peaceful struggle and adopted as their goal "a new capitalist revolution," after the fashion of Chinese leader Deng Xiaoping (Dahal 2013).

13. The elected Constituent Assembly was dissolved in May 2013 for lack of a consensus among major political parties on some of the key constitutional issues, such as federalism. A new election was called.

*This chapter draws in part on S.D. Muni, "The Maoist Insurgency in Nepal: Origin and Evolution," working paper (Singapore: National University of Singapore, Institute of South Asian Studies, 2010).

References

Adhikari, K. K. 1977. "Particulars Relating to the Massacre that Occurred in Kathmandu between the 14th and 15th of September 1846." *Voice of History* 3: 31–39.

Bhattarai, Baburam. 2001. "The Letter of Dr. Baburam Bhattarai on the Palace Massacre in Nepal." *Kantipur*, June 21.

———. 2003. *The Nature of Underdevelopment and Regional Structure of Nepal: A Marxist Analysis.* New Delhi: Adroit.

Conflict Study Center. 2006. "Ratification of International Criminal Court to Just Peace." Situation Update VIII, Sept. 15. www.icc.inseconline.org/download/CS%20Center_Situation%20Update%20VIII.pdf.

Dahal, Phanindra. 2013. "Maoist Party Branching Out Its Base, Transformation from Cadre-Based Party to Mass-Based One." *Ekantipur*, Feb. 7. www.ekantipur.com/2013/02/07/national/maoist-party-branching-out-its-base/366711.html.

Economist. 2011. "Peace, in Your Own Time." Nov. 5. www.economist.com/node/21536635.

Gaige, Frederick H. 1975. *Regionalism and National Unity in Nepal.* Berkeley: Univ. of California Press.

Gersony, Robert. 2004. "Western Nepal Conflict Assessment: History and Dynamics of the Maoist Revolt." International Resources Group Discussion Forum no. 15, Mar. www.irgltd.com/Resources/Discussion_Forum/DF15_Nepal_Maoist_Revolt-03-04.pdf.

Gurung, Harka. 2004. "Rastriyata re Rajniti" [Nationality and politics]. In *Nepal ko Sandarbh ma Samaj Shastriya Chintan* [Social Science thoughts in the context of Nepal], ed. Mary des Chene and Pratyoush Onta. Lalitpur, Nepal: Himal Books.

Hachhethu, Krishna. 2004. "The Nepali State and the Maoist Insurgency, 1996–2001." In *Himalayan People's War: Nepal's Maoist Rebellion,* ed. Michael Hutt. Bloomington, IN: Indiana Univ. Press.

Hutt, Michael. 2004. "Monarchy, Democracy, and Maoism in Nepal." In *Himalayan People's War: Nepal's Maoist Rebellion,* ed. Michael Hutt, 1–20. Bloomington, IN: Indiana Univ. Press.

International Crisis Group (ICG). 2005. "Nepal's Maoists: Their Aims, Structure and Strategy." Asia Report no. 104, Oct. 27. www.crisisgroup.org/en/regions/

asia/south-asia/nepal/104-nepals-maoists-their-aims-structure-and-strategy.aspx.

———. 2007a. "Nepal's Maoists: Purists or Pragmatists?" Asia Report no. 132, May 18. www.crisisgroup.org/en/regions/asia/south-asia/nepal/132-nepals-maoists-purists-or-pragmatists.aspx.

———. 2007b. "Nepal's Troubled Terai Region." Asia Report no. 136, July 9. www.crisisgroup.org/~/media/Files/asia/south-asia/nepal/136_nepal_s_troubled_tarai_region.ashx.

Karki, Arjun, and David Seddon. 2003. "The People's War in Historical Context." In *The People's War in Nepal: Left Perspectives,* ed. Arjun Karki and David Seddon. New Delhi: Adroit.

Khadka, Narayan. 1986. "Crisis in Nepal's Partyless Panchayat System: The Case for More Democracy." *Pacific Affairs* 59 (3): 429–54.

Lawoti, Mahendra, and Anup Kumar Pahari, eds. 2009. *The Maoist Insurgency in Nepal: Revolution in the Twenty-First Century.* Oxon, UK: Routledge.

Lecomte-Tilouine, Marie, and David N. Gellner. 2004. "Regicide and Maoist Revolutionary Warfare in Nepal: Modern Incarnations of a Warrior Kingdom." *Anthropology Today* 20 (1): 13–19.

Lohani, S. C. 1969. "The Birth of Rana Feudalism in Nepal." *Ancient Nepal* no. 8 (July): 46–49.

Manchanda, Rita. 2004. "Maoist Insurgency in Nepal: Radicalizing Gender Narratives." *Cultural Dynamics* 16 (2–3): 237–58.

Mikesell, Stephen Lawrence. 1999. *Class, State, and Struggle in Nepal.* New Delhi: Manohar.

Miklian, Jason. 2009. "Nepal's Terai: Constructing an Ethnic Conflict." South Asia Briefing Paper no. 1, International Peace Research Institute of Oslo. http://file.prio.no/Publication_files/Prio/Nepal's%20Terai%20(South%20Asia%20Briefing%20Paper%201).pdf.

Muni, S. D. 2003. *Maoist Insurgency in Nepal: The Challenge and the Response.* New Delhi: Rupa.

———. 2012. "Bringing the Maoists Down from the Hills: India's Role." In *Nepal in Transition: From People's War to Fragile Peace,* ed. Sebastian von Einsiedel, David M. Malone, and Suman Pradhan. New York: Cambridge Univ. Press.

Parashar, Utpal. 2010. "Prachanda Blames India for Nepal's Palace Massacre." *Hindustan Times,* Jan. 10. www.hindustantimes.com/world-news/Nepal/Prachanda-blames-India-for-Nepal-s-palace-massacre/Article1-495957.aspx.

Prachanda (Pushpa Kamal Dahal). 1999. Interview by Li Onesto. *Revolutionary Worker* no. 1043, Feb. 20.

Ramirez, Philippe. 1997. "Pour une Anthropologie Religieuse du Maoïsme Népalais." *Archives de Sciences Sociales des Religions* 42 (99): 47–68.

Regmi, M. C. 1999. *Imperial Gorkha.* New Delhi: Adroit.

Revolutionary Internationalist Movement (RIM). 2001. "Comrade Prachanda." *A World to Win,* no. 27. www.humanrights.de/doc_en/archiv/n/nepal/politics/170202_interview_pra.htm.

Shah, Akanshya. 2012. "Nepal: Hard Choices for Prachanda." Observer Research Foundation, Mar. 19. www.orfonline.org/cms/sites/orfonline/modules/analysis/AnalysisDetai.htm.

Shakya, Sujeev. 2009. *Unleashing Nepal: Past, Present and Future of the Economy.* New Delhi: Penguin.

Sharma, Pitamber. 2008. *Unravelling the Mosaic: Spatial Aspects of Ethnicity in Nepal.* Kathmandu: Himal Books.

Sharma, Sudheer. 2004. "The Maoist Movement: An Evolutionary Perspective." In *Himalayan People's War: Nepal's Maoist Rebellion,* ed. Michael Hutt, 38–57. Bloomington, IN: Indiana Univ. Press.

Singh, Amrish. 2011. "Dissertation on Terai Discrimination." PhD dissertation, School of International Studies, Jawaharlal Nehru Univ.

South Asia Terrorism Portal (SATP). 2012. "Incidents Involving Communist Party of Nepal-Maoist 2012." Apr. 15. www.satp.org/satporgtp/countries/nepal/terroristoutfits/cpn_2012.htm#.

Thapa, Deepak. 2002. "The Maobadi of Nepal." In *State of Nepal,* ed. Kanak M. Dixit and Shastri Ramachandaran. Kathmandu: Himal Books.

———. 2004. "Radicalism and the Emergence of the Maoists." In *Himalayan People's War: Nepal's Maoist Rebellion,* ed. Michael Hutt, 21–37. Bloomington, IN: Indiana Univ. Press.

Thapa, Deepak, and Bandita Sijapati. 2005. *A Kingdom under Siege: Nepal's Maoist Insurgency, 1996–2004.* London: Zed Books.

Times of India. 2007. "Nepal Maoists to Resume 'Kangaroo Courts.'" Nov. 22. http://articles.timesofindia.indiatimes.com/2007-11-22/rest-of-world/27978895_1_nepal-maoists-parallel-government-kangaroo-court.

Upreti, Bishnu. 2009. "Challenges in the Post-Election Scenario in Nepal." *Economic and Political Weekly* 44 (11).

Yami, Hisila [Comrade Parvati]. 2010. "Women's Role in the Nepalese Movement: Making a People's Constitution." *Monthly Review,* Mar. 8. http://mrzine.monthlyreview.org/2010/yami080310.html.

7

Nepal's Response to the Armed Insurgency, and Its Political Settlement

Bishnu Raj Upreti

For a decade (1996–2006), Nepal faced a bloody armed conflict that decimated the country's infrastructure, paralyzed governing apparatuses, subjected the population to grave human rights violations, and resulted in the deaths of over thirteen thousand people (INSEC 2009). The armed insurgency was rooted in the frustrations with Nepal's ancient, autocratic political and social systems. These systems centralized power and prevented reforms that could correct the social and political exclusion, discrimination, poverty, and subordination in Nepalese society (B. R. Upreti 2004a). Officially, the armed conflict ended with the signing of the Comprehensive Peace Agreement (CPA), which not only brought the UCPN (M) into mainstream politics but also paved the path for the fundamental transformation of the Nepali state. This chapter highlights the different approaches the state used to respond to the armed insurrection, the developments during the different phases of the conflict, the negotiation processes that marked the entire period, and the role of international actors in dealing with Nepal's insurgency. The insights and lessons gathered can be useful for

---

This chapter benefits from the research conducted as part of the Institutions, Governance and Conflict Transformation research program of the National Centre of Competence in Research (NCCR) North-South. Thank you, NCCR North-South, for providing a congenial environment for preparing this chapter.

other countries facing insurgencies. Some of the important lessons derived from the following analysis include using a combination of political, military, and economic approaches; being flexible and open in exploring alternatives; using negotiation as a learning process; sharing power; mobilizing informal facilitators and mediators; dealing with people's expectations; dealing with human rights issues; dealing with actual and perceived risks; using context assessment as part of the response strategies; and engaging proactively with international actors. Most of these issues are recognized to be part of the conflict resolution and broader peacebuilding toolkits. Using them in the right combinations and at the most appropriate times during a conflict is key.

The Context

The decade-long armed insurgency waged by the UCPN (M) officially began in February 1996 and ended on November 21, 2006. It altered the entire political landscape of Nepal (UNDP 2009). During the insurgency, more than 109 armed groups emerged, the proliferation of small arms dramatically weakened human security and increased crime, and the society adopted a radical culture of violence (B. R. Upreti 2010; Upreti and Nepali 2006). The insecurity and instability resulting from the insurgency exacerbated episodes of civil unrest and grave human rights violations (Amnesty International 2005; INSEC 2007; ICG 2005a).

Despite these negative developments, the insurgency and the People's Movement of April 2006 offered a tremendous opportunity for fundamental political and social transformation in Nepal. The nearly two-and-a-half-century-old monarchy was toppled, and Nepal was ultimately declared a republic.

The conceptual framework in figure 7.1 provides an overview of the linkages between major components of the armed conflict and its settlement. It highlights a common conceptual thread that holds together the different aspects discussed in this chapter.

Most analysts and researchers agree that the underlying causes of Nepal's armed insurgency are complex and interrelated.[1] The Nepalese state has long been hindered by a weak governing system, high levels of corruption and nepotism, ethnic and social discrimination, skewed power distributions, and a dysfunctional public sector. Economic inequality and poverty helped escalate the political crises, and the lack of visionary leadership and

1. See Baechler et al. 2008; B. R. Upreti 2006; Thapa and Sijapati 2003; Onesto 2005; Raj 2004; Mahat 2005; Mackinlay and B. R. Upreti 2003; Karki and Seddon 2003; Hutt 2004; Galtung 2004; and Bhattarai 2004.

Figure 7.1. Conceptual Framework

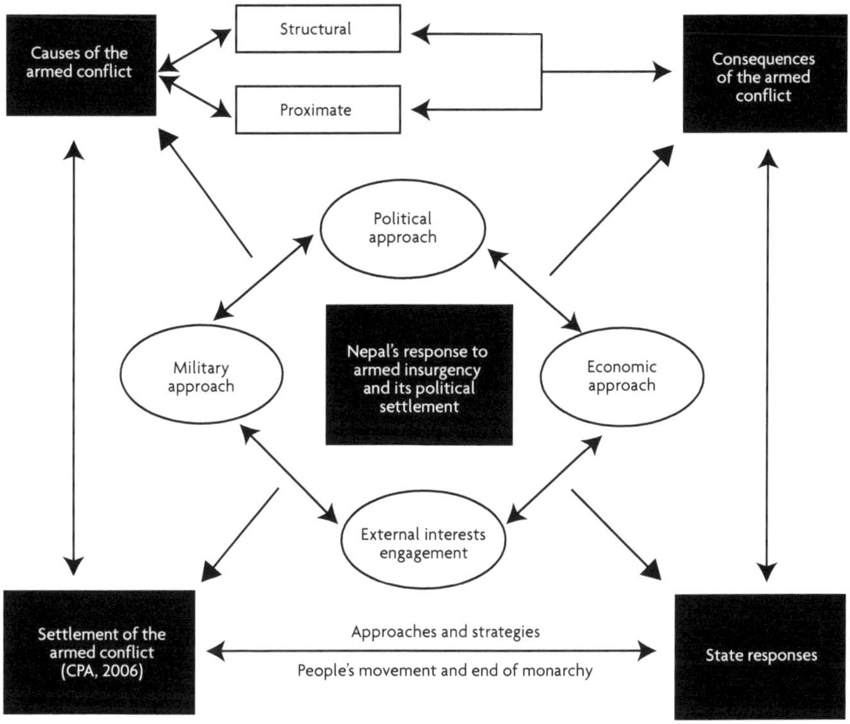

political integrity, a conflict-insensitive media sector, misplaced involvement by international actors, and a severely divided civil society all had direct bearing on the insurgency and its eventual settlement. The UCPN (M) exploited these divisions between rich and poor, oppressors and oppressed, exploiters and exploited, landlords and landless, and bourgeoisie and proletariat to gain popular support. However, once the insurgency was under way, the UCPN (M) changed course and focused its efforts on engendering support from ethnic groups by appealing to their frustrations over restrictions on the right to self-determination.

State Responses to the Insurrection: Dynamics and Approaches

The decade-long insurgency passed through four phases, which are distinct in the severity of the conflict, strategies used by the government and the UCPN (M), and efforts made to negotiate peace. They cover the crisis and war stages on Michael Lund's conflict curve, as well as the post-conflict stabilization phase (Lund 1996, 38–39):

- first phase (February 1996 to November 23, 2001): low-intensity conflict and no mobilization of the army
- second phase (November 24, 2001, to January 2005): high-intensity conflict and mobilization of army
- third phase (February 1, 2005, to November 21, 2006): royal takeover, direct rule by the king, and popular movement against the king
- fourth phase (November 22, 2006, onward): postinsurgency period that began with the signing of the CPA

First Phase (February 13, 1996, to November 23, 2001)

On February 13, 1996, the UCPN (M) initiated violence against the state and the landed elite by raiding police outposts in Rolpa, Rukum, and Sindhuli districts, attacking government offices and seizing landlords' properties. Their aim was to abolish the monarchy and establish a "people's republic" in Nepal.

During the first phase, the state's underestimation of the UCPN (M)'s strength and ability to exploit state weakness while promoting Maoist ideology contributed to the insurgency's rapid growth. The state struggled to determine whether the attacks signified a growing political movement or were merely sporadic acts of terrorism. Consequently, it failed to devise appropriate response strategies and actions to deal with the armed conflict. The state authorities initially brushed off the UCPN (M)'s cause as the unrealistic ambitions of a small radical group to impose an outdated ideology in Nepal.

The state's initial response, emphasizing brute force, was counterproductive. Without formally mobilizing the army, police conducted operations such as Operation Kilo Sierra 2 and 3; Operation Cordon, Search and Destroy; Operation Jungle Search; Operation Delta; and Operation Chakravyuh against the insurgents. These operations ended up suppressing all sectors of society without distinguishing ordinary citizens from UCPN (M) supporters. The home minister and his loyal district administration offices enlisted the police and targeted those who did not support the ruling party, the Nepali Congress (NC) (Thapa and Sijapati 2003). Later, the government also created a paramilitary Armed Police Force to fight the insurgents.[2] As a result of these actions, local grievances against the state expanded and drove much of the population into the arms of the

2. The army was unhappy with this change since its interest lay in strengthening itself, not in diffusing its role. But the military was not formally mobilized to fight the insurgency, and the police force alone was not adequate to the task. This was the official reason cited for creating a paramilitary force.

UCPN (M). In 2000, the state also created an integrated security and development program (ISDP) to disguise military surveillance in some of the insurgency-affected districts (Karki and Seddon, 2003; B. R. Upreti 2004b). The program was quickly withdrawn, however, in the face of opposition from the insurgency-affected districts (B. R. Upreti 2006).

In this phase, only a few genuine political efforts attempted to settle the insurgency. The state vehemently objected to the UCPN (M)'s demands that Nepal be declared a republic via constituent assembly elections. Instead, the government was committed to the twin pillars of multiparty democracy and constitutional monarchy as nonnegotiable guiding principles. Hence, there was little to discuss while these maximalist positions remained intact (S. Sharma 2003; Raj 2004). Even when the government set up a task force in 1997 to suggest possible ways of resolving the armed insurrection, it did not implement the task force's suggestions of exploring primarily political avenues (B. R. Upreti 2006).[3] The same fate befell the recommendations by the government-established High Level Committee to Provide Suggestions to Solve the Maoist Problems. Set up under the guidance of former prime minister Sher Bahadur Deuba (of NC) in 2000, the committee concluded that the insurgency was the result of a weak government system and recommended that the social and economic structures of the state be revamped (B. R. Upreti 2004a).

After six years of violent insurgent fighting, a cease-fire was declared on July 25, 2001, two days after Sher Bahadur Deuba again became prime minister. At that time, the country was attempting to recover from the devastating June 1, 2001, royal massacre, in which the popular King Birendra was killed inside the palace, along with several members of the royal family.[4] The UCPN (M) argued that the royal massacre signified the end of Nepal's traditional monarchy and that it was time to institutionalize the republican system. In this context, the new king, Birendra's brother Gyanendra, was struggling to establish his own legitimacy and believed that the cease-fire could impress the people with the image of a tolerant monarchy.

Sher Bahadur Deuba came to power intent on solving the problem of the Maoist insurgency. The new prime minister wanted to demonstrate his commitment to a political settlement of the conflict. However, he had come to power at a time when relations between the civilian government and the army were extremely tense; Deuba's predecessor, Girija Prasad Koirala, had

3. In April 1997, Prime Minister Sher Bahadur Deuba formed the Working Committee for the Study of Maoist Activities and Finding Solutions, led by Prem Singh Dhami, a member of Parliament. This committee was also known as the Dhami Commission.

4. Prince Dipendra committed the royal massacre, killing nine other members of the royal family and, later, himself.

resigned, citing noncooperation of the RNA. Deuba, in a quest to bring stability to civil-military relations, sought to mend fences. He was related to many senior army officers, which allowed him to move successfully in this direction (B. R. Upreti 2004a; Raj 2004).

With the cease-fire in place, Deuba initiated a dialogue with the UCPN (M). The first round of negotiations began on August 30, 2001, at the Godavari Resort in Kathmandu and concluded without discussing any specific political agenda following the introductory meeting. The second round of negotiations was held in Thakurdwar, Bardiya district, on September 13–14, 2001. The UCPN (M) raised issues concerning the process of institutionalizing the republican system, suspending the present constitution, and authorizing a new constitution (B. R. Upreti 2006).

At these negotiations, the UCPN (M) negotiators also made a proposal for the release of their imprisoned comrades, clarification of the condition of disappeared cadres, withdrawal of the ISDP, dissolution of the Armed Police Force, and demobilization of the RNA. They also demanded an interim government and the development of a new constitution through the constituent assembly (B. R. Upreti 2006). Government negotiators, however, were still wedded to the twin-pillar theory of multiparty democracy and constitutional monarchy (S. Sharma 2003; B. R. Upreti 2004a). A deadlock led the UCPN (M) to withdraw from the negotiations on November 21, and it declared an end to the cease-fire on November 23, 2001. The primary cause of the cease-fire's breakdown was an impasse over the issue of the constitutional assembly (S. Sharma 2003). Further, the UCPN (M) leaders were deeply suspicious of the government's intent, convinced that the government sought to encircle and destroy them during the declared cease-fire.

Ultimately, both sides used the cease-fire period as a strategic pause to strengthen their political and war-fighting capabilities. Specifically, the UCPN (M) used the time to strengthen its political and military positions and to weaken the monarchy by leading a national debate on the conventional monarchy's irrelevance since the royal massacre. In pursuing the former, it formed the United Revolutionary People's Council, established the People's Liberation Army, declared nine regions of Nepal autonomous, and began constructing parallel state structures (B. R. Upreti 2004a, 2009). The UCPN (M) launched effective attacks on army camps in Dang district and acquired weapons a mere three days after the cease-fire ended. The UCPN (M) was also successful in helping its cadres escape from prisons. The cease-fire and attempted negotiations also formally introduced the UCPN (M)'s agenda to the government and enabled it to emerge as a legitimate political force (B. R. Upreti 2004a; Thapa and Sijapati 2003). They also revived, strengthened, and renewed their political linkages.

The government, too, used the cease-fire for strategic purposes. It formulated and implemented ISDP in eight districts, arrested several UCPN (M) cadres, established the paramilitary Armed Police Force, and arranged the transfer of arms and security forces to areas where support for the UCPN (M) was high (B. R. Upreti 2004a, 2004b). Specifically, it transferred a large number of weapons to Ghorahi, in Dang district, during the cease-fire and later used them in attacks against the Maoists (B. R. Upreti 2004a; Thapa and Sijapati 2003).

Second Phase (November 23, 2001, to January 31, 2005)

The second phase of the insurgency differed from the first in both strategy and action. It was during this phase that the state mobilized the army to fight the insurgency. Before then, the state avoided introducing the army, relying only on the police in an effort to portray the insurgency as a mere law-and-order issue (B. R. Upreti 2004a). But after the breakdown of the cease-fire, the state's strategy depended largely on the military protection of the civilian government (B. R. Upreti 2006).

Immediately after the cease-fire broke down on November 23, 2001, the UCPN (M) declared its support for a "national people's government" and launched major violent attacks in Dang, Syanga, and Solukhumbu districts. In response, on November 26, the king declared a state of emergency (B. R. Upreti 2004a). The government introduced the Terrorist and Destructive Activities Control and Punishment Ordinance and designated the UCPN (M), its sister organizations, and supporters as terrorists. This action opened the path to the use of harsh military tactics, which the state employed from late November 2001 to early January 2003.

Fierce fighting between state security forces and the UCPN (M) led to a second cease-fire on January 29, 2003. Again both sides used the cease-fire as a strategic pause to recuperate from the intense fighting of the past two years and strengthen their positions (B. R. Upreti 2006). The government paved the way for a cease-fire after sending a letter to the UCPN (M), stating that it was ready to discuss their three-point demand (roundtable conference, interim government, and the election for a constituent assembly). The real motivation for bringing the rebels to the negotiating table was the monarchy's desire to legitimize the king's direct rule. King Gyanendra believed that if he could successfully forge a settlement, the subsequent wave of public approval would enable him to assert direct rule more easily (B. R. Upreti 2006).

Three months into the cease-fire, the first official talks took place at the Shankar Hotel in Kathmandu. The UCPN (M) was well prepared and had a skillful negotiating team (B. R. Upreti 2004a). Its principal agenda was the election of a constituent assembly. The party also submitted a plan to restructure the state in order to more effectively address social, political, economic, and cultural oppression. But little progress was made because neither party offered any concessions.

A second round of negotiations began on May 9, 2003, to discuss procedural issues. The state agreed to limit the army's operations within a three-mile radius of its bases and to release three central leaders of the UCPN (M) from jail (B. R. Upreti 2004a). But in limiting the army's mobility, the government took a huge political risk that proved costly. On May 30, 2003, the government collapsed following Prime Minister Lokendra Bahadur Chand's resignation, and negotiations were sidelined. On June 5, the king appointed another royal-loyalist as the new prime minister, and two ministers were immediately appointed as government negotiators (B. R. Upreti 2006).

The third round of negotiations took place during August 15–17, 2003, in the Hapure Village of Dang district. The meetings were based on a substantive agenda put forward by both parties. But both remained rigid in their stance on the issue of a constitutional assembly. The government stuck to its positions: sovereignty inherent in the people, constitutional monarchy (it would not agree on any measures that threatened the institution of the monarchy), democracy, and the safeguarding and strengthening of the national territorial integrity and unity (B. R. Upreti 2004a; Hutt 2004). These points undermined the most basic UCPN (M) demand of abolition of the constitutional monarchy. Further complicating the impasse, the army killed seventeen unarmed UCPN (M) cadres and two of their supporters in Doramba village of Ramechhap district (Amnesty International 2005). This situation made it impossible to get both parties back on track for political negotiations (B. R. Upreti 2006).

The second cease-fire ended on August 27, 2003, following a declaration by the UCPN (M) that the government had failed to find an amicable political solution. The UCPN (M) blamed the government—and the army in particular—for arresting and killing UCPN (M) cadres. Moreover, one procedural problem with negotiations during the second phase was the lack of any written documentation of each party's commitment to a political resolution to the dispute.

The government frequently demonstrated its resolve to maintain the status quo and ignore the UCPN (M)'s requests for social, economic, and governance reforms. For one, despite cross-party support for limiting the army's operations within civilian population centers, the government, facing significant pressure from military leaders, revised its initial pledge to draw down army operations. Consequently, UCPN (M) negotiators lost confidence in the government's commitment to the negotiation process and resumed aggressive operations under the assumption that the army would never accept a political settlement (B. R. Upreti 2006). Also, on October 4, 2002, the king thrust himself directly into active politics, suggesting that the central government did not intend to address the country's fundamental governance problems and feudal structures. Observing the negotiation process, Johan Galtung commented, "In Nepal we have negotiation process, although I am not quite convinced that it has started touching the real problems. . . . To touch the military is very difficult but we can make the other force much stronger. Now the first issue deals with the condition that the Maoists give up some of their demands, but the question is whether the king will give up some of his demands. My reading of it is that the Maoists have been more forthcoming . . ." (Galtung 2004, 115–16).

The UCPN (M) believed that senior officials of Nepal's army were under the direct command of the king, who was backed by international powers, such as India, the United States, and the UK, and wanted to continue the war instead of finding a negotiated settlement (B. R. Upreti 2004a). This feeling was reflected in a statement by the UCPN (M) spokesperson, published in the *Kathmandu Post:* "The king must not lead the army and around 200 military officials should resign from their respective posts. . . . There is no constitutional monarchy as the king has control over the army" (J. Pandey 2004).

The brief suspension in fighting did not generate a sustainable peace agreement, but it once again gave both the UCPN (M) and the government ample time and space to bolster their political and fighting capacities. The government bought weapons from India, the United States, and other countries, trained its security forces in counterinsurgency and anti–guerrilla warfare tactics, and recruited new military personnel (B. R. Upreti 2006). The government also amassed intelligence on the insurgents' activities, bases, military strengths, and network of supporters. The negotiations also allowed the state to physically identify many UCPN (M) leaders and cadres (Thapa and Sijapati 2003; B. R. Upreti 2006). And the UCPN (M) benefited from the cease-fire when its cadres were released from prisons and the legal cases against them were dropped. This situation left security forces very dissatisfied with the government. The UCPN (M) used this dissatisfaction to its advantage, sowing confusion concerning the government's confidence in the security forces (B. R. Upreti 2004a). The UCPN (M) also strengthened public relations with the business community, media, political parties, and ordinary people and established and expanded relations with the international community, with the notable exception of India, which remained supportive of the monarchy (Bhattarai 2004; B. R. Upreti 2010). The UCPN (M) also successfully promoted political debate on the need for a constituent assembly. Since wider sections of society also supported this need, the Maoists gained considerable moral and political credibility while the state lost legitimacy in the eyes of the people.

Most importantly, the Maoists were able to improve their fighting capabilities through new recruitment, training, and massive mobilization across the country. Furthermore, in declaring unilateral cease-fires during national and religious festivals and at critical political moments (such as on September 3, 2005, just before the king's departure to attend the UN General Assembly meeting), the UCPN (M) earned public sympathy and endorsement (B. R. Upreti 2004a; Raj 2004).

Having bolstered the army's capacity, the government used various military means to defeat the UCPN (M). It created the Unified Command, an organizational structure aligning all security forces under the command of the army to fight the insurgency, and set up the Village Defense Forces, a force of vigilantes and criminals organized to fight UCPN (M) cadres and supporters. Additionally, the state attempted to weaken public support for the UCPN (M) by declaring bounties on the heads of UCPN (M) leaders, brutally suppressing communities sympathetic to the UCPN (M), torturing and detaining relatives of UCPN (M) members, and giving the military increasing clout over the civilian state apparatus. The state also tried to further delegitimize the UCPN (M) by linking it to the global fight against terrorism. "Red-corner notice" warrants were issued, and Interpol even captured UCPN (M) leaders. But rather than control the insurgency, these heavy-handed measures merely exacerbated the problem.

Third Phase (February 1, 2005, to November 21, 2006)

On February 1, 2005, King Gyanendra, backed by the military, led a coup to assume full control of the state. Previously, the king's role had extended only to dictating government and political processes, but after February 1, the king became head and sole authority of the government. The king cited the Parliament's "grand failure to contain violence, restore peace, control corruption, and improve the deteriorating economic situation of the country" as necessitating his assumption of power (Upreti, Pyakuryal, and Sharma 2008). In his speeches, public comments, and media interviews, the king vehemently expressed his dismay with the political parties. In his address explaining his takeover to the nation, the king referred to parliamentarians' abuse of authority to gain power and fulfill personal and communal interests of political parties at the expense of the nation and citizens. King Gyanendra stated, "We have, by virtue of the State Authority as exercised by us and in keeping with the spirit of the Constitution of the Kingdom of Nepal 1990, taking into consideration Article 27 (3) of the Constitution, dissolved, effective from today, the current Council of Ministers to fulfill the people's desire for the restoration of peace and security and to activate soon the democratic dispensation" (*Kathmandu Post* 2005). The king stressed that it was the duty of the royal dynasty to preserve the national unity of Nepal.

In retrospect, the king had miscalculated the people's wishes on how to achieve peace and his own ability to deliver it. Because he was keen on strengthening his direct rule and acquiring international support in the name of "the fight against terrorism," he relied too much on the security forces and coercion rather than on political negotiations (B. R. Upreti 2006). When the king dissolved the Parliament and extended his own authority, the parliamentary parties and the UCPN (M) signed a peace agreement to coalesce their resources against the king's autocratic rule. This new partnership dramatically altered the course of the conflict. The agreement ultimately led to a Twelve-Point Understanding between parliamentary parties and the UCPN (M), which was signed in New Delhi on November 21, 2005. This agreement was significant because it marked India's fresh alignment with antimonarchy parties. Previously, India had played an ambivalent role, supporting the government's fight against the UCPN (M) while also turning a blind eye to UCPN (M)'s activities within Indian territory. However, after the king took over all power, the relationship between New Delhi and the monarchy deteriorated and, in fact, quickly became confrontational. India stood against the king and facilitated meetings between the UCPN (M) and the SPA—the coalition of parties opposing the king's rule alongside the UCPN (M)—which laid the groundwork for the People's Movement, commonly known as Jan Andolan II. This movement sought to topple the king and resolve the ongoing armed conflict. These objectives were attainable once the relationship between the SPA and the UCPN (M) had transformed from competitive and adversarial to congenial (B. R. Upreti 2010).

In light of this unified opposition, the king tried to convince the international community to help him fight "terrorism" in Nepal. In his address to the SAARC Summit in Dhaka on November 12, 2005, he sharply criticized powerful nations for their failure to follow through on declarations against terrorism across the globe, especially in the context of weak countries vulnerable to the destabilizing effects of violent nonstate actors:

> We cannot make a distinction between good and bad terrorism; terrorism is terrorism. In our region, the Declaration of the 11th SAARC Summit held in Kathmandu categorically stated that "terrorism, in all its forms and manifestations, is a challenge to all states and to all of humanity, and cannot be justified on ideological, political, religious or any other ground." We agreed that "terrorism violates the fundamental values of the United Nations and the SAARC Charter and constitutes one of the most serious threats to international peace and security in the

> Twenty-first century." Nepal has ratified the SAARC Convention on Suppression of Terrorism and its Additional Protocol with the belief that these instruments provide an effective tool to counter terrorism in the region. We call upon the SAARC member states to forge a strong partnership to eliminate terrorism from the region as well as spearhead a coordinated and earnest action against it. (Upreti, Pyakuryal, and Sharma 2008, 38)

By highlighting the double standards and selective approach that governments took in dealing with global terrorism, the king was taking a swipe at the support that India was then giving the UCPN (M) and refuting the demand made by the international community to hand over power to Nepal's political parties (ICG 2005b; B. R. Upreti 2006).

The king's administration also made unsuccessful attempts to undermine democracy and strengthen his power using religion. He mobilized radical extremists and orthodox Hindu clerics to oppose progressive political forces. A former army chief, who was a staunch supporter of the king, publicly asked the government to declare political parties antinationalist forces. The vice chairman of King Gyanendra's cabinet said that monarchy and democracy in Nepal could not go together and that therefore the Nepalese people must choose one (ICG 2006; B. R. Upreti 2006).

The April 2006 peoples' resistance movement was another major development that contributed to settling the Nepalese civil war. The SPA called for a nationwide general strike (*Nepal bandh*) during April 6–9, and hundreds of thousands of people across the country responded through demonstrations in the streets. On April 5, the UCPN (M) declared a cease-fire in support of the general strike. Protesters organized mass rallies and dismantled the statues of the Shah kings (the royal dynasty) (ICG 2006). The royal government mobilized the Unified Command to prevent street protests. It used excessive force, including batons and firearms, to control the crowds. The government also imposed a day-and-night curfew with a shoot-on-sight order. When civil disobedience paralyzed the nation, the RNA used helicopters for surveillance against peaceful demonstrations in various parts of the country and directed ground troops to suppress them (B. R. Upreti 2006).[5] During nineteen days of peaceful protests, twenty-five people were killed and more than 5,500 were wounded. The government mobilized vigilantes, criminals, and pro-king youth on a massive scale to suppress the prodemocracy movement. These measures were unsuccessful in curtailing the protests, however (B. R. Upreti 2008).

The king also tried to use the international community, particularly India and the United States, to back his stance. Karan Singh, an Indian who

5. After the successful April revolution, the revived Parliament changed the name of the Royal Nepal Army to "Nepal Army."

was a relative of Nepal's royal family, was dispatched to Kathmandu as a special envoy of the Indian prime minister.[6] Singh met with SPA leaders and discussed the Indian-sponsored package, which prescribed negotiations between the king and the SPA to ensure the continued existence of the constitutional monarchy and a transfer of executive power from the king back to the SPA (B. R. Upreti 2006). The king accepted this package on April 21 in a public address. But since the main message of his address was that the monarchy was the ultimate custodian of executive power in the country and that the king could assume or return power to the people whenever he wanted, the public vehemently opposed this deal. Protesters vowed to continue protests until their demands were met, namely the return of power to political parties and elections for a constituent assembly.

The international community continued its diplomatic efforts. Even after the king's address, India expressed its hope that the king and the political parties would reconcile and move ahead (Dixit 2003). At the same time, American, French, Swedish, English, German, and Finnish envoys were dispatched to the residence of a senior SPA leader on April 22 to encourage the SPA to accept the king's offer. The public, however, opposed this and continued to expand its protests. On April 23, more than half the country's population filled the streets in protest against the king's rule and demanded elections for a constituent assembly (B. R. Upreti 2006). The UCPN (M) strongly supported the People's Movement by contributing additional protesters and creating difficulties for security forces.

The Unified Command, headed by the army, failed to control the multitudes of demonstrators. The army finally succumbed to the people's power because protesters were threatening to storm the royal palace if the mass demonstrations continued without positive results. The king had to reinstate the dissolved Parliament, which he did on April 26, and Girija Prasad Koirala became the prime minister.[7] In response to the newly appointed prime minister's request, the UCPN (M) announced a fresh three-month cease-fire. By May 2006, the government and the UCPN (M) had begun peace talks, and the Parliament voted unanimously to curtail the king's political power. During the political settlement process, UCPN (M) Chairman Prachanda met for talks with the prime minister and SPA leaders. The SPA and the UCPN (M) signed an eight-point agreement on power-sharing arrangements for the interim government (B. R. Upreti 2006). On

6. Foreign Secretary Shyam Saran (India's former ambassador to Nepal) and Pankaj Saran (joint secretary of Indian external affairs) accompanied him. Shyam Saran also talked with the leadership of the RNA at that time.

7. In announcing the revival of the Parliament, the king said, "We through this proclamation affirm that the executive power of the Kingdom of Nepal, which was in our safekeeping, shall from this day be returned to the people and the exercise according to Article 35 of the Constitution of the Kingdom of Nepal 1990" (*BBC News* 2006).

July 4, 2006, the government and the UCPN (M) invited the United Nations to assist in the peace process and manage demobilization and disarmament. Additonally, on November 8, both parties signed a landmark deal on arms management and political issues, including the Constituent Assembly (CA), interim government, and interim Parliament. On November 21, 2006, the prime minister and Prachanda signed the historic CPA to end the ten-year armed conflict. This agreement also addressed broader issues such as state restructuring, inclusive governance and politics, poverty, inequality, and injustice. The CPA marked the formal end of the insurgency. However, the UCPN (M) retained military combatants, complicating the resolution process.

Fourth Phase (November 22, 2006, Onward)

This phase falls within the sphere of post-conflict recovery and stabilization. As expected, it marked a fundamental shift in tactics, strategies, and actions. The signatories of the CPA focused primarily on political and economic approaches to improve the country. They organized special projects in conflict-affected areas, including generating employment opportunities for youth and bringing the citizenry into mainstream development efforts. National debate shifted to the political issues stated in the CPA: implementing truth and reconciliation commissions, managing transitional security and justice issues, and conducting elections for the Constituent Assembly (B. R. Upreti 2009). The most potent challenge the state faced during this period originated from the people of the Terai (plains), who demanded an equal share in the bureaucratic, judicial, security, political, and economic sectors as outlined in the federal system defined in the interim constitution.[8] The state handled the situation politically for the most part but did occasionally use force to contain the violence and civil unrest among the Terai people (B. R. Upreti 2009, 2010).

From November 2006 to April 2008, both sides refrained from mobilizing forces; the Nepal army was kept in barracks, and the UCPN (M) ex-combatant army stayed in the cantonments (Bhattarai and Wagle 2010). It was also agreed that charges against UCPN (M) leaders and cadres would be dropped provided that partial compensation was paid to the victims. The interim constitution was promulgated during this phase.

When Parliament was reinstated in 2006, one-third of the parliamentary positions were filled by UCPN (M) members, in keeping with the power-sharing agreement. The successful completion of the CA election on

8. The Terai people, Nepal's flatland dwellers, have traditionally reported suffering discrimination in state employment opportunities even though they constitute about half of Nepal's population. They have thus been proponents of a federal rather than centralized structure.

April 10, 2008, was one of the major developments of this phase, and the UCPN (M) emerged with the most votes, surpassing the NC, which previously held the largest share, and the Communist Party of Nepal (Unified Marxist-Leninist) (CPN [UML]), which previously had the second-largest share. These results were unanticipated, with many national and international analysts predicting that the UCPN (M) would end up behind both the NC and the CPN (UML) (B. R. Upreti 2006). Once the UCPN (M) was validated as the most popular political force in the April 2008 elections, it took more than four months for the party to take over government while the NC dragged its feet on relinquishing power.

On May 28, 2008, of the 564 members of the CA, 560 voted to make Nepal a federal democratic republic and approved sending a request to the king to leave the palace within fifteen days. Following the order of the CA, on June 11, King Gyanendra Shah left Narayanhiti Royal Palace, which was later converted into a museum. In a press conference before his departure, Gyanendra said, "Respecting Constitutional Assembly elections and the decision taken by the Constituent Assembly meeting on Jestha 15th, I am cooperating in every way towards the successful implementation of that decision. I have also not thought of leaving the country. I would like to live in my own motherland and contribute in whatever way possible to greater good of the country and peace in this land. I believe that there will be support for this from all sectors" (Gyandendra 2008).[9]

This statement reflected a major shift in the military's strategy, since many had feared that the military would support the king and mobilize to resist the CA's request. By not doing so, the military regained some of the public support it had lost during the insurgency. This was a significant turning point in Nepal's political history (B. R. Upreti 2006).

On July 21, 2008, the CA elected Ram Baran Yadav as the first president of the Republic of Nepal. Pushpa Kamal Dahal (Prachanda) was sworn in as the first prime minister of the Republic of Nepal on August 18. But more transitional pains were yet to come for the Nepalese state. Prime Minister Prachanda's time in office was challenged by interparty tensions. The NC created several problems for the UCPN (M) by asking it to return houses and property seized illegally during the war and by serving as a governmental watchdog to ensure strict adherence to the provisions agreed to in the CPA. Also, the prime minister's adversarial relations with his main coalition partner, the CPN (UML), hampered his ability to run the government effectively (B. R. Upreti 2010).

9. Jestha is a month in the Nepali calendar. *United We Blog* released the transcript of King Gyanendra's speech online on June 11, 2008. The website also links to his original press statement in Nepali.

Tensions between the UCPN (M)–led government and the Nepal army also flared up on several occasions. On April 21, 2009, the government gave the chief of army staff (COAS) twenty-four hours to clarify a recruitment violation, the reinstatement of eight generals without the consent of the government, and the army's decision to pull out its team from the country's national games.[10] But when the prime minister tried to remove the COAS for not complying with these requests, the president—a member of the NC—intervened and insisted that the COAS continue in his post until further notice. Therefore, citing the president's "unconstitutional and undemocratic" decision to overturn the decision of the elected coalition government and retain the army chief, Prachanda resigned from his post as prime minister on May 4, 2009 (B. R. Upreti 2010).

The downfall of the UCPN (M) led to the election of CPN (UML) leader Madhav Kumar Nepal as the republic's second prime minister. The relationship between the UCPN (M) and the CPN (UML) soured when the UCPN (M) characterized the CPN (UML)–led coalition government as a "puppet of foreign power" and headed by a person rejected by the people in the CA election.[11] Even though Nepal has not seen a return to insurgent violence, political tensions have continued, with the CA failing to finalize a new constitution despite getting a number of extensions on its deadlines.

The past three years have seen intense political struggles.[12] The Madhav Nepal government did not last long. Facing pressure both from within his own CPN (UML) party and from the UCPN (M), he resigned in June 2010 and left office in February 2011. The power struggle became so intense that violent protests returned to the streets as the CA failed to elect a prime minister. Even after seventeen ballots, the Parliament could not choose between former prime minister Prachanda of the UCPN (M) and the Nepali Congress Party vice chairman, Ram Chandra Paudel. In an attempt to break the political stalemate, the CA finally changed the provision governing the election of the prime minister. The provision required each CA

10. The National Sports Council had organized the national games, in which the army's team was also participating. Just after the opening of the games, the UCPN (M)–led government decided to include the team from the UCPN (M) cantonments. The Nepal army team pulled out. This situation became one of the prime sources of tension between the UCPN (M) and the army. The COAS strategically used these objections of the UCPN (M) to convince other political parties that the UCPN (M) was deliberately working to dismantle the institution of the army. Consequently, the president, all major political parties, and many influential leaders stood in favor of the army.

11. Madhav Nepal ran and lost in two constituencies in the April 10, 2008, CA, but later the UCPN (M), the NC, and all the other major political parties asked him to lead the Constitutional Committee of the CA. So he was unanimously selected by the political decision makers to be a member of the CA and to head the Constitutional Committee.

12. For a summary of the major political developments in Nepal during 2011–12, see SATP (2012, 2013).

member present on election day to vote. Prachanda finally withdrew from the race, supporting the candidacy of Jhala Nath Khanal from the CPN (UML), who became the thirty-fourth prime minister on February 3, 2011. Khanal managed to secure 368 votes; his closest rival, Ram Chandra Paudel of the NC, had 122 votes. Khanal, relatively more sympathetic toward the UCPN (M) than other Nepalese political leaders, faced tremendous pressure from both the NC and a faction of the UCPN (M) led by Baburam Bhattarai, which had split from Prachanda. Khanal finally resigned on August 14, 2011.

On August 28, 2011, Bhattarai, widely perceived in Nepal as the senior Nepali politician most favored by India, was elected by Parliament as the thirty-fifth prime minister, with 340 votes against the NC candidate's 235. And even his tenure has been controversial, for several reasons. First, the CA has yet to agree on a constitution. More importantly, Bhattarai's decision to announce a new election date without advising the major political parties became a source of deep tension in the Parliament. Once the Parliament–cum–Constituent Assembly was dissolved, no legislative body existed to check Bhattarai's powers. His relationship with the president deteriorated sharply after the latter termed his administration a "caretaker" government. In addition, the hardliners within Bhattarai's party accused him of being antinationalist and pro-India (Adhikari 2011). Also, Bhattarai gave huge amounts of money from the state treasury to his supporters and party cadres. Most recently, his wife was accused of using her influence to appoint her sister to a political position.[13] She has also been accused of accepting bribes from bureaucrats, contractors, businessmen, and criminals.[14]

Since June 2012, political parties in Parliament have tried and failed to replace the Bhattarai government. The president gave several deadlines to establish Nepal's new consensus-oriented government, but the parties were unable to do so. In March 2013, the president appointed the chief justice of the Supreme Court prime minister in order to hold CA elections and thereby create a new constitution. But this decision was widely opposed by the Nepal Bar Association, civil society groups, the radical Maoist Party (which split from the UCPN [M]), and other smaller parties, so there are

13. Bhattarai's wife, Hisila Yami, a three-time lawmaker and Maoist leader, is one of Nepal's most prominent female politicians. Nevertheless, she is a controversial public figure, accused multiple times of nepotism and favoritism for appointing Maoist staffers in state-run offices and corporations. On September 17, 2011, Yami organized a meeting of eleven secretaries of Maoist-led ministries at Baluwatar, Kathmandu, and allegedly instructed them to do her bidding (B. Sharma 2011).

14. Hisila Yami has been accused of running a government "parallel" to her husband's. *Telegraph Nepal* (2011) reports that Yami made her sister, Timila Yami, chair of the Kathmandu Upatyaka Khanepani Limited (KUKL), the state-owned enterprise managing Kathmandu's water supply and sanitation.

doubts whether his appointment will solve Nepal's lingering political stalemate and lead to elections (Kharel 2013).

Post-conflict civil-military tensions. Civil-military tensions played a critical yet complex role in the Nepalese insurgency and the state's response. Before the assassination of King Birendra in 2001, the military was not mobilized. Once Gyanendra was anointed king, he mobilized state forces, and the army took the lead in dealing with the insurgency. At that point, the government was more or less obliged to accept whatever strategy the army proposed. A sharp increase in the defense budget and an increase in arms imports are examples of the military's influence on the state's response to the insurgency (B. R. Upreti 2008, 2009).

The military's resistance was a major obstacle to plans to overthrow the king. Civil-military tensions mounted when the king imposed the state of emergency in November 2001 and mobilized army forces to combat the UCPN (M). Both the army and the UCPN (M) used heavy-handed tactics and strategies in the effort to weaken and defeat each other (Sapkota 2009). The army also used its advantageous relationship with the U.S. and Indian militaries to expand its military capacities (B. R. Upreti 2010). After signing the CPA, the UCPN (M) was constantly pursuing measures that would form a new national army, which included former UCPN (M) combatants and the Nepal army. Consequently, the mistrust and tension between the UCPN (M) and Nepal army mounted. On January 6, 2007, the COAS, Rookmangud Katawal, publicly dismissed the idea of combining UCPN (M) forces with the army. Katawal stated that the army must be kept clean of any particular ideology and political motivation. He went on to say that the state military force should be competent, professional and disciplined, impartial, and obedient to the order of the military chain of command and that a nonpolitical state force must guarantee the stability of the country during the tumultuous democratic periods (Sapkota 2009). In response, the UCPN (M) chair, Prachanda, blamed the army chief for obstructing progressive political changes. Other senior UCPN (M) leaders publicly expressed their dismay on several occasions as well. On the other hand, many senior non–UCPN (M) political leaders and army officials argued that the UCPN (M) wanted to weaken the army (Bhattarai and Wagle 2010). Some even suspected that the UCPN (M) was deliberately trying to damage the army's reputation and, ultimately, dismantle the army.

This issue is still being debated, and consequently, the integration and rehabilitation of UCPN (M) ex-combatants into the state security forces, as mandated by the CPA, has yet to occur. This despite the fact that the UCPN (M), other major political parties, and the government reached an agreement in September 2010 that the Maoist ex-combatants would stay in cantonments under UCPN (M) control. Under this agreement, the management of the Army Integration Special Committee—a constitutional body responsible for the integration and rehabilitation of Maoist ex-combatants—was to accomplish integration and rehabilitation tasks within four months (Bhattarai and Cave 2009).

The bipolar political division between the UCPN (M) and other major political parties—backed by the Nepal army—is deepening. The provisions of the CPA, confusing and subject to many different interpretations, are to blame for this division (B. R. Upreti 2010). The provision of integration and rehabilitation of UCPN (M) ex-combatants is particularly confusing. It led to the conflict over the army's recruitment of some 2,800 new soldiers in the beginning of 2009, to difficulties in extending the contracts of eight retired Nepal army generals, and to the firing of the COAS by the UCPN (M) prime minister—and his subsequent reinstatement by the NC president. Building mutual trust and confidence among the key stakeholders has proved extremely challenging because of the degree of political polarization and the use of the army as a bargaining tool by political forces (Bhattarai and Wagle 2010). Moreover, UCPN (M) leaders are wary of the army's intentions regarding the integration of ex-combatants. They believe that the army wants to disarm and demobilize them. Thus, the entire peace process since the CPA has in no small part been held hostage by the tension between the army and the UCPN (M). And in fact, the success or failure of the peace process now depends largely on the integration and rehabilitation of the UCPN (M) ex-combatants.

Factors Underlying the Insurgency's Settlement

The section above sketched the development of the Nepalese insurgency from 1996 onward and the political developments since. This section highlights the key conceptual issues underlying the decade-long insurgency and, more importantly, its political settlement.

Shifting Conflict Dynamics: From Tripolar to Bipolar Conflict

The shifting course of the Nepal insurgency is unique. Before the February 1, 2005, royal takeover, there was a tripartite conflict between the king, the parliamentary parties, and the UCPN (M). There were episodes of cooperation between the king and parliamentary parties against the UCPN (M), and other episodes when the king and the UCPN (M) worked together indirectly to undermine the parliamentary parties (B. R. Upreti 2009).

But once the king imposed direct rule, the parliamentary parties and the UCPN (M) coordinated efforts to oppose him. The Twelve-Point Understanding reached on November 22, 2005, between the SPA and the UCPN (M) was one of the key turning points that can be credited for settling the armed insurgency (B. R. Upreti 2006). The major political parties finally concluded that the monarchy was the principal obstruction to democracy in Nepal. To most, the king's governmental takeover demonstrated the fundamental incompatibilities between the monarchy and democratically oriented political parties.

Annoyed with the behavior of the king, the political parties began implementing concepts of absolute democracy through a forward-looking restructuring of the state, which necessitated abolishing the monarchy. The monarchy promoted one-language, one-culture practices and centralized power. Therefore, to ensure political, social, and cultural transformation, the political parties worked to terminate the monarchy and establish a democratic government.

To be sure, the success of the People's Movement was largely attributable to the Twelve-Point Understanding (B. R. Upreti 2006). Ironic though it is, it was the ambition, behavior, and actions of King Gyanendra that ultimately led the political parties to unite. If the king had not taken a confrontational approach with the parliamentary political parties—which, until then, were committed to multiparty democracy within a constitutional monarchy—they would not have forged an alliance with the UCPN (M) against the king (Sapkota 2009). If he had not brutally tried to suppress the people's resistance movement of April 2006, the international community would not have turned against him. If he had not taken a military approach to suppress his opponents (not only insurgents but also human rights activists, journalists, parliamentary political parties, and progressive citizens opposing his autocratic rule) under the guise of "fighting terrorism," he would not have been isolated. In this respect, the king's mistakes and aggression proved to be a blessing in disguise for his opponents (B. R. Upreti 2006).

Failure of the Military Approach: The Path to Political Settlement

The Nepalese state used excessive military force during certain periods of the armed insurgency. During such periods, state forces commonly employed media propaganda, psychological pressure, torture, and fear. Mass killings, abductions, destruction of entire villages, and bribing cadres and leaders of the UCPN (M) to expose the antigovernmental organization's weaknesses were commonplace. It is important to note that the UCPN (M) was equally coercive in its tactics. It kidnapped opponents, murdered supporters of the security forces and opposing political parties, tortured family members of security forces and politicians, seized property, and demanded huge monetary donations from the populace. The UCPN (M) maintained control zones where it imposed its own rules and regulations and installed its own security and legal systems. The coercive tactics hurt both sides, although the UCPN (M) fared better because it was more adept at blaming the government forces or presenting its own harsh actions as necessary to maintain strength in the face of government brutality. In fact, the state's heavy-handed approach ended up generating some degree of sympathy for the UCPN (M).

A Weak Economic Approach

An economic approach is believed to be one of the most common means of responding to armed insurgency (B. R. Upreti 2010). In Nepal, the government, regarding the insurgency as essentially a law-and-order problem, did not focus at first on economic measures. But once the insurgency started to gain momentum, the state realized the utility of the economic approach and tried to implement special development projects and programs in the conflict areas. The purpose of these programs was to generate employment and benefits for the poor, marginalized, and socially excluded segments of the society, but these efforts were implemented too late in the day. By that time, the UCPN (M) already controlled most of the territory inhabited by the poor, marginalized, and excluded people. These impoverished communities adopted the slogan "no development without political settlement" and obstructed the government's efforts to initiate economic and development activities (B. R. Upreti 2006).

Further, the state tried to initiate economic policy reforms and trade promotions, create favorable market conditions, invest in basic services—such as education, health, and drinking water—and introduce rural infrastructure development projects following the 2003 peace talks (B. R. Upreti 2004a). The state also tried to modernize agriculture and proposed measures for land reform, including land consolidation, land tenure entitlement to tenants and the landless, land ceiling (the maximum acreage one can legally own), and land-use classification. And it developed rural entrepreneurship, promoted the benefits of biodiversity, and improved access to natural resources (Mahat 2005). The insurgents and their supporters obstructed these initiatives. Economic institutions and development agencies could not implement any activities associated with state agencies in the UCPN (M)–controlled areas (geographically more than 75 percent of the country) (B. R. Upreti 2006). Intercommunity trade was severely disrupted. Moreover, the insecure environment curtailed private investment because many investors withdrew their funds, causing several industries to shut down (B. R. Upreti 2010). The state agencies were also discredited by international aid agencies, which increasingly channeled their assistance through NGOs (B. R. Upreti 2008).

External Dimension of the Political Settlement

International opposition to the king's takeover was another factor leading to political resolution of the armed conflict. Once it became clear that the king was not interested in restoring even a facade of democracy, a number of major powers turned against him.

The United States was among those not happy with the king's takeover. On February 14, 2005, Assistant Secretary of State for South and Central Asian Affairs Richard Boucher issued a press statement highlighting U.S. concerns over King Gyanendra's dismissal of the government; declaration of a state of emergency; detention of politicians, human rights workers, and students; and suspension of fundamental constitutional rights (OHCHR 2012; B. R. Upreti 2009; ICG 2010). The United States insisted that the king restore and protect civil and human rights, promptly release those detained during the state of emergency, and move quickly toward restoration of civil liberties and multiparty democracy under a constitutional monarchy (B. R. Upreti 2006). On February 22, 2005, the British foreign secretary, Jack Straw, similarly urged the king to restore the representative government and democratic freedoms (B. R. Upreti 2009). The British ambassador strongly supported the constitutional monarchy and multiparty democracy in Nepal but opposed the king's dismissal of the prime minister and dissolution of the democratic institutions (*Hindu* 2005). On February 25, 2005, the UK suspended its military assistance to Nepal (B. R. Upreti 2006; Sapkota 2009).

In October 2005, a visiting delegation of the EU warned that without reconciliation, there was a strong risk of a political collapse in Nepal. In a press conference, Tom Phillips, leader of the EU troika mission visting Nepal at the time, urged the king to reach out to the political parties to ensure the return of multiparty democracy. The EU emphasized that Nepal needed the assistance of an independent and credible external partner and the active support of the international community to ensure that the resolution process was inclusive and comprehensive. The troika mission stated that a functional multiparty democracy needed to be in place to engender peace, prosperity, and democracy in Nepal (Forum Asia and ACHR 2005). The EU's stance further isolated the king and encouraged the political parties to unite against the royal takeover (B. R. Upreti 2006).

Perhaps the biggest blow to the king was the loss of India's support. On February 9, 2005, the Indian ambassador met with King Gyanendra and urged him to reverse the takeover, remove restrictions imposed on political leaders since February 1, and seek a national consensus with political party leaders. When the king ignored these requests, India suspended military aid to Nepal on February 25, 2005. But India stated that it would resume aid if the king released detained leaders and members of civil society and restored civil and media rights and multiparty democracy. On March 4, 2005, Indian foreign minister Natwar Singh stated before the upper house of the Indian Parliament, "The development in Nepal constitutes a serious setback to democracy and brings the monarchy and mainstream political parties in direct confrontation with each other. This can only benefit the forces that not only wish to undermine democracy in Nepal but the institution of democracy as well"[15] (B. C. Upreti 2010, 129). The Indian position placed the king in an especially difficult situation and created an international environment that favored the organization of political parties against him.

India's role in pressuring the king and bringing the political parties to a consensus was driven in part by internal compulsions brought on by the expansion of the Maoist insurgent movement into Indian states. Formation of the Coordination Committee of Communist Parties and Organizations in South Asia was led in part by the UCPN (M). Therefore, the massive expansion of Maoist insurgencies in more than thirteen Indian states exerted enormous pressure on the Indian government to bring the UCPN (M) into a negotiated settlement. This development explains India's interest in facilitating the Twelve-Point Understanding between parliamentary parties and UCPN (M) (Sapkota 2009; B. R. Upreti 2009; Shah 2004).

The United Nations built up its own pressure. On April 22, 2005, UN secretary-general Kofi Annan discussed the political situation with King Gyanendra in Jakarta at the Afro-Asian Conference. A week later, Secretary-General Annan organized a press conference in New Delhi to state that the king had failed to implement the promises he had made to Annan (*Kathmandu Post* 2005; B. R. Upreti 2009; Sapkota 2009). The UN Office of the High Commissioner for Human Rights (OHCHR) also spoke out against the circumstances in Nepal, criticizing the king for placing restrictions on the media, calling it a "lack of respect for the rule of law" (OHCHR 2011).

International NGOs also applied pressure on the king through their criticisms of human rights violations. Amnesty International, Human Rights Watch, and the International Commission of Jurists (ICJ) called for travel restrictions on the king, his army officers, and senior advisers and aides. At a meeting organized by the Swiss government in Geneva in 2005, these three international organizations also suggested freezing assets in foreign bank accounts of any person associated with the royal regime (*Web Chautari* 2006). There were also discussions about possibly imposing "targeted" and "smart" sanctions against the king and his aides. These discus-

15. For Natwar Singh's statement on developments in Nepal, see SATP (2005).

sions made it difficult for countries to continue justifying their assistance to Nepal (B. R. Upreti 2009).

Despite the fact that most members of the international community remained supportive of Nepal's twin-pillar theory of governance, the king was unhappy with international statements against his takeover. He continued his confrontational approach. In his address before the SAARC Summit at Dhaka on November 12, 2005 (mentioned earlier), the king criticized the international community for its "double standard." His harshly worded speech isolated him further from his traditional supporters across the globe (B. R. Upreti 2009). The king also remained vehemently opposed to the international mediation that the UCPN (M) had been calling for throughout the conflict.[16] The UCPN (M) deeply distrusted the government and the army and, thus, wanted an international mediator to guarantee that the state would honor any political agreements (Raj 2004; N. Pandey 2005). It also sought the legitimacy and recognition that comes with international mediation. Further, the UCPN (M)'s insistence on international mediation served as a means for establishing international relationships for future political and diplomatic endeavors. During the 2003 negotiations, the chief negotiator of the UCPN (M), Baburam Bhattarai, sought meetings with numerous diplomats—indicative of the UCPN (M)'s dedication to developing relations with the international community (B. R. Upreti 2004a).

Interestingly, the king's reluctance to accept third-party mediation was as much a function of Indian influence on Nepali politics as of the government's need to deny the UCPN (M) international legitimacy. New Delhi, traditionally the most influential external actor in Nepalese politics, was concerned about losing its monopoly if other actors gained a formal role in Nepal's conflict. It changed its stance only after the February 1, 2005, royal takeover, when the UK, the United States, and India developed a common understanding to push the king to reverse his takeover (B. R. Upreti 2006). They later requested that the United Nations play a direct role in resolving the Nepalese conflict.

Conclusion

Perhaps the biggest lesson from the Nepalese experience with armed insurgency is that the settlement process is not linear, instead passing through many phases, favorable and unfavorable for one side or the other, before reaching a conclusion. Moreover, both insurgents and counterinsurgents combine various approaches, which may or may not work out depending on

16. The proposal that the UCPN (M)'s leader, Prachanda, issued through a press release on May 16, 2004, called for a joint dialogue between the king, all political forces, the Maoists, and the representatives of Nepalese civil society, with the help of the United Nations (*Kathmandu Post* 2004).

their goals, implementation mechanisms, and timing. This analysis shows that both coercive tactics, with or without the use of force, and inducements are used, but ultimately, context-specific developments—and even mistakes by the parties—determine the outcome.

In the Nepalese case, the settlement was political. The outcome was shaped by multiple agents and factors. A key dimension was the alignment of the otherwise scattered interests of political actors and focusing the opposition energy on the operational needs of the ultimate objective—in this case, establishing constitutional democracy. The international community also played an important role in helping move the settlement along, especially in the final stages. But it was ultimately the galvanizing effect of people's aspirations that allowed the political parties to unite in calling for a complete abolition of the monarchy.

Finally, while shifts in party alliances and their agendas were important in moving to a political settlement, Nepal's case underscores that what it takes to agree on a settlement is not necessarily sufficient to fix the root causes of the conflict and achieve conflict transformation. It has proved exceptionally difficult for Nepal to bring about the kind of positive change envisioned in the CPA. This observation is crucial for traditional peacebuilders operating in a post-conflict environment and points to the added difficulty in moving the formerly conflicting parties away from tactics and strategies that they believe may (or may not) have paid off and to the different requirements of the post-conflict phase. Nepal's political difficulties since the end of the insurgency highlight the difficulty that even those who received backing from the masses on promises of transformational change and correction of historical wrongs—in this case, the UCPN (M)—face in fulfilling their promises. Nepal's principal bottleneck has not been developmental or humanitarian in nature, although these aspects remain vital. Rather, it has been the failure of the political actors to institute consensual and viable processes that would ensure a "new Nepal" with a clean departure from the underlying problems that led to the armed insurgency in the first place. While insurgent violence has not returned, the country has seen various violent protests over the ineffectiveness of the political class—now including the UCPN (M)—in rising above political tussles and delivering on their commitments to the people of Nepal.

References

Adhikary, Dhruba. 2011. "Nepalese Victor Seen as Pro-Delhi Plant." *Asia Times Online,* Sept. 9. www.atimes.com/atimes/South_Asia/MI09Df02.html.

Amnesty International. 2005. *Nepal: A Long Ignored Human Rights Crisis is Now on the Brink of Catastrophe.* London: Amnesty International.

Baechler, Gunther, Nilamber Acharya, Peter Dammann, Renu Rajbhandari, and Bishnu R. Upreti. 2008. *Nepal Building New Road to Peace.* Kathmandu: Swiss Agency for Development and Cooperation.

BBC News. 2006. "Full Text: Nepal King's Speech." Apr. 21. http://news.bbc.co.uk/2/hi/south_asia/4931498.stm.

Bhattarai, Rajan. 2004. *Geopolitical Specialties of Nepal and a Regional Approach to Conflict Transformation.* Kathmandu: Friends for Peace.

Bhattarai, Rajan, and Rosy Cave, eds. 2009. *Changing Security Dynamics in Nepal.* Kathmandu: Nepal Institute for Policy Studies and Saferworld.

Bhattarai, Rajan, and Geja Sharma Wagle, eds. 2010. *Emerging Security Challenges of Nepal.* Kathmandu: Nepal Institute for Policy Studies.

Dixit, Jyotindra Nath, ed. 2003. *External Affairs: Cross-Border Relations.* New Delhi: Roli Books.

Forum Asia and Asian Centre for Human Rights (ACHR). 2005. "The Chinese Chequer: Split Wide Open in Nepal." Nepal Monthly Human Rights Briefing Paper, Nov. 1. www.achrweb.org/reports/Nepal/Nepal-Oct05.pdf.

Galtung, Johan. 2004. "Transformation of Conflict in Nepal: A Human Rights Perspective." In *Conflict, Human Rights and Peace Challenges before Nepal,* ed. Bipin Adhikari and Rishikesh Shaha, 108–32. Kathmandu: National Human Rights Commission.

Gyanendra. 2008. "Press Statement of Gyanendra (the Last King of Nepal)." *United We Blog! for a Democratic Nepal,* June 11. http://blog.com.np/2008/06/11/press-statement-of-gyanendra-the-last-king-of-nepal/.

Hindu. 2005. "Britain Recalls Ambassador." Feb. 15. www.hindu.com/2005/02/15/stories/2005021514570100.htm.

Hutt, Michael, ed. 2004. *Himalayan People's War: Nepal's Maoist Rebellion.* London: Hurst.

International Crisis Group (ICG). 2005a. "Nepal Dealing with a Human Rights Crisis." Asia Report no. 94, Mar. 24. www.crisisgroup.org/en/regions/asia/south-asia/nepal/094-nepal-dealing-with-a-human-rights-crisis.aspx.

———. 2005b. "Nepal: Responding to the Royal Coup." Asia Briefing no. 36, Feb. 24. www.crisisgroup.org/en/regions/asia/south-asia/nepal/B036-nepal-responding-to-the-royal-coup.aspx.

———. 2006. "Nepal: From People Power to Peace?" Asia Report no. 115, May 10. www.crisisgroup.org/en/regions/asia/south-asia/nepal/115-nepal-from-people-power-to-peace.aspx.

———. 2010. "Nepal: Peace and Justice." Asia Report no. 184, Jan. 14. www.crisisgroup.org/en/regions/asia/south-asia/nepal/184-nepal-peace-and-justice.aspx.

Informal Sector Service Centre (INSEC). 2007. *Nepal Human Rights Yearbook 2007.* Kathmandu: INSEC.

———. 2009. *Nepal Human Rights Yearbook 2009.* Kathmandu: INSEC.

Karki, Arjun, and David Seddon, eds. 2003. *The People's War in Nepal: Left Perspectives.* New Delhi: Adroit.

Kathmandu Post. 2004. "Prachanda Calls for All-Party Talks." May 17. www.ekantipur.com/the-kathmandu-post/2004/05/17/top-story/prachanda-calls-for-all-party-talks/11823.html.

———. 2005. "King Dismisses Deuba Government." Feb. 2. www.ekantipur.com/the-kathmandu-post/2005/02/02/top-story/king-dismisses-deuba-government/30878.html.

Kharel, Pranab. 2013. "March 14 Is a Black Day, Says NBA." Mar. 15. www.ekantipur.com/the-kathmandu-post/2013/03/14/nation/march-14-is-a-black-day-says-nba/246395.html.

Lund, Michael S. 1996. *Preventing Violent Conflicts: A Strategy for Preventive Diplomacy.* Washington, DC: U.S. Institute of Peace Press.

Mackinlay, John, and Bishnu R. Upreti. 2003. "The King and Mao." *The World Today,* Feb., 26–27. www.chathamhouse.org/sites/default/files/public/The%20World%20Today/2003/wt030225.pdf.

Mahat, Ram Sharan. 2005. *In Defense of Democracy: Dynamics and Fault Lines of Nepal's Political Economy.* New Delhi: Adroit.

Office of the High Commissioner for Human Rights (OHCHR). 2011. "Report of the United Nations High Commissioner for Human Rights: Report on the Human Rights Situation and the Activities of the Office of the High Commissioner, Including Technical Cooperation, in Nepal." Dec. 16. www.ohchr.org/Documents/HRBodies/HRCouncil/RegularSession/Session19/A-HRC-19-21-Add4_en.pdf.

———. 2012. "Nepal Conflict Report." Geneva: UN Office of the High Commissioner for Human Rights. www.ohchr.org/Documents/.../OHCHR_Nepal_Conflict_Report2012.pdf.

Onesto, Li. 2005. *Dispatches from the People's War in Nepal.* London: Pluto Press.

Pandey, J. 2004. "Monarchy OK but Rider Attached." *Kathmandu Post,* Jan. 24. www.ekantipur.com/the-kathmandu-post/2010/03/25/most-popular/Unanswered-questions/6547/.

Pandey, Nishchal Nath. 2005. *Nepal's Maoist Movement and Implications for India and China.* New Delhi: Manohar.

Raj, Prakash. 2004. *Maoists in the Land of Buddha: An Analytical Study of the Maoist Insurgency in Nepal.* New Delhi: Nirala.

Sapkota, Bishnu, ed. 2009. *The Nepali Security Sector: An Almanac.* Geneva: Centre for the Democractic Control of Armed Forces. www.dcaf.ch/Publications/The-Nepali-Security-Sector-An-Almanac.

Shah, Saubhagya. 2004. "A Himalayan Red Herring: Maoist Revolution in the Shadow of the Legacy Raj." In *Himalayan "People's War": Nepal's Maoist Rebellion,* ed. Michael Hutt, 192–224. London: Hurst.

Sharma, Bhadra. 2011. "Choosy Hisila Yami Cheapens Her PM Hubby's Resolves." *Ekantipur,* Sept. 28, www.ekantipur.com/2011/09/28/top-story/choosy-hisila-yami-cheapens-her-pm-hubbys-resolves/341490/.

Sharma, Sudheer. 2004. "The Maoist Movement: An Evolutionary Perspective." In *Understanding the Maoist Movement in Nepal,* ed. Deepak Thapa, 362–80. Kathmandu: Chautari Books.

South Asia Terrorism Portal (SATP). 2005. "Statement by External Affairs Minister, Natwar Singh, on Developments in Nepal." Mar. 4. www.satp.org/satporgtp/countries/india/document/papers/india_nepal_natwar05.htm.

———. 2012. "Nepal Assessment 2012." www.satp.org/satporgtp/countries/nepal/assessment2012.htm.

———. 2013. "Nepal Assessment 2013." www.satp.org/satporgtp/countries/nepal/index.html.

Telegraph Nepal. 2011. "Hisila and Timila: Story of Two Privileged Sisters from Nepal." Nov. 23. www.telegraphnepal.com/headline/2011-11-23/hisila-timila:-story-of-two-privileged-sisters-from-nepal.

Thapa, Deepak, and Bandita Sijapati. 2003. *A Kingdom under Siege: Nepal's Maoist Insurgency, 1996 to 2003.* Kathmandu: Printhouse.

United Nations Development Program (UNDP). 2009. *Nepal Human Development Report 2009: State Transformation and Human Development.* Kathmandu: UNDP.

Upreti, Bhuwan Chandra. 2010. *Nepal: Transition to Democratic Republican State (2008 Constituent Assembly Elections).* New Delhi: Kalpaz.

Upreti, Bishnu Raj. 2004a. *The Price of Neglect: From Resource Conflict to Maoist Insurgency in the Himalayan Kingdom.* Kathmandu: Bhrikuti Academic.

———. 2004b. "Nepal on Fire: A Tragedy of Triple Betrayal." *South Asian Journal* 7 (Dec.): 136–46.

———. 2006. *Armed Conflict and Peace Process in Nepal: The Maoist Insurgency, Past Negotiations, and Opportunities for Conflict Transformation*. New Delhi: Adroit.

———. 2008. "Peace Process in Nepal." *Swiss Peace Policy, Publication of the Swiss Federal Department of Foreign Affairs* 2008 (1): 4–13.

———. 2009. *Nepal from War to Peace: Legacies of the Past and Hopes for the Future*. New Delhi: Adroit.

———. 2010. *Political Change and Challenges of Nepal: Reflection on Armed Conflict, Peace Process and State Building*. Saarbrücken, Germany: Lambert Academic.

Upreti, Bishnu Raj, Kailash Nath Pyakuryal, and Sagar Raj Sharma, eds. 2008. *Conflict Induced Displacement: An Emerging Phenomenon of Internal Migration in Nepal*. Kathmandu: Heidel Press.

Upreti, Bishnu Raj, and Rohit Kumar Nepali, eds. 2006. *Nepal at Barrel of Gun: Proliferation of Small Arms and Light Weapons and Their Impacts*. Kathmandu: South Asia Small Arms.

Web Chautari. 2006. "Heads of AI, HRW and ICJ Call for Targeted Sanctions." Apr. 19. http://webchautari.net/news/news_item.asp?NewsID=807.

IV

Sri Lanka

Map 6. Sri Lanka

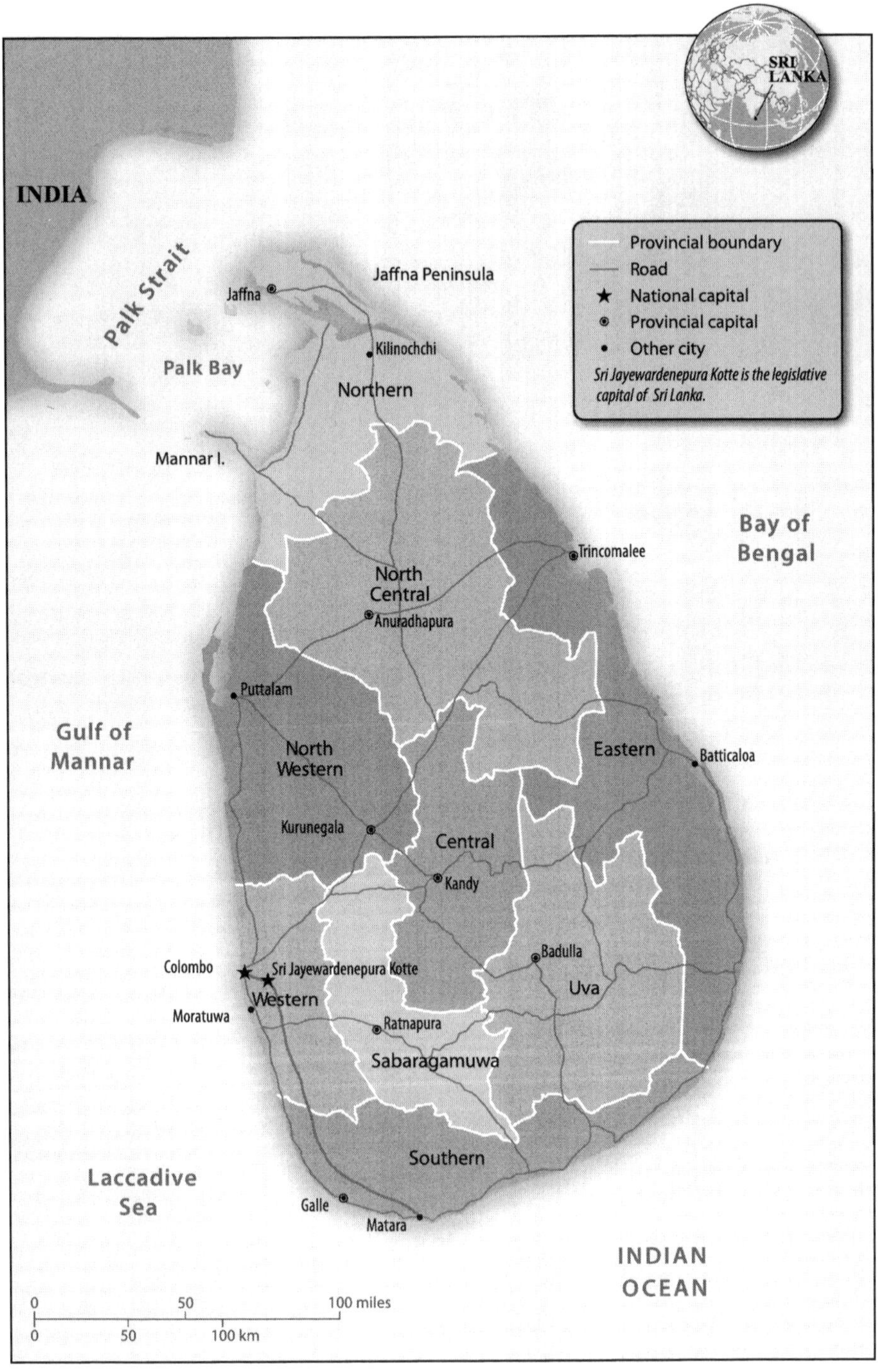

Sri Lanka: Timeline of Events

1939

Indian Tamils form Ceylon Indian Congress, a trade union–cum–political party later renamed Ceylon Workers Congress.

1944

Sri Lankan Tamils form All Ceylon Tamil Congress.

1946

September Three parties representing Sinhalese, Tamil, and Muslim communities combine to form United National Party (UNP).

1948

February Sri Lanka receives independence from the British.
Soulbury Constitution replaces Donoughmore Constitution. The Constitution, as laid out by the British, does not guarantee minority Tamil rights.

November Ceylon Citizenship Act disenfranchises up-country (Indian) Tamils.

1949

December Following passage of disenfranchisement legislation, a subset of Tamils forms Federal Party (FP).

1951

September Sri Lanka Freedom Party (SLFP) forms, becomes the main Sinhalese opposition party.

1956

First anti-Tamil riots follow Prime Minister Kotelawala's statements that Tamil and Sinhalese languages would have parity.

April SLFP wins snap election.

June SLFP passes Official Language Act, or Sinhala Only Act, with Sinhalese replacing English as the country's official language.

1957

July SLFP and FP make the Bandaranaike-Chelvanayagam (BC) Pact to stem ongoing violence. Pact promises concessions to Tamils.

1959

September A Buddhist monk assassinates Prime Minister S. W. R. D. Bandaranaike.

1960

July	Bandaranaike's widow, Sirimavo, is elected prime minister with the help of the FP, but she implements the Sinhala Only Act of 1956, disregarding the BC Pact.
	FP implements *satyagraha* (nonviolent resistance), stalling public administration in the Northern and Eastern provinces and leading government to declare state of emergency.

1961

	Pulip Padai (Army of Tigers) emerges as the first Tamil entity to promote a hard-line response to discrimination against Tamils.

1965

March	UNP and FP sign the Senanayake-Chelvanayagam (DC) Pact, which envisions steps toward greater autonomy for Tamil-populated regions.

1966

January	Tamil Language (Special Provisions) Regulation passes, marking Tamil as an official language in Sri Lanka's northeast.

1969

	FP leaves government after much of the DC pact is abrogated.

1970

	Tamil Students League (TSL) forms to protest communal quotas for higher education, introduced the same year by the SLFP majority government.

1971

April	SLFP crushes Janatha Vimukthi Peramuna–led uprising of Marxist Sinhalese nationalists in the south, killing 10,000–15,000 Sinhalese youth.

1972

	The new Republican Constitution reaffirms Sinhala as the state's sole official language. Ceylon becomes Sri Lanka, and Buddhism is the official religion. FP and other Tamil groups form Tamil United Front (TUF) in response to the 1972 Constitution.
May	Tamil Eelam Liberation Organization (TELO) and Tamil New Tigers (TNT) form.
September	TNT makes its first bomb attack, on a carnival in Thuraiappah Stadium in Jaffna.

1973

Police attack on fourth conference of the International Association of Tamil Research leaves nine people dead, marking a moment of radicalization for the previously nonviolent resistance.

1976

TUF becomes the Tamil United Liberation Front (TULF), changing both name and tactics.

May TULF passes the Vaddukoddai Resolution, formally calling for a separate state of Tamil Eelam. Velupillai Prabhakaran renames the TNT the Liberation Tigers of Tamil Eelam (LTTE).

1977

July After contesting the general elections on a secessionist campaign, TULF, with the second largest number of votes, becomes an opposition party.

August Anti-Tamil violence kills more than 100.

1978

September Second Republican Constitution establishes an executive presidency in place of the executive premiership and contains additional measures that discriminate against the Tamil minority.

1979

TULF supports the District Development Councils Act, but the UNP does not fully implement decentralization of administration.

July Prevention of Terrorism Act (PTA) is passed but results in greater militant activity.

1983

July LTTE kills 13 Sri Lankan army soldiers near Jaffna, sparking anti-Tamil violence known as the Black July riots. An estimated 80,000 Tamils flee to IDP camps. LTTE's ranks swell in wake of anti-Tamil violence.

October TULF is expelled from Parliament for stalling negotiations to end the violence.

1984

January India convenes All Party Conference, where militant groups meet with Sri Lankan government representatives, with India as mediator. Negotiations fail.

1985

December	First attempt at peace talks between LTTE and Sri Lankan government fails.

1987

May	Sri Lankan army launches Operation Liberation against Tamil rebels and institutes concurrent blockade of Jaffna, LTTE's northern stronghold.
July	Indian prime minister Rajiv Gandhi and Sri Lankan president J. R. Jayewardene sign Indo–Sri Lanka Accord, intended to end the ongoing conflict. Devolution of powers to Tamil areas is to accompany withdrawal of Sri Lankan forces and surrender of arms by Tamil rebels. It also provides for an Indian Peace-Keeping Force (IPKF) in the northeast.
September	Clashes between LTTE and rival Tamil groups kill 120 people, mostly civilians.

1988

	LTTE reneges on Indo–Sri Lanka Accord and wages war on IPKF presence, with support from the new nationalist Sri Lanka government, which is now interested in removing Indian presence from Sri Lanka. Peace talks between LTTE and Sri Lankan government follow.

1990

March	IPKF withdraws from Sri Lanka.
June	Eelam War II begins as LTTE ends cessation of hostilities.

1991

May	LTTE suicide bomber assassinates former Indian prime minister Rajiv Gandhi.

1994

October	Cessation of hostilities is announced as negotiations between LTTE and Sri Lankan government resume.

1995

April	Eelam War III begins as LTTE ends cessation of hostilities.

1996

July	LTTE overruns Mullaitivu army camp on northeastern coast of Northern Province, killing more than 1,000 Sri Lankan troops.

2001

July	LTTE attacks Sri Lanka's only international airport, Bandaranaike International Airport, and destroys several planes.

2002

March	Relative calm ensues after LTTE and the United National Front (UNF) government sign a Norwegian-brokered cease-fire agreement (CFA).

2003

April	LTTE withdraws from peace talks, but the cease-fire holds.

2005

August	LTTE-government relations deteriorate. Government declares state of emergency after foreign minister is killed in suspected LTTE assassination.

2006

April	Attacks escalate again as suicide bomber attacks Colombo's main military compound, killing eight.
July–August	Sri Lankan army launches major retaliatory actions, known as Eelam War IV, against LTTE to regain territory and decimate the organization.
	Newly elected nationalist president Rajapaksa's government and LTTE hold talks in Geneva. Talks fail.

2007

	Police expel hundreds of Tamils from Colombo until court order stops the forced exodus.

2008

January	Government formally withdraws from the 2002 CFA, and full-fledged military operation continues.

2009

	Government ignores international calls for a cease-fire despite growing humanitarian crisis over civilians trapped in the war zone.
May	LTTE's leadership is killed, and Sri Lankan army declares defeat of the LTTE and an end to 25 years of conflict.

2010

January	Incumbent President Rajapaksa wins reelection.
April	Rajapaksa's ruling coalition wins parliamentary elections by landslide.

2011

April	UN report finds both sides in civil war responsible for atrocities against civilians and calls for international investigation.

2012

March	UN Human Rights Council (UNHRC) report finds government's Lessons Learnt and Reconciliation Commission lacking in accountability and demands that government improve quality and transparency of its war crimes investigation.

2013

March	UNHRC again passes resolution demanding Sri Lankan government address inadequacies in its war crimes investigation and reconciliation efforts, noting continued reports of human rights abuses.
July	President Rajapaksa formally announces first provincial council elections in Northern Province since its separation from Eastern Province. These are the former war zone's first elections in 25 years. Military says it will close thirteen army camps across Jaffna Peninsula, returning land to original owners.

8

From Postindependence Ethnic Tensions to Insurgency

Sri Lanka's Many Missed Opportunities

Chalinda D. Weerasinghe

Following Sri Lanka's independence from British rule in 1948, tensions between its two largest ethnic groups, the majority Sinhalese and the minority Tamils, boiled over into a devastating insurgency. Historically, the Sinhalese, living mainly in the south and central parts of the country, made up almost three-quarters of the population. Before independence, the island (then named Ceylon) also had a sizable native Tamil population, composing about 10 to 11 percent of the population, spread out over Sinhalese-dominated areas and concentrated in the north and east. This chapter examines three interrelated causal dimensions of hostilities: political, economic, and ethnoreligious. The actions undertaken by the state, which was and is governed predominantly by the majority Sinhalese, are presented along these dimensions. So are the actions of the opposition Tamil minority groups, represented first by moderate Tamil politicians and later by both moderate and radical militant Tamils. The discussion begins by sketching the political and economic, as well as the social and religious, dynamics leading up to the riots of 1983—widely acknowledged as the start of the full-scale insurgency—and then looks at the evolution of the militant Tamil movement through the ascendency of the LTTE. The latter part of the chapter analyzes the evolution of the Tamil insurgency.

The conflict, although multifaceted and complex, stemmed from communal causes and, once begun, evolved predominantly because both ethnic groups continued to think strictly along myopically communal electoral lines. Many occasions arose when both sides, especially the state, could have obviated the spiral of ethnic tensions but chose not to do so for reasons of electoral self-interest. Indeed, the history of Sri Lanka's buildup from ethnic tensions to a full-fledged insurgency can best be described as one of missed opportunities for mutual accommodation and peaceful coexistence. For years after independence in 1948, intransigent, maximalist goals continued to harden positions and forced peace to break down into an active violent confrontation despite clear opportunities to avert such an outcome.

Political and Economic Dimensions

In colonizing the island of Ceylon, the British introduced a plantation economy built around coffee and, later, tea plantations. Unlike coffee production, tea required year-round work. Therefore, from the 1830s onward, the British colonialists brought in a permanent force of south Indian Tamils to do "coolie" labor in the plantations.[1] By 1911, Indian Tamils made up almost 12 percent of the population in Ceylon (Nubin 2003). These new immigrants lived in squalid conditions mostly in the plantation-rich hill country in the center.

The British expropriated land owned by Sinhalese farmers and even Buddhist temple lands—especially in the hill region of Kandy—and used it to expand the plantation economy. The Sinhalese, naturally, resented the move. The British also instituted taxes, which led to further discontent and rebellions. The benefits from cash crops went largely to the British and to low-country, mostly elite Sinhalese and Indian Tamils (Nubin 2003). By contrast, the island's original Tamils, situated mostly in the north, did not have access to these economic opportunities available in the southwest and the central highlands. This forced them to focus their energy on education and entering white-collar occupations (Tambiah 1986).

The seeds of ethnic tension between the Sinhalese and Tamils were sown even before independence in 1948. Amid deliberations for the Soulbury Constitution—Ceylon's first postindependence constitution (named after the then governor general)—the Tamil political leadership called for disproportionate parliamentary quotas. They sought half the parliamentary seats even though, as the largest minority in Ceylon, they were not quite 20

1. For more on the importation of Tamil laborers, see Tambiah (1986), Spencer (1990), and Nubin (2003).

percent of the population. For this insistence, the Sinhalese political leadership, including the main Sinhalese-majority party at the time, the UNP, roundly accused the Tamils of communalism.

When the constitution was eventually enacted in 1948, both the Sinhalese and the native Tamil leaderships voted overwhelmingly to disenfranchise Indian Tamils by denying them citizenship through the Ceylon Citizenship Act. Tamil politicians, all of whom were Ceylonese, had hoped to win favor with the Sinhalese leadership by supporting the disenfranchisement of Indian Tamils, thereby gaining favor for more Tamil representation in Parliament. But some prominent Tamil leaders, such as S. J. V. Chelvanayagam, staunchly opposed these moves. These discontented Tamil political leaders broke away from the majority of their Tamil colleagues and formed the Federal Party (FP) in 1949, calling for fairness and equal opportunity for all Tamils vis-à-vis the majority Sinhalese.

The main Sinhalese-majority opposition party to the UNP, the SLFP, began in 1951. In these early years, language became a major sticking point. The early 1950s saw intense debates over what the country's official language should be. The background of this tussle lay in the preindependence period, when the Tamil community had emphasized fluency in English over the Sinhalese language while the class exclusivism among the Sinhalese meant that less than one-fifth of this demographic—the elites who also happened to be the feudal landholders at the time—attained fluency in English (Krishna 1999). The lower-caste Sinhalese masses were denied any such advantage. The language issue, then, was inextricably bound up with the ethnic misgivings.

Then Governor General Soulbury appointed Dudley Senanayake as Sri Lanka's prime minister in 1952. In 1955, while visiting Jaffna, the major Tamil-dominated city in the north, Senanayake explicitly expressed his desire to give the Tamil and Sinhalese languages parity. This statement sparked the first anti-Tamil riots in the country in 1956 because the Sinhalese perceived this offered concession as a betrayal by the UNP. It also resulted in fissures within the UNP. In the wake of the widespread Sinhalese nationalism that engulfed the country at the time, Sir John Kotelawala, who had taken over as prime minister from Senanayake, reneged on plans for language parity.

The SLFP, under the staunch nationalistic leadership of S. W. R. D. Bandaranaike, wanted to make Sinhala the sole official language.[2] A coalition of parties led by the SLFP won a snap election in 1956 and relegated

2. Bandaranaike, who became prime minister, was initially a member of the UNP, then broke away to form the SLFP. An Oxford-educated "high-class" political leader, he used Sinhalese propaganda to his advantage against the UNP.

the UNP to opposition status. The SLFP also brought forth a three-clause bill, the Official Language Act—also known as the Sinhala Only Act—that same year. The bill made Sinhala the sole official language of administration and governance. Interestingly enough, it was passed with the UNP's support.

It is important to note that not all Sinhalese political parties followed this chauvinistic, nationalist trend. Most notably, the leftist parties remained firm in their stance for equality for both languages. Both the Communist Party of Sri Lanka and the Lanka Sama Samaja Party (LSSP)—the Trotskyite party—opposed the Sinhala Only Act, as did the FP and Tamil Congress. Leslie Goonewardena, a Sinhalese LSSP leader, worried about possible secession by the Tamils, saying, "There is a possibility of their breaking away from the rest of the country." Colvin R. de Silva, another LSSP leader, added, "One language two countries, two languages one country" (Swamy 2002).

The Sinhalese leadership under Bandaranaike instituted Fabian socialist economic policies as Jawaharlal Nehru did in India. The resultant restrictions on the private sector and private profit, and the lack of a significant private sector in the economy, exacerbated the effects of the Sinhala Only Act and other ethnically discriminatory policies that were undertaken concurrently. Most of the available jobs were in the public sector, and to qualify for these jobs, one had to be fluent in Sinhalese—putting Tamils at an obvious disadvantage.[3]

Since Tamils had gained wider fluency in English—even though they represented not quite 20 percent of the overall population at the time—they were disproportionately represented in both public service and educational institutions. When the public sector erected the Sinhala-only language barrier for jobs and entry into secondary educational institutions, the gulf between the two communities widened drastically in favor of the Sinhalese. Some commentators insist that if English had been retained as the official language, much of the ethnic discontent would have been averted.[4]

Amid the ethnic violence that ensued in 1956, the FP held a national convention in the eastern port city of Trincomalee and passed a resolution demanding a federal constitution. Before the start of the convention, thousands of Tamils staged a long march led by members of Parliament. At the convention, they called for parity for both languages, a complete repeal of existing citizenship laws, and an end to the Sinhalese "colonization" of Tamil-majority areas. Tamils also voiced concerns over discrimination in recruitment for government service jobs. At the end of the

3. For more details, see Peebles (2006), Spencer (1990), and Nalapat (2011); they all present these effects succinctly.

4. Both Tambiah (1986) and Nalapat (2011) hold this position.

convention, FP members threatened to launch a regionwide campaign of civil disobedience if their demands were not met (Swamy 2002).

In 1957, seeking to put an end to the ongoing tensions, the SLFP and FP, now the main Tamil party, made a commitment known as the BC Pact.[5] The BC Pact ceded regional autonomy to the Northern Province (NP) and Eastern Province (EP), the non-Sinhalese-dominated provinces (shown on map 6). Tamils would have powers over agriculture and related matters, specifically "land settlement, regional development, law and order, local revenue allocations, use of the Tamil language, and propagation of Tamil culture" (Shastri 1990, 59). Shastri adds, "From the Tamil perspective, the agreement offered the structure of power most compatible with the compulsive realities of a majoritarian democracy at the national level while protecting their distinct needs and identity at the regional level" (Shastri 59–60). By signing the BC Pact, Tamils gave up claims of parity for Sinhala and Tamil languages at the national level. The following year, the Tamil Language (Special Provisions) Act was passed. It called for the use of the Tamil language for education, public service exams, and administration in the NP and EP.

The pattern of the Sinhalese leadership's reaching an agreement with the Tamils only to renege on it later began after the BC Pact. Due to massive and vehement UNP opposition along strictly ethnic lines, the SLFP abrogated the BC Pact in 1958. Ironically, the SLFP's reversal was partly responsible for a split within the FP the following year. A prominent FP member captured the sentiment within the party when he alleged "misery, degradation and loss of respect" to the Tamils through ineffectual leadership (Swamy 2002). Organized militant Tamils who later challenged moderates for leadership would echo this sentiment.

Meanwhile, on September 25, 1959, a Buddhist monk, allegedly perturbed at the BC Pact, assassinated Prime Minister Bandaranaike. Following the assassination, Bandaranaike's widow, Sirimavo, became the leader of the SLFP and ran for prime minister in 1960. The FP held on to the belief that Sirimavo would implement parts of the BC Pact and therefore helped elect her as prime minister. Sirimavo and the SLFP completely reneged on this implicit understanding and instead implemented the Sinhala Only Act of 1956, at the same time ignoring the Tamil Provisions Act. This series of events marked the first major setback in political relations between the two communities.

The 1960 election was a landmark event in many ways. It marked the first time that nearly all the Sinhalese political parties competed against each other by employing anti-Tamil rhetoric. Even Sri Lankan leftist

5. For a discussion of this agreement, see Shastri (1990).

groups, which had previously attracted large numbers of Tamils and had remained secular, embraced Sinhalese chauvinism. This chauvinism was most notable in the case of the LSSP, who promised vital support to the SLFP in the latter's postelection plans of enacting the Sinhala Only Act. These political choices signaled a clear shift among Sinhalese politicians to a more Sinhalese-nationalist platform.

The years 1960 and 1961 also marked the beginning of mass anti-FP sentiment within the Tamil populace. The FP, led by Chelvanayagam, announced its decision to launch "direct action" to assert the rights of the Tamil-speaking people after the public rebuke at the hands of the SLFP in 1960 (Swamy 2002; Tambiah 1986, 1992). They launched a Gandhian nonviolent satyagraha campaign, bringing public administration in the NP and EP to a standstill. Thousands of protesters in both provinces joined the campaign. The UNP, now in the opposition, publicly expressed sympathy with the campaigners. Most notably, many Sinhalese residents in the two provinces aided the campaigners directly or indirectly.

The Sri Lankan government was heavy-handed in its response to what was happening in the north and east. It declared a state of emergency, and a naval contingent laid siege to the main administrative offices in Jaffna. Sirimavo issued a warning to the FP on her way back from a Commonwealth summit in London, to which the FP leadership responded by rebuking the national government and inaugurating the Tamil Arasu Postal Service in Jaffna. Within an hour, they had managed to sell thousands of stamps, stamped envelopes, and postcards. A few days later, another twelve post offices were opened in Chelvanayagam's home constituency (Swamy 2002). This reaction was the most daring challenge to Colombo's authority to date and prompted the army to go on the offensive in Jaffna and attack the *satyagrahis*. Also, a number of FP Tamil parliament members were imprisoned. Several FP leaders expressed reservations about their Gandhian nonviolent tactics at this time, arguing that this would not achieve Tamil political objectives. These calls for stronger forms of opposition to the central government were reinforced when the Sirimavo regime actually started enforcing provisions of the Sinhala Only Act.

Meanwhile, the UNP, led by Dudley Senanayake, signed the DC Pact with the FP, which addressed the establishment of district councils, use of the Tamil language, and "colonization." With the wide support of the Tamils, the UNP won the 1965 elections, but it failed to secure a majority in Parliament and thus was forced to form a national government with the support of the FP, the Tamil Congress, and minor Sinhalese parties. In 1966, the Tamil Language (Special Provisions) Regulation was passed, which gave the Tamil language official status in the northeast. But in July 1968, in the face of strong agitation by the SLFP, the UNP reneged on its commitments to the DC Pact, just as the SLFP had done in 1958. In addition, the 1966 Tamil Language (Special Provisions) Regulation was not implemented. Finally, disgusted and dejected, the FP left the government in 1969.

The 1970 election led to a further decline in Sinhala-Tamil relations. The FP wanted to pit the two main Sinhala parties against each other, while both the UNP and the SLFP used anti-Tamil rhetoric in their party platforms. Although the FP won thirteen of the nineteen seats it contested in the northeast, its performance showed that it was losing the confidence of the Tamil people. Meanwhile, the SLFP, using anti-Tamil and anti-Senanayake rhetoric, managed to win the national elections. Sirimavo established a Constituent Assembly to draft a new constitution. Her government also introduced communal quotas for higher education, which were put into effect in 1971. Higher university entrance requirements were imposed for Tamil speakers, and proposals for parity between the Sinhala and Tamil languages were rejected. This development led many of the moderate Tamil members to withdraw from the Constituent Assembly. The Republican Constitution of 1972 officially made Sinhala the sole language of the state and judicial administration. Government restrictions also made migration by Tamils to foreign countries nearly impossible—India being the only exception. Hence, opportunities for Tamil students to study abroad were also reduced.

One area that witnessed a profound transformation due to the Sinhalese nationalist revival was education. As Peebles points out, before 1971, ideologically driven changes were made to the national curricula and examination systems to bridge the gap between urban and rural, privileged and underprivileged, and Tamil and Sinhalese students (Peebles 2006). Practical education was emphasized over liberal arts, English was taught from grade six on, and science was de-emphasized while cultural studies and socialism studies were emphasized. Universities were brought under central control. Under the Higher Education Act of January 1972, university admission was increased, but only 20 percent of all qualified students were admitted. The communal quotas were instituted, via "standardization" of test scores, to increase admission of Sinhalese students since it was deemed that Tamils had been disproportionately represented in universities before the quotas. Test score standardization meant that a much smaller percentage of Tamil students could attend university than before.

The FP and other Tamil groups came together to form the TUF in 1971, mostly as a reaction to these governmental policies. Although the TUF comprised moderate Tamil politicians, they became increasingly agitated with pro-Sinhala policies. These tensions culminated in the transformation of the TUF into the Tamil United Liberation Front (TULF). This was a change in more than name. The TULF echoed calls for autonomy for Tamil-dominated areas being made by the more militant Tamil elements that had sprung up by this time. In 1976, the TULF passed the Vaddukoddai Resolution, calling for a separate state of Tamil Eelam.[6] Running on a secessionist platform, the TULF won the second-largest number of votes in the general elections of 1977 and became the opposition party for the first time. The UNP, led by J. R. Jayawardene, secured power as the majority government.

The 1978 Constitution, the second Republican Constitution to be adopted in six years, created an executive presidency rather than an executive premiership, among other sweeping changes. The UNP, once again presenting a relatively moderate face, gathered the TULF's support by granting partial concessions to Tamils. One of the main concessions was the decentralization of administration through the District Development Councils (DDCs) Act in 1979. The TULF gave its full support to the DDC Act. In 1981, amid bloody anti-Tamil violence triggered when militant Tamils killed two policemen at a TULF meeting, the TULF won DDC elections in Jaffna, only to have the UNP resist decentralization of administration to the degree called for by the DDC Act.[7] TULF left Parliament as anti-Tamil riots plagued the country in 1983.

By the mid-1970s, the economic viability of an independent Tamil state had become apparent. Although there were legitimate grievances, the realization of the possibility of an independent state occurred when the once economically peripheral areas of the north and east became economic and agricultural centers.[8] By the early 1970s, the traditionally rural and economically unimportant areas of the NP and, particularly, the EP became important rice-producing regions thanks to the government's Mahaweli Development Program. Jaffna, with many small landholders, produced significant crops of chilies and onions. Moreover, by this time, the locus of agricultural production had shifted to the Dry Zone in the EP, with Trincomalee, the province's prominent port city, being hailed as the hub of the next stage of Sri Lankan export-based industrialization.[9] These developments were paramount in driving calls for an Eelam state, which combined not only the traditional Tamil homelands in the north but also the emerging economic power base in the east. This Tamil homeland would be able to

6. For a compelling argument that the timing of vociferous calls for separatism in the north and east of the country corresponded with the region's rising economic viability (discussed later), see Shastri (1990).

7. After a Tamil militant group fired at a TULF public meeting near Jaffna town, killing two policemen and wounding two more, a wave of anti-Tamil rioting erupted in Jaffna. This time, policemen were responsible. Amid looting of houses, shops, and institutions, they went on a rampage and attacked selective targets related to the TULF. The Jaffna library, which housed more than ninety thousand books and many rare Tamil manuscripts, was burned. The violence also spread to the eastern town of Ratnapura, where Tamil property came under attack. Indian Tamils were targeted, and an estimated fifteen thousand had to flee to Vavuniya as refugees.

8. The following discussion is taken mostly from Shastri (1990).

9. The Dry Zone consists of the north and much of the east and southeast.

export agricultural produce and mobilize revenues to develop these regions without the aid of the central government—a previously unimaginable proposition.

The Sinhalese in-migration in previously Tamil-dominated areas in the north and east, primarily undertaken by the UNP under the Accelerated Mahaweli Program in the late 1970s (discussed in the next section), also factored heavily in the calls for separation from the central government. These "colonization" programs—the creation of agricultural settlements in the undeveloped interior of the island, which historically had a population mostly of minority ethnic groups—were undertaken by the Jayawardene regime, ostensibly to redress demographic disparities in these Tamil-dominated regions. But Tamils saw them as blatant ploys to weaken the power base of the moderate Tamil FP and minimize the economic feasibility of a separate Tamil homeland. Colonization was also seen as a means of diverting resources and revenues from these newly emerging agricultural centers in the north and east to the central government—another intolerable prospect. Thus, the start of colonization brought more urgent calls for separation from the rest of the country.

Ethnoreligious Dimensions

The political and economic tensions discussed above are both cause and effect of the social and religious antagonism between the Sinhalese and the Tamils in postindependence Sri Lanka. The merging of the ethnic Sinhala identity with that of the majority religion, Buddhism, allowed Sinhalese politicians to mobilize the majority more effectively than would have been possible through appeals focused solely on ethnic identity.[10]

When Sri Lanka gained independence from the British, the nonelite Sinhalese class led a backlash against the alleged elitism of the UNP's British-educated, English-speaking leadership. In a very short time, this animosity focused on the Tamils as well, who were also viewed as a foreign group. As mentioned earlier, this feeling emanated from the alienation that low-caste Sinhalese felt toward the British and the postindependence high-caste Sinhalese. Some commentators point out that the forces led by S. W. R. D. Bandaranaike ushered in socialist and national forces represented mainly by the underprivileged low-caste Sinhalese, who were driven by conspiracy theories of the influence of the "Catholic cabal" and viewed all foreign, non-Sinhalese influences as existential threats (Roberts 1997; Spencer 1990).

10. For indispensable reading on the origins and evolution of Sinhala-Buddhist rhetoric and its applications in postindependence Sri Lanka, see Tambiah (1992). For a good examination of the rise in Sinhala awareness, see Gunawardena (1985). On Sinhalese nationalist groups, their histories, actions, and later offshoots, see Matthews (1988).

The 1956 general elections were the first manifestation of this Sinhala-Buddhist revival on a massive scale. Tambiah points out, "It is not surprising that the post-independence boiling over of the pot of Sinhalese nationalism resulted in the entirely unexpected landslide defeat of the UNP by S. W. R. D. Bandaranaike, who led the opposition groups and championed their nationalist and revivalist demands and aspirations." He later adds, "The same boiling pot also spilled over in the form of the first Sinhalese riots against the Tamils in 1956 and 1958" (Tambiah 1986, 71).

With the declaration of Sinhala as the country's official language and its language of education and commerce (under the Sinhala Only Act), the seeds of ethnic discontent and rivalry were sown.[11] Since Tamils who held governmental positions were proficient in Tamil and English but not Sinhala, the proportion of Tamils in the public sector fell sharply after the act's implementation. In response to the passage of the Sinhala Only Act, over three hundred FP members, with the support of the leftist Sinhala parties, organized a peaceful sit-in facing the Parliament in 1956. These satyagrahis were beaten by mobs led by several Buddhist monks. The police did nothing to stop the attack. Many prominent Tamil leaders suffered serious wounds. Upon seeing these and other wounded FP members in Parliament later in the evening, Bandaranaike remarked, rather prophetically, that these were "honorable wounds of war!" (Swamy 2002).

Ethnic violence erupted in the country for the first time in 1956. Over 150 people, mostly Tamils, were killed. The FP heeded the SLFP's call for peace and launched a massive campaign of nonviolent civil resistance, pursued despite great adversity and provocation. The resulting BC Pact of 1957 was an attempt to quell the civil unrest. But Sinhalese chauvinism, now embraced by the UNP in addition to the SLFP, ensured that the Pact was abrogated and the Tamil Language (Special Provisions) Act ignored. After the DC Pact was abrogated in 1968, ethnic tensions were stoked once again. As one commentator pointed out, "It was another grievous mistake—one that Tamil guerillas [*sic*] in later years would point out as an example of Sinhalese obduracy vis-à-vis the Tamils" (Swamy 2002, 17).

In addition to reneging on their political commitments to the minority, the majority government actively sought to alienate, demobilize, and humiliate the moderates among the minority. The assault on the Gandhian protesters in 1961 was the first example of this myopic policy. In 1973, the government arrested several Tamil activists, among them members of the TUF. In January 1974, when the fourth conference of the International Association of Tamil Research was held in Jaffna, the police brutally attacked the confer-

11. For a good discussion of some of these issues, see Sahadevan (1999). On the prejudicial nature and consequences of this Act, see Tambiah (1986) and Shastri (1990).

ence, leaving nine people dead. This incident was a turning point for the radical movement and a clear indication that the majority would not tolerate a mobilized, but peaceful, minority (Swamy 2002; Tambiah 1986).

Anti-Tamil violence broke out during the 1977 elections in the south, and as part of the "security protocols," the moderates were not allowed to organize. The government then passed the PTA in 1979, which further increased militant activity in response to crackdowns from the state. As Bloom points out, "Rather than mitigate the occurrences of violence, the PTA escalated Tamil violence in the 1980s, and additional repressive counter measures of the government led to a spiral of increasing brutality and tit for tat violence" (Bloom 2005, 52). These government-led measures to combat militant activity extended to the moderates as well, and they were further alienated.

The 1983 riots proved to be a defining moment in ethnic relations between the Sinhalese and Tamils. In July 1983, the LTTE killed thirteen Sri Lankan army soldiers in an ambush near Jaffna. All the slain soldiers were Sinhalese, and eight of the thirteen were in their early twenties. It was the military's biggest loss so far. In retaliation for the killings, the Sri Lanka Light Infantry went on a rampage, attacking Tamil civilians in Jaffna. After detailed deliberations and in keeping with the wishes of the next of kin, the government decided to bring the bodies of the slain soldiers to Colombo instead of burying them in Jaffna. Violence erupted in Colombo as the bodies were brought back, with mobs attacking Tamil homes, shops, and businesses—killing, looting, and raping. The violence spread from Colombo to other Sinhalese-dominated areas.[12]

In some districts, security forces joined the mayhem and attacked Tamil civilian targets. They even directed some of the violence. Around forty-five imprisoned Tamils, including three militants, were also killed in two separate prisons. Military personnel inside the prisons prevented prison guards from restraining the Sinhalese prisoners. The government first imposed daily curfews but then extended them to nationwide curfews as angry mobs rampaged all over the island. In the weeklong violence throughout the country, hundreds of Tamils died and an estimated eighty thousand fled to refugee camps in Colombo and Jaffna (de Silva 2005; Swamy 2002).

The alienated Tamils emulated the Sinhalese by embracing ethnic chauvinism. Gunawardena (1985) mentions that the Tamils, especially the political elites—mostly from the Vellalar caste—were greatly influenced by Dravidian thought. They maintained that their culture was "pure" Dravidian and thus antedated the "Aryan" Brahmin influence that some Sinhalese

12. For detailed discussions on the July riots and their ramifications, see Swamy (2002) and de Silva (2005).

elites saw as their ethnic origins. Peebles explicitly argues that some Sri Lankan Tamils fell prey to racist rhetoric, calling themselves a "Dravidian" race (Peebles 1990, 31).[13] He adds that these claims, and claims that the northern and eastern regions were "Tamil homelands," found "little support even among Sri Lanka Tamils for secession until the political crises of the 1970s and 1980s" (Peebles 1990, 32).

The majority government explicitly tried to undermine the moderate Tamil leadership in other ways as well. They essentially followed a divide-and-rule logic, reasoning that if the moderates were made ineffectual, then any threat to Sinhalese political dominance would be undermined. For example, Pfaffenberger points out that the Tamil community was sharply divided along caste lines and that "the call for regional autonomy in the Tamil north, and even for the partition of Sri Lanka, emerged first from conservative sections of the Vellalar caste, which deeply resented Colombo's interference in what they considered the 'private' matters of caste relations and temple worship" (Pfaffenberger 1990, 79). The crux of his paper—which deals with the 1968 Maviddapuram temple entry incident between the Vellalar caste and other lower castes—is that as a matter of defensive ethnic nationalism, the FP and later the TULF tried to unite the Tamil community and divert attention from this Jaffna issue, which would have made the Tamil community "fall to pieces."[14] Thus, given legitimate grievances against the Sinhalese-dominated governments, defensive nationalism was another prime reason why the TULF called for separatist politics.

This "interference" from the governments in Colombo first came in the form of the Prevention of Social Disabilities Act of 1957, aimed at outlawing caste discrimination and undertaken "in part to embarrass the Vellalar-dominated Tamil political leadership." He adds, "Although the law proscribes discriminatory acts found sometimes within Sinhalese caste relations, its text specifies the actual forms of intercaste discrimination in Jaffna with an accuracy that would elicit praise from a social anthropologist" (Pfaffenberger 1990, 86). With the enactment of the 1972 Constitution, which provided for state sponsorship of the Buddhist religion, many Hindus feared a government-led onslaught against Tamil culture and Hindu religion in Jaffna. The Tamil leadership was thus further weakened in the eyes of its own people, which was the intent of the Sinhalese-dominated governments.

13. Pamela Price claims that certain aspects of the Sri Lankan Tamil nationalist movement were borrowed from the Indian nationalist movement of the 1950s and 1960s (Price 1996).

14. Maviddapuram temple was a holy temple that the Vellalar-caste Tamils had prevented other, "lesser" castes from worshipping in. The government passed the Prevention of Social Disabilities Act of 1957, aimed at barring precisely this form of discrimination.

"Colonization" attempts undertaken by the Sinhalese in traditionally Tamil areas proved to be the final straw for ethnoreligious tensions. According to Peebles, although both major parties competed for the Sinhalese vote, colonization was associated primarily with the UNP. He blames propaganda surrounding the Accelerated Mahaweli Program for causing further strains in Sinhala-Tamil relations: "During the UNP government of President Junius Richard Jayawardene (1977–1988), both the level of violence and the pace of colonization in the Dry Zone between the Sinhalese and Tamil majority areas increased" (Peebles 1990, 30). He adds, "The Dry Zone has been transformed from a plural society to a homogenous Sinhalese Buddhist one" (Peebles 1990, 40). He quotes Horowitz as saying that the Sinhalese governments perceived the Sinhalese to be a disadvantaged relative to a minority community in the Dry Zone. Thus, colonization was an attempt to redress these inequalities (Horowitz 1985, 141–56). Sahadevan observes, "The resettlement of a large number of rural Sinhalese in the EP was a direct threat to the 'traditional homeland' of the Sri Lankan Tamils" (Sahadevan 1999, 4). He further contends that the Sri Lankan government made no concessions regarding colonization until President Jayewardene met Prime Minister Rajiv Gandhi of India in October 1985. Then there were assurances given that "future colonization would be based on existing ethnic proportions to preserve current demographic balances" (Sahadevan 1999, 46).

From its inception, the FP made colonization a social and political issue for Tamils. Commenting on the 1977 elections, Peebles observes: "The July 21, 1977, elections raised unfulfilled expectations that negotiations between the UNP and TULF, both of whom won sweeping victories, would settle the ethnic crisis" (Peebles 1990, 40). He argues that President Jayawardene thought the 1978 Constitution would resolve the ethnic crisis but adds, "The new constitution modified the wording of passages in the 1972 constitution to which Tamils had objected, and the government resisted Sinhalese extremist demands to further enhance the status of the Sinhala language and Buddhism. The TULF rejected the constitution, however, and Tamil extremists gained strength as negotiations faltered in 1979" (Peebles 1990, 45). Tamil separatists encouraged a backlash in various ways. Chief among them was the Gandhian movement, which resettled Tamil estate workers in the Vavuniya district in 1978–79. The military dealt with these resettlements very harshly: "In July 1979, Brigadier T. I. Weeratunga was sent to Jaffna with orders to 'wipe out terrorism in six months'" (Matthews 1986, 37).

Ultimately, as Peebles argues, "The turning point toward civil war can be traced to two elections in 1982, particularly a referendum in December that extended the life of Parliament rather than hold new elections and initiated the period of accelerated conflict" (Peebles 1990, 45). Parliament expelled the TULF on October 20, 1983, just as violence rose, because the Sinhalese government saw the TULF as possibly inciting the violence and opposition to its rule. Negotiations failed as a result, although they resumed in 1984. Peebles contends, "By the time an abortive all-party conference was dismissed in December 1984, military considerations outweighed negotiations" (Peebles 1990, 46).

Early Militancy and Boilover

The persistence of political, economic, and ethnoreligious tensions between the Sinhalese and Tamils ultimately transformed into one of the most devastating insurgencies in recent history. Tamil radical militancy, which had very humble origins, blossomed into a movement involving more than two dozen separate armed groups with varied ideologies and tactics. The original groups were offshoots of the FP. Nearly all were Marxist in nature, drew from many segments of the Tamil population in the north and east, and held idealistic expectations for the outcome of their struggle. Almost all used violence to achieve their goals. The leading groups were armed, funded, and trained by India and also had help from the Palestine Liberation Organization (PLO) and the Irish Republican Army. What started as a concerted effort by many Tamil militant leaders toward the same goal later became a power struggle to establish dominance and speak for all Tamils.

The moderate Tamil political groups looked ineffectual thanks to the intransigent and myopic policies of the majority governments, and radical Tamil groups attempted to fill the void left in their wake. Radicalism started within the moderate ranks of the FP, with the 1961 emergence of Pulip Padai (Army of Tigers), a group of twenty youths who started off distributing leaflets advocating militancy.[15] Some of these members tried to influence the general direction of FP politics, promoting certain key FP leaders, such as Amirthalingam and V. Navaratnam, who advocated a more hard-line stance against the government and espoused aspirations of a separate homeland for the Tamils. Others in the group started smuggling in arms. Pulip Padai disbanded when the FP publicly supported the UNP during the 1965 elections.

As successive governments in Colombo continued to rescind official commitments, the FP's Youth League broke ranks with the rest of the party in 1968. The split was inevitable, and Pfaffenberger is clear on where the blame lies: "Faced with mounting youth unemployment, the FP's Youth League was showing signs of increasing radicalism in early 1968 in response

15. For details on the group's formation, see Swamy (2002).

to government delays in bringing the District Development Council (DDC) bill before the Parliament; indeed, a Youth League spokesman told a Colombo newspaper reporter that he had lost all confidence not only in the government but also in the Federal Party" (Pfaffenberger 1990, 91).

Thus, as moderate Tamil fortunes waned, radicalism increased in prominence and appeal. When the SLFP government introduced communal quotas for higher education in 1970, the TSL was formed to protest these proposals. According to Swamy (2002), two 1971 incidents greatly influenced Tamil radicals. The first was the radical Marxist Sinhalese-nationalist militant uprising in the south, led by the Janatha Vimukthi Peramuna (JVP). The JVP insurrection was fueled by unrest over perceived societal inequities felt by many youth of lower economic and social classes. The SLFP government mercilessly crushed the JVP, killing ten thousand to fifteen thousand Sinhalese youth. Emergency powers were enacted to accomplish the task. The Tamil radicals learned from the JVP insurrection how to organize a nascent, poorly equipped revolutionary movement against the state. They also learned how the state would respond to such a movement.

The second important lesson in 1971 came from the creation of Bangladesh. The Pakistani army cracked down on the Awami League, which was comparable to the FP, in the eastern half of the country. When millions of Bengalis fled to India as refugees, the Indian government secretly armed them. This action gave the Tamils an invaluable insight: An armed struggle, under India's patronage, was a potent strategy for achieving freedom.

In Jaffna that same year, unsuccessful assassination attempts against government representatives, political and military, were widely attributed to the TSL. In September 1970, a TSL member had tried to assassinate the Sri Lankan deputy minister for cultural affairs (Swamy 2002). In addition to its attacks on Sinhalese government officials, the TSL targeted alleged government "collaborators" among the Tamils. Notable among these attacks were an unsuccessful assassination attempt on a government supporter in Jaffna in 1972 and an attempt on the life of a Tamil Congress member of Parliament who voted for the Republican Constitution (Swamy 2002).

The TSL proved to be the launching pad for many militant Tamil groups, including the TELO and Velupillai Prabhakaran's TNT in May 1972. Tamil Ilaignar Peravai, or Tamil Youth League (TYL), was formed in 1973. It, too, emphasized armed struggle to achieve a separate homeland for the Tamils—quite a departure from the far more modest goal of greater autonomy that Tamil political moderates continued to pursue. When justifying the use of militancy in pursuit of their political goals, all these Tamil groups pointed to past failed political attempts at working with majority governments. In February–March 1973, a series of police arrests crippled the TYL and the older TSL. To escape the crackdown, Prabhakaran and other rebel leaders fled to India.

From 1971 onward, Tamil radicals started experimenting with homemade explosives. TNT members threw bombs at a police jeep in Kankesanthurai and detonated another bomb at the residence of a communist leader who was to be the interpreter for the prime minister on her visit to Jaffna. Almost from the beginning, these groups resorted to lethal force, incuding suicide, to advance their cause. On June 5, 1974, the police trapped a seventeen-year-old TSL leader named Sivakumaran, who, to escape torture, swallowed cyanide. Sivakumaran was the first of many rebels to commit suicide via cyanide. By 2003, more than six hundred Tamil Tigers had done so to avoid capture (Pape 2005). Militant groups started killing police and innocent civilians, both Tamil and non-Tamil. After an earlier failed attempt, TNT finally assassinated the mayor of Jaffna, Alfred Duraiappah, on July 27, 1975. Although a popular man, Duraiappah personified the government regime in the north. Prabhakaran (who changed TNT's name to LTTE in May 1976) was one of the four assassins. Significantly, no moderate Tamil politician condemned the mayor's murder. After this incident, TNT and Prabhakaran became famous not only in Jaffna but all over Sri Lanka. Although the total number of Tamil militants at the time was less than fifty, toward the end of the 1970s they began engaging military targets (Swamy 2002).

In January 1975, a group of Sri Lankan Tamils living in London formed the Eelam Revolutionary Organizers (EROS).[16] EROS drew its cadres mainly from the northeast areas of Batticaloa and Amparai. The student wing of EROS, General Union of Eelam Students (GUES), formed in London in 1975. In an attempt to bring the FP and Tamil Congress, the two main political parties, closer together on a platform of national liberation, TUF became TULF after 1976. TUF's moderate dictates produced resentment within the mainly radical TYL. Some members of the TYL began to see the mainstream Tamil leadership as "half-hearted armchair revolutionaries" (Swamy 2002). In 1975, a split occurred within the TYL: One branch put its support behind the TUF while the other broke away and formed the Eelam Liberation Organization, which advocated armed struggle but remained a reformist organization. In 1980, EROS and GUES went their separate ways, and the Eelam People's Revolutionary Liberation Front (EPRLF), a leftist group with strong Marxist inclinations, was born. Meanwhile, after a bitter split within the LTTE, the People's Liberation

16. Some have argued that "Eelam" (motherland) is simply a synonym for "Sri Lanka." The South Indian Chola kings used this term for regional governance of Sri Lanka. It is also mentioned in reference to imports from the island, circa 200BC–AD200. In this context, Sinhalese have also been a part of Eelam, along with the Tamils.

Organization of Tamil Eelam (PLOTE) was created in 1980. In March 1982, the TULF split into two groups, with the breakaway group calling itself the Tamil Eelam Liberation Front. Around this time, the LTTE, along with the TELO, EPRLF, and PLOTE, began publicly expressing dissatisfaction with the moderate TULF. These radical sentiments echoed the growing dissatisfaction that the Tamil populace in the north felt toward the moderates (Swamy 2002).

Radical groups continued to proliferate. In fact, they mushroomed in the aftermath of the violent July 1983 ethnic riots. According to some estimates, as many as thirty-eight radical groups were created at this time. Many radicals would later cite the anti-Tamil violence of 1983 as the main catalyst intensifying their violent struggle for a separate homeland. From this point on, the insurgency truly took off.

It is important to note that the Tamil radical groups were far from united. Other than their use of violence, their common feature early on (except in the nationalistic TELO) was their avowed espousal of Marxism (Swamy 2002). Moreover, in the beginning, some of the radical groups were idealistic and did not believe in robbing Tamils or targeting civilians. But by the mid-1980s, all the main groups were targeting civilians and armed forces, and many had even abandoned their Marxist leanings.

As the struggle turned violent and solidified to challenge the Sri Lankan state, a parallel vicious tussle arose within Tamil ranks to determine who would be the face of the insurgency. This struggle resulted in significant inter- and intragroup violence among radical Tamil groups and was often behind some of the splits within the groups. For instance, the LTTE leaders, Prabhakaran and Uma Maheswaran, had a prolonged row and ultimately left the group in 1979 and 1980, respectively. Prabhakaran joined the TELO for nearly a year but headed back to the LTTE, while Uma went on to form the PLOTE.

The LTTE, and especially Prabhakaran, was at the forefront of trying to quash any and all dissent. Prabhakaran ordered or directly took part in the execution of many LTTE members he disagreed with. Prabhakaran and Uma also tried to kill each other several times.[17] After many other incidents throughout the first half of the 1980s, on April 29, 1986, the LTTE crippled the second-largest rival rebel group, the TELO, after fighting in the north of the country. Hundreds of rebels died. In his first major interview in the wake of the TELO attacks, Prabhakaran confessed that the LTTE believed in a single-party state and would tolerate

17. For instance, Prabhakaran tried to shoot Uma when Uma stepped out of a movie theater in India in May 1982. Later, the two, along with other members of LTTE and PLOTE, had a shootout in Madras, India.

no opposition (Swamy 2002). He said that only through one-party rule could the dream of an independent Eelam be expeditiously achieved. By the early 1990s, the LTTE was the only radical Tamil group operating against the government. All the other groups were killed off, forced to join the LTTE, or compelled either to flee the country or to make alliances with the government and join the political mainstream.

A number of Tamil radical groups also managed to collaborate almost as often as they fought each other, which was not unusual in the beginning phases of insurgencies. Although intergroup tensions far surpassed the convergences, there were many examples of cooperative behavior. In 1976, the LTTE reached an agreement with EROS and used its training camp in Vavuniya and, with EROS's help, sent cadres to be trained by the PLO in Lebanon. In 1976–77, EROS members themselves trained the LTTE for a while. In April 1984, the EPRLF joined the TELO and the EROS to form an umbrella group called the Eelam National Liberation Front (ENLF). The ENLF coordinated attacks and shared intelligence, and the LTTE formally joined the group in April 1985. In December 1985, when the Sri Lankan army launched a coordinated attack on an LTTE base, guerrillas from the TELO, EPRLF, and Tamil Eelam Army joined the battle on the LTTE's side. In January–February 1986, when battle-weary Sri Lankan soldiers began moving out of one of their main camps in the north, rebels belonging to the LTTE, TELO, and EPRLF fought together against them. And as late as October 1989, the EPRLF, Eelam National Democratic Liberation Front, TELO, and PLOTE formed the Tamil National Congress to coordinate their actions (Weerasinghe and Lichbach 2006).

The Sri Lankan government played an interesting role amid all these developments. In the aftermath of the 1983 riots, the government blamed the violence on the TULF and forced it to leave Parliament. The government then blamed the leftist parties for orchestrating the violence. Once the radical groups started mushrooming and the violence escalated, the government took the rebels on militarily, yet they let the rebels kill each other during the internal conflicts. When, by the mid-1980s, it was obvious that the LTTE would emerge as the dominant militant group, the government forces, along with other Tamil rebel groups opposed to the LTTE, started waging war against it. Ultimately, however, the government could never retain a consistent enough policy and wavered, at one point even arming the LTTE to oust the Indian presence, as discussed below.

The External Dimension of Tamil Militancy

Tamil radical groups had strong international connections and derived part of their strength from external patronage. The PLO started training some of the Tamil groups in its camps in Lebanon as far back as 1976. The pleas of the Sri Lankan government did not persuade the PLO to halt this assistance. Support also came from sympathizers in India. Until the 1977 riots, the government of Tamil Nadu, the south Indian Tamil-majority state—led by Maruthur Gopalan Ramachandran, who headed the All India Anna Dravida Munnetra Kazhagam (AIADMK)—had been indifferent to the Tamil situation in Sri Lanka. After the riots, however, the Tamil Nadu assembly voiced its indignation. The Dravida Munnettra Kazhagam (DMK), a leading Tamil party in Tamil Nadu, organized a general strike in the state (Swamy 2002).

By 1980, Tamil militant groups were getting support from rival sponsors in New Delhi and Tamil Nadu, including the AIADMK and DMK, and they were trained and armed by the Research and Analysis Wing (RAW)—India's external intelligence agency—and the Indian army. Under Prime Minister Indira Gandhi's leadership, India supported the Tamil rebels. Retired Indian military officers began training the LTTE and other groups in New Delhi with the Indian government's full knowledge, as the rebel leadership fled Sri Lanka following powerful governmental military operations during 1979–81. Even when LTTE leaders such as Prabhakaran and Uma Maheswaran were arrested in Tamil Nadu in 1982, India refused Sri Lanka's requests for their extradition, thanks to agitation by the DMK.

In India's official support of Tamil insurgents, especially the LTTE, geopolitical considerations were paramount. The most pressing concern for Indira Gandhi was not the plight of the Tamils in Sri Lanka but the fact that Sri Lankan president Jayawardene was aligned with the United States, China, and Pakistan—three nations that were working together to support the jihad against the Soviet occupation in Afghanistan in the 1980s. From the Indian perspective, these three powers were cooperating with Sri Lanka in lessening Indian influence regionally and within Sri Lanka. Also, Tamil Nadu's support of Tamil insurgents in Sri Lanka pushed New Delhi to back the rebels.[18]

Tamil militant attacks waned in 1980, following the radical leadership's escape to India and internal bickering among the groups, but picked up the following year when military action against Tamil radicals stopped. After the 1983 riots, Indian Tamil youth arrived in Sri Lanka by boat to fight the Sri Lankan government alongside the rebel groups. The Indian government's response to this violence was interesting. On the one hand, New Delhi launched intensive efforts to secure rights for Tamils within a unitary Sri Lankan state. Thereafter, it even started assisting the Sri Lankan government in countering Tamil militants. In 1986, the Indian government

18. For details, see Krishna (1999). For a succinct analysis, see Nalapat (2011).

seized communications equipment belonging to the LTTE and even held Prabhakaran temporarily under house arrest in Madras.

On the other hand, however, India took steps that ran counter to the Sri Lankan government's interests. In 1987, the Sri Lankan army launched a massive military campaign, Operation Liberation, against the rebels and concurrently instituted a blockade of Jaffna that extended to food, fuel, and medicine. Indian prime minister Rajiv Gandhi, departing from the policy of his mother, Indira Gandhi, had been insistent on not overly supporting the push for a separate Tamil state. But he began a process of arming the LTTE when it seemed that its northern stronghold might fall. Again, geopolitical considerations were significant in Rajiv's intervention in Sri Lanka in 1987. India feared that if Sri Lanka emerged victorious in its war against the rebels—as it was close to accomplishing in 1987—it would align with the U.S.-China-Pakistan triumvirate and strengthen the anti-India bloc on India's borders (Krishna 1999; Swamy 2002; Nalapat 2011).

After an unsuccessful attempt to send a ship filled with supplies, India parachuted food and medicine into Jaffna despite the Sri Lankan government's curfew. The next step was to initiate diplomatic negotiations between Colombo and New Delhi. Ironically enough, this effort resulted in the Indo-Lanka Peace Accord, providing for an IPKF in the northeast of the country. After Indian persuasion, the LTTE agreed to surrender large caches of arms and ammunition. Official Indian funding for the rebel groups, and training supervised by the RAW, were cut even though clandestine funding from Tamil Nadu continued to flow. The LTTE was also forced to accept a cease-fire.

The fissures between the LTTE and the Indian government became apparent soon afterward. Prabhakaran insisted on formal independence from Sri Lanka. India was adamantly opposed to such a move for fear of inciting secession within its own borders. Not surprisingly, the LTTE's acceptance of this arrangement did not last long. But in 1988, it overplayed its hand and began to wage war on the IPKF presence. In yet another twist, the newly elected UNP government of Sri Lanka took a nationalistic stance soon thereafter, branding the IPKF presence as a grave threat to Sri Lankan sovereignty. President Premadasa proceeded to fund and arm the LTTE to overwhelm the IPKF and then ordered the IPKF to leave. Amid troubled India–Sri Lanka relations, the IPKF finally withdrew in 1990, leaving behind an even stronger LTTE. Some of the Sri Lankan state's worst years in its failure to tackle the LTTE insurgency were to follow.

Conclusion

The ethnic conflict between the Sinhalese and Tamils had multidimensional causes, and yet it ultimately spiraled out of control due to the shortsighted and intransigent actions of both ethnic groups. The

Sinhalese-majority governments, however, must take the larger share of the blame for letting electoral and communal gains prevail over more rational and farsighted motivations. Once radicals had occupied the bargaining space left by the alienated Tamil moderate groups, there was little hope for a political solution to the conflict. This is the primary lesson from the Sri Lankan experience: The time for settling ethnic tensions through political means occurs in the beginning, when parties are amenable to discussion and the use of violence has not been entertained by the minority—somewhere in the unstable peace phase of the conflict curve. It is imperative to seize these opportunities before organized violence enters the fray and the conflict curve shifts from the peaceful stage to the crisis and war stages. The onus will always be on the majority group to accommodate the minority and ensure that the moderate parties within the minority speak for the minority as a whole. Militant groups, if they are present, need to lose their appeal due to the powerful presence of more moderating forces within the minority.[19] A prescient majority government realizes that if it gives minority moderates power and credibility, it will have not only a favorably disposed minority but also a unified and peaceful regime.

The Sri Lankan case clearly exemplifies this recommendation. From the beginning, majority governments were not interested in credibly committing to the minority. As time went by, the majority governments, in their quest to win and maintain power, pandered to extremist sentiments within the majority population, stoked Sinhala nationalism, and repeatedly isolated the moderate Tamil leadership. To make matters worse, the majority governments used the Tamil parties to win electoral coalitions by guaranteeing concessions (most notably, the BC and DC Pacts) on which they reneged when confronted with agitation from Sinhalese opponents. As these bargaining failures began to mount, growing calls came from the Tamil moderates for a stronger stance in relations with the government and from the Tamil population for credible agreements. When it was clear that these calls were not going to be heeded, radicals within the Tamil population started gaining influence, even among moderates.

When the government actively tried to undermine the moderates' influence (by passing the Prevention of Social Disabilities Act, for example) and break their ranks, the moderates had no choice but to join the radicals in an attempt to maintain their own power structure. Thus, the Tamil calls changed from initial insistence on political settlements, with guaranteed civil liberties and relative autonomy, to demands for complete autonomy

19. For a preliminary examination of whether the existence of many radical groups in the Sri Lankan context helped or hindered the ability to make credible commitments, see Weerasinghe and Lichbach (2006). This by itself is an important question, but only if the conflict is allowed to escalate to this level.

within a separate Tamil Eelam homeland. The Sri Lankan case leads to a fundamental query: Will the majoritarian democratic system actually undermine ethnic politics, especially in cases where there is a large majority coalition? The Sri Lankan experience suggests that it can potentially do so, necessitating a great effort by the majority to include and accommodate the minority. This can be done very effectively using "credible commitments"—arrangements in which parties to an agreement are assured that all those involved have strong enough incentives to adhere to it and, therefore, will not unilaterally renege on the understanding.[20] Also, the minority needs to help the majority realize the shared benefits of such cooperative actions. Both groups may need to forsake short-term electoral gains for long-term sustainable agreements that strengthen ethnic relations. Thus, the overall spirit of just distribution across factors that underpin the tensions in a society becomes central.

Another important consideration in the Sri Lankan situation is the involvement of third parties, particularly India. Many other state and non-state actors played a role in the Sri Lankan conflict, but India's role was pivotal. As the regional hegemon, India had unusual clout and undertook actions unilaterally, such as parachuting supplies to Jaffna amid an embargo enforced by the government in Colombo. India was also influential in forcing parties to accept treaties that they would not otherwise have concluded. Also, India's Tamil population played an instrumental role in the way the country conducted its policies surrounding the ethnic conflict in Sri Lanka. In essence, by helping the radicals and subsequently curtailing this help, New Delhi may have contributed to prolonging the conflict. Counterfactually, one could envision a very different Indian policy in support of the Sri Lankan state, which would have produced markedly different results.

Sri Lanka provides a cautionary tale of ethnic relations, and yet the underlying dynamics are anything but unique. Credible commitment mechanisms will be vital in situations where such power disparities exist. This should be the focus of internal and external parties that have stakes in these ethnic relationships. All actors need to be made aware of the advantages of long-term strategic thinking over myopic electoral considerations. Third-party stakeholders may need to be monitored to keep them from exacerbating existing ethnic tensions. Ethnic friction need not drag a nation into protracted violence with incalculable costs to all. Foresight and vigilance can help prevent such an unfortunate chain of events. This is the key mes-

20. For more on a model of credible commitments in a general ethnic conflict setting applied to the Sri Lankan conflict, see Weerasinghe and Lichbach (2009).

sage for peacebuilders seeking to prevent conflicts from igniting in the first place or—more pertinent to Sri Lanka today—reigniting.

References

Bloom, Mia. 2005. *Dying to Kill: The Allure of Suicide Terror.* New York: Columbia Univ. Press.

De Silva, Kingsley M. 2005. *Reaping the Whirlwind: Ethnic Conflict, Ethnic Politics in Sri Lanka.* New Delhi: Penguin.

Gunawardena, R. A. L. H. 1985. "The People of the Lion: Sinhala Consciousness in History and Historiography." In *Ethnicity and Social Change in Sri Lanka: Papers Presented at a Seminar Organized by the Social Scientists Association, December 1979.* Colombo: Karunaratne and Sons, 55–107.

Horowitz, Donald L. 1985. *Ethnic Groups in Conflict.* Berkeley, CA: Univ. of California Press.

Krishna, Sankaran. 1999. *Postcolonial Insecurities: India, Sri Lanka, and the Question of Nationhood.* Minneapolis: Univ. of Minnesota Press.

Lichbach, Mark I., and Chalinda Weerasinghe. 2009. "Mobilizing for Peace: Majority Credibility, Minority Power, and Ethnic Politics." Unpublished working paper, Dept. of Government and Politics, Univ. of Maryland, College Park, MD.

Matthews, Bruce. 1986. "Radical Conflict and the Rationalization of Violence in Sri Lanka." *Pacific Affairs* 59 (1): 28–44.

———. 1988. "Sinhala Cultural and Buddhist Patriotic Organizations in Contemporary Sri Lanka." *Pacific Affairs* 61 (4): 620–32.

Nalapat, M. D. 2011. "Defeating Terrorism—Why the Tamil Tigers Lost Eelam . . . And How Sri Lanka Won the War." Jewish Institute for National Security Affairs, Mar. 11. www.jinsa.org/publications/global-briefing/defeating-terrorism-why-tamil-tigers-lost-eelamand-how-sri-lanka-won-wa#.UTlYWWdGb8k.

Nubin, Walter, ed. 2003. *Sri Lanka: Current Issues and Historical Background.* New York: Nova Science.

Pape, Robert A. 2005. *Dying to Win: The Strategic Logic of Suicide Terrorism.* New York: Random House.

Peebles, Patrick. 1990. "Colonization and Ethnic Conflict in the Dry Zone of Sri Lanka." *Journal of Asian Studies* 49 (1): 30–55.

———. 2006. *The History of Sri Lanka.* Westport, CT: Greenwood Press.

Pfaffenberger, Bryan. 1990. "The Political Construction of Defensive Nationalism: The 1968 Temple-Entry Crisis in Northern Sri Lanka." *Journal of Asian Studies* 49 (1): 78–96.

Price, Pamela. 1996. "Revolution and Rank in Tamil Nationalism." *Journal of Asian Studies* 55 (2): 359–83.

Roberts, Michael. 1997. "For Humanity. For the Sinhalese. Dharmapala as Crusading Bosat." *Journal of Asian Studies* 56 (4): 1006–32.

Sahadevan, P. 1999. "Ethnic Conflict in South Asia." Working paper, Joan B. Kroc Institute for International Peace Studies, June.

Shastri, Amita. 1990. "The Material Basis for Separatism: The Tamil Eelam Movement in Sri Lanka." *Journal of Asian Studies* 49 (1): 56–77.

Spencer, Jonathan, ed. 1990. *Sri Lanka: History and the Roots of Conflict.* London: Routledge.

Swamy, M. R. Narayan. 2002. *Tigers of Lanka: From Boys to Guerrillas.* 3rd ed. Colombo: Vijitha Yapa.

Tambiah, Stanley Jeyaraja. 1986. *Sri Lanka: Ethnic Fratricide and the Dismantling of Democracy.* Chicago: Univ. of Chicago Press.

———. 1992. *Buddhism Betrayed? Religion, Politics, and Violence in Sri Lanka.* Chicago: Univ. of Chicago Press.

Weerasinghe, Chalinda D., and Mark I. Lichbach. 2006. "Ethnic Conflict in Sri Lanka: Does Fractionalization of Minority Radicals Influence Credible Commitments?" Unpublished working paper, Dept. of Government and Politics, Univ. of Maryland, College Park, MD.

9

Sri Lanka

Tackling the LTTE

Kumar Rupesinghe

The nearly three-decade-long protracted territorial conflict between the government of Sri Lanka (GoSL) and the LTTE ended on May 18, 2009, at Nanthikadal, with the insurgents being militarily defeated and their top leadership killed or captured. The LTTE has been described as one of the deadliest terrorist organizations in the world. It took nearly three decades to end what was one of the longest civil wars in modern times. This analysis focuses on the LTTE's rise from a small insurgent group among many to a formidable fighting force and reviews successive Sri Lankan governments' strategies for addressing terrorism, with special emphasis on the military and political strategies adopted by President Raj apaksa and the armed forces in finally defeating the LTTE.

Brief Description of the Conflict

When Sri Lanka gained independence in 1948, the Soulbury Constitution bestowed on Prime Minister D. S. Senanayake by the British did not guarantee protection of the fundamental rights of the minority Tamils. This issue was left to the discretion of the Sinhalese leaders. Before the final discussions regarding the constitution, however, the Tamil national leadership demanded equal representation in the governance structure of the country—a demand that aroused fears among the Sinhalese leaders. They believed that this demand would be the first step toward establishing a separate state, and this belief, in turn, led them to take a strong stance against the Tamils' demands.

The Sinhalese constitute more than 70 percent of the population, and the Tamils, concentrated in the north and in the Hill Country in Central Province, constitute about 18 percent. The Hill Country Tamils are of Indian origin, having been brought to Sri Lanka by the British, and while they are a minority population in Sri Lanka, over fifty-five million Tamils live in the southern Indian state of Tamil Nadu. The Sinhalese therefore feel that they are a minority in the broader region despite being a majority in Sri Lanka itself. The demographic contours of Sri Lanka, the minority-majority complexes, and the threat perception emergent from these issues have led to self-fulfilling prophecies, "chosen people" syndromes, and demonization of the "other."

Added to the demographic pressures that laid the basis for civil war in Sri Lanka's north were discriminatory policies by successive national governments, which deprived Tamils of the right to use the Tamil language for administrative purposes in public institutions; discrimination, both real and perceived, in employment and land policy in Tamil-majority areas (namely the north and east); and discrimination through quotas for higher education. The combination of these issues deprived the Tamils of a partnership role in building the country as a multiethnic and pluralistic democracy. These indignities served to underpin future Tamil militant movements insisting on the right of self-determination for the Tamil people. Moderate Tamil leaders attempted to address these issues through peaceful means, largely through Parliament and occasionally through nonviolent protests in various parts of the country, but they were often met with violence and intolerance. This resistance ultimately led them to abandon satyagraha—a philosophy and practice that employs nonviolent means of resistance—to win their rights, since they felt that a minority employing satyagraha against a majority community would never achieve the desired results (Rajakulendran 2005).

The nonviolent struggles of the early stages generated a spirit of Tamil nationalism and mobilized the Tamil people into a collective national force poised against the Sri Lankan state in demanding separatism. A younger generation of Tamils, however, was prompted to take up arms and resort to violence to establish a separate state of Eelam. As a result, for the first time in the postindependent history of Sri Lanka, people witnessed the radicalization of the Tamil youth. Manifestations of this radicalization appeared in the demands put forward in the Vaddukoddai Resolution of May 14, 1976, adopted at the First National Convention of the TULF, demanding a separate Tamil Eelam state.[1] Campaigning based on this resolution, the

1. The Vaddukoddai Resolution's main provisions included that the State of Tamil Eelam should consist of the people of the northern and eastern provinces and should also ensure full and equal rights of citizenship of the State of Tamil Eelam to all Tamil-speaking people living in any part of

TULF received the overwhelming vote of the Tamil people in the parliamentary elections of 1977. These actions were precipitated by events that took place with the breakaway of East Pakistan and the establishment of a separate state, Bangladesh, toward the end of 1971. This historical backdrop may have led the armed militant youth to believe that setting up a separate state of Tamil Eelam in the north of Sri Lanka could easily be done.

The declaration of Tamil Eelam as the avowed objective of the Tamil national movement enhanced existing prejudices of the Sinhalese majority. The activities of the armed Tamil groups provoked retaliation from the extremist Sinhala nationalist movements against Tamils living in the south. This retaliation culminated in a massive pogrom in July 1983, which resulted in the displacement of over 250,000 people and considerable destruction of property and businesses owned by Tamils. This is when the civil war began in earnest.

Evolution of the Tamil Armed Struggle: LTTE's Journey to Center Stage

In the early stages of the armed resistance, India played a central role in empowering the major Tamil militant groups. The Indian government, through its external intelligence agency, RAW, could control almost all the armed Tamil groups at this stage. From August 1983 until May 1987, RAW provided arms, training, and monetary support to six Tamil militant groups: the LTTE, TELO, PLOTE, Eelam Revolutionary Organization of Students, EPRLF, and Tamil Eelam Liberation Army. As Rohan Gunaratna explains, "The need to have leverage over Colombo was adequately demonstrated by the Research and Analysis Wing (RAW), the agency also responsible for advancing India's secret foreign policy goals. Within her [Indian Prime Minister Indira Gandhi's] inner circle, the decision was justified. Geopolitics and domestic compulsions validated the rationale." Moreover, before 1983, there had been very few Tamil insurgent training camps in the Indian state of Tamil Nadu. But after Indira Gandhi decided in August 1983 to support the Sri Lankan northern insurgency, thirty-two training camps sprang up in Tamil Nadu, and by mid-1987, over twenty thousand Sri Lankan Tamil insurgents were receiving sanctuary, funding, training, and weapons from the Tamil Nadu state government or insurgent groups (Gunaratna 1988).

Ceylon and to Tamils of Eelam origin living in any part of the world who may opt for citizenship of Tamil Eelam. For the full text of the resolution, see SATP (2001).

India financed these groups and provided training and weapons, but it was not their only patron. They received training from many other entities, including the PLO, the Irish Republican Army, British mercenaries, and Israel.

Initially, the LTTE, then known as the TNT and colloquially as the Tamil Tigers, functioned as a political-military organization. Soon after the promulgation of the Republican Constitution of Sri Lanka in 1972, Velupillai Prabhakaran, then eighteen years old, formed the TNT with a small group of young people on May 22, 1972. Prabhakaran attended training camps organized by the Eelam Revolutionary Organization of Students and gradually emerged as a leader within the overall militant movement. Prabhakaran sailed to India in 1972 with others, including Thangadurai and Kuttimani, leaders of the TELO, for further military training, returning to Sri Lanka in 1974 (Jain Commission 1997, Section 7.1).

From 1972 to 1976, the TNT engaged in low-intensity violence masterminded by Prabhakaran. Its success in carrying out attacks—for example, the attack on a carnival in the northern town of Jaffna in September 1972; the assassination of Alfred Duraiappah, the SLFP's mayor of Jaffna in 1975; subsequent assassinations of police officers; and bank robberies—encouraged the group, stimulated its military spirit, and lent it enough confidence to pursue reorganization.[2] In 1976, Prabhakaran made structural changes and renamed the organization the LTTE. Anton Balasingham, later to become the LTTE's chief negotiator, joined as its main ideologue in 1979 and added depth to the LTTE's politics, contributing to its social restructuring. This significantly changed the way the world viewed the LTTE.

The LTTE continued its low-intensity operation against the state, particularly policemen, and quickly became the most dominant militant group. By 1983, hundreds of youths, driven by the LTTE's violent successes and the government's flawed policies, had come forward to join the group, which continued to develop into a militia with the help of the RAW. With increased manpower, in 1984, the LTTE intensified its attacks against the Sri Lankan troops, even launching attacks on government fortified areas. It founded its much-renowned Sea Tiger Wing the same year.

In 1987, the LTTE established its Black Tiger Wing, an elite unit of members responsible for conducting suicide attacks against political, economic, and military targets. The first LTTE Black Tiger was "Captain Miller," who volunteered to drive a vehicle full of explosives into the makeshift army camp in Nelliady, Jaffna, on July 5, 1987, killing himself and over fifty Sri Lankan soldiers (Sri Kantha 2001).

2. On Tamil militancy during this period, see Swamy (2002).

The war quickly became more about Prabhakaran's determination to form an independent Tamil state under the exclusive control of his Tigers than about addressing legitimate Tamil grievances. Evidence of this objective can be found in the number of moderate Tamil politicians killed by the LTTE who would have been willing to cooperate politically with the GoSL (*Wall Street Journal* 2009). The LTTE convinced the youth that the only way Tamils could attain freedom was by establishing a separate state, thus enticing them to join the LTTE. Also, the group used child conscription and child abduction to swell its ranks, particularly in the east. According to a November 22, 2008, report by University Teachers for Human Rights, Jaffna, the LTTE had conscripted nine thousand "very young" persons since early 2008 (UTHR[J] 2008). According to military intelligence reports released on December 24, 2008, the LTTE also directed over eight thousand students who sat for the General Certificate of Education O-Level Examinations in the Kilinochchi and Mullaitivu Districts in the country's Tamil-dominated north to join combat training (SATP 2009). Before finally losing the war in 2009, the LTTE had even trained old women to use arms against government forces. These recruitment patterns meant that an organization that began with about twenty members in 1972 grew into one of the world's biggest and most ruthless terrorist groups in the ensuing three decades. It should be noted that where the LTTE exercised hegemonic control, the distinction between Tamil civilians and auxiliary forces was blurred.

The LTTE had a two-tier structure—a military wing and a subordinate political wing—with the Central Governing Committee, headed by Prabhakaran, in charge of both. This body was responsible for directing and controlling several specific subdivisions, including the Sea Tigers, headed by Colonel Soosai; the Air Tigers, headed by Colonel Shankar, alias Vythialingam Sornalingam; the Black Tigers, the suicide commando unit, and the intelligence wing, headed by Shanmugalingam Sivashankar, alias Pottu Amman; and the political wing, headed by Thamil Chelvam. By far the most critical of these subdivisions to the LTTE's success was the intelligence wing, the Tiger Organization Security Intelligence Service. Not only did Pottu Amman receive training in India after joining the LTTE in 1981, but Prabhakaran also requested the top-notch LTTE cadres residing abroad to obtain intelligence manuals from the CIA, FBI, Mossad, and other intelligence agencies, which were translated into Tamil (Weerakoon 2009). This effort helped the LTTE build a vast and solid intelligence network, which was later even able to infiltrate the GoSL's security establishments. Pottu Amman was responsible for collecting intelligence from across the island, especially Colombo, and feeding information to Prabhakaran to use in planning operations. It is a well-documented fact that Pottu Amman was the brains behind most of the LTTE's successful military operations (Weerakoon 2009).

In addition to the locally based subdivisions, the LTTE had an International Secretariat headed by Kumaran Pathmanathan, widely known as KP. The International Secretariat's three main functions were publicity and propaganda, fund-raising, and arms procurement and shipping. KP was also responsible for gathering international political support for Prabhakaran's dream of an independent Tamil state. By May 1998, the LTTE's International Secretariat was believed to have offices and cells in at least fifty-four countries. The largest and most important centers were located in western states with large Tamil expatriate communities: the UK, France, Germany, Switzerland, Canada, and Australia. Key cells were also in Cambodia, Burma, South Africa, and Botswana (Chalk 1999).

The LTTE's international propaganda war was quite sophisticated and, for a long time, far more powerful than any opposing campaign of the GoSL. Using satellite phone links, battlefield reports were transmitted directly from Sri Lanka to the LTTE's international offices daily (Chalk 1999). The atrocities committed by the GoSL forces were captured in graphic detail on film, and these videos were distributed among the Tamil diaspora. The Internet was also used as a communications tool, with several websites that pushed visitors to websites and publications from internationally renowned humanitarian and development agencies and, more recently, to YouTube. Through these efforts, the LTTE's massive diaspora network ensured that the heat was turned on the government via the international community.

By the late 1990s, the LTTE's annual income thus collected was between \$175 million and \$385 million, with estimates of its total asset value as high as \$1 billion. It is believed that \$100 million to \$250 million of the total income came from drug trafficking. Local taxation and extortion are thought to have contributed about \$30 million; human smuggling and funds siphoned off from NGOs, \$3 million to \$5 million; contributions from the Tamil expatriate community, \$40 million to \$50 million; and profits from businesses, \$35 million to \$50 million (Strategic Foresight Group 2006; Reddy 2006).

The LTTE's annual military expenditure, both in Sri Lanka and abroad, was estimated at close to \$8 million. Reports indicate that the LTTE spent minimally on its cadres, with the bulk of these funds spent on sustaining a war economy and an international support base (Reddy 2006). It was through these global financial operations that the LTTE managed to acquire most of its weaponry and munitions. In the early 1990s, an LTTE member, Dharmakulaseelan, played a key role in a multinational operation whereby money raised in North America was forwarded to the Philippines and used to buy weapons from Southeast Asian arms dealers.[3]

From 1995 onward, although it lost Jaffna, the LTTE controlled most of Eastern Province and the whole of the Wanni region in the north. It overran strategic camps, such as Elephant Pass, Pooneryn, and Kilinochchi, during the mid-1990s. The northern army camp of Mullaitivu was the last to be taken over, on July 18, 1996, through an operation that resulted in the deaths of more than one thousand GoSL soldiers. Through these operations, the LTTE managed to capture sophisticated arms and ammunition, including long-range artillery and mortars. Until its defeat in May 2009, the LTTE controlled one-third of Sri Lanka's total coastline, including the Exclusive Economic Zone. This area included over two hundred miles of the strategically important A-9 Road, linking the north of the country to the south, which remained under LTTE control for twenty-three years. It was a cash machine for the LTTE, who taxed everything that entered north of Kilinochchi—a town about one hundred kilometers southeast of Jaffna—from the south. The LTTE set up its own police, judiciary, and administration system centered at Kilinochchi, which served as the capital of the de facto state of Tamil Eelam in northern Sri Lanka (see map 7). In the areas under LTTE control, the civilians fell completely under the writ of the LTTE, whose totalitarian control was uncontested. The slightest deviation or nonadherence to the laws imposed by Prabhakaran, or suspected disloyalty to him, resulted in dire punishments. This was even the case for his most trusted lieutenants, as evidenced by the 1994 incarceration and killing of Mahaththaya, Prabhakaran's onetime confidant and deputy.

Prabhakaran's success in sustaining the conflict for over a quarter century came from a combination of his own cunning and the GoSL's lack of purpose, unity, and determination. Also, the LTTE leader owed much of his success to his ability to adapt quickly in fast-changing environments. In fact, this ability was the linchpin not only of the group's effectiveness but of its very survival. In a recent book, General Mehta, former commander of the IPKF that was stationed on the island in 1987 following a deal between the Indian and Sri Lankan governments, quotes security expert Zachary Abuza as crediting the LTTE's tremendous originality and inventiveness for the longevity of its phenomenal success (Mehta 2010, 16).

Although it may have had its parallels elsewhere, the LTTE was the group that institutionalized the suicide bomber as an offensive weapon both politically and militarily. The LTTE used suicide bombers repeatedly with great success. In the south, from 1984 to 2006, the group is reported to have

3. For more details, see Chalk (1999).

Map 7. Jaffna Peninsula

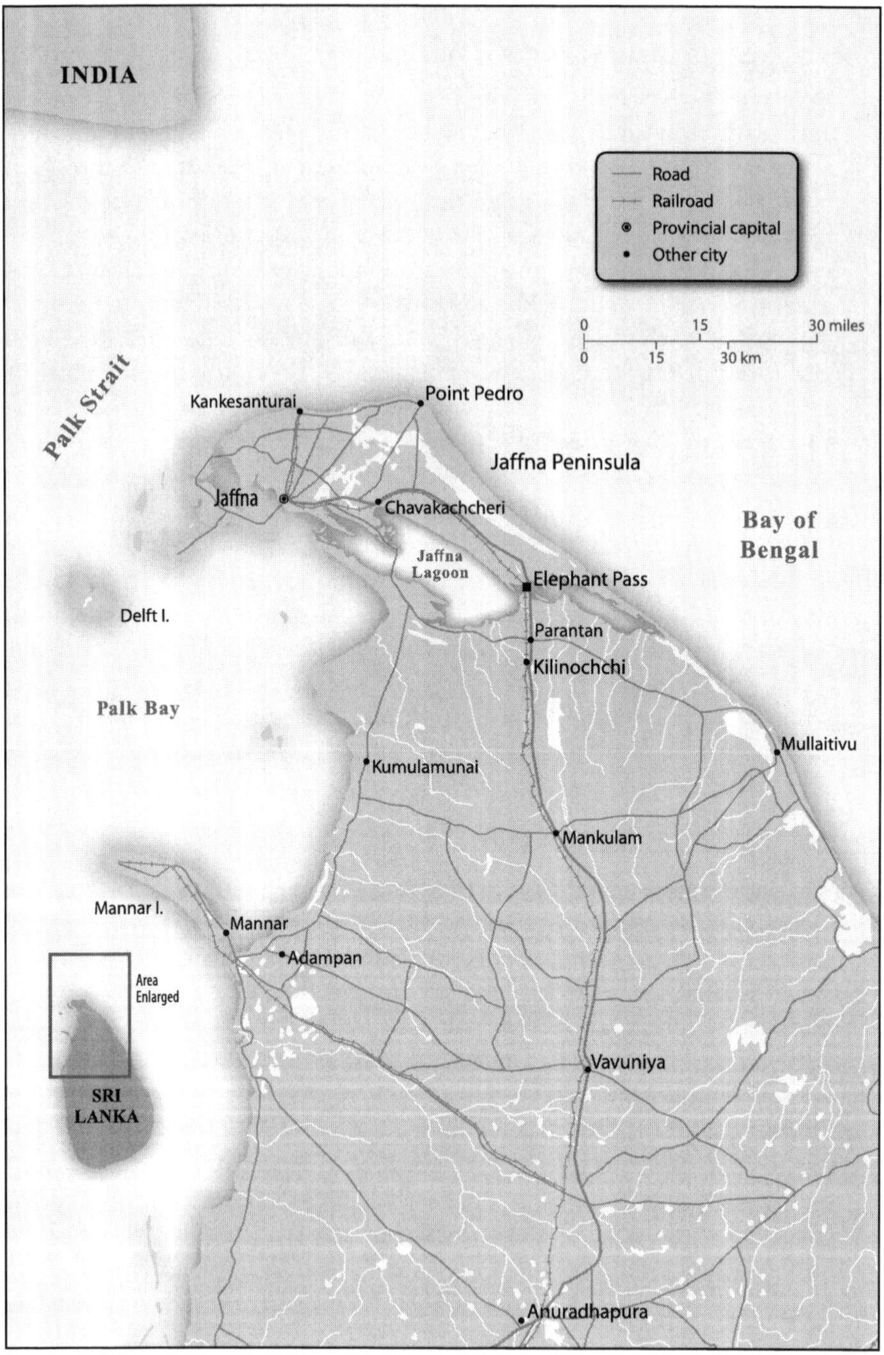

carried out 168 suicide attacks—the most by any terrorist organization in the world during that period—and assassinated 3,262 civilians in 346 targeted attacks across the country. In 2008 alone, the LTTE killed as many as 158 people in no less than ninety incidents outside the war zone in the north and east (SATP 2009). Reviewing Mehta's work, Tammita-Delgoda says this about LTTE's genius for improvisation:

> [It] found its outlet in the great variety of mines, booby traps and improvised explosive devices, which were invented out of the most basic materials, with the simplest technology. The LTTE's ability to camouflage, disguise, surprise and trap was one of their greatest strengths and it was the rationale behind many of their fortifications and defenses. While General Mehta mentions the ditch cum bund, there were also many other types of defenses: the elevated sniper points, the tiny armored bunkers, the tank pits, and the booby traps. (Tammita-Delgoda 2010, 26–27)

Response by Successive Sri Lankan Governments

Initially, the governments of J. R. Jayawardene (1978–89), Ranasinghe Premadasa (1989–93), and Chandrika Kumaratunga (1994–2005) attempted to force the LTTE to the negotiating table. While engaging the LTTE militarily on the battlefield, each government—thanks largely to pressure from India and the broader international community—tried to engage the LTTE in negotiations. CFAs were concluded between the GoSL and the LTTE in 1994–95 and then again in 2002–05 when Ranil Wickramasinghe became prime minister under President Kumaratunga. But each time, the LTTE found a reason to withdraw from the negotiation process, triggering an immediate return to violence against the GoSL forces and civilians.

The governments of the day found defeating the LTTE difficult for a variety of reasons. During the Jayewardene regime, interference from India, which was unwilling to oppose the Tamil militant movement, was a major impediment. In the 1987 Vadamarachchi battle, when the government had imposed a successful blockade of Jaffna and was about to crush the LTTE—which held only parts of Jaffna at the time—India air-dropped vital supplies into Jaffna. India also threatened to attack Sri Lanka unless the GoSL troops immediately halted their advance (*India Today* 1987). India changed its stance toward the LTTE only after the group assassinated Indian prime minister Rajiv Gandhi on Indian soil in 1991 (Vasudevan 2012; BBC 1991).

Previously, in 1984, India convened the All Party Conference (APC), inviting all the militant groups of the time to participate along with the Sri Lankan government with India as mediator. At the conference, the Tamil parties made four demands:

1. recognition of the Sri Lankan Tamils as a distinct nationality
2. recognition of an identified Tamil homeland, and the guarantee of its territorial integrity
3. based on the above, recognition of the inalienable right of self-determination of the Tamil nation
4. recognition of the right to full citizenship and other fundamental democratic rights of all Tamils who look upon the island as their country (Edirisinghe 1999, 169–87)

The entire conference was characterized by positional bargaining. The Tamil delegation, dominated by militant groups, failed to put forward a concrete set of proposals. After the failure of the APC, the Tamil militants continued their guerrilla attacks on civilians as well as GoSL forces, killing and injuring many.

By 1987, in an unrelated development, the People's Liberation Front (JVP), a traditionally communist party of Sinhalese youth, which was banned at the time, started causing havoc in the south through active violence. Since the GoSL's military strength was insufficient to contain two insurgencies, President Jayewardene signed the Indo–Sri Lanka Accord with Indian Prime Minister Rajiv Gandhi in 1987. This Accord provided for the IPKF to be based in Sri Lanka's north and east to battle the LTTE (Premdas and Samarasinghe 1988), which essentially made the northern insurgency India's problem. After a lackluster start, the IPKF was beginning to improve its performance and had managed to drive the LTTE out of its strongholds, thus weakening it considerably (Ispahani 1992, 224). At this point, Jayewardene's successor, President Premadasa, who believed in maintaining the country's sovereignty and territorial integrity at all costs, provided the LTTE with arms and ammunition to fight the IPKF and ordered the IPKF to withdraw from Sri Lanka in 1989.[4] This came as a major humiliation for India. Nonetheless, Premadasa initiated peace talks with the LTTE. These talks lasted for about a year, during which the LTTE, as a "goodwill gesture," announced a cessation of hostilities. The LTTE ended this cessation abruptly, just months after the last IPKF contingent pulled out of Sri Lanka in March 1990. In June 1990, the LTTE attacked and overtook several police stations in the Eastern province, taking captive some six hundred police personnel. The government gave the police orders to surrender, only to have the LTTE murder most of the captives in cold

4. For a brief discussion of India's military intervention and withdrawal from Sri Lanka, see Ispahani (1992), 222–32.

blood (Dissanayaka 2005, 142). Violence resumed thereafter with some frequency as before.

The Kumaratunga government, which succeeded Premadasa, was similarly characterized by further bloodshed. Initially, Kumaratunga did try to engage the LTTE in negotiations, and the LTTE reciprocated in 1994–95 with another declaration of cessation of hostilities. But from the very beginning, the negotiations floundered over several issues. The LTTE wanted confidence-building measures to precede formal talks and argued that the people's suffering should be addressed first. The government maintained that confidence-building measures should be carried out simultaneously with discussion of core issues. On the ground, there were difficulties in dismantling a regime of controls, and the embargo imposed by the military made for considerable complications, arousing the LTTE's suspicions that the government was not sincere in allowing essential goods to reach the people. An exchange of letters between the leaderships of the two sides became increasingly hostile over time. The end result was that the LTTE withdrew its cease-fire pledge in 1995. Thereafter, the government engaged in a "war for peace" strategy and launched a massive military operation. Although it managed to recapture the northern LTTE stronghold of Jaffna in 1996, during these Kumaratunga years, the military suffered spectacular losses on the battlefield, with thousands of soldiers killed. In 2001, the LTTE even attacked the country's sole international airport, causing massive losses of civilian and military aircraft. Sri Lanka recorded a negative economic growth rate that year for the first time in its postindependence history. The Kumaratunga period ultimately witnessed a series of military disasters and a further emboldening of the LTTE.[5]

Political interference in many forms impeded the GoSL forces from ending the war in its early stages (Ministry of Defence 2010). The reason for this is widely believed to involve the vested interests of certain politicians and those in the defense establishment who stood to gain financially from purchasing ammunition and other necessary equipment for the GoSL forces. The more prolonged the war effort became, the more these officials stood to gain, motivating them to drag out the war effort. Some security force commanders who wished to stay on the correct side of the political fence simply overlooked these deals, which resulted in the purchase of substandard weapons and poorly maintained aircraft. This decline resulted in thousands of troops sacrificing their lives on battlefields, such as Pooneryn and Mullaitivu, or dying in aircraft lacking antimissile protection. Asked about the procurement of such outdated equipment, the governments of the day claimed a lack of funds to buy the more sophisticated equipment.

5. For a brief discussion of the war during the 1990s and the military's efforts, see Smith (1999).

During the Kumaratunga period, electoral expediency also played a role in the decisions made by the defense establishment. Deadlines were given to military commanders to capture particular areas so that the party in power could ride to election victory on the wings of the military victory. Despite awareness of insufficient time, manpower, and equipment, the commanders agreed to the deadlines in order to please their political masters and secure their own personal goals. They did so knowing that those on the front lines would have to sacrifice their lives. The few commanders who were uncompromising on their principles were shown the door.

Compounding these issues, whenever the LTTE declared a cease-fire, the government stopped recruiting to the armed forces and training troops. Combat readiness was neglected, resulting in poorly trained soldiers—sometimes with as little as three months training—being sent into battle each time the LTTE launched new attacks.

The period from 2002 to 2005 saw relative tranquility, when Ranil Wickramasinghe of the United National Front (UNF) became prime minister even as Kumaratunga, who did not necessarily see eye to eye with the UNF on the LTTE issue, remained president. Nonetheless, the UNF government signed a CFA with the LTTE in February 2002. Six rounds of talks, facilitated by the Norwegian government, took place in various foreign cities until the LTTE abruptly pulled out again. Only Anton Balasingham, political adviser and negotiator of the LTTE, kept reiterating his group's commitment to the CFA. Politically in Sri Lanka, however, a situation of dual power existed, with President Kumaratunga, from the People's Alliance Party, as commander in chief of the armed forces, impeding every attempt by the prime minister (who belonged to the competing party) to resume negotiations and eventually dismissing three of his key ministers and calling for snap general elections in 2004. Finally, President Kumaratunga, under vociferous pressure from her coalition, forced abandonment of the negotiations strategy altogether.

Prime Minister Wickramasinghe's efforts to bring the LTTE to the negotiating table and achieve a negotiated solution provided a short respite from the violence. The prime minister's greatest failure was that he couldn't create a bipartisan consensus with the president. Kumaratunga's oft-repeated strategy of undermining the CFA publicly at every turn also led to the end of the UNF government because it turned the public against the Wickramasinghe regime. An additional factor was the Wickramasinghe government's stringent economic policies, which alienated him from the people. Wickramasinghe lost the snap elections.

The LTTE, meanwhile, showed utter disregard for the CFA. It committed a number of CFA violations, including continuing to recruit child soldiers and to engage in extortions, abductions, and assassinations of intelligence personnel and political rivals. In essence, during the protracted period of negotiations, the LTTE used a variety of subterfuges to use the negotiations process itself in politically advancing its cause and consolidating its military gains (Gunaratna 2009).

It was against this backdrop that the presidential elections were announced in 2005. Ranil Wickramasinghe (UNP) and Mahinda Rajapaksa from the United People's Freedom Alliance (UPFA) were the two main contenders for the post. But Rajapaksa faced problems from within his own party, since President Kumaratunga opposed him and sought to publicly undermine his campaign. This opposition necessitated some quick thinking on Rajapaksa's part, and it is now well known that before the elections, the UPFA candidate signed agreements with the two ultranationalist parties, the JVP and Jathika Hela Urumaya (JHU). The foundation for these agreements was that if Rajapaksa came to power, he would abrogate the CFA and try to defeat the LTTE militarily. This agreement provided the Rajapaksa campaign with much-needed drive at the grassroots level, led by these two parties, both of which were against a negotiated solution backed by the UNP candidate. The propaganda campaigns by the JVP and the JHU helped whip up nationalist spirit among the Sinhalese, who came to see Wickramasinghe's CFA as offering one-third of the country on a platter to the LTTE. The presidential elections were closely contested, and Rajapaksa won, although with a very narrow margin of 180,786 votes (CEPPS 2005). A majority of Tamils in the north and east did not vote during the presidential elections because the LTTE had asked them to boycott the polls. This was a common practice for the LTTE, continued from previous presidential elections.

The Decisive Push under Mahinda Rajapaksa: 2005–09

Unlike all previous Sri Lankan heads of state, who were from elite Colombo families and had reaped the benefits of Western education, President Rajapaksa came from a very strong Sinhala Buddhist background. From the outset, he was determined that his government would not engage in negotiations with the LTTE. But at the time he assumed the presidency, the CFA was still officially in force, and international pressure pushed him toward resuming negotiations. Two desultory sessions were held in Geneva in 2006 with little forward movement. A third round, scheduled to take place in Oslo, never got off the ground after the LTTE, having arrived in Oslo, refused to sit at the negotiating table with the government delegation (*Colombo Telegraph* 2013). During this time, despite the CFA, the LTTE made several attacks against the government, chief among them being failed attempts to assassinate army commander Sarath Fonseka and Defense Secretary Gotabhaya Rajapaksa (the president's brother) through suicide bombings. These two incidents goaded the president into action, and after a lull of several years, the military received instructions to carry out retaliatory attacks. As military analysts had noted, the president demonstrated a basic resolve: "Given the political will, the military can crush terrorism" (Shashikumar 2009). His winning strategies were not planned. Rather, they evolved according to the situation. The two failed assassinations were a decisive factor in that both targeted men returned to wage a war to the finish. From here on in, victory was defined solely in terms of military tactics. Eelam War IV—the final push under President Rajapaksa—was beginning. The strategy meant that the GoSL made a conscious decision to let go of any nonmilitary means to end the conflict. Ironically, controversial though such a mind-set was guaranteed to be, supporters of the GoSL argue that this single-minded focus was instrumental in the ultimate decimation of the LTTE.

Soon after assuming presidential duties, President Rajapaksa appointed his brother Gotabhaya, who had been in the army, as defense secretary. Thereafter, one of the president's boldest decisions was to appoint Lt. Gen. Sarath Fonseka, then serving as chief of staff of the Sri Lankan army, as the army's new commander over more senior officers. Even at that time, Lt. Gen. Fonseka was a much-decorated hero in the military. In 1991, when the LTTE held the Jaffna Fort under siege, then colonel Fonseka led the Midnight Express operation to rescue the besieged troops. Several hundred soldiers were saved. He was also the deputy general officer commanding during Operation Riviresa, which led to the recapture of Jaffna in 1996.

It is reported that soon after his appointment, Fonseka requested permission to recruit a handpicked team to recapture the approximately fifteen thousand square kilometers of land under LTTE control in the east and in the Wanni region in the north. The team chosen by the army commander by August 2006 consisted of five divisions.[6] Meanwhile, in the east, the Sri Lankan army's task was made significantly easier through the assistance and advice of Karuna, the LTTE's former eastern commander, who had defected in 2004 due to a disagreement with Prabhakaran, and, in no small measure, through the GoSL's exploitation of the tension the disagreement had caused between them. Niel Smith concludes that Karuna's split "deprived the LTTE of several hundred experienced fighters and significant support. . . . Over time, this weakened the LTTE's grip in the eastern portion of the

6. These included the Fifty-Third Division, led by Maj. Gen. Kamal Gunarathne; the Fifty-Fifth Division, led by Brig. Prasanna Silva; the Fifty-Seventh Division, led by Maj. Gen. Jagath Dias; Task Force One and Fifty-Eighth Division, led by Brig. Shavendra Silva (which eventually chalked up the most victories against the LTTE); and the Fifty-Ninth Division, led by Maj. Gen. Nandana Udawatta.

country," ultimately making it easier for the GoSL troops to capture Batticaloa, the LTTE's eastern stronghold (Smith 2010, Hull 2008).

Also in 2006, the LTTE blocked the Mavil Aru, which supplies water to parts of the east. This blockage denied water to fifteen thousand villagers, and the GoSL troops finally had to engage the LTTE to reconnect the water supply. This was followed by victories in Vakarai, Sampoor, Muttur, and by January 2007, Thoppigala, the last LTTE bastion in Eastern Province. Military analysts have pointed out that the LTTE gave up territory in the east without too much of a struggle and retreated to the Wanni in the north, its stronghold, under the assumption that the GoSL troops would never be able to beat them in their chosen battlefield. The LTTE also assumed that the GoSL would not have enough troop strength to safeguard the newly liberated east while also waging war on the LTTE in the Wanni. During this period, Prabhakaran issued many provocative statements warning that the GoSL forces would meet their waterloo if they tried to capture the Wanni.

But as it turned out, at the same time the east came under the GoSL's dominion, the army commander's five-pronged attack headed by the Fifty-Seventh Division's Maj. Gen. Jagath Dias began military operations north of Vavuniya. By January 2009, the army had captured Kilinochchi, the LTTE headquarters, and the LTTE moved its headquarters to Mullaitivu.[7] Simultaneously, Brig. Shavendra Silva's Fifty-Eighth Division achieved a string of victories in the Mannar area, from Silavathurai to Pooneryn and Paranthan. It then took the vital Elephant Pass bastion and, together with the Fifty-Seventh Division, moved to Sundarapuram, Puthukudiyiruppu, and finally to the Mullaitivu district. At the same time, Maj. Gen. Nandana Udawatta's Fifty-Ninth Division opened a new front in the Welioya area in January 2008, enabling the five divisions of the army to reach the Mullaitivu area within one year. Facing this massive artillery firepower, the LTTE leadership took the unprecedented step of taking hostage three hundred thousand civilians living in the area. The LTTE retreated with them to a small strip of less than 1,235 acres in Mullaitivu, where it used the civilian hostages as human shields. All along, the army had been able to achieve its spectacular successes with generous tactical support by the air force, which carried out massive aerial bombardment in the earmarked areas before the ground troops marched in. But with the LTTE's decision to use civilians as human shields, the international community intensified the pressure on the Sri Lankan government to halt the aerial attacks, declare a safety zone, and enforce a lull in battle to allow the civilians to escape. Even after being limited

7. For details of the military strategies and developments on the battlefield during Ealam IV, see de Silva (2012) and Mehta (2010).

to ground battles, the GoSL forces carried on, with the final battle starting at Vellamullivaikkal, where 250 LTTE members formed a ring around Prabhakaran and other top leaders. The GoSL troops successfully overcame this obstacle and annihilated the LTTE and its top leadership, completing the task it had taken on nearly three years earlier (Jayasekara 2009).

The navy also played a major role in the LTTE's defeat. Once the LTTE was limited to the Wanni area, its land supply routes were completely cut off, and it had to depend on the sea route to obtain its supplies, weapons, and other essentials. It is reported that the LTTE had eight "warehouse" ships, which transported "artillery, mortar shells, artillery shells, torpedoes, aircraft, missiles, underwater vehicles, diving equipment, radar, electro-optical devices and night vision equipment" (Shashikumar 2009). These ships dropped anchor close to the Sri Lankan coast but beyond the area under the navy's control. In this manner, the LTTE had obtained the latest weapons for decades.

Once Eelam War IV began, the GoSL Navy, with the help of the Indian Navy and its naval intelligence establishment, which provided information on the movement of LTTE-owned merchant navy vessels, managed to sever the sea route supply of weapons for the LTTE. Starting from 2006, the GoSL Navy destroyed all eight of the LTTE's warehouse ships, thus starving it of weapons. This effort is considered one of the major turning points in the battle.

Drivers of Success: Factors That Made Victory Possible

Several factors came together to make the GoSL's military victory against the LTTE possible. While some elements may have been unique to the Sri Lankan situation, a number of aspects have wide applicability. The following strategies led to the ultimate destruction of the LTTE.[8]

Unwavering Political Will to Defeat the Insurgency

The president gave the army commander and the defense secretary a free hand in defeating the LTTE. He made sure the armed forces were equipped with the latest weapons and befriended countries that were willing to give Sri Lanka the massive loans required to pay for the arms and ammunition. When India and Western countries showed reluctance to sell offensive weapons to Sri Lanka, citing concerns about international humanitarian law and human rights, the president obtained weapons from Pakistan and China. As the following chart indicates, Sri Lanka's defense expenditure kept increasing continuously after the Rajapaksa regime came to power.

8. The broad categories of factors discussed here approximate those presented by Shashikumar (2009).

Table 9.1. Sri Lanka military expenditures, 1983–2009

	1983	1986	1995	1996	1998	2001	2004	2005	2006	2007	2008	2009
Rupees *(Billions)*	1.7	6	24	38	56	63	56	56.3	69.5	139.6	166.4	177.1

Source: Adapted from appropriations bill for the 2009 budget (*Sunday Leader*, Oct. 5, 2008).

The army commander, in turn, saw that his troops were well trained and in optimum physical condition and that their morale was high. Instead of simply giving orders from Colombo, as had been the practice until then, the commander and the defense secretary were often seen visiting the battlefront. This fostered a sense of admiration in the soldiers on the battlefront and raised their spirits and confidence. Also, the army conducted a major recruitment drive. Its total manpower was forty-thousand personnel in 1987. This number had increased to 220,000 by 2008. According to Gen. Fonseka, once the GoSL abrogated the CFA and started waging war in earnest, the army managed to attract around three thousand new recruits every month. Toward the end of the war, morale among the youth was so high that monthly recruitment had increased to five thousand (*Financial Times* 2009). This sustained increase in manpower, coupled with high morale, meant that during the late stages of battle, troops were able to fight longer at a stretch than they had in the past. The LTTE had not factored these changes into its strategy. The drop in the desertion rate and the enthusiasm to join the fighting forces demonstrated the public support for the war, and the efficacy of the government's communications campaign showed the public that the war was winnable.

And there was no political interference. The president's orders were very clear: He wished to eliminate the LTTE from the country, irrespective of domestic, political, or international pressure. Western countries, especially the United States and the EU, and even the United Nations raised concerns about the rising numbers of civilian casualties and human rights violations being committed during the war and tried to insist that the GoSL return to negotiations with the LTTE, even threatening to impose international sanctions. But the president stood firm and insisted that a political solution would follow only after the military battle was over. A cease-fire was never considered at any point. Indicative of the mind-set within the government at the time, Mahinda Samarasinghe, minister for human rights and disaster management, said, "Human rights violations during war operations and the humanitarian crisis that engulfs civilians caught in the cross fire have always been the trigger points to order a military pull-back. . . . The LTTE would always play this card in the past. They would use the cease-fire to regroup and resume the war" (Shashikumar 2009).

The Rajapaksa government tried to show the international community that the LTTE did not represent the legitimate interests of the Tamils. Rather, they were simply engaged in terrorism, and the GoSL was not willing to negotiate with terrorists. The president also echoed the same view when he said, "We will finish off the LTTE, we will finish terrorism and not allow it to regroup in this country ever; every cease-fire has been used by the LTTE to consolidate, regroup and re-launch attacks, so no negotiations" (Shashikumar 2009). Even when foreign dignitaries visited the country, this was the message conveyed to them by both the president and the defense secretary. The Sri Lankan government had clearly adopted a very controversial position in the international community's eyes, but that position was in line with its singular goal of military victory.

Appointments and Freedom of Action without Political Interference

Under previous regimes, the various presidents and defense secretaries often had differences of opinion since they saw each other as a threat to their political aspirations. Therefore, the different actors often gave the military contradictory commands, which hurt the war effort. With President Rajapaksa's regime, the appointment of his brother as defense secretary meant there were no such contradictions, since both acted in unison and with a common goal. Moreover, as Gotabhaya had formerly served in the GoSL army, the army considered him a legitimate voice. He understood that political goals and deadlines should not affect military strategies. Also, he had retained his long-standing friendship with Gen. Sarath Fonseka, allowing Fonseka a free hand in planning and executing military strategies as and when required. At the same time, the defense secretary took on the role of conveying the military's needs to the president, who, in turn, ensured that these needs were met.

The army commander employed some unusual strategies when he accepted the job of planning the LTTE's demise. One was to appoint young but efficient officers to lead the battle instead of following the usual practice of appointing officers based on seniority. Lt. Gen. Fonseka is reputed to have visited the lines personally and handpicked capable officers to lead the battle. He created a merit list and a common list, whereby only those who performed exceptionally well were put on the merit list (*Financial Times* 2009). Those on the merit list had to continue to maintain their high standards or they were "demoted" to the common list. These lists served as incentive for the rank and file to perform at their best. To build synergy, he created a clear single-command leadership across all divisions and task forces. He made the point that no brigade, battalion, or division can win a war in isolation, and thus, the backup facilities were also carefully planned under one leadership (Athukorala 2009). Lt. Gen. Fonseka remarked, "I thought seniority was immaterial if they could not command the soldiers properly. I restructured the Army and changed almost all the aspects of the organization. I made the Sri Lanka Army a more professional Army. Everybody had to work with a sense of professionalism" (Shashikumar 2009).

Innovative Military Tactics

The GoSL forces also marked a departure from sticking solely to methods of conventional warfare, as they had done previously.[9] When the war started in the Wanni, the GoSL decided to kill as many LTTE cadres as possible to reduce their manpower, while ensuring minimum casualties on the GoSL side, rather than attempting to capture territory. To implement this strategy successfully, it used Long-Range Reconnaissance Patrols to great effect in hunting down and assassinating kingpins in the LTTE, dealing strategic blows to the group. It was only after the LTTE captured Kilinochchi in 2009 that the army decided to concentrate on capturing territory as well (*Sunday Observer* 2009).

Also, the GoSL military leadership decided to launch nighttime attacks, which took the LTTE by surprise on many occasions. Using a five-pronged attacking structure also became a feature of the new military strategy. In previous wars, Sri Lankan armed forces had attacked from only one direction. This time several operations were launched simultaneously on various fronts—a capability the Tigers did not think the army possessed. While the Fifty-Fifth Division worked its way down the coast, two other divisions, the Fifty-Third and Fifty-Eighth, advanced eastward across the land toward Puthukudiyiruppu, the last town on the coast. Once they had taken the town, their objective was to link up with the Fifty-Fifth Division. Meanwhile, another infantry division, the Fifty-Ninth, advanced through the jungles of Mullaitivu and Oddusuddan, stopping on the edge of the Nanthi Kadal Lagoon (Tammita-Delgoda 2009). By employing this strategy, the army denied the LTTE access to regroup, thereby putting it on the defensive. In the past, the LTTE had always been able to rest and regroup in order to counterattack. But during Eelam War IV, the army never let the momentum slacken. Also, instead of the large formations it had used in the past, it adopted the practice of fighting in small groups of four- and eight-man teams. This strategy succeeded in confusing the enemy, who did not know where the GoSL troops would be or what they would do (Tammita-Delgoda 2009).

Toward the final stages, the military conducted its campaign across lagoons. It was not only a military factor but also a logistical and engineering challenge. The LTTE defenses had been constructed in such a manner that

9. See de Silva (2012) and Mehta (2010).

they could be guarded by a minimal number of cadres. This strategy was aimed at slowing down the army's advance and causing massive loss of life. But the LTTE made the fatal mistake of assuming that anyone advancing on such a narrow front could do so only at the risk of enormous casualties and that the GoSL would not attempt such a maneuver.

Rohantha Athukorala notes that the GoSL forces turned Sun Tzu's advice to "attack the vulnerable points" on its head, by deciding to instead target the most challenging fronts:

> For example, it took the army eight months to take Thambapanni, which was just four kilometers from the frontlines, and at that time, many were wondering whether the army could actually win the unconventional war that the LTTE was waging. The army leadership did not change course but kept its focus on the bigger plan. The troops finally broke through the lines, creating a psychological advantage. The enemy, on the other hand, became weaker from this strategic loss. (Athukorala 2009)

As a result of highly specialized training given to the GoSL forces, they were mentally and physically conditioned to battle on for several days at a stretch, even when the battlefield changed to the flat terrain in the arid zone. Where even the LTTE assumed that it would hold the upper hand due to its familiarity with the territory and climate, endurance was a key factor.

Finally, another new practice was to hone the skills of the GoSL's intelligence wing. Thus far, the LTTE had an edge over the government because of its superior intelligence-gathering capabilities. This capacity was often credited for most of LTTE's success in attacks against the GoSL targets. During Rajapaksa's tenure, this weakness was rectified. Several of the GoSL's military successes in the final year of the war can be attributed to this shift. These successes include the air force's targeted aerial bombardment that killed Tamilselvan, leader of the LTTE's political wing—a major blow to the group.

Media Blackout

The aim of total military victory also ended up benefitting from a number of rather controversial policies that concerned the international community. These policies included the president's ability to authorize the use of absolute force, in part due to the imposed media blackout. No foreign or local reporters were allowed inside the battle zone. When the war reached a decisive stage, these restrictions extended even to local and international NGOs engaged in humanitarian work in the battle zone. No foreign dignitaries were allowed to visit the battlefronts, no matter what country they represented. Only the government version of battlefield events and casualty rates was released to the media. Although pro-LTTE media and websites portrayed the "other" side of what was happening, this information could not be verified because the media had no firsthand access to the battlefront. Thus, the military had a free hand to use whatever battle tactics it saw fit. Interestingly, proponents of absolute war commend this approach for providing an added impetus to the military to "go for the jugular." For them, this was a positive lesson that the present government had learned by observing Presidents Premadasa's and Kumaratunga's regimes: When the government's forces were nearing victory, the international community, fearing high civilian casualties, asked them to stop. For many others watching the proceedings, the media blackout was a highly unfortunate and unacceptable development that ran contrary to the ethics and even the laws of war. The conduct of the Sri Lankan armed forces ultimately resulted in widespread accusations of human rights and international humanitarian law violations from the international community and human rights groups.

Strategic Alliance with India and Other Friendly Countries

As soon as Mahinda Rajapaksa assumed the presidency, he made India a vital cog in the government's campaign to eliminate the LTTE. He made frequent visits to India and, at times, sent his youngest brother, Basil, a member of parliament and a senior presidential adviser, as his emissary there. A triumvirate consisting of Defense Secretary Gotabhaya Rajapaksa, Senior Adviser to the President Basil Rajapaksa, and Secretary to the President Lalith Weeratunga visited India often to consult and inform New Delhi. The two sides were able to agree on a strategic partnership of sorts on tackling the LTTE. The November 26, 2008, multiple terrorist attacks in Mumbai further reinforced the Indian government's will to stick to its policy of noninterference, despite pressure from pro-LTTE political quarters within the state of Tamil Nadu. Although it refused to provide offensive weapons to Sri Lanka, India came to play a crucial role in the GoSL's military operations by providing continuous military intelligence. In one instance, the Indian navy had detected some LTTE warehouse ships located about 1,700 nautical miles southeast of Sri Lanka, close to Australia's exclusive economic zone (Shashikumar 2009). This information was vital for the Sri Lankan navy to destroy the ships and thereby prevent the LTTE from obtaining any new weapons via its sea routes.

Moreover, the Indian request to end the war against the LTTE before the Indian elections in 2009 also helped the Sri Lankan government's cause. Not wanting to annoy its Tamil Nadu allies, such as the DMK, unnecessarily, the Congress government in New Delhi had urged Colombo to try to conclude the war against the LTTE before the summer of 2009, when India was expected to hold the general elections (Gokhale 2009).[10]

10. This information was confirmed to the author by the LTTE's Kumaran Pathmanathan (aka KP) in an interview in 2012.

Also, the president personally managed key relationships with China, Russia, Libya, Iran, Israel, and Japan to keep global support available for Sri Lanka. This support was particularly essential once the Eelam War IV started and Western countries raised concerns about human rights violations being committed by the GoSL. This dented the LTTE's hopes of using the Tamil diaspora to lobby powerful Western countries to pressure the government over military choices and strategy. China and Russia, both permanent UN Security Council members, blocked any such moves thanks to some adroit diplomacy on the GoSL's part. Also, some of these countries provided the latest, most sophisticated weapons, which the GoSL used during the latter phases of the war.

When the LTTE used its rudimentary Air Tiger Wing to carry out attacks on vital areas in Colombo and its suburbs during 2007–08, Russia and the Czech Republic responded to the GoSL's request for assistance in destroying it. India, too, provided radar that could detect low-flying aircraft (SATP 2009). All this took place against the backdrop of the LTTE's desperate efforts in at least twelve countries, including the United States, to pressure Colombo to stop its military onslaught. At one point, the Obama administration threatened to block US$1.9 billion in aid from the International Monetary Fund to the Sri Lankan government if human rights violations did not stop (Gunasekara 2009). Ultimately, though, even some of these capitals helped the outcome of the war as they moved to freeze Tiger fund-raising by the Tamil diaspora residing in these countries (*Wall Street Journal* 2009).

The LTTE's international efforts were also defeated because of the GoSL's broader "encirclement campaign" aimed at getting LTTE banned by foreign governments. This campaign was originally formulated during President Chandrika Kumaratunga's regime. The post-9/11 context led to UN Security Council Resolution 1373, which requires all member states to legislate suitable laws and take appropriate action to curb global terrorism. Before 9/11, only the United States, India, Malaysia, and Sri Lanka had taken individual actions to designate the LTTE as a terrorist organization. By the end of Eelam War IV, the number rose dramatically to reach thirty-two countries (Bhattacharji 2009).[11] Banning the LTTE had a significant impact, in many ways, on the group's ability to fight the GoSL. The LTTE could not collect funds from the Tamil diaspora with impunity, and in some cases, organizations that were collecting funds were taken to court and indicted. There was continuous surveillance on the LTTE front organizations, leading to the arrest of key members. Arms procurement also became

11. The countries included India, the United States, the UK, EU countries, Canada, and Sri Lanka.

more difficult. The sharing of intelligence information among the countries that had banned the LTTE further helped impede its efforts.

LTTE's Failings That Helped the Cause

In addition to all the above factors, certain errors of judgment by the LTTE also led to its defeat. The greatest mistake was the decision to take three hundred thousand civilians hostage, limit itself to less than two square miles of jungle in Mullaitivu, and engage in conventional warfare rather than use the guerrilla tactics that it had mastered over the years. The LTTE based this decision on the mistaken belief that the Tamil diaspora would be able to whip up enough pressure from the Western countries to force the government to halt the war on humanitarian grounds, giving the LTTE a brief respite and time to regroup and rearm.

The LTTE also banked heavily on the 2009 elections in the Indian state of Tamil Nadu, where a victory by the pro-LTTE parties was expected. In the days leading up to the elections, pro-LTTE elements, especially the well-known politician Karunanidhi, engaged in fasts and various other demonstrations. These efforts gathered a lot of momentum, with the help of the Tamils in the south Indian state, to pressure New Delhi to intervene in Sri Lanka. The pro-LTTE parties publicly announced that if they won, they would openly support establishment of a separate state of Eelam in the north of Sri Lanka. The actual election results were a major blow to the LTTE when these parties failed to achieve the kind of outcome they had expected.[12]

Thus, two of the main strategies that the LTTE had banked on for survival failed. Since Eelam War IV's start in mid-2006, the LTTE had followed three broad military strategies—conventional warfare, guerrilla warfare, and suicide attacks—against the government forces. At the conventional level, the Tigers' main aim was to resist the rapid advance of the Sri Lankan Army toward Kilinochchi. But they found it difficult to hold back the government forces. For one, they had expected the monsoon rains to slow down the army's advance. The LTTE also mistakenly believed that it could overstretch the army into the unfamiliar terrain of the Wanni by giving less resistance to advancing forces from the south. In the past, the LTTE had regained lost territories by inflicting heavy damages on government forces at the appropriate time. The LTTE's "strategic retreat" from the east was initially seen as a ploy to conserve its energy, men, and matériel for the battle in the Wanni (Manoharan 2008). But none of these ploys worked, because this time the LTTE faced a very determined the GoSL armed force with high

12. The DMK and its allies won twenty-seven of thirty-nine seats. The LTTE did not overwhelmingly back any one party; thus, it did not significantly influence the election.

morale and orders to fight for absolute victory. The LTTE forces employed ingenious tactics to slow down the GoSL forces, for example, by having three rings: the outer ring manned by women, children, and RAW recruits, and the middle and inner rings by battle-hardened commandos who set booby traps and land mines to further slow the progress of the GoSL forces. But the armed forces ultimately overcame all these obstacles. The LTTE did not anticipate that the GoSL troops would employ LTTE-like unconventional tactics. In effect, the armed forces innovatively used guerrilla tactics and subterfuge, while the LTTE relied on conventional strategies.

Also, the massive improvement in the GoSL's intelligence network, made up of the Directorate of Military Intelligence, State Intelligence Services, and the police's Terrorist Investigations Division, resulted in the army's being able to outwit the LTTE through counterintelligence operations. In the final weeks, when the LTTE was occupying less than two square miles of territory, even the top LTTE intelligence cadres were unaware that GoSL intelligence operatives had infiltrated their area. When the government forces opened up seven fronts to mount the final assault, the LTTE was caught totally off guard.

Prabhakaran's ferocious Black Tigers let him down on perhaps the two most important assignments they were ever entrusted with: the attempted assassinations of General Fonseka and Gotabhaya Rajapaksa. This failure was an indication that the Black Tigers' efficiency and commitment were dwindling. It also indicated that the LTTE's celebrated intelligence chief and Prabhakaran's most trusted lieutenant, Pottu Amman, was not invincible. This was important because, until the last few weeks of the war, the LTTE's media machine had portrayed it as indestructible. Also, the group proclaimed to be backed by the people whose grievances it professed to represent. The first sign that the LTTE was cracking came with the defection of Karuna, its eastern commander, in 2004.

The next sign was visible in the final weeks when, once the GoSL declared a safety zone, the hostages that the LTTE had taken started escaping to government-controlled areas at the first opportunity, even when threatened with death. This finally shattered the myth that the LTTE had the universal backing of Sri Lanka's Tamil population.

To recap, Eelam War IV was not a conventional war. The GoSL had attempted conventional techniques on several previous occasions without much success. This time, the GoSL embarked on unconventional stratagems, adopting the very tactics that the LTTE had used with such efficacy. The army's multifaceted approach—employing a many-pronged attack, small groups of four to eight commandos in simultaneous attacks on many fronts, and nighttime surprise attacks—denied the LTTE any respite. The LTTE, on the other hand, made the classic mistake of relying on conventional battle strategies that amounted to abandoning its traditional advantage of guerrilla warfare.

Conclusion: Is "Victory" Complete?

President Rajapaksa's entire policy was based on military victory. It all but left out all nonmilitary aspects—political, social, or economic—that fall within the broader counterinsurgency doctrines. Giving up on a political solution and blocking opportunity for outsiders seeking to find a less brutal way of ending the war was bound to irk the Western world.

After the war was "won," the president had the opportunity to unite the entire country by moving toward reconciliation and reconstruction. In quite a few instances of wars between and within states, road maps and visions were created for the betterment of the country. The dilemma for Rajapaksa's government was that he drew his support from the nationalistic constituencies. This created a paradox. Precisely because of the nature of his coalition, he could persist with the military war, but the makeup of his coalition also meant that he had little freedom to introduce genuine power-sharing arrangements after the war, since this might have caused fresh divisions within his rightist enclave. On the other hand, ignoring Tamil rights—such as the right to use the Tamil language, the right to employment, and other freedoms—had much to do with the rise of Tamil discontent, and the GoSL could ill afford to repeat the mistakes of the past. Doing so could easily nullify any gains from the military victory. Unless the government created inclusive policies, sustainable peace was likely to remain elusive.

Some of the government's steps after the end of the war did inspire some hope. First, both leading Sinhalese-majority political parties, the SLFP and the UNP, invited minority leaders to join government. Almost all the minority parties, including those representing the Tamil plantation workers, began to work with the government. Many of the Tamil parties, except the Tamil National Alliance—a party composed of Tamil moderate and hardline elements with an extremely soured view of the Rajapaksa government—also served in coalition with the government. Rajapaksa also set up a Lessons Learnt and Reconciliation Commission, which invited citizens to present their testimonies, and many did so. The commission also visited many from the former war zones and heard the testimony of large numbers of war victims.

The government's real postwar problem, however, has come from international quarters. The international community has put the Sri Lankan state under the scanner and raised deep and fundamental questions about its conduct of war. International concerns strike at the heart of questions of international law, especially rules of war, ethics of war, and human rights, among many others. There are allegations that the Sri Lankan armed forces encouraged Tamil civilians to flee toward the safe zones established by the military and, once they were inside the safe zones, killed them in large numbers. In the documentary *Sri Lanka's Killing Fields,* the British TV station Channel 4 produced a series of gruesome footage recounting the atrocities allegedly committed by the Sri Lankan government (Channel 4 2012). The Channel 4 videos were given maximum television coverage in many capitals of the world and repeated screenings in Tamil Nadu.

The prelude to this sequence of international action was the 2009 visit of UN secretary-general Ban Ki-moon, who flew over the war-affected areas and later signed a joint statement with the president compelling the GoSL to initiate an investigation into violations of humanitarian and human rights law in the last phase of the conflict. The final paragraph of the joint statement reads, "Sri Lanka reiterated its strongest commitment to the promotion and protection of human rights, in keeping with international human rights standards and Sri Lanka's international obligations. The Secretary-General underlined the importance of an accountability process for addressing violations of international humanitarian and human rights law. The Government will take measures to address those grievances" (UNSG 2009).

The UN secretary-general later appointed a panel of experts to advise him on the issue of accountability related to the alleged violations of international human rights and humanitarian law during the final stages of Eelam War IV. The panel's work revealed "a very different version of the final stages of the war than that maintained to this day by the Government of Sri Lanka" (UNSG 2011). The panel found "credible allegations" that, if proven, would confirm that the Sri Lankan military and the LTTE committed war crimes and crimes against humanity. The panel's findings suggest that as many as forty thousand civilians may have been killed in the final months of the civil war, mostly as a result of indiscriminate shelling by the Sri Lankan military.[13] The UN secretary-general's panel of experts recommended that he conduct an independent international investigation into the allegations (UNSG 2011). The Sri Lankan government has rejected the entire report, calling it "fundamentally flawed in many respects" and based on "patently biased" and unverified material (MEA 2011). Nonetheless, the government of Sri Lanka has been under pressure to implement the report's recommendations.

In its March 2012 session, the United Nations Human Rights Council (UNHRC) passed a resolution urging the government to appoint an independent commission to investigate the crimes that may have been commit-

---

13. These figures are a matter of serious contention in Sri Lanka. A counterview is provided by a comprehensive study of the last phase of Eelam War IV, from January to mid-May 2009, produced by the Independent Diaspora Analysis Group–Sri Lanka (IDAG-S). The study challenges the numbers reflected in the panel's report. See IDAG-S (2013).

ted by the Sri Lankan armed forces and the LTTE (*BBC News* 2012). In March 2013, the UNHRC session again put forth a U.S.-backed resolution that got the support of twenty-five countries, including India. India called for an "independent and credible investigation into allegations of human rights violations and loss of civilian lives" (Manjesh 2013). The Indian state of Tamil Nadu has seen this issue become highly political, with the Tamil Nadu assembly pressuring New Delhi through a unanimous vote on the assembly floor to introduce a resolution in the UN seeking a referendum in Sri Lanka to carve out a Tamil Eelam state (*Madhyamam* 2013). The resolution also asked India to impose economic sanctions on Sri Lanka (*Deccan Herald* 2013).

The extreme international pressure that Sri Lanka has been facing is not unexpected. The international community had called for rethinking the military strategy even when Eelam IV was ongoing. On the other hand, for many observers, it raises fundamental issues about use of force and the extent to which absolute victory is justified when the human costs are so high. To be sure, the Sri Lankan experience throws into sharp focus the debate between the realist school, which had argued for the use of force against terrorism, and those promoting an alternative model for ending civil wars (i.e., peacebuilding). The key question for peacebuilders, however, is a counterfactual one: What alternatives could GoSL have employed, given its bitter history of a quarter century spent trying various military and non-military tactics to placate the LTTE? The answer to this question could provide crucial insights for comparable circumstances in the future.

References

Athukorala, Rohantha N. A. 2009. "Lessons From the War for Business," *Sunday Times* (Sri Lanka), July 12. www.sundaytimes.lk/090712/FinancialTimes/ft308.html.

BBC. 1991. "Bomb Kills India's Former Leader Rajiv Gandhi." May 21. http://news.bbc.co.uk/onthisday/hi/dates/stories/may/21/newsid_2504000/2504739.stm.

BBC News. 2012. "UN Adopts Resolution on Sri Lanka War Crimes Probe." Mar. 22 www.bbc.co.uk/news/world-asia-17471300.

Bhattacharji, Preeti. 2009. "Liberation Tigers of Tamil Eelam (aka Tamil Tigers) (Sri Lanka, Separatists)." Council on Foreign Relations, May 20. www.cfr.org/terrorist-organizations/liberation-tigers-tamil-eelam-aka-tamil-tigers-sri-lanka-separatists/p9242.

Chalk, Peter. 1999. "Liberation Tigers of Tamil Eelam's (LTTE) International Organization and Operations: A Preliminary Analysis." Canadian Security Intelligence Service Commentary no. 77. www.fas.org/irp/world/para/docs/com77e.htm.

Channel 4 (UK). 2012. "Sri Lanka's Killing Fields." Mar. 14. http://srilanka.channel4.com/.

Colombo Telegraph. 2013. "WikiLeaks: MR Had No Intention of Going to War, LTTE Behavior at Oslo Would Strengthen Hard-Liners—Palitha to US." Feb. 14. www.colombotelegraph.com/index.php/wikileaks-mr-had-no-intention-of-going-to-war-ltte-behavior-at-oslo-would-strengthen-hard-liners-palitha-to-us/.

Consortium for Elections and Political Process Strengthening (CEPPS). 2005. "Election Guide." Nov. 17. www.electionguide.org/results.php?ID=171.

Deccan Herald. 2013. "Lanka Reacts Strongly to Tamil Nadu Assembly Resolution." Apr. 8. www.deccanherald.com/content/324725/lanka-reacts-strongly-tamil-nadu.html.

De Silva, K. M. 2012. *Sri Lanka and the Defeat of the LTTE*. New York: Penguin.

Dissanayaka, T. D. S. A. 2005. *War or Peace in Sri Lanka*. Mumbai: Popular Prakashan.

Edrisinha, Rohan. 1999. "Constitutionalism, Pluralism and Ethnic Conflict: The Need for a New Initiative." In *Creating Peace in Sri Lanka: Civil War and Reconciliation*, ed. Robert I. Rotberg. Washington, DC: Brookings Institution Press.

Finanacial Times. 2009. "New War Strategies Succeeded against the LTTE." Speech by Lt. Gen. Sarath Fonseka at the PIMA annual Counterpoint Seminar, Aug. 30.

Gokhale, Nitin. 2009. *Sri Lanka: From War to Peace*. New Delhi: Har-Anand.

Gunaratna, Ranjith. 2009. "Retiring the LTTE." *Harvard International Review*, Mar. 12. http://hir.harvard.edu/retiring-the-ltte.

Gunaratna, Rohan. 1988. "International and Regional Implications of the Sri Lankan Tamil Insurgency." *Tamilnation.org*, Dec. 2. http://tamilnation.co/ltte/98rohan.htm.

Gunasekara, Tisaranee. 2009. "Blinded by Hubris." *Asian Tribune*, May 3. www.asiantribune.com/node/17235.

Hull, C. Bryson. 2008. "Sri Lanka Can Defeat Tigers, Top Ex-Rebel Says." *Reuters India*, Nov. 13. http://in.reuters.com/article/2008/11/13/idINIndia-36488720081113.

Independent Diaspora Analysis Group–Sri Lanka (IDAG-S). 2013. "The Numbers Game: Politics of Retributive Justice." www.satp.org/satporgtp/countries/shrilanka/document/TheNG.pdf.

India Today. 1987. "Journey to Jaffna." June 30.

Ispahani, Mahnaz. 1992. "India's Role in Sri Lanka's Ethnic Conflict." In *Foreign Military Intervention: The Dynamics of Protracted Conflict*, ed. Ariel E. Levite, Bruce W. Jentleson, and Larry Berman. New York: Columbia Univ. Press.

Jain Commission. 1997. "Interim Report: Growth of Tamil Militancy in Tamil Nadu". http://tamilnation.co/intframe/india/jaincommission/growth_of_tamil_militancy/bgsec2.html.

Jayasekara, Shanaka. 2009. "Strategic Miscalculation by the LTTE." *Asia Tribune,* Feb. 6. www.asiantribune.com/?q=node/15489.

Madhyamam. 2013. "Tamil Nadu Advocates Tamil Eelam in Sri Lanka." Mar. 27. www.madhyamam.com/en/node/10451.

Manjesh, Sindhu. 2013. "India Votes against Sri Lanka, but Skips Amendments to US-Backed Resolution at UNHRC." *NDTV,* Mar. 21. www.ndtv.com/article/cheat-sheet/india-votes-against-sri-lanka-but-skips-amendments-to-us-backed-resolution-at-unhrc-345284.

Manoharan, N. 2008. "Eelam War IV: Military Strategies of the LTTE." Institute of Peace and Conflict Studies. www.ipcs.org/article/sri-lanka/eelam-war-iv-military-strategies-of-the-ltte-2707.html.

Mehta, Ashok. 2010. "Sri Lanka's Ethnic Conflict: How Eelam War IV Was Won." Center for Land Warfare Studies Manekshaw Paper 22. Reprinted in *Sri Lanka Guardian,* May 20. www.srilankaguardian.org/2010/05/sri-lankas-ethnic-conflict-how-eelam.html.

Ministry of Defence. 2010. "Why Could We Not Defeat LTTE for 25 Years?" Ministry of Defence, Sri Lanka, Dec. 30. www.defence.lk/new.asp?fname=20090629_02.

Ministry of External Affairs (MEA). 2011. "The Government of Sri Lanka States that the Report of the UN Secretary General's Panel of Experts Is Fundamentally Flawed in Many Respects." Ministry of External Affairs Sri Lanka, Apr. 13. www.mea.gov.lk/index.php?option=com_content&task=view&id=2730&Itemid=75.

Premdas, Ralph R., and S. W. R. Samarasinghe. 1988. "Sri Lanka's Ethnic Conflict: The Indo-Lanka Peace Accord." *Asian Survey* 28 (6): 676–90.

Rajakulendran, Victor. 2005. "Where Does Sri Lanka Go after Their Leaders Have Spelt Out Their Political Positions?" South Asia Analysis Group Paper no. 1644, Dec. 12. www.saag.org/%5Cpapers17%5Cpaper1644.html.

Reddy, Muralidhar. 2006. "Conflicting Signals." Strategic Foresight Group, Oct. 7–20. www.strategicforesight.com/media_inner.php?id=321.

Shashikumar, V. K. 2009. "Lessons from Sri Lanka's War." *Indian Defense Review* 24 (3). www.indiandefencereview.com/spotlights/lessons-from-the-war-in-sri-lanka/.

Smith, Chris. 1999. "South Asia's Enduring War." In *Creating Peace in Sri Lanka: Civil War and Reconciliation,* ed. Robert I. Rotberg, 26–32. Washington, DC: Brookings Institution Press.

Smith, Niel. 2010. "Understanding Sri Lanka's Defeat of the Tamil Tigers." *Joint Forces Quarterly* 59 (4): 40–44.

South Asia Terrorism Portal (SATP). 2001. "Vaddukoddai Resolution." www.satp.org/satporgtp/countries/shrilanka/document/papers/vaddukoddai_resolution.htm.

———. 2009. "SL Assessment 2009." www.satp.org/satporgtp/countries/srilanka/index.html.

Sri Kantha, Sachi. 2001. "Prabhakaran Leader of Tamils Phenomenon, Part 6." http://velupillaiprabhakaran.wordpress.com/2011/10/09/the-prabakaran-leader-of-tamils-phenomenon-part-6/.

Strategic Foresight Group. 2006. "Cost of Conflict in Sri Lanka, 2006." www.strategicforesight.com/publication_pdf/79052Cost%20of%20Conflict%20in%20Sri%20Lanka.pdf.

Sunday Observer. 2009. "Fall of Pooneryn Triggered LTTE Downfall." Dec. 13. www.sundayobserver.lk/2009/12/13/sec04.asp.

Swamy, M. R. Narayan. 2002. *Tigers of Lanka: From Boys to Guerrillas*. Colombo: Vijitha Yapa.

Tammita-Delgoda, Sinharaja. 2009. "Sri Lanka: The Last Phase in the Eelam War IV: From Chundikulam to Pudumattalan." Center for Land Warfare Studies Manekshaw Paper no. 13. www.claws.in/administrator/uploaded_files/1251699653MP%20No%2013%20%202009.pdf.

———. 2010. "Sri Lanka's Ethnic Conflict: How Ealam War IV Was Won—Ashok Mehta." *Sunday Island Online*, Oct. 30. www.island.lk/index.php?page_cat=article-details&page=article-details&code_title=10164.

United Nations Secretary-General (UNSG). 2009. "Joint Statement by UN Secretary-General, Government of Sri Lanka." SG/2151, United Nations, May 26. www.un.org/News/Press/docs/2009/sg2151.doc.htm.

———. 2011. *Report of the Secretary-General's Panel of Experts on Accountability in Sri Lanka*. New York: United Nations. www.un.org/News/dh/infocus/Sri_Lanka/POE_Report_Full.pdf.

University Teachers for Human Rights (Jaffna) (UTHR[J]). 2008. "Unfinished Business of the Five Students and ACF Cases: A Time to Call the Bluff." Special Report no. 30, Apr. 1. www.uthr.org/SpecialReports/Spreport30.htm.

Vasudevan, R. 2012. "Rajiv Gandhi Assassination: Vidyadharan's Role in Undercutting LTTE." *Asian Tribune*, Nov. 7. www.asiantribune.com/news/2012/11/06rajiv-gandhi-assassination-vidyadharan%E2%80%99s-role-undercutting-ltte.

Wall Street Journal. 2009. "Sri Lanka's Victory." Opinion Asia, May 20. http://online.wsj.com/article/SB124276225317535897.html.

Weerakoon, Ruwan. 2009. "Pottu Amman: Patient but Ruthless Tiger—Untold Story of LTTE Intelligence Leader and LTTE Network." *The Nation*, Apr. 10. www.nation.lk/2009/10/04/militarym.htm.

Conclusion

Lessons for Peacebuilders

Moeed Yusuf

The preceding chapters have provided useful insights into the dynamics underpinning the progression of conflict in the four cases examined in this volume. The contributors studying the causes have analyzed contexts and factors responsible for tensions that can potentially build up to violent insurgency. Those examining counterinsurgencies have closed the loop by looking at South Asian states' responses to insurgencies and the insurgents' counterreactions.

This chapter will not summarize the cases studied. Rather, it highlights the key observations on the onset and progression of insurgencies; the approaches, strategies, and outcomes of counterinsurgency operations; and the opportunities and potential pitfalls in the post-conflict stage within the South Asian context. The focus will be on identifying how these observations create space for, or challenge the work of, peacebuilders seeking to promote nonviolent interventions at various stages of a conflict.

The stages identified in Lund's conflict curve—from stable peace to crisis/war, in the crisis and war stages, and during the post-conflict phase—serve as a useful framework (Lund 1996). Three questions guide the discussion that follows:

1. For the preinsurgency period, what can states and the would-be insurgents do to avoid moving along the conflict curve from stable peace to crisis and on to the war stage?

2. After the onset of the crisis and war stages, how can the conflict be de-escalated and terminated to result in the least violence possible?

3. What opportunities and constraints exist to steer the situation toward sustained peace in the post-conflict stage?

The answers to these questions emphasize lessons on the timing and nature of peacebuilding interventions and the roles of third-party actors.

From Stable Peace to Crisis/War

The period before the onset of violence is the most ignored stage in the conflict cycle. Thus, it presents a tale of missed opportunities for the state to address underlying risk factors *before* they translate into conflict drivers and eventually into violent insurgency.

Timing of Peacebuilding Interventions

The first hint for peacebuilders is that insurgencies seem to come out of situations where durable peace has not existed for a long time. Each of the South Asian cases studied began in a state of stable peace as tensions ebbed and flowed even when peace prevailed. Long-standing underlying tensions and historical disconnections on issues seen as vital by a segment of society were common to the insurgencies examined. Therefore, although each conflict had immediate triggers, the underlying risk factors lay somewhere in the years and decades preceding the move into the crisis and war stages on the curve. In the Sri Lankan and Kashmiri insurgencies, for example, the problems dated back to decolonization—a process that entrenched communal and geographic distortions. These root causes, exacerbated by the exclusionary policies of successive governments in Sri Lanka and also India, proved intractable over time. In Nepal's case, the problems were even more structural. S. D. Muni holds the very makeup of the Nepali state and the nature of the monarchy responsible for the process gave rise to the insurgency. Since these underlying tensions may not always be visible, it is crucial for peacebuilders to be well versed in the local context so that they can identify the risk factors and warning signs peculiar to the environment where they are operating.

Perhaps the single most crucial lesson that peacebuilders can draw for the precrisis phases from the South Asian cases studied is that the movement from stable peace to unstable peace and on to crisis is gradual and offers a number of opportunities along the way for both sides—though especially for the state apparatus—to resolve matters nonviolently. Violence is not preordained. Often it is the myopic and exclusionary policies of the central authorities, driven by trivialization of the underlying risk factors and conflict drivers and by a lack of any sense of urgency to mitigate them, that amounted to a denial of even the most basic rights of the disgruntled peoples and, consequently, moved the situation to the tipping point. Although specific actions differed, the heavy-handed and dismissive nature of state policies toward the grievances of the alienated people was strikingly similar across the case studies. Repeating themes include a denial of democratic rights, a pattern of political manipulation, promises broken to accommodate immediate electoral concerns, and aversion to lasting compromise. Examples include the Indian central government's propensity for responding to political demands from J&K with manipulation of politics and dismissals of popular leaders (e.g., Sheikh Abdullah in 1953, Farooq Abdullah in 1984); the Sri Lankan government's constant reneging on formal agreements, such as the BC and DC Pacts; and King Mahendra's unprovoked dismissal of the Nepalese parliament.

Interestingly, some of these self-defeating policy measures were employed even when the concessions demanded by the disgruntled segment of society would not have fundamentally undermined the interests and incentives of the actors representing the state. Perhaps most obvious—and, according to Weerasinghe, entirely avoidable—was the successive Sri Lankan governments' pattern of formal promises of concessions to the Tamils, and the subsequent failure to deliver on these promises. It is not at all clear that following through on the BC and DC Pacts would necessarily have altered the hold of Sinhalese-majority parties over Sri Lankan politics—an outcome that parties such as the SLFP seemed most worried about. But the paranoid outlook of successive governments in Sri Lanka forced them to miss obvious opportunities to address Tamil demands. Pakistan's case is even more unfortunate: The political and socioeconomic neglect of the people of the Federally Administered Tribal Areas (FATA) was built into the constitutional arrangement for this tribal belt. The state could only have gained by mainstreaming FATA in the years following its merger with Pakistan; instead, the neglect was perpetuated in the name of "autonomy" and the FATA residents' dislike of interference by the central government. This despite the fact that, in reality, the state had been deeply involved in using FATA as the launching pad for the anti-Soviet jihad, and its policies were having a profound impact on the society by enabling the clerics' and non–blue-blooded radicals' rise as key power brokers.

This pattern of state heavy-handedness and indifference seems to hold across the four cases, implying that the *type* of government—pluralistic democracy in India, majoritarian democracy in Sri Lanka, constitutional monarchy in Nepal, and military-dominated policymaking in Pakistan—does not correlate with that government's exclusionary tendencies in the troubled areas within its country. But each time a state implements such policies, thereby neglecting underlying problems and often prompting an adverse response from its alienated segments, it has missed an opportunity to correct historical flaws and to prevent movement up the conflict curve toward violence.

The key for peacebuilders is to identify contexts with an explosive potential and pursue legitimate nonviolent procedures to settle differences as soon as such potential arises, and at least when tensions become evident—typically, in the durable peace stage or, less preferably, early in the unstable peace phase. Identifying such contexts is especially important since the case studies suggest that not only the state but also the nonstate party to the conflict becomes less flexible as the list of exclusionary actions by the state grows. The most obvious warning signal is the gradual rise of radical voices within the disgruntled segment of the population. Evidence from the case studies suggests that once the radicals establish themselves as the principal voice for the alienated group, the onset of the insurgency becomes a matter of when, not if.

Within the alienated segment, the tendency of the moderates to gradually lose credibility and space to the radicals, who portray them as ineffective and weak, is evident across the four cases studied. For example, in Sri Lanka, the Tamil moderates were alienated because they couldn't gain concessions from the Sri Lankan state. This alientation triggered a split in the Tamil-majority FP; then organizations, such as the Tamil United Liberation Front and the LTTE, continued on the path of increased radicalization. In FATA, the gradual rise of the non–blue-blooded jihadis and the growing importance of the clerics at the expense of the tribal maliks should have been ample warning of the troubles to come.

The state makes matters worse when it resists making concessions that would keep moderates relevant and instead co-opts these popular, moderate representatives of a disgruntled people, thereby discrediting them and providing an obvious opening for the radicals. In India, for example, the MUF emerged directly out of the vacuum created by the Congress Party's political manipulation and co-option of the NC. The "king's communists" in Nepal were also discredited for doing the state's bidding, and this created a vacuum that more radical Maoist groups were eager to fill.

The actual triggers for insurgencies tend to be varied and unpredictable. Thus, for peacebuilders, early intervention is key. Only then can they initiate sustained interventions grounded in the local context and predicated on mutual political incentives for the potentially conflicting parties. The rigged 1987 elections in Indian Kashmir, the disqualification of United Communist Party Nepal (Maoist) in the 1996 Nepalese elections, and the 1983 Sri Lankan riots all proved to be triggers for the formal onset of the insurgencies, but in none of these cases did the state expect the situation to boil over into violence. The states' complacency and their having been caught unawares are not surprising—after all, several comparable incidents had happened in the past without triggering an insurgency. Why did Farooq Abdullah's dismissal from the J&K government in 1984, the Sri Lankan government's brutal reaction against the satyagrahis, or Nepal's Jhapali revolt not lead to sustained violence? The cases studied here do not point to any single useful predictor. But we can learn this much from the analyses in this volume: It is dangerous for states (and peacebuilders) to let the situation slip so perilously close to a trigger point that one further action by the state can serve as the final straw—the catalyst for a full-fledged insurgency. Peacebuilders should engage long before the crisis phase, since the probability of getting the conflicting parties to an acceptable compromise seems inversely proportional to the time elapsed since the start of the unstable peace phase.

The dilemma for peacebuilders is that the periods without manifest violence are the least likely to get the needed attention of the future antagonists. As is evident from the cases, states are reluctant to acknowledge problems that merit compromise at a time when the marginalized population is not willing or able to threaten violence. In each of the four cases, it is clear that the states felt no compulsion to compromise early on. In fact, complacency led to heavy-handed responses, which, in turn, further galvanized the insurgents and their support base. But this is precisely why local and external peacebuilders are so crucial: They can force awareness of the potential repercussions of intransigence upon the principal actors long before sustained violence breaks out.

Nature of Peacebuilding Interventions

The task of peacebuilding is not simply to introduce nonviolent tools but also to make them relevant and effective in a particular context. In Pakistan, the move from unstable peace to crisis was extremely compressed due to the black swan event of 9/11 and international pressure thereafter. The other three cases, however, featured political debate, dialogue, and negotiations before the onset of the insurgency. Thus, we see that an emphasis merely on holding dialogues and negotiations may be purely cosmetic. The real challenge is to counter the lack of desire and incentives, particularly on the part of the state, and to show flexibility regarding the aggrieved party's concerns. As we have seen, intransigence, maximalist positions, and unwillingness to stick to commitments made during negotiations are evident in all the chapters that focused on the preinsurgency phase. Also (most obviously in the Sri Lankan case), as political negotiations break down, states tend to respond with an even heavier hand—all this in the name of "national interest" and maintaining the integrity and sovereignty of the state.

The mantra of "national interest" was also the principal justification for the Congress Party's policies toward J&K. The real challenge for peacebuilders, then, seems to be to examine and understand the context and devise political incentives—typically, both carrots and sticks for both the conflicting parties—that are compelling enough to entice them to compromise and adhere to mutual commitments. In none of the cases did the state apparatus and insurgents achieve this goal. This failure explains in part their eventual move to the war stage on the conflict curve.

Tied to this objective of successful pact making must be the goal of helping the state relegitimize itself in the eyes of the alienated cohort. The mantra of "winning hearts and minds" is usually applied to counterinsurgency contexts, but the analysis in this volume suggests that achieving this goal may be equally, if not more, important in the preinsurgency phase. It is precisely the loss of confidence among the aggrieved segments of society—and the ability of the radicals among them to take advantage of the widespread resentment against the state—that allows an insurgency to find support among the people. In each of the cases, years of discrimination eventually led the aggrieved segment to see the state as an enemy and the insurgents as a genuine alternative for change. An obvious conclusion to be drawn from the analyses in this volume is that moderates seeking political means of resolving differences are vastly better partners than radicals. Peacebuilders can find a role in seeing that neither a state's shortsighted policies nor the strategies of the radicals will send the moderates on both sides into oblivion.

Role of External Third Parties

While the analyses in this volume put the onus of corrective measures to prevent a move up the conflict curve toward crisis and war largely on the conflicting parties and primarily on the states, third parties removed from the conflict are also crucial to nudging the antagonists to open their eyes and look for visionary solutions. Indeed, much of peacebuilding literature focuses on third parties as principal agents of peacebuilding in conflict-ridden environments. Here we focus specifically on external third parties.

From a collective analysis of the four case studies, no consistent pattern emerges in the type and effect of third-party roles in the precrisis stage. Third parties can definitely act as peacebuilders, but they can also play a spoiling role. In its international dimension, the Kashmir issue saw a positive, albeit ultimately unsuccessful, role of the United Nations in mediating and proposing solutions to the problem. Pakistan, meanwhile, played a pivotal role in keeping Kashmiri resentment alive and in assisting the radicals when the situation began drifting toward crisis. In at least two of the remaining three cases, external parties were directly responsible for accelerating the move toward an insurgency. The clout of the Indian state of Tamil Nadu on India's policies toward the Sri Lankan conflict and New Delhi's support for Tamil radicals in the run-up to the insurgency helped set the stage for a violent insurgency. The evidence of a third party's role as spoiler is clearest in FATA's case, where the United States and the entire Western world backed and glorified the anti-Soviet jihad in the 1980s. Then, after 9/11, external pressure on Pakistan proved to be the trigger for the FATA-based insurrection. Nonstate actors, too, can have significant impact. The training of Tamil radicals by militant groups around the world and the inspiration that Nepalese Maoists received from Maoist organizations in South Asia, Latin America, and elsewhere emboldened both groups to take on their states.

Interestingly, except perhaps in the case of Kashmir, where Pakistan wished for instability, the external parties did not want the insurgency to take off. But their actions were driven more by their own foreign policy interests than by peacebuilding objectives. In pursuing the former, they, like the antagonists, often ended up making shortsighted choices that ultimately hurt their own interests. This is true for both India and the United States in the Sri Lankan and Pakistani cases respectively—and, for that matter, for Pakistan in the case of Indian Kashmir. Each faced a significant backlash because of its prior policies in the country in question.

Reversing the Tide: From Crisis/War Back to Unstable Peace

The chapters on the counterinsurgencies present interesting findings that both confirm and question the conventional wisdom on counterinsurgency environments. And in the process, they provide interesting insights on intervention options for peacebuilders.

Timing of Peacebuilding Interventions

The single most recurring theme in these chapters was the absence of a holistic counterinsurgency approach by the states in question. All four states led with a security-centered strategy heavily focused on the use of force, intelligence-driven action plans, and heavy-handed measures in dealing with the local population. Authors of the Kashmir, Pakistani, and Nepalese case studies criticize this approach and emphasize the need for broader methods, including political and economic interventions. A closer examination, however, points to a fundamental paradox for those seeking to use a peacebuilder's toolkit: Although state-perpetrated violence and heavy-handed approaches contributed to additional support for the insurgents and perhaps even prolonged the conflict, they also appear to have undermined, to a point, the insurgent force's ability to continue fighting the state effectively. Rupesinghe's analysis of the Sri Lankan case takes this thesis to an extreme. He maintains that it was the Sri Lankan government's unwavering commitment to war and the near perfect civil-military coordination—even as the state trampled basic human rights and defied international law—that ended the active armed insurgency. And in the Pakistani case, paralleling Qadir's criticism of the state's lack of a holistic strategy is his admission that only after a successful military operation in Swat—at a cost of millions of internally displaced persons—did the state begin to pull the situation back toward normality. Even Chowdhary, who is quite candid in blaming the state's security-heavy approach in J&K, nonetheless acknowledges that the might of the Indian state, exhibited in its heavy-handed measures in the initial years—although it further alienated the people—led many insurgents to lose faith in the prospects of their violent struggle. In Nepal, the opposite was true. The failure of the state's military approach, combined with the Maoists' successful counterresponse, was one of the main reasons preventing the Nepalese state from truly gaining the upper hand. But again, it was violence that paid off—this time, for the insurgents.

To add to the conundrum, while the authors in this volume have lamented the lack of a holistic counterinsurgency approach, it is not clear *when* broader political and economic interventions are most effective. South Asian states have tended to bring in political corrections and economic uplift plans at the back end of military successes. While counterinsurgency theorists and peacebuilders would prefer to see those corrections introduced earlier, empirical evidence of their feasibility and efficacy is divided across the case studies. Nepal's case suggests that once all-out conflict is under way, insurgents may well find reason to prevent or target economic development plans in the troubled regions for fear that the state may relegitimize itself in the eyes of the people. Chowdhary's analysis suggests that New Delhi's political and economic overtures did have a positive impact in J&K, but this change came after the peak of the insurgency had passed and the state had regained enough control—through use of force—to be able to implement them successfully. In Pakistan, Qadir's contention, that a window for peacebuilding existed immediately after the U.S. ultimatum to Musharraf, was never tested. But when the state did attempt numerous rounds of talks and peace deals in the early part of the counterinsurgency campaign, these failed, and the army ultimately had to fall back on excessive and dedicated use of force. On the other hand, the economic sanctions imposed by the state against the insurrectionist tribes in FATA early on did not deliver any useful result.

The point here is not to support violent responses in counterinsurgency environments. Rather, it is to highlight that those studying these cases are likely to conclude that violence did pay off, and therefore, this pattern is likely to be repeated in future conflicts. The question that needs more attention from peacebuilders is *why* states such as India, Sri Lanka, and Pakistan, who had experience with counterinsurgencies, favored security-centered methods even after volumes have been written criticizing such approaches—and even though, when taken to an extreme, these approaches can create serious international condemnation and calls for legal proceedings against the state's rulers, such as the Sri Lankan regime faces today. Are we looking at a situation where those using force see it as an effective tool to undermine the opponent's strength at the front end of dealing with insurgent violence—before nonviolent peacemaking efforts are seriously entertained? Is the utility of violence real or perceived? And what is the way to break through this pattern, reducing the violent aspect of strategies at the front end? The case studies in this volume do not provide the answers, but these questions merit greater attention in future work.

The pattern of high levels of violence being employed at the front end by both parties implies that the move up from crisis to war on the conflict curve can be rapid. Indeed, in each of the four cases, the full-fledged onslaught of violence came soon after the key precipitating events. Less than two years elapsed between the 1987 elections in Kashmir and the beginning of the sustained insurgency in 1989. Similarly, the disqualification of the Maoists from the 1994 elections came less than two years before the formal onslaught of insurgent violence in 1996. In Pakistan's case, the window was even more compressed.

One possible reason for high levels of violence occurring at the front end and only later being followed by concerted attention to broader approaches could be both antagonists' overriding need to attain a position of strength. Indeed, the experience with interventions such as dialogues and negotiations in counterinsurgency contexts seems to point to their ineffectiveness until one side has gained a decisive advantage in the field—an advantage inevitably reached through violent means. Direct, indirect, and third-party-mediated dialogues were part of the mix in all cases, but all ultimately failed to bring about a peaceful resolution. When they were conducted, they became a vehicle to rehearse maximalist positions; cease-fires, when agreed upon, were used as little more than strategic pauses by both sides. Dialogue took center stage in a positive way only when the military strategy had limited the insurgency to some extent (Kashmir) or when the opposition to the status quo had decisively united and was in a position to dictate terms to the state (Nepal). Otherwise, even when the Pakistani state attempted outright appeasement through peace deals favorable to the insurgents—a policy that, incidentally, finds criticism among peacebuilders—including from Rana and Qadir in this volume—the Pakistani Taliban saw it as a sign of weakness and took advantage of the situation to strengthen its hand. Again, what alternatives peacebuilders could recommend for the early part of the war stage in the conflict remains an open question. Or is it simply a choice between counterproductive talks and outright military action?

This leads us to a counterintuitive observation: If both sides are looking to achieve a position of strength before conducting a sincere dialogue, a violent insurgency should be tougher to pacify in the early stages after the eruption of the insurgency than later, when the war stage has been persisting for some time. Other factors reinforce this view. For one, the first batch of militants seems to be the most ideologically motivated and is often from the segment of the disgruntled population directly affected by the state's preinsurgency tactics. Thus, they are less likely to give up. The first batch of Kashmiri insurgents came from the MUF, who felt betrayed by the rigging of the 1987 J&K state elections. And the early LTTE cadres were those affected by anti-Tamil quotas introduced by the state or were at the receiving end of the 1983 anti-Tamil riots. Key defections came only when the insurgency had persisted for some time and individual insurgents grew disillusioned with the struggle or when the insurgency's core got diluted by less dedicated or differently motivated insurgents joining the fight. In Kashmir, for example, the Ikhwani phenomenon discussed by Chowdhary grew from the resentment toward Pakistan-backed Islamists and from the Ikhwanis' ability to gauge the futility of their struggle. Of course, not all insurgent ranks weaken over time; they never did in Nepal.

States are even more unlikely to give up early in the war stage. They are likely to fight until left with no choice. It was only after the Nepalese state's many contradictions and internal tussles—between the monarchy, political elites, army, and within the political enclave—had allowed the Maoists a decisive advantage that the monarchy and army had no option but to concede. And not all conflicts see a force-heavy front end followed by broader interventions. Violence peaked in Sri Lanka right before the conflict's termination.

The overall conclusion is disappointing: Peacebuilders promoting nonviolent solutions to a conflict may have an extremely hard time breaking through a conflict situation when a full-fledged insurgency has taken off and violence levels are still rising. This conclusion mirrors the need for "conflict ripeness" often stressed in peacebuilding literature.[1] It is only later on in the conflict mitigation phase that nonviolent interventions may be able to make a real difference. A troubling corollary is also noteworthy: In counterinsurgency environments, the most effective peacebuilding may come at the tail of excessive violence.

1. For literature on "ripeness," see Zartman (2000, 2001).

Nature of Peacebuilding Interventions

Perhaps the key lessons to be drawn from the case studies regarding the nature of peacebuilding interventions are that (a) the interventions must be chosen to suit the specific context and (b) they must address true underlying causes of the conflict. Identifying the risk factors and the core conflict drivers is the first step to devising effective responses. Jacob's distinction between "core" and "add-on" factors that underpin a conflict is an important one for policymakers. It implies that even inclusionary and conciliatory policies, if based on a misreading of the central issues of concern, may not produce the desired outcomes. In the four cases studied, political and identity-based alienation stand out as far more significant than issues of socio-economic concern—at least, by the time the conflict has progressed to the crisis and war stages.

Evidence across the case studies substantiates this observation. While Chowdhary maintains that New Delhi's economic interventions in the late 1990s helped ease tensions, her argument, confirming Jacob's assertion that politics was the basis of J&K's alienation, clearly points to the need for a political solution as the silver bullet. Sri Lanka's and Nepal's cases were also dominated by political concerns during the crisis and war phases, and economic interventions had no effect. In Nepal, the Maoists stalled the state's efforts to bring about economic development, and impoverished communities adopted the slogan, "No development without political settlement." In the Sri Lankan case, the Accelerated Mahaweli Program in the late 1970s actually made the Tamil radicals believe that an independent state of Eelam had become even more viable. This is not to suggest that economic development should not have taken place amid the violence but only that measures not addressing what the disgruntled segments of society perceive to be their pivotal demands and concerns are unlikely to push the situation toward resolution. Pakistan's case was the most complex. The state did correctly identify the key issue: the insurgents' ideologically (identity) driven demand to be allowed a free hand in using FATA as a launching pad to attack the foreign presence in Afghanistan. But the international context simply did not allow the state to agree to this.

The observations about the substance of negotiations and dialogues between the antagonists, made earlier for the preinsurgency phases, bear repeating here. The key is not in holding dialogues per se—each crisis saw numerous attempts through direct interactions, through committees, or brokered by third parties. Rather, it is to create a framework attractive enough to induce both sides to climb down the conflict curve. Nepal is one example where the political parties and the insurgents managed to converge in such a manner that they brought about a swift end to the conflict by isolating the monarch. Perhaps the best example of this approach, however, is the Pakistan-India peace process, which worked on an agenda driven by the interests and compulsions of both sides and which very nearly achieved a breakthrough in an extremely complex dispute.

Finally, theorists see the question of public opinion and "winning hearts and minds" as central to any counterinsurgency's success. The Pakistani and Nepalese cases are good examples, though at opposite ends of the spectrum. Qadir's chapter suggests a strong correlation between popular support for the Pakistani state and the strategies the state employed vis-à-vis the Taliban. In Nepal, the state's failure to win over public opinion—and the Maoists' success—determined the winner of the contest. Even in Sri Lanka, while the state completely disregarded Tamil sentiments, it was the government's confidence in having the backing of the Sinhalese nationalists who had brought it to power that allowed it to undertake an extremely controversial military-focused strategy despite obvious ethical, legal, and international diplomatic concerns. The Sri Lankan government's propensity to block any access to independent information from the war zone in Eelam War IV also points to the importance it accorded to preventing popular opposition to the military's tactics, in this case turning the logic on its head from a peacebuilder's perspective.

Its importance notwithstanding, public support does not necessarily lead to the path of least violence. In Kashmir, once the insurgents began to lose local support, violence did decrease significantly. But in Pakistan, public support was instrumental in allowing the military to launch a full-scale operation in Swat, as well as several later operations. In Sri Lanka, support of the rightist nationalists was instrumental in getting a controversial force-dominated strategy put in place to begin with. This raises a pertinent question for peacebuilders: Where should they stand on the issue of generating popular support for conflicting parties? Should the decision of how seriously to help achieve popular backing (or even to see it as positive or negative) depend on what its impact on the violence in a given situation is likely to be? What effect might this stance have on the length of the conflict? Or should the conventional wisdom that peacebuilders must keep their neutrality be upheld at all costs, irrespective of how this affects the conflict trajectory? These are questions that require greater attention from peacebuilders.

Role of External Third Parties

The potential for external third parties to influence a conflict is qualitatively different in the crisis and war stages than in the preinsurgency phases. In each case study, both the state and the insurgents engaged external parties to further their own interests and even entertained their suggestions and demands to varying degrees. This interaction implies greater eagerness and receptivity for third-party engagement. Incidentally, this is also the stage when external actors are most likely to pay attention and show willingness to help mitigate and terminate the conflict.

The Nepalese king constantly sought external support for his heavy-handed measures in the post-9/11 context. Sri Lanka accepted India's intervention in the 1980s and a Norwegian-backed peace process in the following decade. President Rajapaksa reached out to countries to cultivate support and was instrumental in getting states such as China and Russia to back him when much of the Western world had shunned Eelam War IV. The Indian state, despite its resistance to outside intervention, ultimately initiated dialogue with Pakistan, and it was also affected by international human rights organizations raising the profile of its human rights abuses in Kashmir. As for the insurgents, the Nepalese Maoists and the LTTE were extremely conscious of the need for international support and, to secure it, made a determined effort through direct outreach and expatriates, respectively. Kashmiri insurgents looked to Pakistan for survival and support.

The influence of third parties in the crisis and war stages of the conflict is obvious across the four South Asian case studies. As in the precrisis phases, however, their behavior does not always seem to further the agenda of peace. India's mixed role involving initial support to the Tamil radicals, deployment of the IPKF against the LTTE—even as support for the insurgency continued from political parties such as AIADMK and the DMK in Tamil Nadu—and partial Indian support to the Sri Lankan government during Eelam War IV had a profound impact on how the conflict progressed. The Sri Lankan conflict also occasioned an unequivocally supportive role by a neutral party in seeking a peaceful resolution of the conflict: The Norwegian efforts in brokering a cease-fire, even though ultimately unsuccessful, created a chance for a peaceful resolution. On the other hand, the LTTE's hope that Tamil expatriates would get the international community to make Colombo stop its martial assault in Eelam War IV went unfulfilled.

In Kashmir, Pakistan was central to sustaining the insurgency and later giving India greater space to manage the conflict internally through the bilateral peace process. In FATA, even as the United States and other external actors wished for peace in the tribal belt, their presence next door in Afghanistan became a major rallying point for the insurgents and is in no small part responsible for the insurgency's continuation. Finally, India's and the international community's shift from an ambivalent stance on the Nepal conflict to one that opposed the king's 2005 royal coup—and that ultimately isolated the king—was instrumental in helping terminate the conflict.

In each of these cases, the trend is clear: the most helpful third-party roles—and their ability to achieve positive outcomes—come after violence has persisted for some time—not at the front end of the crisis and war stages. For peacebuilders, the key is to be able to judge the context and preferences of various external players with direct interests and nudge them to minimize their negative roles at the outset and instead encourage the use of their diplomatic, political, and economic leverage to help resolve the conflict in peaceful ways. Coalitions, including neutral actors such as the Norwegians in Sri Lanka or the United Nations in Kashmir, can also be instrumental in generating collective pressure. Again, the need to devise the right incentives for all parties to converge on the path most likely to lead to conflict termination is the most obvious challenge to overcome.

Toward Sustainable Peace: The Post-Conflict Phase

Only two of the four case studies in this volume have reached the post-conflict stage. Both had very different conflict termination patterns, and neither reflects substantial progress toward durable peace.

The most obvious conclusion we can draw, says Bishnu Upreti, is that "what it takes to agree on a settlement is not necessarily sufficient to fix the root causes of the conflict and achieve conflict transformation." The statement is applicable beyond Nepal—in Sri Lanka, for example. At least in these cases, the fundamental post-conflict problems seem to arise in the political arena. Therefore, while the broad spectrum of peacebuilding interventions—including recovery, rehabilitation, and the like—are important, there is a need for greater focus on political processes as a vehicle for conflict transformation. Peacebuilders have traditionally neglected this aspect (Cousens and Kumar 2001).

The Nepalese case suggests that tensions and mistrust developed during the prolonged period of violence are not easily overcome. The past seven years of Nepalese political history have been turbulent and full of tensions—between the civilian and military sectors, between political parties, and within the party representing the triumphant insurgent movement. Since 2006, the Constituent Assembly has been unable to draft a constitution. Fundamental questions about the fate of the Maoist fighters and the Nepalese army also remain unaddressed. And the postinsurgency state, despite multiple promises made during the insurgency and efforts thereafter, has been unable to satisfy the socioeconomic demands of the marginalized segments that so wholeheartedly backed Jan Andolan II. Moreover, while neither Muni nor Upreti sees a return to the insurgency as likely, both have pointed to the split within the leadership of the former insurgents and the dangers in a lingering political stalemate.

In the Sri Lankan case, the celebratory tone of Rupesinghe's chapter must be highly disturbing for peacebuilders. But anyone promoting nonviolent means of conflict resolution must take it as an intellectual challenge. Given that the Sri Lankan state did attempt negotiations on multiple occasions before Eelam War IV, peacebuilders must ponder what negotiating strategy or inducements might have compelled the state to prefer a peacebuilding approach to end the conflict even during Eelam War IV. Still, even Rupesinghe acknowledges that the state's inability to give moderate Tamils a larger stake in the country may reverse the gains of the military victory. Sri Lanka, despite some preliminary efforts by the government, remains rife with deep-seated mistrust. It is clear that Eelam War IV may have suppressed Tamil grievances, but it has certainly not addressed them.

Even Kashmir, though formally still not in the post-conflict phase, has seen both a drastic reduction in violence and progress in political dialogue, both with the separatists and with Pakistan. Yet the difficulties of making the final leap from this much improved situation to a stable and peaceful one—to stable peace—are all too obvious. As Chowdhary argues, the Indian state has remained unable to isolate the radicals; its failure to seize on improving conditions by making substantive political concessions to moderates keeps the radical separatists relevant. In fact, their importance is on the rise again.

One observation common to these cases is the lasting domestic institutional implications of security-centered strategies during the conflict. In Nepal and Sri Lanka—and, for that matter, Kashmir—the states' reliance on the security apparatus, civilian or military, has left the security establishments with bloated mandates and operational space. As counterinsurgency builds up to the war stage, states inevitably introduce new laws to give security forces maximum operating space, and new units or formations are set up specifically to tackle the insurgency. This happened in both Nepal and Sri Lanka. These cases suggest that having started down that path, states find it very hard to pull the security presence back. The disproportionate influence that security forces become used to as they operate in the insurgency environment seems to last, and the special laws invoked to protect them prove terribly difficult to reverse. Tensions continue between the Nepalese army and the Maoists on the fate of Maoist insurgent fighters and the army's powers. Although Rupesinghe does not report it in his analysis, Sri Lanka's victory against the LTTE ended with army chief Fonseka blaming the civilians for undercutting the military and with the government charging and imprisoning him (Izadeen 2009). Even the Indian state, the most mature democracy in the region, despite years of promises, has found it impossible to withdraw its security presence completely from the Kashmir Valley or to reverse laws giving the security personnel excessive powers. The lesson seems to be that civilian-dominated systems are just as susceptible as quasi-democratic or undemocratic systems to falling into the trap of giving security forces too much impunity and policy space and then being unable to reverse this at will. Peacebuilders ought to highlight this troubling reality, in the process emphasizing the merits of less security establishment–dominated strategies.

Finally, the Sri Lankan case raises a fundamental question about the end goal of conflict resolution. Unlike for warring parties, the ultimate goal of peacebuilders is not necessarily "victory." Rather, peacebuilders are much more interested in attaining a state of durable peace. A victory that fails to address broader root causes of violence over time and risks returning to tensions or violence negates the very essence of peacebuilding. In this regard, the current attention on the Sri Lankan case is welcome. Calls for war crimes investigations must be heeded and, if international law was indeed violated, perpetrators punished suitably, regardless of which side they were on. While questioning the laws and ethics of fighting a war remain beyond the scope of this volume, they are no trivial matters. Inaction by the international bodies mandated to act in such situations, despite evidence of gross transgressions, would set a bad precedent and make the task of peacebuilders promoting nonviolence over absolute "victory" through use of excessive force elsewhere more difficult. Equally damaging, however, are the double standards for how closely specific conflicts are scrutinized. Not that excesses of the type and magnitude alleged in Sri Lanka necessarily occurred in any of the other three crises studied, but excesses occurred all the same, and the international community has certainly been far less willing to highlight the reports of human rights excesses committed by the Indian state in Kashmir (or, for that matter, by the Pakistani state against the Taliban).

Peacebuilding in the South Asian Environment: Final Thoughts

The analysis in this volume comes down heavily in favor of peacebuilders channeling their energies to the most underdeveloped aspect of peacebuilding: conflict prevention. The broadest option set, with the highest probability of success for nonviolent approaches to conflict resolution, is likely to be in the early stages of the unstable peace phase in Lund's conflict curve. This period provides multiple opportunities for states to resolve issues without allowing deterioration toward the crisis and war stages. Triggers for the onset of an insurgency tend to occur some time after radicals have taken charge of the disgruntled population, and once this happens, the choices for peacebuilders armed with a nonviolent toolkit narrows significantly and abruptly. Peacemaking seems to have the worst odds. Probability of success rises again in the conflict mitigation phase, when one party begins to

Figure 10.1 Conflict progression and the probability of successful nonviolent intervention

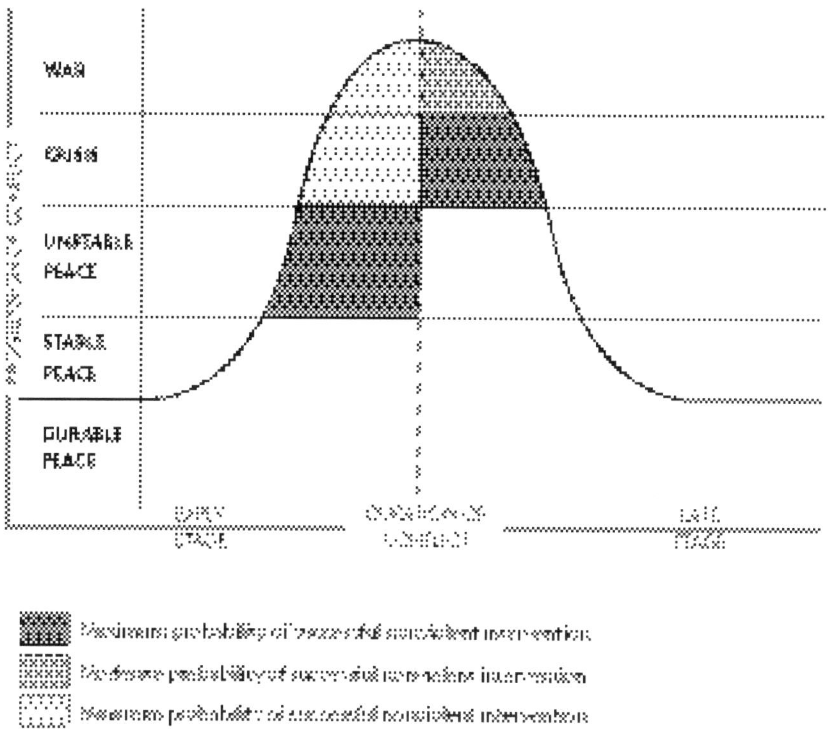

achieve a position of strength or where the inability of either to do so leads to greater efforts seeking alternatives to force-heavy strategies. But this is still nowhere near as attractive a situation for peacebuilders as the preinsurgency period, when moderates still hold sway among the alienated population. In all four cases in this volume, excessive violence had already taken place before the conflict mitigation stage arrived. Figure 10.1 illustrates the relative probability of successful nonviolent interventions during the various stages of conflict, and figure 10.2 summarizes the key developments along the conflict curve for the cases examined in this volume.

The single most important determinant of a peacebuilder's success, then, may well be the *timing* of the effort. The real value of peacebuilding is to engineer meaningful dialogue with realistic incentives for both sides at a time when violence has not broken out and the issue is ripe for resolution.

Figure 10.2 Key developments along the conflict curve for the studied cases

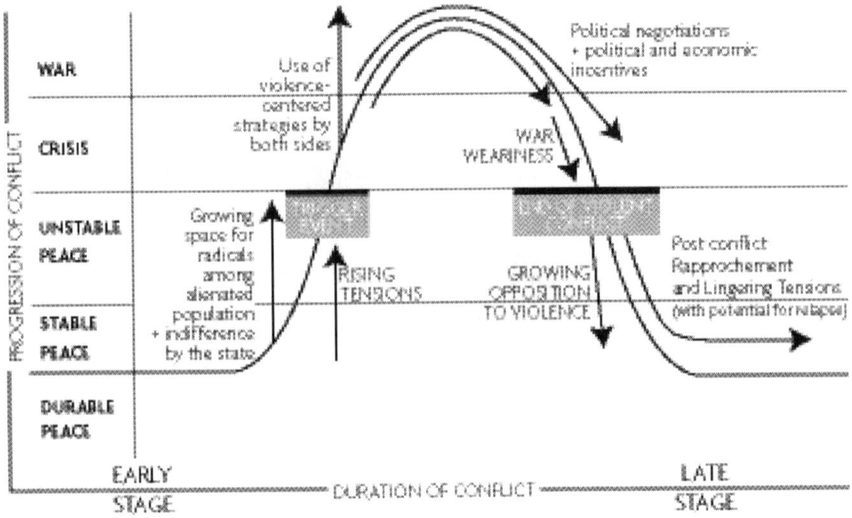

Source: Adopted from Lund (2009, 290).

Peacebuilders then need to generate pressure to ensure implementation of the understanding reached between the relevant parties.

Based on the analysis in this volume, it is safe to say that the track record of South Asian states in managing tensions before the onset of insurgency, as well as in tackling insurgencies after they have taken off, has been dismal. Judging by the similarities among their actions and reactions, if anything, South Asian states seem to have repeated each other's mistakes in pushing situations from stable peace on to crisis and war. Even the structural differences among the cases do not seem to have significant bearing on behavior before and during the insurgencies. Democratic, quasi-democratic, and undemocratic dispensations all adopt fairly exclusionary policies until it is too late to prevent conflict. The insurgents, too, seem to have many similarities, especially in the rise of the radicals from within moderate ranks, their internal rivalries and competition, their ability to throw up charismatic leaders, their success in gathering internal support and external patrons, their propensity to commit excessive violence, and their ability to bog down major military forces for years.

Peacebuilders never have it easy, and South Asia seems to provide no exception to this rule. The South Asian cases examined here all developed into full-blown insurgencies. Each of these insurgencies was avoidable, but after a point, they became inevitable. Moreover, once they began, violence—and a lot of it—was on display, and none offered a quick or easy recipe for termination. Finally, even when the armed conflict ended, "victory" did not imply a resolution of the core problems.

The task is cut out for peacebuilders to promote nonviolent resolution in tense environments. They must grasp the context, jump in, time their interventions right, and ensure that their interventions have incentives attractive enough for all parties concerned to resolve the conflict as peacefully as possible. This is no mean feat. But peacebuilders must continue thinking creatively and making concerted efforts, for the alternative is often the unacceptable resort to greater violence.

References

Cousens, Elizabeth, and Chetan Kumar, with Karin Wermester, eds. 2001. *Peacebuilding as Politics: Cultivating Peace in Fragile Societies*. Boulder, CO: Rienner.

Lund, Michael S. 1996. *Preventing Violent Conflicts: A Strategy for Preventive Diplomacy*. Washington, DC: U.S. Institute of Peace Press.

———. 2009. "Conflict Prevention: Theory in Pursuit of Policy and Practice." In *The SAGE Handbook of Conflict Resolution,* ed. Jacob Bercovitch, Victor Kremenyuk, and I. W. Zartman, 287–308. London: SAGE.

Izzadeen, Ameen. 2009. "Why Lankan War Hero Fonseka and Rajapaksa Broke Up." *Rediff News*, Nov. 13. http://news.rediff.com/special/2009/nov/13/why-lankan-war-hero-fonseka-and-rajapaksa-broke-up.htm.

Zartman, I. William. 2000. "Ripeness: The Hurting Stalemate and Beyond." In *International Conflict Resolution after the Cold War*, ed. Paul Stern and Daniel Druckman. Washington, DC: National Academy Press.

. 2001. "The Timing of Peace Initiatives: Hurting Stalemates and Ripe Moments." *Global Review of Ethnopolitics* 1 (1): 8–18. www.peacemaker.un.org/sites/peacemaker.un.org/files/TimingofPeaceInitiatives_Zartman2001.pdf.

Index

Page numbers followed by *n* indicate footnotes.

About the Contributors

About the Editor

Moeed Yusuf is the Director of South Asia Programs at the U.S. Institute of Peace. A native of Pakistan and a political scientist by training, before joining USIP, Yusuf was concurrently a fellow at the Frederick S. Pardee Center for the Study of the Longer-Range Future at Boston University and a research fellow at the Mossavar-Rahmani Center at Harvard Kennedy School. His coedited volume, *South Asia 2060: Envisioning Regional Futures,* was published by Anthem (UK) in 2013. He is also the coeditor of *Getting It Right in Afghanistan* (U.S. Institute of Peace Press, 2013) and editor of *Pakistan's Counterterrorism Challenge* (Georgetown Press, 2014).

Rekha Chowdhary, presently ICSSR National Fellow, retired as professor at the University of Jammu, where she worked on issues related to Jammu and Kashmir, ethnicity, nationalism, identity politics, religion, democracy, conflict, and peacebuilding. Her most recent book is *Identity Politics in Jammu and Kashmir.* She has been a Fulbright fellow (Johns Hopkins University School of Advanced International Studies, 2005), Commonwealth fellow (QEH, University of Oxford, 1997–98), and Ford Foundation SAVSP visiting scholar (Oxford, 1992–93).

Happymon Jacob is an assistant professor of disarmament and diplomacy at the School of International Studies, Jawaharlal Nehru University. Jacob is a regular columnist with the Srinagar-based daily *Greater Kashmir.* Before joining JNU, Jacob worked with the University of Jammu's Department of Strategic and Regional Studies and with the Nelson Mandela Centre for Peace and Conflict Resolution, Jamia Millia Islamia University, New Delhi.

Khalid Mahmood served in many Pakistani missions abroad—including Paris, Accra, Brussels, and Ankara—and served as ambassador in Oman,

Poland, Belarus, and Czech Republic. He also worked as the head of the foreign minister's office in Islamabad. He holds master's degrees from Government College, Lahore, and John F. Kennedy School of Government at Harvard University. He is currently working on a book with former foreign minister Kasuri on Pakistani foreign policy.

S. D. Muni is a visiting research professor at the Institute of South Asian Studies, National University of Singapore. Formerly a professor at Jawaharlal Nehru University, he has written and edited more than twenty books and 150 research papers. He also was the founding editor of *South Asia Journal* and *Indian Foreign Affairs Journal*. The government of Sri Lanka bestowed on him its highest national honor, Sri Lanka Ratna, in 2005.

Shaukat Qadir spent thirty-five years in the Pakistani military. He began his military career as a pilot in the air force and concluded it as a brigadier in the infantry. While in uniform, he held command, staff, and instructional assignments at all levels. Since retirement, he has headed a government-funded think tank, served as visiting faculty member at various universities, and been a part-time journalist. He speaks Pashto and has spent considerable time in Pakistan's tribal areas.

Muhammad Amir Rana is a security and political analyst and the director of Pak Institute for Peace Studies, an independent Islamabad-based think tank. He worked as a journalist with various Urdu and English-language daily newspapers from 1996 until 2004 and has been a visiting fellow at the Institute of Defence and Strategic Studies, Singapore. He is also the editor of *Pakistan Annual Security Report*, the English-language research journal *Conflict and Peace Studies*, and the Urdu monthly magazine *Tajziat*.

Kumar Rupesinghe is the chairman of Knowledge City, an organization devoted to education. From 2002 to 2009, he served as chair of the Foundation for Co-Existence. He spent ten years as a fellow and research director at the International Peace Research Institute and has edited or written over fifty books on the transformation and resolution of conflict. He has a master's degree from the London School of Economics and a PhD from the City University London.

Bishnu Raj Upreti, director of the Nepal Centre for Contemporary Research, is active in teaching and research focusing on conflict, peace, and unconventional security. His research focuses on South Asia. He has written or coedited thirty books on conflict, peace, statebuilding, and security and is frequently published in peer-reviewed international journals and anthologies. One of his latest coedited books is *Human Security in Nepal: Concepts, Issues and Challenges* (2013). He holds a PhD in conflict management from Wageningen University, Netherlands.

Chalinda Dilesh Weerasinghe is completing his doctoral studies in government, politics, and economics at the University of Maryland, College Park. His specializations are international relations, econometrics, political economy, and development economics. He has master's degrees in economics and international relations from the Georgia Institute of Technology and a bachelor's degree in mathematics, economics, and history and political science from Shorter University in Rome, Georgia. He hails from Sri Lanka.

United States Institute of Peace Press

Since its inception in 1991, the United States Institute of Peace Press has published more than 175 books on the prevention, management, and peaceful resolution of international conflicts—among them such venerable titles as Raymond Cohen's *Negotiating Across Cultures*; John Paul Lederach's *Building Peace; Leashing the Dogs of War*, by Chester A. Crocker, Fen Osler Hampson, and Pamela Aall; and *The Iran Primer*, edited by Robin Wright. All our books arise from research and fieldwork sponsored by the Institute's many programs, and the Press is committed to extending the reach of the Institute's work by continuing to publish significant and sustainable works for practitioners, scholars, diplomats, and students. In keeping with the best traditions of scholarly publishing, each volume undergoes thorough internal review and blind peer review by external subject experts to ensure that the research and conclusions are balanced, relevant, and sound.

Valerie Norville
Director

About the United States Institute of Peace

The United States Institute of Peace is an independent, nonpartisan institution established and funded by Congress. The Institute provides analysis, training, and tools to help prevent, manage, and end violent international conflicts, promote stability, and professionalize the field of peacebuilding.

Chairman of the Board: Stephen J. Hadley
Vice Chairman: George E. Moose
Acting President: Kristin Lord
Chief Financial Officer: Michael Graham

Board of Directors

Stephen J. Hadley (Chair), Principal, RiceHadleyGates, LLC

George E. Moose (Vice Chair), Adjunct Professor of Practice, The George Washington University

Judy Ansley, Former Assistant to the President and Deputy Security National Advisor under President George W. Bush

Eric Edelman, Hertog Distinguished Practitioner in Residence, Johns Hopkins University School of Advanced International Studies

Joseph Eldridge, University Chaplain and Senior Adjunct Professorial Lecturer, School of International Service, American University

Kerry Kennedy, President, Robert F. Kennedy Center for Justice and Human Rights

Ikram U. Khan, President, Quality Care Consultants, LLC

Stephen D. Krasner, Graham H. Stuart Professor of International Relations, Stanford University

John A. Lancaster, Former Executive Director, International Council on Independent Living

Jeremy A. Rabkin, Professor, George Mason School of Law

J. Robinson West, Chairman, PFC Energy

Nancy Zirkin, Executive Vice President, Leadership Conference on Civil and Human Rights

Members ex officio

John Kerry, Secretary of State

Chuck Hagel, Secretary of Defense

Gregg F. Martin, Major General, U.S. Army; President, National Defense University

Kristin Lord, Acting President, United States Institute of Peace (nonvoting)